IN
PURSUIT
OF KNOWLEDGE

A PUKHTUN'S LIFE, FROM EAST TO WEST

SHER M. KHAN

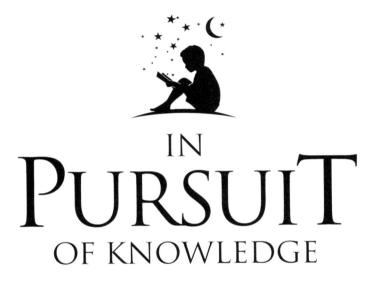

IN
PURSUIT
OF KNOWLEDGE

A Pukhtun's life, from East to West

SHER M. KHAN

MEREO
Cirencester

Mereo Books

1A The Wool Market Dyer Street Cirencester Gloucestershire GL7 2PR
An imprint of Memoirs Publishing www.mereobooks.com

In Pursuit of Knowledge: 978-1-86151-527-8

First published in Great Britain in 2015
by Mereo Books, an imprint of Memoirs Publishing

The address for Memoirs Publishing Group Limited can be found at
www.memoirspublishing.com

The Memoirs Publishing Group Ltd Reg. No. 7834348

The Memoirs Publishing Group supports both The Forest Stewardship Council®
(FSC®) and the PEFC® leading international forest-certification organisations. Our
books carrying both the FSC label and the PEFC® and are printed on FSC®-certified
paper. FSC® is the only forest-certification scheme supported by the leading
environmental organisations including Greenpeace. Our paper procurement policy
can be found at www.memoirspublishing.com/environment

Typeset in 10/14pt Plantin
by Wiltshire Associates Publisher Services Ltd. Printed and bound in Great Britain
by Printondemand-Worldwide, Peterborough PE2 6XD

CONTENTS

Dedication
Acknowledgements
Foreword

Part One: A Pukhtun Life

Part Two: A Pukhtun in England

Part Three: Return to the National Health Service

DEDICATION

Dedicated to my grandchildren: Sarah, Dawood, Yusra, Hanna, Raneem, Danish, Dina, Daneen, Abdullah and Eissa. Hopefully they will practice and preserve the "Pukhtunwali" of generosity, hospitality and honour wherever they live in the "Global village" and strive for peace, progress and prosperity individually and collectively in the land of their ancestors, who left their abode not far from the Oxus River because of unparalleled cruelty to their kith and kin (Yusufzais) and then settled west of the Indus River.

IN HONOUR OF

Malik Ahmad Baba, the founder of Yusufzais in Khyber Pukhtunkhwa.

Pisha Khan Baba, founder of Mashar Khel and Kashar Khel in upper Swat.

In memory of my great grandfather Paacha Gul, and of my grandparents and parents.

GENEALOGY OF PAINDA KHEL SWAT

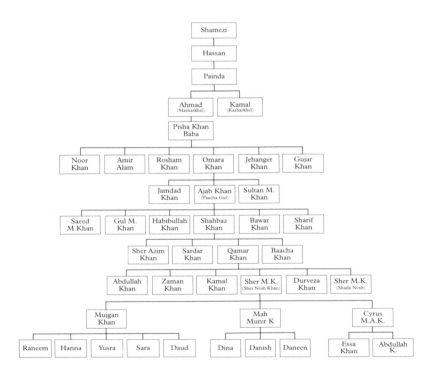

ACKNOWLEDGEMENTS

First of all, I am very grateful to Professor Charles Lindholm for suggesting and making sure in his own nice way that I start writing my memoir and then continue doing so. It would have not been possible without his active support at all the stages of writing, editing and publishing. I know he would not want me to dedicate the book to him. I am also grateful to Sir Michael Green, who suggested in passing that I should pen down the past and present about village life when he came to Swat after visiting Hindukush.

Dr Farooq Swati was kind enough to go through some parts and suggested the title "In Pursuit of Knowledge". Professor Rasul Jan has also been helpful whenever I wanted advice or help from members of the university faculties.

Shazia Shah and Saima Nawaz went through some sections and patiently tried to correct my English writing. Salman Usama, Danish and Atif Rose helped with the computer work, for which I am thankful.

I am most grateful to the former Engineer In Chief of the Army and Rector of NUST University, Shujaat Hussain, former Governor of Sind Province Moin Haider, Professor Abdullah Sadiq and Professor Gregor Prindull, who were gracious enough to send material which I have included in the book .

I used the facilities of Rehman Medical Institute (RMI) and I must thank Chairman Muhammad Rehman, his talented CEO, Shafique-ur-Rehman and his colleagues in the Management Department.

My wife Shahnaz made sure that I was regularly provided with jugs full of green tea, coffee, walnuts and given breakfast in bed when I was busy writing. Leaving her beautiful home in Isfahan and settling in strange place and then helping in the education and marriages of my nephews and nieces were all great feats which need to be mentioned. No wonder Charles and Cherry Lindholm named her "Guardian Angel".

I will be failing in my duty if I do not acknowledge the help in my education in early and later life of my teachers, mentors and friends. Baidara Ustad, the village prayer leader, taught me "Quaeda" without any indoctrination or hatred for other religions and sects. Chaghwar Ustad taught me the Pushto and Urdu alphabet in the village shop in return for a daily bowl of fresh milk. Recently I discovered that his family Roghanis came from Dir and that his relatives A. Rahim and M. Shaw have become renowned Pushto poets.

In the formal primary teaching school in Swat, I am glad to have been taught by Lala Jan Ustad, who had a great sense of humour and never resorted to "spare the cane and spoil the child." Hussain Khan, Abdur Rashid, Serai Ustad and Sambat Ustad are fondly remembered from my days in Jehanzeb College. I am grateful to the Wali of Swat who devoted his energy to development of education, health and infrastructure in Swat, and who made sure that the teachers in the College had high standards not only in education but also in building the character of students. The teacher of English, Shuaib Sultan Khan (SSK), was the top student of Lukhnow University in

India. Ashraf Altaf, who was from Karachi, encouraged me and made me editor of the English section of the college journal, for which I am grateful. The fact that our Urdu teacher also played the harmonium made me think that there is more to learning than mugging your books. Danishmad Khan was not only kind but wanted me and my friend Sherin Jan learn how to type.

Haji Roshan Tota (HRT) offered me the help of his son Hazrat Bilal, who was studying at King Edward Medical College Lahore. Ahmad Hilal, HRTs able cardiologist son, who is settled in the US, has always been supportive of our work in education for underprivileged children in my home village. It was a pleasure for me and Shahnaz to name the Science Hall in Shin Bagh School after him and the Library after Haji Roshan Tota.

The teachers of the medical college knew their job well because late Dr. M.K Afridi, an internationally known malariologist and retired British Officer, made sure that medical teachers had the proper degrees and the proper attitude. He inculcated ability, accessibility and affability (3A) in future health workers. Inayat Khan and the Bengali teacher made me act in a humorous Pushto skit, "Da Wache Khan" (Good for nothing Khan), which helped me to get over my shyness. Medical teachers are role models and Nasiruddin Azam Khan was not only my role model because of his clinical teaching in the wards but also his ethical approach.

Among the senior students at the Medical College, Bakth Biland (high luck) and his English wife Jill have remained family friends. Amjad Hussain of Toledo, Ohio was an important member of the football team and he continues to call me "goalie"- goalkeeper. My class fellow Jauhar Khatoon not only wore the hijab in the class but was pretty and brainy. Her husband Dr. Shafiuqe, as well as his brothers and their spouses, have become family friends. Imran, who is a gynaecologist in

Delaware USA, has been a good host but introduced me to gambling games in Atlantic City. He used to lament that he had failed to instruct his children in the Pushtun values of respect for elders that were traditionally taught in Hujras.

My senior and in-charge of the Saidu Hospital, Swat, Dr. Najibullah Khan Chuhan, taught me that you do not have to be a super specialist of a narrow medical speciality to help your patients. He was a physician who did surgery on all parts of the body. This helped me in my future health work for the patients. From him I learned the need for self-training and for making facilities available, for which I am grateful.

My good friend Fazli Ali helped and facilitated my trip to Great Britain and Majid Khan of Manchester put me on the right path to apply for jobs in NHS. Ali Nawaz Babar recommended me for the Royal College of Radiologists and has always remained supportive.

Seeing me dejected coming out of Khyber Medical College because I had not got a job, Tariq Nishtar and the late Dr. Shams advised me to knock on the door of Pakistan's Atomic Energy Commissioner (PAEC), where I met Chairman Munir Ahmad Khan, whose golden words I still remember: "I am trying to establish institutions so that our qualified people have places to work when they return from abroad and I am also trying to build Nuclear Reactors for Electricity Generation as we will have power shortage in future".

There were many in PAEC who helped facilitate my work in the peaceful uses of atomic energy, including, most notably, Inam-ur-Rehman and Abdullah Sadiq. Durre-Sabih was kind enough to arrange a Sher M. Khan day in Multan, many years after I had left the Seraiki Belt. Meeting the generous people of Multan who still send me delicious mangoes every year was exhilarating. Sultan Topian, who hails from the same area but is settled in Paris, is a man of many talents who keeps his friends and acquaintances all over the world amused not only by sending the Sufi poetry of Bulle Shah and Pathane Khan over the internet, but also by forwarding mouth-watering still pictures and moving pictures.

I am also thankful to Chris Newton and Tony Tingle for their help in editing and publishing this memoir.

There are many who helped and gave advice during the writing of the book and during my career. Space does not allow me to mention them individually. For them, I will if I may use the letters IBM, which I first heard from Catherine Sahovic. It stands for "In-Sha-Allah, Bukra, Ma-Sha-Allah".

I do not have to acknowledge the help and support of Mah Muneer, Mujgan, Cyrus Khan and their life partners Gohar, Shoab and Sidra, because Pukhtuns take help and support for granted from their near and dear ones.

FOREWORD

I first met Dr Sher Muhammad Khan while I was doing anthropological fieldwork in Swat in 1977. We became good friends, and it was mainly through him that I kept up with events in the valley and the village in the years that followed. For a number of reasons, I never went back to Swat, but Sher always brought Swat back to me, and I am honored that he has asked my wife and myself to write forewords to his memoir.

Now, after reading this sensitive, wide ranging and often very funny autobiography, I have learned much more than I knew before about Swat and the people who live there. I have also learned about Pakistan in general and about the medical professionals and other middle-class Pakistanis whose lives are not usually recorded by anthropologists.

Dr Sher's story is unique to him, of course. But it is also similar to the biographies of many other village boys around the world who have somehow learned the skills and attitudes that allowed them to succeed as professionals in the international arena. His father, Muhammad Qamar Khan (Khaista Dada – 'beautiful dada' - to his juniors), was highly regarded throughout

Swat as a person of honor, a leader of men, and a staunch ally. But, like most of his generation, he was also illiterate, and his horizons were limited. The world he lived in was harsh and impoverished; luxuries were absent, while pain and sickness were rampant, as Sher's memoir documents without any beautification.

At the same time, as Sher's memoir also shows, the Swat of his youth was less isolated than outsiders tend to think. Some village men did travel great distances to find work, even to Bombay, and they came back with many stories of the strangeness of these foreign places and the people who lived there. Others, like his uncle Major Nisar Khan, achieved positions of authority in the Pakistani military, providing a personal example of worldly accomplishment. But the village and its values of generosity, hospitality, and honor still remained the touchstone for personal and collective identity. In that environment, roles and relationships were regulated by custom, and ties of allegiance bound patron and client together in mutual dependency. Swat certainly wasn't paradise, but it was a stable place, woven together by shared kinship ties and the values of Pukhtunwali – the code of conduct.

All that is clear enough in Sher's memoir. At the same time, he corrects fundamental errors that many outsiders, including myself, made about traditional life in Swat. For example, the interdependence of villager and townsman, farmer and merchant, has generally gone unremarked in anthropological accounts of Pukhtun life. But without the financial help and influence of his father's storekeeper allies from nearby towns, the path out of the village would have been closed to Sher.

Another theme is the dishonesty, favouritism, and profiteering that pervaded Pakistan after independence. Partly this was the result of the intrusive power of the state and the social disruption caused by the expansion of free-market capitalism. Customary laws and local mediation by respected village khans and mullahs were superseded by an inefficient and often unfair judicial system. Meanwhile, feudal ties of patronage were transformed into easily severed relationships between employers and employed, so that absentee landlords could abdicate their customary responsibility for their poor clients and tenants.

As Sher's stories reveal, these insidious external influences acted in unexpected tandem with traditional values. Tribalism has its virtues – it promotes solidarity and protects kin from predation. But at the same time it can lead to supporting unworthy relatives and the envious persecution of able individuals who are outside the circle of kinship. Corruption is the inevitable outcome. Dr Sher's traditional training in the moral responsibilities of being a khan, following the example of his father, was combined with his schooling in the achievement-based English system, and with his experiences as a doctor and world traveler. These influences combined to make him very conscious of the damage that can result from the distorting conjunction of tribal consciousness with modern institutions.

It is Sher's awareness of injustice that makes his memoir more than simply a personal story, written to amuse and inform family and friends - though it does that admirably. It also makes it more than a valuable description of a vanished world and of the new world that is replacing it. With sensitivity, modesty, and humor, Dr Sher's story portrays the life of a wise and kind man - a khan, a village boy, a Pukhtun, Yusufzai, Paindakhel, who is also a world traveler, doctor, expert in nuclear medicine, philanthropist, paterfamilias, - who is striving to overcome the inequity and suffering he sees around him. Acting on that generous impulse, he has built and supported clinics and schools in his home village, healing the sick and training young people – girls as well as boys – to learn and to excel, and to live larger lives than their parents.

Is it possible for one man to make a difference in this world? Dr Sher's memoir demonstrates that it can.

Charles Lindholm, University
Professor of Anthropology Emeritus, Boston University

When I first arrived in Sher's home village in Swat in the spring of 1977, what struck me was not only the physical beauty of the place - the fields full of bright yellow mustard flowers, the surrounding mountains of the Hindu Kush, the sparkling icy River Swat rushing through the valley, and the colors and textures of the river stone and mud houses that made up the ancient village – but also the sensation that it was all somehow very familiar. I found myself unexpectedly at home in this strange place, where everything was new and unknown and where I could not understand a word of the language that sounded to me rather like the river – an unbroken and unintelligible rush of sound.

During the year I lived in the village, I managed to pick up a few basic phrases – mainly from the children. I had the vocabulary of a two-year-old, but sufficient for my needs. I was indeed like a small child in my new environment – naive and unaware, but able to learn. I am grateful to the women, children and men who were gracious enough to welcome a stranger and to tolerate my ignorance.

What life in the village lacked in modern amenities, it more than made up for in the richness of its emotional canvas, and I think it was the intensity of this chemistry that was responsible for my feelings of familiarity when I first arrived – the basic chemistry of all human beings coming together anywhere in the world. It was indeed rather like falling in love, that sudden rush when the stranger becomes the beloved.

I will never forget my time in Swat, the beauty of the

landscape, the river, the changing seasons, and especially the people; and I thank Sher for writing this autobiography, which will help enrich my already rich memories.

Cherry Lindholm

We first met Sher Khan when we visited Pakistan in 1999. Our tour took us from Rawalpindi along the road up to the Hunza area, close to the Chinese border. We arranged to meet Sher, when we were in Swat. We had known about him for a long time because our student Chuck Lindholm had done his dissertation research while living with Sher's family. On the day we met Sher, he told us we were lucky, a strange thing to say since, unfortunately, a death had just occurred in his family. The funeral was to be held that day. As a consequence of his association with Chuck, Sher knew how interesting funerals were to anthropologists since they revealed the social structure of the society.

Sher is unique in that he has lived in two very different worlds. First he is an important leader among his own people, establishing a school for community children in which English was taught. Second, he lives in the modern world of western medicine, being a Professor of Cancer and Nuclear Medicine. Some years ago, the Wali of Swat told his own story. We are delighted that Sher is now telling the story of his life.

Paula Rubel
Professor of Anthropology Emerita
Barnard College, Columbia University

Abraham Rosman
Professor of Anthropology Emeritus
Barnard College, Columbia University

PART ONE
A Pukhtun Life

CHAPTER ONE

LIFE IN THE VILLAGE

I am a member of the Yusufzai tribe of the Pukhtun people, born in the village of Lower (*kuza*) Durshkhela in the picturesque valley of Upper Swat in Northwest Pakistan, the region where my tribe has lived for at least four centuries. Our legends say that we fought our way into the valley from Afghanistan.

Yusufzais left Afghanistan some five hundred years ago following a massacre of their *maliks* (chiefs) when they were invited by the then ruler of Kabul to a banquet. Out of seven hundred only six survived, and one of the six was Malik Ahmad, who led the tribe through the Khyber Pass to come to the plains of Peshawar and ultimately settle in their present fertile and picturesque, if not peaceful, lands of Swat, Dir, Malakand and Mardan. The population of Swat at that time was Jehangiris, who left Swat along with their peace-loving ruler Sultan Owais to the east of the Indus River and are settled in Hazara, where they still call themselves Swatis and Jehangiris. The Sultan lived in Manglawar, where recently the grandson of the former Wali of Swat died in a roadside bomb blast.

Buddhism was the predominant religion in Swat before the invasion of the armies of Mahmood Ghaznavi. Monasteries and the statues of Buddha can still be found in Swat, some with their heads defaced. One professor of archaeology mentioned that Buddha was born in Swat and people travelled from Tibet and India for their pilgrimage. Archaeological sites depicting settled populations and monasteries all over Swat are evidence that Swat was peaceful and tranquil, and people followed their daily routines without fear.

However, fierce fighting did take place when the army of Mahmood Ghaznavi invaded Swat, and the commander of the army was killed, along with his son. Martyrs in this war were buried in my village (Kuza Durshkhela) and Bara (upper) Durshkhela, which are thought to have derived their names from the martyrs (*dursh*) who are buried there. Upper Swat has been the site of many battles since; some internal, between families and parties, some external, against the neighbouring kingdom of Dir. Most recently, it was the centre of an uprising of religiously-inspired rebels (Taliban) against the Pakistani Government. This rebellion was only put down by massive military intervention and the use of tanks and jet planes. As this is being written, Upper Swat is still occupied by the Pakistani army.

The date of my birth is not known. At that time, there were no records of births or deaths, although I have heard that during British rule the records were kept in police stations. However, I must have been born around 1940, since one of my first recollections is of the times during the Second World War when men gathered in my father's cousin's *hujra* (hujras are community centres used mainly by men to accommodate guests and for entertainment) to listen to the village's only radio, which was battery-powered. People were either on the side of Germany or the Allied forces. Whenever there was news of one side's victory over the other, half the listeners would rejoice, while the others would lament. Those supporting Germany were called 'Germanian' and those on the side of the Allied forces were called 'Angreezan'. I also distinctly remember the celebratory fires lit on the mountaintops in 1945 at the end of the war.

My mother, Bakht Bisyar (meaning plenty of luck), was the second wife of my father, Mohammad Qamar Khan. She was a very intelligent and tough lady; domineering, yet kind to all those who worked for her. Though she could not write, she taught herself to read and was fond of the Shahnama of the great Persian poet Firdausi, the poems of Rahman Baba, the Pukhtun Sufi mystic, and other books translated into the Pashto language. On the tenth day of the month of Muharram, marking the martyrdom of Prophet Muhammad's (PBUH) grandson Hussain at the hands of the Caliph Yazid in the battle of Karbela, the ladies from our house and the neighbours' houses gathered around my mother as she read aloud the sad stories of that fatal event. The women cried loudly at these recitations, as it was believed that the more tears you shed, the more your sins would be forgiven. When men heard these tales, they would abuse the villain Yazid, but the women never indulged in such abuse, saving their energy for wailing.

Pukhtuns have been Muslims for a very long time. When Islam came from Arabia to the Pukhtun territories, the Pukhtun quickly adopted it because many of its elements appealed to them. First, Islam was a warrior religion, and horses, swords and battle attract Pukhtuns. Strong notions of honor (*ghairat*), hospitality and generosity were other characteristics of Islam that they found compatible. Pushtun converts were important in spreading the Muslim religion in India and probably also into Central Asia. The emergence of Pakistan after partition in 1947 is to a large extent due to Pushtuns, who were the pioneers in spreading and preaching their adopted Muslim religion. When I was a boy, it was taken for granted that being a Pukhtun meant being a Muslim, though most Swatis did not know much about Islamic doctrine, except that a devout believer should, if possible, pray five times a day, try to go on the *hajj* (pilgrimage) to Mecca, keep the fast during the holy month of Ramadan, recite the *shahada* (there is one God, Allah, and Mohammad is his Prophet) and give alms. Most people were content with that. We knew nothing of sectarian differences - that wailing was essentially a Shi'ite ritual, not followed by Sunnis, which is what we were. In fact, we did not know that Shi'as existed. Nor did we know that our tradition of jumping over fires in the springtime is a remnant of Zoroastrianism, or that the custom of paying devotion to Saints' tombs is forbidden by Wahhabi zealots. The Pukhtun customs of paying bridewealth, excluding women from inheritance, forbidding divorce, were all assumed to be Islamic. Only recently have Muslim teachers and preachers informed us that this is not so.

My mother's family came from the neighbouring village of Baidera, where I often visited my maternal relatives, who always looked after me very well. Like her daughter, my Baidera *abai* (grandmother) was a tough lady who was gentle to me. My mother's mother was Mamatkhela and she was the first wife of my mother's father, who also took two more wives. In Baidera I was cared for as well by Akbar Sultana (Big Sultan). Her respect name was Shahi Bibi, meaning Royal Lady, and she was the youngest sister of my mother. Shahi Bibi was talented, elegant, and pretty, but she was blind in one eye as a consequence of smallpox during childhood. She had been engaged as a child, but her mother broke the engagement off because of a feud against the family of her husband-to-be. Later she was happily married to a friend of her brother and moved to her husband's home in the Katlang Mardan area, south of Swat.

Our house in my father's village of Lower Durshkhela was large and was shared by my father's mother, my father's two brothers, one older and one younger, their respective wives and children, and also by the female household servants. My father's first wife, Shan Baha, who we called Bodigram Bibi because Bodigram was her home village, lived in the same house in a separate room. As a competing co-wife (*bun*), she was not liked by my mother, and was not invited to her readings from Firdausi, Rahman Baba, and from her account of Hussain's martyrdom. My father, a peaceful man, usually did not dare go near Bodigram Bibi for fear of my mother's sharp tongue. Nevertheless, one pregnancy did take place and when the baby was being delivered, my mother stayed awake all night and kept on asking whether the new baby was male or female. When it turned out to be a girl, my mother was very happy, since a boy baby would have been my rival.

The antagonism between my mother and Bodigram Bibi could be terrible. Once I asked our local religious teacher if he could offer up *dua* (prayers) or supply *taweez* (holy texts placed in amulets and worn for protection) that would stop the two women from arguing so much. His efforts were ineffective. At times the shouting coming from our compound was so loud that it could be heard in the hujra, which was about two hundred yards away. Noisy fights between co-wives or between neighbouring women were common in the village, and were a major form of popular entertainment. Women's loud verbal exchanges usually started as a result of quarrels between their respective children, which could escalate to involve adults. Mostly, the women shouted at each other from their rooms, but sometimes they ventured forth to pull each other's long hair. When a fight broke out, children ran out onto the streets to eavesdrop and bring reports of the choicest insults back to the women secluded in their compounds. If a hair-pulling fight occurred close by, women and children climbed onto their roofs to look and listen with avid interest.

Writing about hair pulling reminds me of an incident in the late sixties when Maulana Abdul Qadir, founder and director of the Pashto Academy and a sophisticated, pious, and cultured person, was visiting London in search of a Pashto book in the British Museum. The book was written by Pir Roshan of the Burki tribe in Waziristan. Cricketer turned politician Imran Khan, who was married to a pretty, elegant, rich lady, Jemima Goldsmith, also belongs to the Burki tribe. The book was burnt, as the writer, known as Pir Roshan to western Pushtuns, who speak the soft dialect of Pashto, and Pir Rokhan, to the eastern Pukhtuns, who speak the hard dialect of their language Pukhto, was declared heretic by a Mullah during the time when India was ruled by Moghuls (note – in this book I use Pushtun and Pukhtun more or less interchangeably). The Mullah had declared that anyone who burned the book would straightaway go to Heaven. The result was that Pukhtuns burnt the book '*khair-ul-byan*' wherever they got hold of it. Professor A. Qadir ultimately found the original copy in a library in Germany. Pukhtuns will do anything right or wrong if they are told that ultimately they will get 'Hurrahs' or 'Ghilmans'. It was, I think, Lenin who said 'if you keep on repeating a lie, people will start believing it'.

Maulana Abdul Qadir was living in a hotel in Charing Cross. When I went to visit him I found him extremely excited. He told me that while walking on the street he had just seen two ladies shouting, fighting and pulling each other's hair. This respected, serious scholar enjoyed the spectacle tremendously. It is true that wrestling and boxing are spectator sports in many other cultures, but in my opinion, the Pukhtun probably like watching any sort of fighting more than anyone else.

Despite my mother's hostility towards her and the fights between them, my stepmother was kind to me. When I was a pre-school child, I used to sit with her in her room while she fed me and took good care of me. At times I asked my mother why she was not on good terms with her co-wife, but there would be no answer. I also had two stepbrothers and two stepsisters. Unlike our mothers, we generally got along well, though there was some jealousy over the fact that my mother was my father's favourite. This jealousy increased after my mother produced three more sons: Shad Mohammad Khan (Shada Nosh), Mohammad Kamal Khan and Abdullah Khan. Shad Mohammad eventually became a lawyer (*wakil*) in the local courts and Kamal Khan received a religious education and was an important leader in the Muslim community in England until his early death. Abdullah Khan emigrated to the USA, where he now works as an insurance broker. He has one pretty, intelligent daughter, Marjan, and a son, Zakir. Zakir stutters and is in special school in New York, but someone told his parents that if he is taught the Quran, his stuttering will disappear. The best place to send him, his mother Shahida thought, was to England to Kamal Khan's sons, who are all 'Hafiz-e-Quran' - they had learnt the Quran by heart. Twelve-year-old Zakir landed at London Heathrow Airport alone and the immigration officers rightly sent him back because of his age and his statement that he had come to study in the madrassa. When I heard about it I told Abdullah Khan off, but he blamed Zakir's mother and I had to exchange harsh words with her, saying that there had been no mullahs for generations in their family nor in our family, so why did she want to make her son a mullah? In Pukhtun families, the elders in the family are at liberty to tell off, swear at or abuse the younger and their wives for good reasons, without the younger ones questioning or retaliating, but this is changing. I described the episode of my nephew Zakir to a friend and he said that old beliefs acquired during early life are difficult to change and told me the saying of a Persian Sage, Shaikh Saadi: 'Khare Essa gar Maka rewad, choo beayed hunooz khar bashad' - even if the donkey of Essa goes to Mecca, on return he will remain a donkey.

Unlike me, my older stepbrother, Durveza Khan, was known for his mischief. Nonetheless, after getting an education in good schools and colleges, he joined the banking service and reached the position of vice president, but his jealousy towards me and my mother remained until the end. Because of my blue eyes, he called me 'Shintagh,' which is the name of a noisy bird with blue-green feathers. This was not a compliment. He also insulted me by calling me 'da mateze khaze zwe' - the son of a runaway lady. I asked my father about this, and his reply was not to mind, my brother was Omarkhel (the tribe of Durveza's mother). A tribal background is often quoted in Swat to explain people's behaviour and characteristics. The Omarkhel, according to my father, were naturally jealous.

Paacha Gul, my great grandfather, was chief of the Painda Khel tribe in Upper Swat. He died of a wound in his chest which he had sustained during tribal fighting, presumably because of infection leading to an accumulation of pus. A British adventurer or an intelligence agent at that time had seen his suffering and sent a message that he would treat him provided he was given protection, but it was too late and he died before he got the message. One Omar Khel in Bodigram village had bragged that he was the one who had shot Paacha Gul. My grandfather, Shahbaz Khan, who was known as Sinpora Khan, a Khan of Sinpora, came to know about it and killed the persons who had bragged about injuring Paacha Gul.

Revenge is ingrained in the psyche of the Pukhtun right from childhood. Recently in a village near Peshawar hardly a hundred yards from where I live, a young man was told during a brawl in a village street that if he was so brave why had he not avenged the murder of his father? He took a Kalashnikov, went to the mosque and started shooting, and killed twenty people who were praying. The targeting of Police Force, Army and Frontier Constabulary is probably because of the psyche of revenge.

Bodigram village is perched high on the right bank of River Swat. As a child I went with Durveza Khan to visit my stepmother when she went to her father's house. I used to look forward to it because they looked after me, feeding me well with milk, rice and butter, which were in abundance because they kept buffaloes next to their house. I used to enjoy looking at the river flowing in a zigzag manner from the north to the south. At night time I could hear the rushing sound of the river, the barking of dogs, braying of donkeys and howling of foxes from distant mountains. In Pukhtun traditions, young visiting children were extended all the facilities of hospitalities and not harmed during fighting, but Pukhtuns also have strange and at times destructive traditions.

It was on one of these visits to Bodigram village that I heard that Biradar Khan (Brother Khan), brother of my stepmother, whom I called Mama, Maternal Uncle, was lying in bed because of injuries he had sustained during the marriage ceremony of his brother. In those days, the bride was brought in a *dooli*, carried by two relatives of the bridegroom in front and two relatives of the bride at the back. At the entrance of the bridegroom's house the bride's brothers used to say that their sister had to be given the prized place for sitting near the open hearth - 'da naghari bar taraf'. If the bridegroom's brothers refused because of their egos, a fight would start, and this was how Biradar Khan was injured. Only fists and kicks were used, no guns or rifles. This was probably an excuse for indulging in fights, because of lack of healthy sports.

Bodigram village and the next two villages, upper Bamakhela and Lower Bama Khela, belong to a 'Kashar' (younger Khel) of Painda Khels, while the lower Durshkhela belonged to a 'Mashar Khel' (elder Khel) of Painda Khel. They came from the same stock and shared the lands in the village to which I belong. Bodigram is also the village to which a 'commander of Taliban' - Bakht Farzand belonged. He was dreaded and was responsible for attack on the vehicle of Afzal Khan Lala, popularly known as Khan Lala, and his nephews. Mohammad Rahim Khan, a Painda Khel from our village, rescued them by firing in the air and the attackers entered the thick olive grove near the road and walked away.

It is said that it was also a revenge attack because they had given refuge to the murderers of Bakht Farzand's Father. During the Army Operation, Farzand escaped to Indus Kohistan, where he was killed in an 'encounter' and his body brought to Swat by the Army Personnel and exhibited in different villages in Upper Swat.

My other half-brother was Zaman Khan. He was my junior by six months. Unlike Durveza Khan, Zaman Khan was always friendly to my mother and me. He had a good sense of humour and we used to share our secrets. Zaman Khan was never cruel like his brother, but he too was mischievous. He found that it was easy to pilfer grain from our house because the containers for rice, wheat, maize or flour were made either of dried mud or wood. It was a simple matter to punch a small hole at the bottom of these containers and drain small amounts of the grain periodically without it being noticed. This grain could then be sold or exchanged. He also liked to remove the handmade silk embroidered pillows covers that were kept for guests in the hujra and sell them to buy peanuts, *gur* (brown sugar), homemade sweets or rubber for slingshots from the few shops in the village.

As a young man Zaman Khan was also quite a chaser of

women. He hid his girlfriends in a long wooden storage container that was kept in the hujra. This went on until one day our father opened the box and found a girl inside. Zaman was not keen on his studies, but he was very talented at repairing and mending things; he was always ready with a joke, and was an expert at making friends. Later he became a teacher and now runs a private school. In Swat, there was no recognition of a person's aptitudes or talents. In those days, men were expected to grow up to follow their fathers' occupations; women were expected to be housewives.

I had six sisters. Asmane Rome (sky of Rome) was the eldest stepsister. She was engaged as a child to a cousin, Dir Mohammad Khan (DMK), who was much older, and he left for Bombay before partition to seek work. He was a spendthrift and even in Bombay his lifestyle was like Pukhtun Khan, with a small hujra and hospitality for whomever sought his help. He returned after partition to the village, got married and continued his lifestyle of music and dancing at night time until the cash which he had brought finished. He was the only person in the village who knew how to drive and later became a personal chauffeur of a businessman from Punjab, which he resented. Pukhtun did not have any idea of investment and saving for a rainy day. One of DMK's sons, Sattar Khan, joined UNHCR and was sent to Iran, where he was declared persona non grata because he would not compromise on the treatment of refugees by the Iranian Government. Pukhtuns by and large, when given certain duties, especially outside their region, will interpret rules and regulations rigidly because of the code of loyalty instilled in them, right from the childhood. In big cities like Karachi, Pukhtuns are sought after as personal bodyguards and for security duties in private houses, because of their dependability and bravery.

The eldest of my sisters was named Sucha Bibi (unpolluted bibi). She was blonde, with blue eyes and fair colouring. My mother got her married to a cousin of ours who had more land than us. Her husband died soon after marriage because of a brain haemorrhage. As in Pukhun traditions, she had to be married to the brother who was already engaged to his mother's niece. Sucha had a tough time to adjust to her new environment because of her younger age and domineering mother-in-law.

Pukhtun ladies played the dominant role in marriage because of accessibility and continuity of close relations. Like her mother, Sucha would not allow her husband, Mohammad Qavi Khan, popularly known as Bacha Lala, to go near her 'bun'. She had six pretty daughters but no son of her own. Male issue is important in Pukhtun society and a couple will continue to have children until they have at least one boy. All her daughters are happily married.

During the recent man-made disasters, followed by the natural disaster of devastating floods, there was a shortage of all items, including life-saving medicine. Swaties suffered a lot. On the one hand the Taliban scared people, while on the other hand the trigger-happy law-enforcement authorities made life very hard because of curfews, search operations, displacements and checking. Sucha died because of the non-availability of insulin. Someone remarked that Sucha 'starved to death in the midst of plenty', meaning that there were three well-qualified doctors in her family and her husband was a retired school principal. But Pukhtun blame everything on 'pa qismat ke ye ba lekeli wa': it must have been written in her fate.

Jehan Pass (top of the world), the second sister, had the respect name Liaquat Bibi, but my father, who was good at nicknaming people, called her 'Levanae', meaning mad person. She got married in Baidara, the village of my mother's family.

The third sister was named Taj Mahal and her respect name was Risalat Bibi. My father nicknamed her 'sandori' because as a child she was 'roly poly'. She married a cousin and had two sons and four daughters. The girls were well educated, unlike the girls in our family. Naheed, the eldest girl, is headmistress in the high school in our village.

The youngest sister, Sahib Jamala, lived with us in Peshawar. My wife Shahnaz looked after her very well and trained her in household work. In return Sahib Jamala looked after our two daughters, Mah Muneer and Mujgan, and later on our son Cyrus. The children loved her because she was quiet, never lost her temper and would agree to what the children wanted. She had inherited the genes of our father rather than our mother. Some outsiders from the family wanted her to be engaged to be married, but Shahnaz wanted her to be married within the extended family. She was engaged to Inam Khan, son of Nisar Khan, and she is happily married and has two daughters and two sons. Mah Muneer, Mujgan and Cyrus have fond memories of their childhood in the company of Sahiba, whom they all recall affectionately.

Jehan Pass's husband-to-be had seen her during Eid festivities: after Ramadan, the month of fasting, people in general and children and adolescents in particular wear new clothes, visit each other's houses and exchange gifts. In our village on the first day of Eid the girls, wearing bright new multicoloured clothes, used to go to the *banr*, graveyard, which had tall olive trees and grassy ground with a stream flowing in the middle. The place was described by a foreigner as the most beautiful place in the village. During these gatherings, the girls used to sing and dance. Boys would also go to the same place separately with their flutes, sitars and drums and enjoy themselves. Strong ropes (*narae*) made from the skins of animals were tied to the tall trees and used as swings. On the second and third day the boys and girls, in separate groups, went to other villages such as Pir Kali Mian Qasam Baba, where the son of Mahmood Ghaznavi is supposed to have been martyred some thousand years ago when Buddhists were living peacefully in Swat. These festivities are no longer celebrated in upper Swat because of religious militancy.

A woman by the name of Zerqeshun was given the task of looking after me, since I was my young mother's first child. My nanny came from another village to work in our house, leaving her own newborn son with her family. She took care of me, fed me and was very fond of me. I was a pretty baby: chubby, blue-eyed, fair coloured, with light brown hair. Later in my life, when I lived in England, I was always mistaken for a European.

At times my mother accused Zerqeshun of disobedience and of being too friendly with her enemy, Bodigram Bibi, and banished her from the house, but Zerqeshun would wait outside and when she saw me alone in the cot would run in, grab me and take me away with her. My mother had no choice but to allow her back in.

Zerqeshun was a freedom-loving woman. When she came to us, she had already married once, left her husband, and then remarried a *balkay* (dancer) in the service of my eldest uncle. She later left him and married yet again to a man in another village. She had one daughter with him who was given as a child bride to a musician and trained to be a singer in marriage ceremonies. There she performed for gatherings of women, but she was not used as a dancer because of her dark complexion. The strict Pukhtun tribal ideals of honour and character that prohibited divorce and remarriage for women were applied to some but not to others, depending upon which caste one belonged to. Zerqeshun, a poor woman, actually had more liberty than my mother, though she earned much less respect.

Zerqeshun always carried me with her to orchards and other people's houses. If she wanted to eat apricots, mulberries or pears she would say to the owner 'Khan Jari, 'Mewa Ghwari" (the Khan is crying 'I want fruit'). No one could refuse. Since everyone, including Zerqeshun, slept in a courtyard in the summer, whenever there was a sound of farting coming from us at Zerqeshun's side she would say 'Sher Nosh Khan, Loy sha au kha sha' (Shair Nosh Khan, get older and better).

Children learn how to impose and get what they want in their homes. If I wanted anything such as food or money and my mother would not give it to me, I used to run out of the house, go to the neighbour's house, climb up the wooden ladder to the roof and throw stones at the house until my mother agreed or my father or uncle persuaded me to come down. Every house had ladders and the roofs were flat and interconnected with the other houses. The roofs leaked during the rainy season and in winter because of snow. The walls were made of mud and river bed stones. The streets were muddy during rain and we wore wooden high-heeled shoes called 'kanawe', made by carpenters. People had to learn how to walk in these. I was stubborn as a child and it is only recently that I learned that the Japanese had done research on blood groups and those who have group A are stubborn and cannot relax, but their positive characteristics are peace, harmony and organization. Dina, one of my ten grandchildren, who daily visits us as Mah Muneer lives next door to us, is thought to have the features as well as the characteristics of granddaddy Gul Dada (Flower Dada – my respect name) according to Shahnaz, unlike MM's other children, Danish and Daneen. The rest of my grandchildren live in the United Arab Emirates and the USA, so we do not know yet how they behave.

My father's mother, who lived with us in Durshkhela, was very elderly, and since it was extremely cold during the winters, she would ask all the children to sleep next to her so that she could keep warm. Matches were either not available or were too expensive, so our job was to cover the smouldering fire with ashes for rekindling in the morning. The source of light at night was a burning piece of pine tree (*shontae*) brought from the mountains by tenant Gujars (a caste of cattle herders). Other sources of light included a wick soaked in mustard oil and put in a special earthenware pot. There was no smoke emanating from it, unlike the smoky kerosene oil lamps that were introduced at a later stage.

Gujars are interesting people in Swat. The majority of them live in mountains as tenants and sharecroppers on the land owned by the Khans of Swat. They pay annual *oalang* - rent - to the Khans and share fruit, such as berries and walnuts. The women come to help in the household of the property owner during marriage ceremonies and other festivities. The men are supposed to bring the wood from the mountains to be used in the houses as firewood for cooking and in the mosques in winter for heating. The Shahkhel - leather worker - was supposed to collect the annual galang and to make sure that firewood - *gaidaes* - is regularly brought and able-bodied men and women come to work when needed.

I was be sent to the hill areas by my father and uncle to attend Gujar funeral ceremonies and offer *fatiha*, as it was the tradition in Pukhtun society to help their Gujar tenants at times of bereavement or other domestic troubles. Shahkhel Khuna Gul, meaning 'olive flower', used to accompany me to these far-off places such as Mairamay, Brinjal and Gul Dheri, where we had property from the time of Paacha Gul, my great-grandfather. Khuna Gul was slim, dark, loyal and trustworthy. I also went to his house to eat the cooked and barbecued intestines of animals. Shahkhels also acted as butchers in the village. The intestines, head and feet made up their share.

Khuna Gul (KG) had lost four wives because of illness. Once he was in the bathroom in the mosque, as only mosques had bathrooms in the village for men. My father, who was known for his sense of humour, peeped through the cotton curtain and saw KG having a bath and remarked 'now I know why your wives die, it is because of your huge organ'. KG was also dreaded by our tenant Gujars as he was a no-nonsense man and the Pukhtun Khans kept people like him: clever, diplomatic at times and forceful when the occasion demanded.

During the season of migratory small birds like thrushes in winter and spring, I used to accompany my father to these areas where Gujars lived. We carried slingshots and air guns only. Rifles were strictly prohibited for certain families by the then ruler of Swat, especially to those who had been powerful during the time when there was no formal government. We hunted in a place where there were collections of trees, mainly wild olive trees, usually in graveyards, because in Swat people would plant trees in cemeteries and would forbid cutting trees. In one *banr* - collection of trees in a cemetery - called 'bejawra' (insane), people were brought and tied to a tree for treatment.

My father, Handsome Dada, used to disappear for hours, leaving us to shoot birds. Later I discovered that he had a Gujar girlfriend. Girls from Gujar families were sought after because of their shapely, athletic figures. One of my uncle's second wives belonged to a Gujar family and one of my father's great-grandfathers had a wife belonging to one. The Gujar women brought milk and fruits such as figs, wild black berries to sell in the villages. Once I overheard Jalat Mama (JM), meaning in Pashto 'executioner maternal uncle', in hujra talking about one of these Gujar women bringing milk to the village for selling. JM tricked the woman to his home where he was living alone in a narrow street, put her pitcher full of milk down and told her to sleep with him. JM was a loyal worker of my uncle Tra-Dada and had come from Dir, a neighbouring autonomous state ruled by a Nawab from the Painda Khel tribe. JM was married to a maid working in the house and my uncle educated his children; one became a school headmaster and the rest went to UAE. JM's one grown-up grandchild became a gangster, and during the Taliban uprising he forcefully collected money from people along with his four accomplices until a 'commander' from Bodigram - Omar Khel area came to know about it, called them to him, and executed all four. Another of the four was also the grandchild of one of our past loyal workers, Bakhtak, who was a weaver by profession. This group of four was probably also instrumental in writing me letters to give them three crores of rupees equivalent to three hundred thousand dollars, otherwise they would confiscate the land near Shin Bagh Medical Clinic. I did not accede to their threats, nor did I give the letter to the Army or other law-enforcing authorities for further action.

I never saw an obese Gujar man or woman because of their living conditions; they worked in mountainous regions, eating unrefined food and fruits. Recently some of the Gujar families have amassed wealth by working in the UAE and have bought the land on which they worked as tenants. Some have also become politically active. In the recent uprising of the Taliban in Swat, young Gujars also played an active part as they resented the treatment meted out to them by certain landowner Khans, but not all Khans. In the case of our tribe, when there was an uprising during Bhutto's time of 'Roti Kapra, Makan' - bread, clothing and shelter, and people called it 'Kissaani' - peasants revolted, and when some Khans had forcibly removed Gujars from the land, my father categorically said that no one should touch their tenant Gujars, as they had lived with us for generations. An old short-bearded man named Khachan (unkept) Gujar, still recalls my father's actions.

The origin of the Gujars is disputed, but they probably came from Punjab, because they speak Gujro which is like 'hindko' and Punjabi languages. One of the Presidents of Pakistan in Bhutto's time, President Chowdry, was Gujar. Once an army brigadier asked me 'how are our people in Swat?' meaning Gujars. Some Gujars have left Swat, Dir and Bunner and settled in plains down country such as the Mardan area. One family from our area of Upper Swat settled in Skhakot and are known for kidnapping for ransom, car lifting and gangsterism. They have the protection of some politically-strong Khans in the area. One has the name of Rawan, meaning always on the go, but if you remove the 'a' the meaning in Pashtu becomes mischievous.

Rawan or Rwan was known for kidnapping people, mainly from Punjab. He happened to be my patient when he was on his deathbed and told me some of the stories about his encounters with police. In one encounter he had jumped from a railway bridge into the mighty Indus river near the Mughal Attock fort swam to safety. My car was stolen from the bazaar in Peshawar Cantonment in broad daylight, allegedly by the same family. I had gone to their house in Skhakot, against the advice of some friends. They remembered how good I had been to their father and relatives, showed me the pictures of Rawan., I did not say a word about my stolen car as I thought, and said, that they probably needed the car more than I did.

Some of the Gujar families migrated from Dir, Swat and Buner and became religious teachers and Imams - prayer leaders. They also run religious schools, some, but not all, of which are hotbeds of militant Talibans and suicide bombers.

The ladies, especially those belonging to Khan families or other respectable households, could not talk face-to-face to unrelated men, but were allowed to speak to a man who stood on the other side of a wall. Therefore, our multiple family household had an open space that was walled off from the main house. Without breaking purdah (female seclusion), the ladies of the house could talk to the male workers through that wall and order them to do various jobs as well as give instructions and encouragement to the men whenever there were skirmishes between opposing parties (*dullahs*) or family feuds within the village.

For privacy, the house had the facility of a 'toilet' reserved only for women, which simply consisted of a walled-off place in a corner. The hujra also had a place where guests could urinate. As children we went outside to a pit near the house for our various bathroom needs. The garbage was also put in that pit, and the compost was used, mixed with animal dung, to manure the crops in the fields once a year. Once I was squatting at the edge of the pit to answer the call of nature and at the same time eating roasted corn. A passer-by remarked 'Khana, jaranda ta che dana ache nah ala warna raozi' - Khan, if you put grain in the flourmill then flour will come out of it.

The small village flourmills were powered by the rushing water of a nearby stream. People carried their grain in leather or cotton cloth sacks to the *jaranda* (mill) where a village carpenter performed the task of milling in return for a share of the flour. Everything was done in turn, according to a strict system. A Pukhto proverb probably comes from this practice: 'Jaranda ka da plar de kho pa waar de' - even if the watermill belongs to your father, you still have to wait for your turn. Rice, which is a staple diet in Swat and is eaten at least once a day, was refined by the *paiko* - a stone attached to a thick hard piece of wood and run by water. This was also looked after by carpenters employed collectively by villagers. They were given a share of grain at harvest time twice a year, as well as a piece of land to sharecrop.

Our water came from a canal connected to the main river Swat, which flowed through the eastern side of the village. The canal had been dug some years back by the villagers, who also looked after it collectively. The canal water was used for cooking and drinking, and watering and washing the cattle. We also used to swim in it by tying up our baggy pants (*shalwar*) to our legs and then blowing in them at the waist to inflate them. Abai often had us bring her water from the nearby stream. At times she stood in the door and simply asked passers-by to fill her pitcher. Once I asked her why she asked strangers to do this for her and she replied, 'They are our *azizan* (close dear people)'. When I was older, I visited the houses of our azizan in our *tul* (neighbourhood association) to organize collective festivals, get people to help one another in harvesting or at times of crises, or to lend money to someone in need. Members of the tul shared a common mullah, barber (*nai*), and *shahkhel* (leatherworker). The tul also included carpenters, shopkeepers, weavers, *kulalan* (makers of earthenware pots) and others who did not own land and were not considered to be Pukhtuns. These service people had been associated with our family for generations and were very loyal. My father told us not to call them by their given names, but by respectful titles such as 'mama' (mother's brother). We trusted and relied on them, and provided for them when they were no longer able to work.

However, these mutual relationships were eroded when Swat became more modern and a money economy prevailed over old obligations. Instead of entering into a lifetime relationship, servants and specialists became employees who worked for hire, and could be fired. As a result, in recent years some of the younger generations of these workers in Swat joined the Taliban and fought against their former masters. But during my youth, all of the members of the tul association attended each other's marriage ceremonies and cared for one another during illness and death. Food to the bereaved family was given in turn by the various members of the tul. Membership was voluntary, and people could shift their allegiances, but generally it was a stable group of neighbourhood allies, clustered around a powerful khan household - in this case, the household of my father and his brothers. In my village, as in most villages, there were rival tuls.

Right from a very young age, children (mostly girls) were taught to look after babies and younger siblings, carrying them on their hips, feeding them when they cried and making sure that the flies did not disturb them too much in the summer. Children were not only trained to look after their younger brothers, sisters and cousins, they were also expected to help in cleaning, washing, and carrying cooked items to and from their neighbours and relatives in the village. They also ran errands from their houses to hujras, bringing tea and bread to the men lounging there. By keeping their ears open while running these errands, children were often able to bring home some gossip to entertain their housebound mothers.

For entertainment, we played marbles and girls played jacks with stones. Both girls and boys played hide and seek, especially at night-time. I was a willing partner with the older girls from the neighbourhood in these night games. But in general boys and girls were discouraged from mixing. The elder ladies told the girls that they would develop horns on their heads if they played with boys. Chasing and shooting small birds with a slingshot was another major pastime for us; later the lucky boys whose families could afford them had air guns and rifles. Bullets were expensive, and we learned not to waste any. We also learned to snatch flies clustered on a piece of brown sugar (gur). The boy who caught the most was the winner. We boys learned how to wrestle down other children and to fight rival gangs with sticks, punches, kicks and stones from our slingshots. In the old days, there were regular battles with neighbouring villages in which boys were occasionally seriously injured, even killed. Quail fights, cockfights, dogfights and bull fights were popular entertainments. None of my friends knew anything about cricket or soccer or any of the other healthy games that boys in Pakistan and India play today. Rather, our games were mostly preparations for war, the Pukhtun hobby.

Older children also taught the younger ones some unhealthy habits such as taking *naswar* (chewing tobacco). I remember that my stepbrother, Durveza Khan, who was about three years older than me, used to gather four or five boys together, take them to the nearby fields, sit them in a row and teach them how to masturbate using chewed mild mint plucked from the fields for lubrication.

My name was taken from the name of my maternal uncle, whose name was Faramosh Khan. In Swat, there are no family names as there are in the West. The term Khan, which is given to all Pukhtun, simply means one is a land-owner and a member of a *khel* or tribe, although when one is actually addressed as Khan it is a sign of deference. Among intimates, people are known by their *adab* (respect) names. My respect name is Gul Dada (Flower Dada), though poor people, workers and my subordinates call me Khan or Khan saib (sahib). Respect names in Swat are quite simple; the first word often refers to appearance, character, kinship relationship, or residence. The second is usually a nonsense word such as Lala or Dada. My brother Durveza's *adab* name was Tor Lala (Black Lala), because of his dark colour. My father's older brother, Baacha Khan, was known as Khan Dada in reference to his authority, while his younger brother, Sher Azim Khan, was known to us as Tra Dada (Uncle Dada). My mother's great grandfather, Masum Khan, was called Totki Dada because he dominated a village called Totki when he was young. Elsewhere, adab names can be more ornate. Among the Mangal tribe of Afghanistan, for example, common girls' pet names include Selae (breeze), Diwa (source of light), or Brekhna (twinkling). Mangal men are usually named after flowers or plants or precious stones.

My given name was originally Shair Nosh Khan (milk drinker). Faramosh is a Persian word meaning forgetful and Shair Nosh is also Persian. In Swat people studied Persian books such as Saadi's and Hafiz's books Gulistan and Bostan and some other books, like Musnawi of Roomi and Hadith translated from Arabic. Later I read about the Greek historian Herodotus travelling through this region where Pukhtuns now live. Herodotus had mentioned Cyrus the Great displacing some turbulent tribes from Iran and settling them west of Indus River more than two thousand five hundred years ago. Cyrus is known for his benevolence, according to the Jewish Chronicles, but he is also known to have displaced tribes who would make trouble in his vast kingdom. As I write this, the region where Pukhtuns are living such as Afghanistan, Baluchistan and Khyber Pukhtunkhwa (KPK), formerly known as North West Frontier Province (NWFP), is turbulent.

My father's adab name, appropriately, was 'Khaista Dada' - Handsome Dada. Handsome Dada had a great sense of humour and, as his name suggests, he was also very fond of women. Once as he was telling his rosary, which one usually does by quietly saying 'Allah' or 'Subhanallah,' he was asked by a young serving maid, 'Khaista Dada, what are you saying as you are fingering the beads?' The answer was *'jenai, jenai, jenai'* - 'girl, girl, girl.' I also remember as a child that traders used to call loudly in the village streets, 'Zor pa newi bande' - old stuff for new. Most of our beautiful local handicrafts were lost to these men, who relied on the villagers' desire to possess cheap modern goods. Sometimes I see old Swati embroidery and carved furniture from my home place selling for huge prices at specialty shops in the West. I wish I could buy them and return them to the village. One day my father met the trader in this village street as he was calling 'old one for new one' and asked jokingly 'Can you bring me a new wife in exchange for my old one?' The trader was unwilling to make this bargain.

Of course, philanderers like my father were careful to keep their extramarital affairs secret because of the danger that a cuckolded husband might try to take revenge, and out of fear of their own wives' anger. Nonetheless, my mother was quite well informed about my father's illicit liaisons. Once, when she found his nightdress soiled with blood, she asked the mother-in-law of a pretty married lady nearby whether her daughter-in-law was menstruating. She wasn't. It turned out instead that there was a middle-aged widow in the village with whom he was having relations.

My father was a moderately religious man who kept the fast, said his prayers five times a day, and read the Koran in Arabic without understanding the meaning. Just reciting the Koran aloud was considered a virtuous act, although sometimes the local religious teacher did explain what the words meant. He was fond of hunting and kept falcons (*bashae*) and raised fighting quails. He loved his dogs and used them to flush out the birds he liked to shoot. This hobby was a family tradition. According to my father, his paternal grandfather, the great warrior Ajab Khan (Paacha Gul), had a hundred dogs that he fed and cared for, as well as a hundred *karimars* - 'eaters of curry' - men whom he also fed and cared for, and who in return served as his private army.

Even though my father was greatly respected by all his family, his sons sometimes wished that he did not exist. Hostility between fathers and sons is common in Pukhtun society. The probable reason is that fathers are autocratic and keep their sons dependent. I remember that one day my elder stepbrother, Durveza Khan, got me, Zaman Khan, Shad Mohammad Khan, Mohammad Kamal Khan and Abdullah Khan together to ask our father to give us our rightful share of his property (in Swat women are not entitled a share in the inheritance). Khaista Dada was incensed and told us that as long as he was alive, he was not going to distribute any property to us. He frankly said, 'You people are trying to turn me out of my own house.' As a result, we had to ask the court to make a decision in our case. Sometimes, close relatives even take the law into their own hands with the result that fathers, sons, brothers and cousins kill each other in disputes over inheritance and land distribution. The British were right when they reduced the causes of problems in Pukhtun society to the three Zs: *zun* (women), *zar* (money) and *zamin* (land).

I do not remember my father ever losing his temper. When people complained to him about his sons' mischief, all he would say was: 'Khudai de warta hidayat ooki' - God give them lessons in good behaviour. One of the only orders I remember him ever giving us was to tell us not to make noise if his elder brother Baacha Khan (Khan Dada) was sleeping in the hujra. Uncle Baacha Khan spent most of his time there and rarely visited our compound. His wife beseeched his mother, my abai, to send messages asking him to come to the house as his family missed him, but he only stopped by very occasionally in the night.

My father's younger brother, Sher Azim Khan, whom we called 'Tra Dada' (Uncle Dada), was even less likely to come home. His character was very different from that of his two brothers. He was one of the few people in the village who could read or write. Although he was supposed to be living in the same compound with us, he spent all of his time in the men's house and slept in his own separate room there. He was officially married to Qavi Bibi, a fair skinned, brown haired, blue-eyed lady. Unlike the other ladies living in our joint household, she kept her room neat and always wore clean clothes. Because she did not have children of her own, my stepbrother Zaman and I often sat with her around the open hearth in her room as she gave us something to eat. We children were always happy to get some extra food. She entrusted me to ask her husband to come home at least once in a while, but he had a life of his own that did not involve her. He only came home at lunchtime to see abai, his mother. Like my father, when he went about the village, he was always surrounded by his dogs, which he used for flushing birds. He also hunted birds with falcons, and was often seen with one on his wrist.

At night time, especially in winter, people gathered in Tra Dada's room in the hujra and listened to him recite stories from Firdosi's Shahnama, the great epic poem of Persia, which he knew by heart. After everyone left, he would sleep with a young friend of his. We often went to his room in the hujra to have breakfast with him in the morning. Breakfast with Tra Dada always consisted of tea and maize bread. At times the young friend of Tra Dada was still sleeping in my uncle's bed at breakfast. My father was upset that we children should see this, but I do not remember him saying any harsh words to his younger brother or to his friend. Meanwhile, Qavi Bibi had a friend in the village who was a transvestite. She (or he) would secretly scale the wall at night, spend the night with Qavi Bibi and go home before dawn.

My elder uncle, Khan Dada, was tall and weather-beaten, and as tough and harsh in his dealings with his own family as he was in disputes with other tribes. At that time, Upper Swat was divided into two *dullahs* (parties), which were named after their dominant tribal clan (*khel*). The party of my father and his brothers was the Painda khel and their traditional opponent was the Mamat khel. These two parties had allies throughout Swat. Though they often intermarried with one another, nonetheless the parties fought regularly over rights to land, taking revenge for slights, and other matters. Khan Dada was a leader in these battles, and once even took a shot at his own maternal grandfather, Totki Dada, who was Mamat Khel. Totki Dada much regretted this.

Totki Dada was my father's maternal uncle. He was an intelligent and peace-loving man who travelled widely and introduced new plants and other novelties into Swat, and as a result owned many orchards. As it happened, Totki Dada did not have a son, but only daughters, including, of course, my abai. According to Pukhtun custom, girls are not given a share of their father's inheritance, but must pass it on to their male relatives. This meant that Totki Dada's daughter's sons (my father and his brothers) would ordinarily have inherited his large tracts of land. However, because of the feud between the families, none of his property fell into our hands, although my abai continued to claim produce from it.

When I was three years old, a girl was born to the third and youngest wife of Khan Dada. Childbirth was usually managed by a self-trained lady in the village, and many women died as a result. Babies were swaddled for one year. The *saizn*i (tying rope) was woven with either multi-coloured silk thread or cotton thread. It was thought that keeping the baby tied in this way prevented it from putting out its eyes. It certainly did not prevent infants from crying loudly, and one of the most noticeable sounds of the village, along with the bellowing of cattle, was the crying of infants.

My mother, who wanted an alliance to maintain her position in this house of multiple women, including my stepmother, clipped a part of the dress of the baby, which meant that Khan Dada's baby was now engaged to me. Marrying a boy to his father's brother's daughter was considered the best possible marriage in the village, though often such marriages led to a great deal of bad blood and arguing between the families. This engagement would cause me considerable trouble in later life when I decided I wanted to marry someone else, but as a young boy it meant nothing except that my prospective mother-in-law and father-in-law now treated me especially nicely. They often invited me to eat special food with them and gave me presents. Khan Dada brought me my first pair of embroidered silk shoes from Bombay when he visited that city before 1947.

More important to me in my life than either of my father's brothers was my mother's brother Faramosh Khan, whom I was named after and whose adab name was 'Khkwale Khan' (Beautiful Khan). My father used to take him by bike to school in Thana near the Malakand area and stayed there with him for weeks. It was during one of those stays that the good news of the birth of a son (me) was brought to my father by one of the loyal workers of the family.

Faramosh Khan later changed his name to Nisar Khan and at the same time changed my name to Sher Mohammad Khan, which is the name I am still known by. Nisar Khan always remembered the support of my father during his formative years. He called him 'Khan', stood when my father entered the room, did not smoke or take naswar in front of him, and showed him all the other traditional signs of respect.

Mohammad Nisar Khan was a paragon of Pukhtun virtues: handsome, intelligent, courageous and generous. He was also extremely ambitious and tried his best to loosen the tyrannical grip of the powerful khans in Upper Swat. As one of the few educated men in the valley, he not only wanted his nearest and dearest to be educated, but other people as well. He guided me and paid for my schooling, and did the same for my stepbrother Durveza Khan, much to the disgust of my mother (Nisar Khan's sister). When Nisar Khan found out about an elite school started by the Pakistan Air Force, he paid to have Durveza Khan coached, so that he could pass the entrance examination. When Durveza did pass and was admitted my mother was furious. She said that Nisar Khan was 'fattening her enemies.' But he retorted that her son's turn would come, and it did come, as he promised, so that I too went to that school, which I shall discuss in due course.

Nisar Khan had two wives. The first was from a powerful sub-tribe called the Shamakhel. She was married by arrangement, in order to make an alliance, as was usually the case among the khan families. She was very short but was also very talented. I especially relished the *paratha* (buttered flatbread) that she cooked. She knitted beautiful gold threaded caps as well. Unfortunately, she turned out to be infertile. Nisar Khan had heard about the beautiful sister of his friend from Gham Jabba village in the Kabal area of Swat. Her given name was Paree (fairy), but we called her 'Willayat Bibi' (England Bibi), a name given to her by Nisar Khan. She was very kind to people and, in contrast to my mother, did not quarrel with her *bunna* (co-wife). Willayat Bibi was soft-spoken, helpful, and respectful to her husband. Unlike most Swati women, she did not gossip about her husband's extramarital affairs in the village or the sexual relations he had with the maids working in the house. Much later, I had the good fortune of looking after this fine lady when she was seriously ill.

Although Swat is primarily rural, it has urban centres too. Mingora is the biggest town in the valley. It has two main communities: the business people were called Parachkan, while the land-owning khans were the Pukhtana. Close relations such as intermarriages were not common between the two communities. Business, shopkeeping and trade were considered below the dignity of the Pukhtana. The result was that after property was divided up among various sons or sold to pay for debts, land-owning khans were often impoverished, leading many to migrate in search of their fortunes. Only those such as the Suhrab Khan family in Mingora prospered in Swat because they went into business and other trades instead of depending on land only. The business community made sure that their children were well educated. Nasir-ul-Mulk, who became a Judge of Pakistan's Supreme Court, and Shaheen Sirdar, who became Health Minister, were from this community. Business families also produced prominent medical doctors and teachers who have contributed in their fields not only in Swat but also in the wider world. In contrast, the Pukhtana community preferred to go into government services such as the police, militia and other positions of political authority. Mingora's two communities were not immune to the jealousy prevalent in Pakhtun society.

Like the villagers, city people originally belonged to the Yusufzai tribe, but those who started businesses or became shopkeepers instead of farming were usually called *seth*. The rural khans kept their money with the businessmen in the commercial town of Mingora, who were reliable and honest. Many of these families contributed greatly to the development of Swat and the community in terms of trade and commerce. The families of Ghani, Shamshi, Ismael Seth and my father's friend Haji Roshan Tota come to mind. Later in life, when I was in college in Saidu Sharif, close to Mingora, I used to often visit Tota Seth in his shop in the bazaar in the centre of town. My father told me that if I ever needed money in an emergency, then I should go to Tota Seth.

Kamran Khan and his family were also important businessmen. They had entered the timber business, a major source of income in Swat, which was then surrounded by dense virgin forest (most of it is gone now). Kamran Khan was an intelligent man who had good personal relations with the then ruler of Swat, Jehan Zeb, the Wali, who used to stop in the bazaar so that Kamran Khan could accompany him swimming in the Swat River. We students heard that Kamran Khan and other intimates of the Wali attended parties where they were entertained by handsome boys from the Wali's bodyguards and by professional dancing girls. It was during these sessions that the Wali fell in love with the pretty dancing girl Zaiba, whose story I will soon relate.

Mohammad Rawan Khan, one of the two men who could write and read in our village (my uncle Tra Dada was the other) was employed by Kamran Khan. He negotiated the contracts for them in Indus Kohistan on the silk route. This was no easy task. He took along people from our village and other nearby places as helpers, and they walked for days through difficult country in order to reach the deep forests that were suitable for logging. They told us stories of the habits of people and of their strange ceremonies during circumcision. When Rawan Khan fell ill from tuberculosis, the family of Kamran Khan looked after him very well, as business families customarily did with their loyal workers, just as khans used to care for their loyal retainers.

Although we lived in a remote village, our people regularly went to Bombay, Hyderabad, Ahmadabad, Delhi, and Calcutta to seek employment, or to Arabia to perform the hajj. Perhaps because there is little chance for advancement in their homeland, Pukhtuns have always been great travellers and adventurers, roving far and wide in search of work and opportunity. They typically become merchants, truck drivers, taxi drivers, night watchmen, bodyguards, labourers, sailors, businessmen - almost any job where hard work and perseverance lead to success. If you look, you will find Pukhtuns in every part of the world.

The railway built by the British was efficient and stretched from Durgai, not very far from Swat, all the way to Nowshehra, Rawalpindi, Lahore, and then into India. After partition in 1947, many people from the north-west tribal area went to Karachi seeking jobs. There they had to face terrible hardships as they built Karachi up from nothing with their blood and sweat. The sole communication with these migrant labourers was through letters, which were generally delivered very efficiently by the postal system developed by the British. There were sub post offices scattered all over Swat. The main post office in the big town of Saidu Sharif was headed by a moustached, burly but polite man, who was held in great respect.

Because the literacy rate was very low, people had to find educated people to write letters for them. In our village my younger uncle Tra Dada (Sher Azim Khan) and my cousin Mohammad Rawan Khan were the only two people who could read and write. Tra Dada would never refuse to write letters for the villagers, but he had a wicked sense of humour. He would write the letter, put it in an envelope and ask the man who wanted to send it to go to Saidu Sharif, put a stamp on the envelope and drop it in the red postal box, making sure to shout in the hole of the postbox 'da raghe' - the letter is coming. Some would actually follow his instructions.

When a villager returned after sometimes as many as 15 to 20 years away, ladies of the house beat drums (dumamai) and celebrated day and night. We children listened amazed to the returnees' tales of travelling or working in the big cities of 'Hindustan.' I heard about India's sacred cows as a small child. One traveller said the Hindus treated them as mothers, and I wondered how a cow could be the mother of a human being. The returnees talked excitedly about the films of Laila Majnoon. They told stories of travelling by train without a ticket, hiding when the ticket checker entered the compartment. If caught, they were thrown out on the next station but would not be handed over to the police. They would then board the next train and ultimately reach the big cities, where they lived as guests with their relatives or friends until they could find jobs.

Despite being disinherited by his maternal grandfather Totki Khan, Baacha Khan was still a fairly rich man, since besides land he had inherited quite a lot of wealth, mainly gold and silver coins. He spent the inherited wealth on buying shotguns, rifles and horses for hunting while also providing for the karimars who were his private army. Sometimes a person killed someone in a feud and was given refuge from his enemies by Khan Dada, following the Pukhtun custom. Khan Dada also purchased supplies to be used whenever fighting broke out among the different tribes or between dullahs. He was very fond of music and kept troops of *balkay* (boy dancers) and women dancers. Some of the male dancers were feminine in their talk and actions and were called *badaghs* (homosexual).

In our hujra there was entertainment almost every night, beginning soon after the evening prayers, as musicians performed on the rubab, sitar, harmonium, and *duprai* (tabla). They always began by smoking *charas* (hashish) in their typical way, putting a thin slice (a *chita*) on a smouldering lump of charcoal, sipping water and inhaling the smoke through a dried wheat straw. When exhaling, they spat out the water and shouted 'Yahoo!' This exclamation does not come from American cowboy movies, as Western readers might think, but is derived from the Sufi cry 'Allahu'. Once the musicians reached a proper state of *nusha* (intoxication), the music would start and the dancers began.

The dancers - both boys and girls - wore expensive dresses as well as jewellery. They usually danced energetically for twenty or thirty minutes, and then sat while the singers performed. They would begin with what we call *tappa*. In one popular song, a girl beseeches her lover to bring her an embroidered shirt from Peshawar: 'Laar sha pekhawar ta, kamis tor mala rawra.' In another, she begs him to bring fresh red flowers: 'Taza, Taza gulona range sur mala rawra.' Red is the favourite colour of

Pukhtuns. No wonder Ghaffar Khan, the frontier Gandhi, selected red to symbolize his Khudai Khidmatgars (the so-called 'Red Shirts' who joined Gandhi's campaign of passive resistance against British occupation).

Other songs were taken from the works of the great Sufi poet Rahman Baba, who lived near Peshawar in the 17th century, during the reign of the Mughal king Aurangzeb. His tomb was a place of pilgrimage until it was destroyed by the Taliban in 2009. One stanza I recall is: 'Kar da gula ka che seema de gulzar shi. Aghzi ma kara pa akhpo ke ba de khar shi' - Grow flowers so that your world becomes a garden. Don't grow thorns for they will prick your own feet. The warrior poet Khushal Khan Khattak was also much quoted. Then would come the second type of performance, the recitation of *char beta*, which consists of four stanzas recounting the heroic deeds of our ancestors, especially those who fought to free our homeland from oppression by the Nawab of Dir.

Musicians and dancing girls were required at all marriage ceremonies in the villages of Swat. At night men and children sat and watched the performers entertain, while ladies perched on the roofs, so they could see but not be seen. The dancers marched around the audience, stopping to prance, shake and sing in front of any man whose friends beckoned. To everyone's amusement, the dancer snatched rupee notes which the man's friends placed on his head and shoulders, sometimes slapping him quite hard in the process. After watching these lively singing and dancing ceremonies in the village, I was always depressed for one or two days. Whether this was a physiological, psychological or environmental reaction is still not clear to me.

Along with musicians and dancers, writers and poets, the Yusufzai also are fond of comics. Men gathered in their hujras and the women sat on the roofs to listen to local comedians. One of the most famous was Sharab (Sharif) Gul of Paithai village (since changed to Fathehpur) who was also a court jester. The ruler once sent him with his militia to Kashmir, where he went to the Indian side of Kashmir dressed as a Sikh. The next time he was asked to do this he politely refused, saying he had no enmity with Hindus or Sikhs. Sharif Gul was often invited to marriages and other functions. He was accompanied by one heavily-built but mentally abnormal young man and one transvestite - *putlae* - who joined him in dancing and cracking jokes of all sorts.

I remember one of Sharif's stories. He dreamt he was transported by angels to 'Aasman' - the sky or heaven. There he was shown all sorts of things. In one place there were lots of holes of various sizes. He asked what they were and the angels replied that the size of these holes depicted how much fortune one was destined to have. He asked to be shown his 'hole of luck,' which he was disappointed to find was very small. So he put his finger in it to make it larger. He woke up and found that his finger was in his anus.

Another of the performers I distinctly remember went by the name of Multanae, because he was dark coloured, like people from Multan, south of Swat. Multanae was a dancer to start with but then became famous and organized his own group of musicians and dancers to provide entertainment at celebrations of births and marriages. He was a very intelligent man and an expert in playing the harmonium. He was also innovative and made up many new tunes and steps. Multanae travelled widely with his troop throughout the subcontinent. Once, after Multanae returned from a trip, he asked me to inform my mother that he had a message for her from his Murshid (Sufi guide) in Ajmer Sharif in India. My mother spoke with Multanae from behind the household wall, greeted him, and asked him about his wife and children. Multanae told my mother that he had asked his Pir Murshid to pray for my family so that it could once again attain its past glory. But it turned out that his prayers went for naught. Those days of heroic grandeur were gone forever.

Multanae had a pretty niece named Niawata who was a famous dancer in his troop. She was very popular with the men, who paid large sums of money to spend time with her. Niawata did not accompany anyone who was willing to pay for her time. She was choosy, which made her even more desirable. Eventually, she found a permanent place with the Nawab (ruler) of the neighbouring valley of Dir. The Nawab was a Pukhtun of the Painda khel. He loved luxury, was fond of keeping hunting dogs and had a harem of girls. Niawata was his favourite and she was very well looked after in terms of food, clothing, and lodgings, but had a miserable life. Multanae told me that every night she had to go to the Nawab's room. He was usually drunk and half-conscious in bed, and covered with sweat, but she had to dry him with a towel and then make him lie on her for sexual intercourse. People in Dir and Swat had not heard of the book 'Kama Sutra' and knew nothing of various sexual positions.

Some of these professional dancers (*dumma*) became quite famous, and men competed for their attention. One of them was named Zeba. She entranced the second ruler of Swat, the Wali, who banned her from dancing in public and built a special road to her house, which was known as 'Dummano Road'. He could have kept her as a mistress, but being an honourable man, he actually married her, much against the wishes of his family and of his eldest son, Aurang Zeb, the Crown Prince. The family stipulated that Zeba be sterilized so she could have no offspring of her own who would be called 'da dumma bachi' (children of a dancer) and who might compete with theirs.

This charming, intelligent, and lively woman was accustomed to the limelight because of her profession, and sometimes accompanied the Wali when he made foreign trips. Because she had no support from the Wali's family and had no family of her own according to Pukhtun traditions, the Wali made sure that she was secure after his death. However, property, a fat bank balance and the palace she inherited did not make her happy, and she often complained about her complicated life.

CHAPTER TWO

RIVALRIES AND POWER

☪

My favourite uncle, Mohammad Nisar Khan, was in the Swat militia. In 1947 we saw him off to fight in the first Kashmir war. After returning he often talked about this cruel conflict and especially about the unnecessary killing of innocent civilians. Because Nisar Khan was a charismatic and ambitious man, the powerful local leader, Sultanat Khan (also known as Jora Khan after his home village of Jora and later by his title as Khan Bahadur), felt threatened by him and accused him of running away from a battle in Kashmir. As a result of this accusation, Nisar Khan was dishonourably dismissed from the militia, but he took positive steps by going to study in a college in Campbellpur, Punjab. After graduating he joined the Pakistani Air Force and eventually attained the rank of squadron leader - the equivalent of a major in the army. But since Pukhtuns never forget any wrong done to them, no matter how much success he had outside of Swat, Nisar Khan continued to scheme to defeat Sultanat Khan and avenge himself.

Sultanat Khan, Nisar Khan's deadly enemy, was a tall, bearded, well-built man who originally belonged to a small landowning family. He started his political career with meagre resources, and was a subordinate ally of my forefathers. However, he later became the most powerful man in Upper Swat by tactics such as libelling his personal enemies - including Nisar Khan - as enemies of the Wali's father, the previous ruler, Miangul Abdul Wadud, also known as Badshah Saib. Sultanat Khan told the Badshah 'It is true that the people of Upper Swat are against me, but when I am removed, then they will turn against you.' As a result, the Badshah made mass arrests of Sultanat Khan's enemies. I remember that when I was a child in the first class at school I sat in the hujra of the sons of Khan Bahadur overlooking the road from the Badshah's palace and heard Khan Bahadur insult the men whom the ruler's police were marching off to prison.

Sultanat Khan made clever use of tribal jealousies and old animosities, fomenting internal feuds between the Mamat khel and Painda khel dullahs in Upper Swat, which led to interventions by the ruler, who gave Sultanat Khan permission to confiscate the warring khan's rifles and their other sources of strength such as horses or lands. Sultanat Khan also did not hesitate to imprison and assassinate his opponents. In return for his help in maintaining peace and subduing the unruly khans of our region, the Badshah awarded him the title of Khan Bahadur (a Mogul honorific) and gave him a free hand to collect taxes and punish his enemies.

Whenever the Badshah tried to rein his ally in, Khan Bahadur would go to visit the mamat khel dullah, while at the same time making sure that an official of the ruler was informed of his whereabouts. The Badshah could not trust the mamat khel, who were his old enemies, and so acquiesced to Khan Bahadur's demands in order to keep him from going over to their side. One reason for the enmity between the mamat khel and the ruler was that a great leader of the mamat khel, Habib Khan (popularly known as Darmae Khan) of our neighbouring village of Bara Durushkhela, had died under mysterious circumstances when he was on a friendly hunting trip in Buner with the ruler and his party. It was said that he had fallen to his death, but his son Abdul Hamid Khan said his father was not some animal who was likely to slip and die in the mountains. Abdul Hamid Khan was blind in one eye because a bird had pecked at it in his childhood. All through his life, whenever he saw flocks of these birds, he shot at them. Because of the enmity of men like Abdul Hamid Khan and the rest of the Mamat Khel, the ruler thought it best to keep Khan Bahadur on his side, whatever the cost.

The Badshah himself was an outsider to the valley. His family was Miangul - a religious lineage - who originally hailed from the Safi Mohmand tribe; his grandfather, Saidu Baba, was considered a holy man, a saint who arbitrated disputes in Swat and united the people against their enemies. His tomb is in the capital of Saidu Sharif, which is named after him. Miangul Abdul Wadud was originally appointed ruler in 1915 by a *jirga* - a counsel of tribal elders, which was convened in Kabal, in Southern Swat, to arrive at a consensus as to who should succeed the previous ruler, Sayyid Abdul Jabbar, who was also an outsider from a religious family, but who had proven to be incompetent and was dethroned. Khan Dada, my eldest uncle, attended the jirga. He took his beloved pistol, a German Mauser, with him, but it had been decided that no one would bring arms into the counsel, so he had to set it aside.

According to Khan Dada, Miangul Abdul Wadud impressed

everyone when he arrived riding a horse and leapt from the saddle to the ground. When he left, he also jumped into the saddle from a distance. His athletic ability, religious background, his reputation for trustworthiness and credibility, combined with his status as an outsider uninvolved in dullah feuds and therefore capable of fair arbitration (and also the fact that he was in the good books of the British) led the jirga to acclaim him as their ruler. However, his Miangul relatives must have done some intensive groundwork, since Abdul Wadud was the only candidate for the post.

Miangul Abdul Wadud was short and had a dark complexion and a beard. He was staunchly religious but not a bigot. Although illiterate, he was extremely intelligent and clever and used all his skills to stabilize the anarchic conditions in Swat, so that he and his son and eventual successor, Jehan Zeb, could concentrate on bringing education, healthcare and a better communication system to the valley. To a large extent, they succeeded in their ambitions until 1969 when Swat state was fully amalgamated into Pakistan, which resulted in deterioration, instability, corruption, and militancy. It has been said: 'Give me good people, good things will happen.' The converse is also the case.

Habib Khan, whom the Badshah was said to have murdered in the hills of Buner, was the father of Afzal Khan, who was popularly known as Khan Lala. Afzal Khan swore to take revenge against the Badshah and his family, and left the valley to study in Peshawar's Islamia College. Along with his friend from Bandai village, he incited opposition to the Badshah's regime, writing leaflets and pamphlets against him and distributing them in Swat. As a result, he was banned from returning to his homeland. Although he was a talented, intelligent and charismatic leader, Afzal Khan's opposition movement did not succeed. What were the reasons for his failure? One was that he was motivated by personal revenge rather than seeking the overall good of the people. Another was that in 1949 Miangul Abdul Wadud voluntarily handed power over to his son Jehan Zeb, who was a progressive man, pro-education, pro-health care and therefore popular with the masses. Khan Lala's self-interested campaign could not make any headway against the well-liked new ruler.

Jehanzeb - now known as the Wali of Swat - was suspicious of his father's old ally, Khan Bahadur, but could not do much against him because of Khan Bahadur's entrenched position and because of his father's continued support for his friend. The old man once even asked my father to convince his son, the Wali, to stop harming Khan Bahadur. Otherwise, Badshah threatened to do Kuda -that is, leave Swat in protest. For Swatis, friendship was and is considered to be much more important and binding than relations with sons or brothers, which are often hostile due to rivalries over property.

Khan Bahadur used to say that he was wrestling with Jehan Zeb and that they were 'Akhre Pakhre' - meaning both had fallen to the ground, but side by side rather than one on top of the other. In other words, they were at a standoff. To help break the stalemate, the Wali allowed Afzal Khan to come back to the valley in return for his support - a shift in allegiances quite common in Swati politics. Later, Afzal Khan became the leader of the National Awami Party (NAP) in Swat and was a powerful figure in Pakistani politics. We students would sometimes come to the courts to see this famous man when he visited. 'Daghe de, Khan Lala, Daqla de Khan Lala' - There is Khan Lala, that's Khan Lala.

To offset Khan Bahadur's power, the Wali also made friends with my uncle, Nisar Khan. As I mentioned, Nisar Khan neither forgave nor forgot Khan Bahadur's accusation that he had run away during the Kashmir debacle. During my school days, he would periodically visit Swat while he was working for the Pakistan Air Force. Encouraged by the Wali, he organized a group of like-minded people bent on breaking Khan Bahadur's iron grip on Upper Swat. When he travelled around the valley he always took my father with him in the front seat of his van. This was not only in recognition of my father's long friendship, it was also because he knew that no one would dare fire on Khaista Dada and instigate a feud with our family and the Painda khel dullah.

However, despite the friendship between Nisar Khan and my father, my family could not afford to antagonize Khan Bahadur. In fact, my elder uncle Khan Dada visited Khan Bahadur's hujra once a week to show his loyalty. During these visits, Khan Bahadur often recalled how one of his uncles had tried to kill him many years ago, and how my paternal grandfather, Shahbaz Khan (also known as Sinpora Malik, because he had once ruled Sinpora) had saved his life. As a result, Khan Bahadur favoured the sons and grandsons of Shahbaz Khan. However, he was dead against the family of Shahbaz Khan's younger brother, Sharif Khan, in spite of the fact that his daughter was married to Sharif Khan's son Subedar Khan. When they were young both Sharif Khan and Khan Bahadur had been exiled to Dir, the kingdom north of Swat, and their rivalry began there.

But another reason for their hostility was that Sharif Khan had once forcibly confiscated a caravan laden with grain destined as a tribute for the Badshah Shahib, saying that Upper Swat came under his dominion. The booty he took from the Badshah formed a big part of the wealth that my elder uncle Khan Dada later inherited and spent on guns and dancers. This episode was the start of a feud between our family and the

Badshah, who wanted to consolidate his rule. To earn the Badshah's support, Khan Bahadur also opposed Sharif Khan and his people. However, as I have mentioned, when the Badshah's son, Jehan Zeb, came into power, he began to favour some his father's old rivals as a way to challenge Khan Bahadur's power. Thus, the old enmity between our people and the Badshah was, if not forgotten, at least ignored. Furthermore, Jehan Zeb had a soft spot in his heart for Khaista Dada because my father often brought him gifts of the game birds he had shot on expeditions with the Wali's cousin.

There are many more stories to tell about Sharif Khan. When he was in exile in Dir, his paternal nephew, Malik Nawab Khan, turned against him and confiscated a part of his property. This caused a violent feud. As a child I witnessed a fight in our village between Malik Nawab Khan and Sharif Khan's son Subedar Khan (in Swat close paternal cousins [tarbur] are often so antagonistic that their relationship [tarburwali] is a term of enmity). Malik Nawab started the fight with the excuse that Subedar Khan had cut down a tree on his property without asking permission. The real reason was that he wanted to please his patron, Sultanat Khan. Sharif Khan was very elderly then, but brave. I remember him raising his hands and saying that he was ready to die if Malik Nawab wished to shoot him. My father was neutral in this dispute, which allowed him to intervene and stop the fighting.

Another story about Sharif Khan tells of how the Badshah once imprisoned him in a notorious jail, Shalatraf, in the remote region bordering Buner. Somehow he managed to tunnel his way out and escape into the countryside. In those days, quail hunters used captive quails to call the wild ones. Nets were spread over the fields and pointer dogs flushed the birds. That morning, when the dogs started barking and the hunters came near, they found Sharif Khan hiding in the fields. A *Mian* (religious) family gave him sanctuary instead of handing him over to the police. The local jirga sought the help of Khans of Thana of the Malakand Agency, who were friendly with the Badshah. They negotiated a compromise so that Sharif Khan could return home.

In his old age, Sharif Khan lived quietly in his home village of Lower Durshkhela, keeping bees, tending his chickens and enjoying the pears and grapefruits he had planted in his hujra grounds and in the small orchard nearby. We used to call him Baba and he gave us honey. He died peacefully, and was mourned by everyone.

Sharif Khan's enemy, Khan Bahadur, eventually died of a heart attack and left a vast estate. I vividly recall attending his funeral as a child. Hundreds of people were there, and at the end of the funeral ceremony, people raised their hands to say the usual prayer of 'Khudai de Obakhi' - God forgive him. But the impression was that very few of them said 'Amen.' Khan Bahadur was feared rather than loved. His sons tried to keep his political authority, but ended up feuding among themselves. However, they acted together to take revenge on Jehan Zeb, the Wali, by actively supporting the centralization and amalgamation of Swat with Pakistan, thus helping to end his family's skilful running of the Principality of Swat and sending it down the pathway toward ruin.

The Wali's son, Crown Prince Aurang Zeb, would have been a good ruler. He was a straightforward person, transparent and helpful in his dealings and unable to keep a secret about anybody. He also had great sense of humour, and went out of his way to help people. Because he took sides with some who were his father's political opponents, he sometimes aroused his father's anger, even though his father had often done the same thing himself. Aurang Zeb was educated in the famous Dhera

Dun School in India, became a Captain in the army and ADC of General Ayub Khan, who later became the President of Pakistan. Aurang Zeb married Ayub Khan's daughter Naseem, a fine lady who tried to help the women of Swat by starting vocational training centres. Unfortunately, her good intentions went for naught, as these centres were not sustained over time. As often happens, the good work fizzled out once the person who started it lost interest.

The Wali also had a very pretty daughter named Noor Jehan. She later married into the well-known Pukhtun family of Mardan. The Wali had three other sons, Hafiz Baacha, Amir Zeb and Ahmad Zeb. Prince Ahmad Zeb met a tragic death. Hafiz Baacha married Khan Bahadur's daughter. Feuding between the brothers undermined the authority of the ruler's family, but the Mianguls still remain powerful in Swat, in the region, in Pakistan, and even internationally. Hafiz's children were intelligent and his daughter later married Akbar S. Ahmad, who later became a Political Agent in Waziristan and since then gained international reputation as an anthropologist, writer, broadcaster, scholar and filmmaker. He wrote several books about the Pukhtun, and his daughter has recently written a book about changes in Swati society.

While the Badshah and the Wali were sometimes cruel and dictatorial, they did have a progressive vision of the future, and worked to improve the lives of the people. In contrast, although the powerful khans of the past were intelligent, honourable and courageous, they were also ignorant and self-interested, so they did very little for the common good. Is Pukhtun society unique in this respect, or is it simply human nature for the strong to oppress the weak? Is behaviour a result of nature (genetics) or nurture (environment) or both, and how important is it to manage children's upbringing during childhood and education to make a better society and more peaceful world? In my experience, some people will turn out selfish and cruel no matter how they are raised, but most will turn out better if they are raised well and educated.

CHAPTER THREE

VILLAGE ISLAM

☾

My education in Islam began when I was very young. All the small children in the village were supposed to learn how to pray at home as well as in the mosque. However, most of my instruction came at the mosque. Unlike my extremely pious grandmother in Baidera, my mother did not pray five times a day and was not particularly religious. When devout people used to say to her 'Allah rizaq rasaan de' - Allah provides everything we eat - she would reply 'Spee la pa deran hum rizaq warki' - a stray dog is provided food from the garbage pit. My mother was not one to rely solely on Allah's beneficence.

There is a story that makes this point. Once a man asked the Prophet Muhammad (PBUH) whether he should tie up his camel or rely on Allah to keep it near. The Prophet answered: 'Rely on Allah, but tie up your camel.'

Unlike many others, our local religious teacher could read and write, and spent most of his days scribbling in the mosque.

Like other religious scholars, he was very poor and reliant on charity for his livelihood. Sometimes he asked me for spare paper. He was called 'Baidare Ustad' and was recognizable by his long white beard, which was mandatory for men of his holy status. Baidare Ustad belonged to a Pukhtun family, but after getting an education in religion, he adopted the religious profession and his sons and grandsons were then called Mullahs. Baidare Ustad's Friday sermons mainly consisted of preaching that people ought to be good to each other, help each other at times of illness or difficulties and resolve disputes without resorting to fighting. He gave examples from the Prophets of all religions and illustrated his sermons by telling stories from the life of the Prophet Muhammad (PBUH) and of the Caliphs. I do not remember that he ever instigated people against any other sects or religions.

In those days, the religious specialists in the village were subservient to the khans, who provided them with food, lodging, and protection. In Pukhtun society mullahs were not well respected, and for some unknown reason were often the butt of jokes. My eldest uncle, Khan Dada, had a strong grip over the affairs of the mosque where he worshipped, and no one would dare to start the prayers unless he was present. Once the imam (prayer leader) did begin the prayers before my uncle arrived. When Khan Dada appeared at the mosque, he was furious and kicked the imam out of the mosque. However, because of his respect for the occasion, he did not then use his favourite curse 'aurat kwase' (aurat is the Urdu word for woman and kwase is Pukhto for vagina), nor did he wield the bamboo stick that had been brought for him from Bombay, which he usually applied to the backs of those who crossed him. Other members of our family had the same proprietary attitude toward the village's religious figures, whom they regarded as servants. For example, when one of my cousins was late for prayers he ordered the prayer leader to prolong the first part of the service so that he could join in. We children prayed in the last row, where we often nudged each other and sometimes giggled. At the end of prayers, the adults scolded us.

In those days, some Taliban (the word 'Taliban' literally means religious students) from other villages and regions travelled around Swat, living in mosques and studying with local *maulanas* - mullahs trained in a religious seminary who have expert knowledge of certain religious books. Different maulanas had different kinds of knowledge. Some taught Arabic grammar, others taught *tafseer* (commentary on the Koran), while others were experts in *hadith* (the sayings of the Prophet and his companions). In our village there was one of the latter and students came from as far as Afghanistan to study with him. These young talibs were generally from underprivileged families. Most of them were young and shaved their heads, but the older ones kept their hair long in the old style.

At times the Taliban would set '*atun*' (a trance-inducing dance) and gyrate through the night in the mosque grounds. The only sign of their evening activities was that when people came for the early morning prayers, the dried hay spread on the floor for worshippers to kneel on was strewn about and some could even be seen stuck to the ceiling. The youngest Taliban were sent to different houses to beg for sustenance. Following Pukhtun custom, whenever there was a stranger staying in the mosque or hujra, he was automatically provided with food, tea and shelter without questions being asked. We boys brought food and tea for the guests and served them. There were no organized religious seminaries during my boyhood. It was only under the rule of the Badshah that one seminary was built and funded, in the capital of Saidu Sharif. This was the beginning of the gradual rise in power and authority of the religious classes in Swat.

Today, no one could imagine a khan beating and cursing an imam for starting prayers too early.

Other, more prestigious, religious personages lived in Swat. These were the Sahibzada and Miangan, who were land-owners. Their *tseri* lands were strips between villages that had been granted to them by the Pukhtun. Unlike their Pukhtun neighbours, the Sahibzada and Miangan did not carry weapons, and were known for their sanctity. Because it was unheard of to attack such people, whenever there were skirmishes or fighting, combatants sent their womenfolk and their other precious items to be protected by them. They were not only neutral but also trustworthy, having established their credibility and piety over many years. As a result, they were often called upon to mediate disputes. However, some of these religious lineages did not follow the tradition of pacifism and more or less became Pukhtun, carrying weapons and pursuing honour. For example, in the region of Lalkoo, local Miangan, hoping to take high-quality rice land from their neighbours, secretly manufactured a cannon and attacked the town of Bodigram. They were only defeated with difficulty. The Miangan of Sir Sirdari were known for their ferocity and fought alongside my ancestors in the war against Dir.

In the old days of periodic land exchange (*wesh*) these respected religious families remained on their tseri strips, while the Pukhtuns had to change their location according to the set rules of Sheikh Milli (the founder of wesh in the 17th century). Every seven years land exchange took place among the villages in Upper Swat, and every 21 years the people of Upper Swat were obliged to change their lands with the people of Thana, which was originally a part of Swat, but later annexed into what is now the Malakand agency. The ancient 21-year cycle of wesh migration and land exchange was terminated in a jirga (counsel) called by a British political agent in Malakand - I believe his name was Dundas - who was fluent in Pukhto and well versed in the culture of the area. The spokesman from Upper Swat in this jirga was an intelligent and articulate person named Abu Kaka from the Painda khel dullah.

To my knowledge, Taliban fighters first came to Swat about a hundred years ago. They gained influence because Upper Swat was being tyrannized by the soldiers of the Nawab of Dir, who ruled the area at that time. Like the Swatis, the people of Dir were Pukhtun, as was the ruler, but while Swat was a relatively fluid, competitive and egalitarian society, Dir was a tyranny. The Nawab extended his dominion over Upper Swat, where his police, soldiers and officials were hated because of their arrogance. Whenever they came to a village, they insisted on drinking *mastuh* - sour milk - and refused ordinary milk, saying they had had enough from their mothers during childhood. A new and better cap would be taken by force from the person who was wearing it and an old one given in return. My father said they would even tie the belt of a man's *shalwar* (pantaloons) to their own shalwar belt and pull it out if it happened to be new. People were fed up with these actions, but they could not unite because of tribal and dullah jealousies. They were only able to come together and liberate themselves from the tyranny of the Nawab under the leadership of a holy man from the Sendakai area, east of the Indus River. Sendakai Baba came to Upper Swat accompanied by his *chatti* Taliban, so called because they grew their hair long. These men arrived in our villages carrying their sticks and special *tubergai* (small axes). They did not threaten the local khans, but they did put people on the right path - obliging them not to rob or steal or keep mistresses.

Under Sendakai Baba's influence, the Mamat khel and Painda khel dullahs of Upper Swat, joined by the Miangan of

Sir Sirdari, who were known for their toughness, rose up in arms and battled the Dir army near the Katkalaye ravine. The *char beta* verses recited in our hujra commemorate that epic struggle, fought with muskets, swords and horses, and sometimes in hand-to-hand combat. My father's eldest brother, Sirdar Khan, the leader of the Painda khel dullah, was killed in the struggle. Sword in hand, he chased down and captured soldiers of Dir Nawab. In surrendering his rifle, one of the Nawab's men accidentally shot my uncle in the stomach. My abai told me how brave her son was, because he did not complain of the fatal bullet wound but complained instead of a pain in his right arm. The Mamat khel leader was also killed in the struggle, but the people of Upper Swat expelled the outsiders from Dir once and for all. This was probably the only time when the Mamat khel and Painda khel dullahs joined together for a common cause. It required an external threat and the leadership of a holy man to accomplish this feat.

The influence of the Taliban waned after that, and Sandakai Baba's followers now are just a small sect living in a remote village, of no importance in Swati politics. But in the seventies a new kind of religious revival began in Swat. Partly as a result of the violence in Afghanistan and the influx of religious zealots from the Middle East, and partly in reaction to social changes in Swat that eroded the authority of the Khans and the ruler, religious seminaries started and mushroomed, teaching a fundamentalist version of Islam. People in Swat began sending their children to these seminaries, mostly for economic reasons, since they were free. People also donated land and money to the seminaries. Charity collection, which had previously been haphazard, became organized and some rich people from the Middle East began sponsoring these new schools. Loudspeakers were installed in the mosques and were used to convince people to donate. Some of the fundraisers among these new Taliban were so expert that ladies even donated their jewellery to the cause.

In Swat, mullahs stepped out of their subservient roles and began taking an active part in politics. Some won seats in Parliament and became ministers. The Taliban and religious teachers who formerly were given food, clothes, and respect from the people began to be feared instead. They used modern technology such as loudspeakers, FM radios, printing and the distribution of leaflets to spread propaganda and incite the people against the khans and against the government. In Swat, during the rule of the Wali and his father, it was very dangerous to print or distribute anti-government literature, and no one dared to talk about rebellion in the village mosques. Once, during the reign of the Badshah, a religious person in Shangla, a part of Swat, inspired many people to come to him for his blessing. The Badshah saw him as a threat to his authority, and had him dropped into a dry well and killed. The ruler's tight control over the State coincided with an emphasis on development in education, health, and infrastructure, and so his sovereignty was supported by the masses. The khans too were close to the people and were respected.

But this changed when Pakistan took over and corruption and bribery became rampant. Justice was for sale and enforcement of rules no longer appeared to coincide with any benefits for the population. Population pressure also increased the incidence of poverty and hunger in the Valley. Meanwhile, the traditional relationships of obligation between the khans and their retainers and servants were replaced by cash payments and work for hire. Many khans moved to Peshawar, where they could live a more modern lifestyle, away from the demands of village life. Another destabilizing factor was the American invasion of Afghanistan, which led many Afghans to flee into Pakistan, and also made Swatis aware of the wider battle between al Qaeda and the West.

New religious schools reflecting these changes appeared in Swat and nearby, funded by Saudis and others, preaching a fundamentalist form of Islam. Teachers in these schools and the new religious leaders in Swat called for implementation of a pure form of Islamic law (Shari'a) that would take the place of Government courts and the rule by custom. In Kuza Durshkhela, the Taliban were recruited mostly from boys between thirteen and sixteen. They belonged to Khan families as well as to other castes, such as barbers, Gujars, muleteers and mullahs. They all defied their parents, which is very unusual in Pushtun culture.

Two incidents occurred in my village that may shed some light on the nature of this rebellion. My nephew Wali Mohammad Khan, who is a pious man and a *tabligi* - itinerant religious preacher - made some unfavourable remarks about the Taliban. They heard about his remarks and sent armed young boys to handcuff him and bring him to their makeshift court in the village. One fourteen-year-old boy was the son of the accountant in our local school. His father tried to restrain him but the boy said his Taliban leader was more important than his father.

During their uprising, the Taliban raided the building where I held a clinic outside the village. They defaced the buildings and took all the furniture and medical equipment. The government-sponsored girls' school three hundred yards away from my school for under-privileged children was burnt down at night. The Taliban policy of destroying schools in tribal areas and Swat has multiple reasons, but the predominant reason is probably revenge against the authorities, both civilian and military. My guesthouse was also raided, the people blindfolded, the doors broken and articles including medical instruments taken away. My family and I had to stop going to Swat.

A week later I got a phone call from someone who claimed responsibility for the attack. He said he was a suicide bomber and that all the stolen items had been put aside in a safe place. The caller then asked: 'Do you know me? I studied in your school until the eighth class. You gave us books and paid our tuition. But I had to stop my schooling because of poverty.' A few days later, when the rebels were under ferocious attack by the Pakistani army, he called again to tell me where I could find my goods, which had been protected. I later recovered them intact.

CHAPTER FOUR

EARLY SCHOOLING

☪

In the early 1940s there were no schools worth mentioning in Swat. The only school in the British era was in Thana, Malakand District, which was a long way from my village. Children learned the Quran and the Arabic alphabet in mosques, but those parents who were keen to impart reading and writing to their children either employed special teachers or sent them to other places to be tutored. I was sent to the nearby village of Baidera, where my mother's parents lived.

In Baidera a shopkeeper had started a school in his one-room store. The teacher was called 'Chopan Mirza' because his eyesight was weak (probably as a result of trachoma) and he blinked often. He had a long stick with which he beat children. His pupils were of different ages. One older child liked to expose his private parts to other children when the teacher was busy with the shopping, which involved exchanging the agricultural goods for items such as tea, gur, spices, and sweets. My stepbrother Durveza Khan also attended the same school and was my champion if anyone threatened me. We stayed overnight in Baidera in my abai's house. Once there was a commotion late at night. It was said in the morning that Durveza Khan had got up to search for something. My maternal great-uncle almost shot him, thinking he was an intruder.

I do not remember much of my early education in the village shop except the long stick of the shopkeeper teacher and the long dick of an older boy in the class. Afterwards, I was sent to Saidu Sharif, the capital of Swat state. There I joined two of my older maternal uncles who were already studying in Wadudia School, named after and started by Abdul Wadud, the Badshah, who had no formal education himself but wanted the people of Swat to be educated. He enticed good people from other parts of the North West frontier province as teachers.

I was admitted to *adna* (kindergarten) under my new name of Sher Mohammad Khan, and my approximate date of birth was entered in the record books. Our first teacher, Lala Jan, came from Mardan. He was a good teacher in the sense that he was not harsh, did not carry a stick with him, and did not believe in the 'spare the rod and spoil the child' philosophy that was the norm in those days. Instead, he encouraged the children and had a good sense of humour.

In Saidu I lived in a house with my two uncles, Jehan Sher Khan, and his younger stepbrother, Jehan Zeb Khan. The person looking after us was a middle-aged man named Pacha Syed who had spent some time in Bombay. His wife was young and I used to help her in cooking by arranging the fire in the open hearth. I also looked after Pacha's child, while my uncles went out to play. I had no choice but to help in the house because Pacha's wife would not give me enough food unless I worked for it. Next door in the hujra lived two grown-up students, a young man named Mohammad Khan and his nephew Gulbar. Their family had furniture business in Bombay. An older lady cooked for them. I visited whenever she cooked bread and she gave me buttered paratha, which I relished; when I ate it tears would roll down her cheeks and at times she would cry loudly. Later I learned that she had a son, her only one, who had died and who had looked like me. The free daily bread ended when the cook was replaced by a younger woman. Soon I started witnessing frequent quarrels between the nephew and uncle. The cause was the new young cook.

I was promoted to class 1. In the class, all the boys sat on mats, which they wrapped up after finishing the class. This is the source of the saying 'the por waar terawal' - one's turn to stay at the end of the class - with the implication that one would be fondled by the teacher. I dreaded my Islamyat instructor because he slapped me once when I could not recite the Arabic writings. Prayers were held during recess time and there was a roll call for each class, but some of the students would leave as soon as the roll call was over. The last period of the class was given over to teaching the multiplication tables, which were to be learnt by heart. Rognath, a Hindu boy, and I were given the task of reciting the multiplication, followed by repetition by the rest of the class. This is how we became best friends. In fact, a number of Pukhtun made best friends with Hindus, who were outside of tribal jealousies. Nowadays very few Hindus remain in the valley, since they left after partition.

Even at a young age we knew which family and ethnic or religious group the other students belonged to. There were students from well-to-do families from Mingora who belonged to named groups such as 'parachkan'(businessmen), 'lalagan' (sayyids related to the mianguls of Swat), 'Pukhtuns' (land owners), Hindus, 'khanans' (chiefs) and others such as mullahs. Whenever there was a quarrel, we boys used to call one another 'you son of so-and-so.' The so-and-sos were mainly weavers, barbers, mullahs and parachkan. No one was insulted by being called a son of a Khan or Pukhtun.

There were a few other students I remember. One was called 'Lala Sahib' because he was related to the ruler; he became a politician later in life and a government minister. He was mediocre in studies. 'Kaki' was a tough boy and the rest of the students were scared of him. He could break the wooden writing pad by hitting it with his head. He told us lurid stories of his sexual encounters with other boys in Mingora. The last I heard about him was that he had been murdered by his own son. Another class-fellow, Habib Nabi, was a good student and became a leading paediatrician in Swat. He belonged to a business family, but the great fire of Mingora town, which was next to Saidu Sharif, destroyed their house and businesses, along with many others. We schoolchildren were asked to contribute to help rebuilding. I contributed two annas out of my pocket money, which was equivalent to a tenth of a rupee. I still joke with the sons of Mingora businessmen who eventually became doctors that I had a role in the prosperity of their families because of my two-anna donation.

When I was about eleven years old, I changed to a new school called Shagai, which was nearby in the Saidu area. I walked to school and passed near the ruler's residence. The guards were well dressed and disciplined. Sometimes the Wali could be seen watching the passers by. He was held in awe and respect, but not in fear. Every Friday he distributed money among the poor. My father approached his first wife, Begum Sahibe, for intervention whenever there was a difficulty affecting our extended family. She was the sister of prince Bahramand, with whom my father was friendly because of their mutual interest in falconry and dogs and hunting. Babramand was a hospitable, generous, and courageous man who later became one of the

Khudai Khidmatgars. He was murdered after the creation of Pakistan. The perpetrators were never caught.

In Shagai school, I was made the monitor, since I was good in my studies and obedient. There was only one girl in our class and she sat somewhat apart from the boys. We called her by her adab name of *Ghwara* (literally oily, but meaning a girl who is well-behaved and obedient). She was quiet and had a dusky complexion; she did not wear the conservative niqab (mask) or the toadstool-like Afghan burqa but wrapped herself simply in the local chador. Her father was an employee of the Ruler, and her family lived in Saidu. In later life, she entered the Medical College in Lahore and became the second qualified lady doctor in Swat. She married a dental surgeon who happened to be younger brother of my childhood friend Qazi Fazli Ali. In Swat at that time and even now there were only two respectable professions women could enter: medical (specializing in female complaints) or teaching (in girls' schools). Both were necessary occupations, since traditional Pukhtun women would never think of seeing a male doctor, or of allowing their daughters to be taught by men.

I remember there were no toilets in the school and we went to the nearby fields. One finger was raised if we wanted permission to go for urination and two fingers if we were to go for moving our bowels. Wild boars were prevalent in the nearby mountains and it was somewhat dangerous to go to the fields, since the boars would come close to eat the faeces just as they were being produced. For urination we squatted in any open place and then dried the drops of urine with a *loota* - dried piece of mud - which we put into our baggy shalwars with our left hands. People from the villages used to carry these loota to big cities and even onto the hajj. They caused many blockages of Western-style toilets. The Wali hated the local practice of squatting to urinate in public places, and his bodyguards would chase people they caught squatting during his daily afternoon trips in car to the surrounding areas of the Capital Saidu.

Teaching at first was in my mother tongue of Pukhto, but later it was replaced by Urdu. We learned by rote. The maths questions were mostly about simple interest and compound interest. Elementary English was taught, and we wrote our English in a special notebook with four coloured lines on which we were taught to write small and big letters. I do not remember any teaching of science. Passing the annual examinations was generally on merit but 'putting in a word' and thus changing 'fail to pass' also worked. I know this because one of my maternal uncles passed and he was known in the class as *safarshi* - influence. He did not complete his later studies despite the intervention of his important elder brother. His sons also did not complete their studies, unlike his elder brother's sons, who became doctors and engineers.

There were three class fellows from Shagai whom I especially remember. One was a *sayyed* (a person supposedly descended from the Prophet) from the Sar Sardari area. He always made trouble by influencing other students against me, since I had been appointed monitor and had to make sure that the only girl in the class was respected. Monitors had direct access to the headmaster and I complained to him about this boy. The headmaster said I had to present a solid case before action could be taken. It was at this early age that I learnt that a person cannot and should not be punished on flimsy charges. There were two other students, Syed Mohammed Kabir and Shujaat Ali Khan, whom I recall in a more positive way. Kabir was quiet, well-behaved and good at his studies. He later became a leading surgeon in Swat. Shujaat Ali Khan was a son of Khan Bahadur, the ruler of Upper Swat. We were neighbours in Saidu and he occasionally invited me to join him for meals during recess.

These meals were brought to him by his servant and consisted of rice, milk and pure ghee. I was often hungry and was glad to eat these rich foods. Shujaat Ali later became a minister in the Pakistani government.

As I look back, it is clear to me that gaining further education and achieving a respectable position in Swati society depended on three things: scholastic ability, family background and financial status. In my case it also depended on guidance by Nisar Khan, my selfless, literate and far-sighted maternal uncle, who consistently helped me and advised me in my education.

I had to change my school once again because my maternal uncles moved into hostels and I could no longer afford to stay in Shagai on my own. Moreover, a middle school had opened near our village, and I could commute from my home. Matta school was situated on a raised ground near the local courts (*tehsil*) where disputes were solved by *rewaj* (custom) and by Qazis (interpreters of Quranic law). Bicycles were used for travelling to school. Tongas (horse-driven carriages) were also used for transportation. The fare was one *anna* (about a penny) from the village to school. There was only one car in the area. It was a Chevrolet that belonged to Nisar Khan's father. The driver was a local man who had learned how to drive in Hindustan. My mother at times was given a ride home in it at night time after she had visited her parents in the next-door village of Baidera.

The teachers at Matta school were mainly non-local, except for the Islamyat teacher, who had a long beard, as one could not be a religious instructor without one. Another local man (Munshi Fazal), who been educated in India, was well versed in Urdu poetry. Most of my classmates were older than me. There was Masoom Jan, who was called saib in the village because he belonged to a Sahibzada family, a lineage of religious people. The other classmate who was about the same age as me was

Fazli Ali. As I mentioned, his younger brother eventually married Ghwara, my classmate at Shigai school. He was later a great help to me when I migrated to the United Kingdom. Fazli Ali had come to study in my school because of a friend of his father's who was an official *tehsildar* (official) in that tehsil (administrative district). Qazi Sahib, father of Fazli Ali, wanted his son to devote maximum time to study away from the distractions of his village of Barikot. We became close friends and he often came to our village to stay in our hujra over the weekend. During long vacations I also went to visit him in his village. As our comings and goings became more frequent, one day I overheard my father saying 'Da Halakan Tekdi?' He was asking, 'Are these boys all right?' In other words, were there any sexual relations between us? There weren't, but such relations were not unusual among schoolboys deprived of any female companionship.

This tendency is why my maternal uncle wanted me to shave my head regularly, right from kindergarten. It was only much later that I realized that my combination of brown curly hair, fair skin and blue eyes was sought after by sexual predators. He told me that I had to shave because otherwise lice would grow in my hair. Nits and lice were indeed common in those days. Body lice were multi-coloured and white, while head lice were black. Rightly or wrongly, I attribute my abundance of head hair today to shaving and lice. In the pre-DDT era, special combs were made for the extraction of lice from scalp hair. Various tricks were used to keep children still and quiet when the nits and lice were physically removed. In my case, body and head lice were put in my palm and the fascinating fights between them distracted me.

In Matta School, I was in the seventh class and was known as *mazoob*, a person who does not speak much. Hussain Khan, the Headmaster, was a fine, intelligent man who talked in the class about his own wife and daughters. We students would later make fun of him, since this kind of talk is not acceptable in Pukhtun society. My older classmates told me to be careful about Headmaster Sahib, because he corrupted fair-haired boys. However, I found no evidence of this.

The Islamyat teacher was a local man from Matta Tehsil. Unlike the other religious teachers, he was not very strict nor would he try to intimidate the students in any way. If anyone came late to class, he would ask 'Katkalaye ta tale way' - has someone taken you to Katkalaye? This was a ravine near the school that was usually dry but was flooded during rainy season. It was the scene of a great battle between my ancestors and the soldiers of the Dir Nawab in which my eldest uncle was killed.

CHAPTER FIVE

A BRITISH EDUCATION: THE AIR FORCE PUBLIC SCHOOL

☪

After I had completed my schooling in Matta, Nisar Khan took me to Rawalpindi and hired a Warrant Officer named Mr Shah to teach me and groom me to answer questions in the entrance exam and interview for the Pakistani Air Force Public School, where Durveza Khan had already been admitted. My interviewer was Air Force Officer Station Commander Trurowich, who was Polish but had dedicated his life to working for the Pakistan Air Force. He eventually retired as Air Vice Marshall. He had visited Swat and was an enthusiastic hunter, well known to my father. My uncle knew what sort of questions he would ask and what sort of birds are found in Swat, and where the best place to hunt them was. I answered all the questions and passed the entrance examination to the PAF public school Murree Hills. It is rightly said, 'If you do not plan, you are planning to fail.'

During the Korean War, Pakistan had earned a lot of foreign exchange because of the jute produced in East Pakistan (now Bangladesh). With this surplus, the Pakistani Government, probably on the advice of Iskandar Mirza, who was an official during the British era, decided to establish two schools on the pattern of British public schools. This is how PAF Public School Murree Hills was established. The school grounds had previously served as a base for the British Royal Air Force and featured well-constructed buildings as is the case with so many places in Peshawar that were designed by the British.

Half the students were from East Pakistan and half from West Pakistan. Admissions were based on merit and one of the British teachers oversaw the interview board to be sure no unqualified students were admitted. When I entered school, it was the month of March and the Murree Hills were covered with heavy snow. I was placed in Corfield's House, which was named after our Housemaster. The name was later changed to Sir Syed House in commemoration of Sir Syed Ahmad Khan, the famous reformer and founder of Aligahr Muslim University in Uttar Pradesh, India. Durveza Khan, who had joined the school earlier, was in Kiddell's House. He took me to visit him and was surprisingly friendly and kind unlike the angry stepbrother I had known back in the village. In my experience, Pukhtuns behave differently when they are away from home. They become far more peaceful, friendly, and hardworking on the whole. Examples can be found in the big cities of Pakistan and United Arab Emirates, where many Pukhtun migrate for work.

As I mentioned, Corfield's House took in boys from all over Pakistan, both West and East. Those from East Pakistan were good at indoor games as well as outdoor games. They were also skilled at singing and dancing. The boys from Karachi were much advanced in their general knowledge. Zamir, from Karachi, knew a lot about the actors and actresses from Bombay. He subscribed to a magazine called 'Film Fare', which we were sometimes allowed to look through. My eyes were drawn to the actresses' lower bodies revealed beneath their tight clothes.

I was made a house monitor after the first term and then promoted to School Prefect after my House Master and other teachers made sure that I knew my responsibilities. These involved making sure that the beds were made properly, that the students' uniforms were clean and well pressed, and that the boys were disciplined. I also had to make sure that nobody smoked. I stood outside the lavatories which were in the open grounds outside the Corfield's House to be certain that rule was followed. As I was waiting outside the lavatory door a student came out, and I said, 'You people have been smoking'. When he said 'no,' smoke came out of his mouth. Once I noticed that one of our Assistant House Masters was very friendly with a good-looking boy from East Pakistan. I reported him to the Head Master, Mr. F.H. Shaw, and the Assistant House Master, who was an Englishman, did not return to school the next term. Presumably his contract was terminated on moral grounds.

The British House Masters of the school and the Assistant School Masters, except one or two, were inspiring role models. The Headmaster was tall and always well dressed. His wife was pretty, but the boys always talked about the Bursar's wife. Whenever we heard that she was coming towards the school, some of us rushed out to catch a glimpse of her and fantasize about her. The Deputy Headmaster, Mr. Hill, was a strict disciplinarian and students were scared of him. He punished anyone who spit, even though spitting was considered a normal part of Pukhtun life and not an offence.

Mr. Hill had a grown-up daughter who liked to play tennis with other teachers, especially with Mr. Banaud, who was single. The students watched the game because of her. I had never imagined a lady wearing shorts that showed her shapely legs. I was born and brought up in a society where women had to cover themselves completely, even in front of their near relatives. However, unlike Afghans, women in Swat did not hide their faces behind the *niqab* or cover themselves with the *hijab* (which covers everything but the face and hands). Rather, they wore the Iranian-style *chador*, drawing their headscarves across their mouths in public.

There was one teacher who was very fond of Pukhtun students. He even formed a Pashto Society. His name was Mr. Eastgate, and he was a well-built, moustached Englishman who was also quite strict with students. Later on I learned that when he was in the British Army he had once bailed out of his aircraft and landed in Waziristan, where he was shown traditional Pushtun hospitality and generosity. He had one son whom he called 'Sikandar', the Pukhto name for Alexander, referring to Alexander the Great, who had once fought the Pukhtun and married a Pukhtun woman. I do not know whether he persisted with this name after returning to the UK, but it revealed his father's appreciation of Pukhtun people. Mr. Eastgate often invited the four or five Pukhtun students to his house for tea and talk. He told my Housemaster, Mr. Corfield, that in future I should go into the diplomatic services. I soon realized that good teachers observe you and know your aptitudes and then guide you. However, the diplomatic service was not to be my fate.

The ladies who looked after the students' uniforms were Pakistani Christians. The one in Coggan's House was busty and young. The Housemaster, Mr. Coggan, was friendly with her and once a student told us that he saw him embracing and kissing her. We were curious and I asked him, 'How do they kiss?' He explained mouth-to-mouth touching. In my village, people kissed, but only on the cheeks. This is probably the reason why cheeks are mentioned so much in Pushto romantic poetry. I had also never heard of lipstick or nail polish. The ladies in the village made use of dried walnut bark (*dundasa*) for cleaning teeth and making their lips red.

The school had all the facilities for extracurricular activities. We played sports and learned woodworking and aeroplane modelling under the tutelage of British teachers. One I remember was Clifford Leach, a gentleman who knew his job. Even though he was a Christian, he also made sure the students followed the rituals of Islam. He came early in the morning to make sure that we got up at the right time for 'Sehri' during Ramadan, the month of fasting. He then took us up to a mountain called Monkey Hills for what was called a 'treasure hunt' and other tough physical activities such as climbing and jumping using ropes, and so on.

There was a *pir* or holy man in the area near the school whom we sometimes saw. People all over the county came for his blessings. He always beat these seekers; the more harsh the beating, the more wishes would be granted, according to the myths. Once I was watching him as he was beating his supplicants. He saw me and shouted 'Pakro Pakhtun Ko!' - get hold of the Pukhtun. I ran away as fast as I could. His followers ran after me but did not get hold of me, since when they got close they told me to run faster. There were several stories spread by people about him. One was that a rich lady had come to beg him to save her two children from execution. He told her to take off her shalwar (pants). She obediently removed her shalwar from one leg, but then hesitated. As a result, one son was released but the other was executed. Another local pir used to see ladies in his separate dark room. As the lady entered he would tell her to untie the belt that holds the shalwar up. If the woman became angry, he would say that he meant the rope hanging from the ceiling above her head. As everyone knows, ignorance leads to all sorts of personal and societal complications.

Mr. Eastgate was in charge of boxing. He trained and prepared my stepbrother Durveza Khan for a match with another boy from the Military School who was visiting us. There was a lot of excitement prefight, and we all hoped Durveza Khan would win. The robe, which Durveza Khan wore before the fight, had written on it 'Strength comes from Cleverness.' However, Durveza was not a clever fighter. In the first round he threw some good punches, but his opponent was agile and knew how to deflect the blows. Durveza Khan charged after the other boy, who cannily retreated and kept on hitting him in the face. Finally my brother's face started bleeding and the fight was stopped. Durveza Khan lost, but his courage was much praised by the teachers. Mr. Eastgate had another chance to impress his colleagues about the courage of the Pukhtun, who will not retreat in spite of odds.

This characteristic was not always appreciated by the other boys. For example, there was only one radio in the school, which was kept in the canteen. The students listened to Urdu and Bengali stations, as speakers of those languages were in majority, but whenever Durveza Khan came in he would change the station to Peshawar to hear Pashto. The Bengalis got tired of this high-handed behaviour decided to punish him. Durveza Khan knew about their plan but still went into to the canteen, and as usual changed the radio station. On this the students from East Pakistan pounced on him and started punching him. Durveza got hold of the ringleader, wrestled with him and pushed him to the floor. Seeing this, the rest of the gang disappeared.

The school allowed us to visit the Murree Bazaar on Sundays, provided we had permission and were in groups. We looked forward to it, because that was the only place where we could see girls clad in their bright-coloured dresses. The students were also taken to see films in Murree, accompanied by our English teacher. I remember Mr. Eastgate took us to see the film of 'Julius Caesar.' He explained the story prior to the film, but all I saw was the dagger piercing the body of the hero and another person making a long speech. It was later that I realized this was the famous speech by Mark Antony. We were all much more interested in Indian films: boy meets girl, accompanied by lively dances and melancholy songs. I already knew about the Bombay films (Bollywood now) during my preschool days in my village from the returnees from India, as well as from the silent films shown in Saidu about heroines and heroes, especially Dilip Kumar Medhobela and Nargis.

During one of these visits I saw a tall, graceful bearded gentleman walking on the Mall Road, near the Cecil Hotel. People were saying, 'He is Ghaffar Khan.' I approached him and said 'Baba 'Pa Khair Raghle' - welcome Baba. He replied 'Bachia Pukhto Waye' - Are you speaking Pukhto? Yes was my answer, and I saw a broad smile cross his awe-inspiring face. 'Sake' - what are you doing?' 'I am studying in school. 'Education is the best, my son' was his last remark after he patted me on the head. This great man is now almost forgotten, though it was he who led the successful Pukhtun struggle against British colonialism with his organization of the Khudai Khidmatgars, the Red Shirts. Even more impressively, he turned the warlike tribesmen away from the path of violence and onto the Gandhian mode of passive resistance. Fighting, he showed, is not the only way, nor the best way, to be a man of honour. But because he opposed the partition of Pakistan from India, his memory has almost been erased from official memory.

Like the other boys, I left the school after my matriculation examination with a heavy heart. My days there were probably the best time of my young life. I was very happy, and also healthier than ever, thanks to my physical training teacher, the British Doctor Dr Unwin and the Head Nurse, Miss Boyd, who removed the nits and lice from my hair after shutting the door to make sure that other boys did not know about it. I often wondered whether all English ladies were as kind as Miss Boyd or whether her kindness was due to her nurse training.

In the school our teachers, the majority of whom were English, prepared us to enter the wider world, not just as good citizens but also as leaders. Although the school was meant for airmen, the Head Master, Mr. Shaw, and his British colleagues made sure that the school's status was changed so that the boys could make their mark in whatever roles they entered in to. My classmates became businessmen, professors, bankers, medical doctors, engineers, as well as generals and air marshals. The school was later discontinued but has lately been reinstated, with local teachers. Was the success of the students in their later lives due to the fact that they were selected on merit, or was it due to the free schooling, or the excellent teachers? Or was it a combination of all three? Time will show whether the success story of the school can be replicated today.

My school mates from Lower Topa are all over the wide world: Australia, Europe, USA and Canada. They have been successful in whatever they are doing and contributing in a positive way to the humanity. Was it because of the "quality education" imparted to them or due to "character building" by their educated teachers? I suppose both. So for peace, prosperity and progress, good institutions with good teachers are essential.

Below are some writings from my friends from school days.

Engineer Khaleel Choudhri of UK wrote to me as follows: "About 10 years ago I met up with Sher Khan after nearly 50 years at the PC Hotel, Lahore during my visit to Pakistan from the UK whilst Sher was visiting Lahore from Peshawar. Since then we keep in regular contact via emails or phone. Friends come and go, but with a precious few you should hold on."

Oh those days at the Topa hill,
Those were the days my friend
We thought they'd never end
For we were young and sure to have our way.
Those were the days, oh yes those were the days.

The School Lower Topa gave us the foundation,
Set us on a path of confidence to surmount the world.
I find those memories grow more precious now,
As I'm just a wise old Hajji, Uncle, a Buzurag.
Buzurag may be but 'Masha Allah' still young at heart.
It's an issue of mind over matter.
But I don't remember getting old,
It shouldn't happen yet.
Who said my joints ache!
I'm really not that old.
Our body doesn't understand
It won't do what it's told.
Other than that, I am in my prime you know.
I am still a 'gorgeous Topian-Boy'.

May Allah bless, and good health.

Our headmaster in Lower Topa was Mr. Frank Shaw. After moving from Lower Topa he had been Headmaster of King's

College School Winbeldon UK. His reflections on 20 years of head mastering, *No Memorial*, by Frank Shah, and on Lower Topa are as follows:

"I never knew what true happiness was until I became a headmaster. Then of course it was too late. But If Fortune did smile upon me, it was most certainly in contriving that my first Headmastership should be in Pakistan. There I enjoyed two blessings that were never again to be bestowed upon me. My governing body met rarely and only in Karachi, some eight hundred miles from the school I founded in the Himalaya foothills. It included therefore no old boys who could only by considerable and sustained effort be persuaded to return to the agenda from their reminiscence of triumphs in unbeaten School XVs of the distant past. I have known indeed a governing body that lacked only a veteran fullback and a second-row forward, deficiencies which the universities of Oxford and Cambridge stubbornly overlooked in selecting their representatives. And the second blessing was that of all the hundreds of parents whose sons attended the school, one only in the course of five blissful years visited the academy. His, to be sure, was a memorable visitation. He strode unannounced into my study, a Pathan of huge proportions, chest engirdled by a bandolier and attended by three wild-eyed, silently menacing tribesmen. He had come in response to a letter I had incautiously sent him in mild criticism of his son. This son, he declared, he now intended to kill. Where was he to be found? He had many other sons to bring him honour in his old age. This miserable offender was dispensable. Happily the youth had observed his father's arrival from a distance and had secreted himself. The father returned to the Frontier, mission unaccomplished, and I vowed never to communicate with a Pakistani parent again."

Appetite for learning

"For the young Pakistanis I formed an immense respect. They responded magnificently to a nineteenth-century regime, its object to ensure that by lights out they were incapable of further activity. I can recall no anxieties over drink, drugs or smoking. Sex was certainly no problem for them; they revelled in it. Their appetite for learning was prodigious. I once saw 70 pupils gathered round their teacher, eyes and ears fixed avidly upon him, as they sat in the open air in a village in the North West; among them were 20 greybeards, eager to keep pace with their grandchildren. Nothing saddened me more on my return to England than the apathy of the young and their affected distaste for intellectual effort. I had been badly spoiled by the Pakistanis.

"The selection of Pakistani staff was an exacting and at times heart-breaking task. How can one deal fairly with over a thousand applications for one appointment? Their testimonials, doubtless drafted by professional letter-writers in the bazaars, spoke eloquently of their surpassing virtues. How could one fail to appoint the Punjabi graduate who ended his letter of application with the words 'in the name of Jesus Christ whom you so closely resemble?' He hadn't even met me.

"Forty miles and 6,500 feet down a precipitous, zig-zag road lay Rawalpindi and its golf course where water buffalo grazed the fairways and failed to replace divots. A ball lying adjacent to their vast bodies could be dropped without penalty - that is, if you were careful where you dropped it".

CHAPTER SIX

JAHAN ZEB COLLEGE

☪

After leaving the Murree Hills, I very much wanted to join the armed forces like my uncle. But when I returned to the village, I was not able to apply on time because a close relative collected all the proper forms from the village post office and destroyed them. This was a case of jealousy, which is unfortunately an all too common trait among my countrymen. As a result, I had to reconsider my future. At that time, there were two avenues normally available for literate young people seeking employment: to become a teacher in a local school, which paid next to nothing, or go to Karachi, find more lucrative work there, and send money back home. My mother favoured that course, but my father, though uneducated and illiterate, had developed a broader view from associating with Nisar Khan and other educated friends and associates. He wanted me to continue my education at Jehan Zeb College in Saidu Sharif, which was founded and named after the Wali of Swat.

I was indeed admitted to the college. The paperwork was facilitated by a senior student there who happened to be the son of Ronial Khan, a good friend of Khaista Dada. Friendship in Pushtun society was a valuable resource, as is the case in other societies.

The problem was money. How could my father support my living away from home? Produce from our family land was our sole source of income, and that had to be shared with the tenants, including the Gujars, whose herds were on the land, as well as our other servants and dependents. Some khans used brute force to extract money from these people, but that was not Khaista Dada's way. He was kind to the tenants, Gujars and servants. As I mentioned earlier, we children were told to treat them well when they visited and show respect by calling them Mama (maternal uncle) or Kaka (elder) and not by their proper names. As a result, cash was not available. Instead, Khaista Dada again made use of his friendship network in order to provide my brother and me with a place to live while at school. He also borrowed money from his well-to-do friends to pay for our expenses.

One friend of my father's said that I could live with him in Qambar village a few kilometers away from the College. Originally, this man came from Hashtnagar, the area where the Khudai Khidmatgars of Ghaffar Khan began. He was in exile in Swat because he had killed his tarbur. As I mentioned earlier, the British in their time had analyzed the disputes leading to serious crimes as a consequence of the three Zs (zun - women, zar - money and zamin - land). Here it was the third Z that had caused the fatal quarrel. Like many others, he avoided vengeance by leaving his home place and taking refuge elsewhere with a strong Khan family - in this case with my father and his brothers. According to Pushtun traditions, anyone seeking refuge (*panah*) had to be given protection with no questions asked. At first, this man lived in our hujra; after things cooled down he moved to Qambar village, where he drove a *tonga* to earn his living. I lived in his hujra, which was also a kind of casino where gambling took place. I went to his house for meals. He and his people treated me as their guest. However, I only lived in Qambar for a short time and then Khaista Dada moved me to a rented room in Mingora.

The college was a two-storey building, kept clean and painted in bright colours because it was on the main road and the Wali, who was fond of architecturally good buildings, made sure it was kept neat and clean. The Wali had provided all the facilities, including residences for the college teachers. Their bungalows had all the amenities, piped water, bathrooms and lavatories. The Wali was keen to hire competent people as college administrators and teachers. The principal of the school, Hafiz Osman, was brought in from Islamia College in Peshawar.

One teacher I remember was Shah Dawran Khan, who was educated in Lahore and instructed us in Botany and Zoology. The father of S.D. Khan lived in the village but would occasionally come to stay with his son in the college residences. He was asked by someone in the village, 'How is your son, the Professor?' His answer was, 'He is good, because he respects his parents and takes care of his near and dear ones. He helps the village needy in spite of his high education, but he is *baisharum* (shameless) because whenever he wants to pass urine or stools, he ought to come home.' In the Pakistan tradition, men are not supposed to talk about their calls of nature, especially in front of women and children.

We liked our Physics teacher because he would use humour and story-telling in his lectures. The English teacher, Ashraf Altaf, was a cheerful, short man who always wore his coat buttoned to the neck. The Urdu teacher was a poet who played the harmonium and who also talked about his wife's ability at the same instrument. It sounded very strange to us that a lecturer's wife would play the harmonium.

College elections were held regularly, with the purpose of introducing us to the democratic process. But in fact tribal and village loyalties were brought into the canvassing campaigns. Although I was elected as class representative unopposed, presumably because I was good at studies, the other elections were much more hotly contested. Sometimes Swatis and non-Swatis split the vote, which was not liked by the Principal, but the students learnt how to cast votes and whom to vote for. Mahmood Khan, who became the student body President, eventually joined the bureaucracy and retired as Chief Secretary, but the people of his area of Shangla did not speak well of him saying he had not done much for his area, presumably because he did not use his influence or accede to their illegal demands. There is a saying that people often quote: 'Kha kar har Sarea kawale she. Khpal Kho hagha de che tala ghalet kar ooki' - Everybody can do things according to law and according to merit, but anyone who is willing to do unlawful acts or use influence is your near and dear one.

The Wali encouraged sports at the school and had built large pitches for football, hockey and volleyball. Cricket was not played in the 1950s in Swat, but a squash court was built for officials of the Swat Government because the Wali had seen the British playing squash in Peshawar. The legendary world champion Hasham Khan was a Pukhtun. He eventually settled in Denver, Colorado in the USA and was honoured by his adopted country, but his country of birth and the Pukhuns took a long time to recognize his and his family's talents. We students watched the squash players from the court gallery. As Swat was becoming a tourist spot, film stars occasionally visited. Once Rukhshi, a famous actress, played squash with a male doctor.

We whispered to each other about the full erection that was visible beneath his shorts. Because of my height, I was the goalkeeper of our football team and took part in the tournament in Peshawar. When we lost, people blamed me because I had not caught the ball - 'Da gooli waja wa.' In Pukhtun society, you usually blame others for mistakes, but take credit yourself if there is a victory.

At this time, Durveza Khan and I were living in a rented room in Mingora with a family who were acquaintances of my father. The owner of the house was an old man, but his wife was young, pretty, and smart. We had to leave after few months because he suspected us of sexual hanky-panky with his wife, which was not true in my case but could well have been true of Durveza, as he was already keeping a runaway married woman as his mistress in town. Once he told me I could go to such and such a place to make my acquaintance with this young woman. I went, but found that the girl had a rash on her hands and face, which repelled me. I promised to return once her rash was cleared up, but never did. Later, this girl was seduced by a Mingora businessman who kept her as his mistress, but, like Zerqeshun, my old nanny, she preferred a free life, and eventually ran away.

Life in the hostel was comfortable. I was not hungry; I met other students, and I did not have far to go to attend the call of nature since the common lavatories were inside the hostel. I shared a room with an older classmate who came from Charsadda. Like many others from the Charsadda and Mardan area, my roommate's family grew sugar cane. The Swati students called the boys from this area 'da gwaro Khanan' - Khans of gur. They were sent to Jehanzeb College by their wealthy parents because of the quality of education and the discipline. There was no concern with teaching children to be good citizens.

Mardan now is home to many rich land-owning clans such

as the Hotis, the Khankhels, the Torous and others. The land around Mardan was dry and barren until the British built the Malakand tunnel, which diverted the Swat River into irrigation canals and was used for the generation of electricity. One of the grandsons of Khan Bahadur, Ibrahim Khan, told me that at the time when the tunnel was being built, the British instructed his grandfather to buy land in Mardan as it was soon going to become fertile. We joked that the Swatis should dam up the river, leaving the rich boys from Mardan to carry stuff on their donkeys and mules to sell in Swat in exchange for rice, as they did in the old days. The famous Guides' Cavalry was also stationed in Mardan. It is also said that camel drivers from the Mardan region were sent to Australia and that a railway in Australia is named the Ghan Railway after the word Afghan.

My roommate was soon given a single room by the warden because he offered him gifts of *gur* with nuts (Misldara Gwra) which be brought from his home village, and I started sharing the room with another classmate from Thana. He was quiet boy with a thin but sonorous voice and considered to be lazy. Whenever students passed by in the corridor to fetch water, he would call from inside the room 'Rora mala hum oba rawra' - brother bring me water as well. As he was one of the older students, nobody refused his request. It was and still is considered disrespectful and against the norm of Pukhtun culture to disobey an older person. Students learnt how to avoid his frequent requests by tiptoeing by our room.

I can recall some other hostel mates. There were two Iqbals, both from Takht Bai, an archaeological site from the Buddhist era. They were friendly with each other. One Iqbal became a medical doctor and added Safi to his name, becoming Iqbal Safi. Safi is a clan of the well-known Momand tribe that straddles the border between Pakistan and Afghanistan. They are known for their love of independence and self-respect and for supporting each other. I have yet to see a Momand begging for alms. They did all sorts of jobs everywhere in the region, but were especially known for carrying firewood and roasting corn. If a Momand falls ill you will always see a crowd of relatives and friends accompanying him or her to the clinic and hospital, much to the annoyance of the nurses, doctors and administrators, who know very little about the highly collective culture of these people.

Dr Iqbal Safi later on joined a religious organization started by another medical person, Dr Israr Ahmad, who is internationally known and who happened to be a class fellow of another internationally known person, Chairman Munir Ahmad Khan of the Pakistan Atomic Energy Commission, which is famous for promoting the peaceful use of atomic energy.

Jehan Zeb Khan was another hostel friend I remember. He had severe diarrhoea once. Diarrhoea was not uncommon because of the unhygienic conditions and poor sanitation. We students looked after him and took him to the hospital. He survived and always remembered that I had helped him during his severe illness. I suppose people remember the help rendered to them very well if it is done selflessly. I thought this trait was due to Pakhtun culture, but an American lady, Catherine Sahovic, always introduces me as 'the person who saved my life,' although I had not done much except advise her husband, Dr Sahovic, about what to do when his wife fell seriously ill in Kashghar, China while travelling on the silk route towards the Karakoram Highway into Pakistan. What a pleasure it is to meet people who kindly recall whatever good you rendered them, no matter how small.

I once heard a Harvard cardiologist talking about 'stress management.' He said that stress cannot be avoided, but you can minimize it by thinking about something you like or love. If you are religious, pray and recite the name of God. Telling a rosary can help too. Avoiding people who are negative is also helpful. But when Pukhtuns get together, they mainly give sarcastic accounts of the bad points of others. During my ten years in England serving in the National Health Service, I rarely encountered people talking in this manner. Once, while sipping tea in a British hospital, I mentioned something negative about the character of a person. My English companion merely said 'I am sorry for him' and there was no further discussion or comment. Whether I met people from a particularly genteel strata or whether sarcastic discussion is not part of English culture is not clear to me.

In the college, I had to study hard as there was heavy competition for entrance into graduate studies. Biology students were supposed to go into medicine, while the mathematics students were called pre-engineering. Once the biology teacher asked the students what questions we had attempted to answer in the annual examination. I had chosen a question about Mendel's experiments on pea flowers in the monastery, which was foundational to the discovery of modern genetics. This story fascinated me, so I had read up about it on my own. Since the professor had not taught us that topic, he told me: 'You are a genius.' In those days, and today as well, teaching was completely examination oriented. To produce better graduates, it has to change to a more knowledge-oriented approach.

While I was attending college, my father often visited Saidu to see me and, more importantly, to pay his respects to the Wali and his father Badshah Sahib, who had long since handed the affairs of the state over to his son. I sometimes accompanied my father, who would ask Badshah Sahib to pray for me. At this time, the former ruler was old and frail, but his mind was active. He fasted daily and constantly read the Quran. He had also built a tomb for himself. He was very fond of hunting and even in old age asked to be taken to the reserve to do some shooting. His eyesight was weak, but his servant told him when the birds were flying overhead, and he aimed his shotgun and shot at them.

The laws against hunting in the areas reserved for the royal family were strictly enforced and violators were fined or imprisoned, but people used to break the laws anyway. Once our goshawks and falcons were confiscated when the Badshah discovered that my father and uncles were using them to hunt in his reserve. As it happened, Ataullah Khan, popularly known as Wakil Sahib, had reported my family to the ruler, not knowing whom he had seen.

Ataullah Khan and his family were from Punjab and belonged to the prominent Chuhan family. They played a dominant role in the development of Swat, especially in the fields of healthcare and education. He originally emigrated to Swat at the behest of Miangul Abdul Wadud, the Badshah. Wakil Sahib was a remarkable man, elegant, well dressed, soft spoken, intelligent, loyal and polite. He was crucial in establishing friendly relations with the British as he was educated, spoke excellent English, and was able to correspond correctly with officials. That an outsider who did not know the Pukhto language was so important in establishing and maintaining the state was a remarkable feat in itself. Later he and his sons amassed considerable wealth legally by trade and in timber, but they avoided close relations and marriages with the business families of Swat and never took an active part in politics, wisely preferring to remain neutral. He also drove a small car and kept a low profile so as not to arouse the jealousies of the Swati Pukhtuns. His nephew, Dr Najibullah Khan, played a vital role in establishing quality health care in Swat state. He also had a great influence on me, as I will show later.

CHAPTER SEVEN

HOW TO GET INTO MEDICAL SCHOOL

☪

There was a first division, second division and third division in the premedical examination results in the Faculty of Science (FSc). In 1958, I passed in the first division. After passing. I wanted to realize my old dream of joining the Air Force. I had studied in the PAF Public School, my maternal uncle, Nisar Khan, was a squadron leader, the uniform was attractive, and the prospect of a free education with an income for my household, especially for my mother, was appealing. Unfortunately, I was now too old to enlist. Moreover, Nisar Khan wanted me to become a medical doctor.

My father was also in favour of this, perhaps because one of his maternal uncles had been admitted to study medicine in King Edward's Medical College in Lahore, a prestigious institution established during the British era. However, when he entered the dissection hall, he fainted. Whether it was due to the smell or from seeing dead bodies is not known. After he left medical studies he excelled in politics and became a Federal Minister in later life. But my successful passage through medical school would redeem this old family disgrace. Finally, I also remembered the bad health I had experienced as a child in the village. Perhaps I could do something to alleviate the conditions that caused so much suffering to my people.

As Omar Khayyam said: 'Life is like a bridge: there are holes at the beginning into which one falls, followed by fewer holes in the middle. But at the end of the bridge, there are chasms which one cannot escape.' In the Swat of my youth, there were many holes that people could easily disappear into. Sudden inexplicable deaths were attributed to the *balla* (witches) that prowled about at night-time. People attributed any unexplained bruises to blows from balla. Rumours of such attacks spread rapidly in the village and to other villages without contradiction from any quarter. We children were scared to go outside because of witches and *djinns* (evil spirits).

Another danger for children was the evil eye. Conjunctivitis, for example, was said to be due to the evil eye of envious people. Casting an evil eye was usually unintentional. A man with the evil eye could inadvertently cause disease and sometimes the death of an infant - including his own son - when he looked at the baby with admiration. This is the reason fathers were kept from viewing their baby sons for some weeks after birth, and why ash was smeared on babies' foreheads to make them ugly. Similarly, cow skulls were hung off the roofs of new buildings to make them unattractive and fend off an admiring and envious evil eye. For the same reason, Pukhtuns do not openly praise anyone or anything. Doing so can be taken as putting the evil eye on whoever or whatever has been admired. Some people - especially those with blue/green eyes like mine - were thought to have especially powerful evil eyes. Secretly, some men were proud to have this destructive power, and bragged among friends that their glance was responsible for the downfall of an envied neighbour.

Diseases were rampant in the village. Loose bowel motions and fever were normal in summer time because of flies and unclean water. In winter, there were coughs, colds, and pneumonia, although I do not remember any children having asthma. Intestinal worms were common and one could see worms crawling in the uncovered cesspits. There was no escape from infectious diseases like whooping cough, measles, chickenpox, and smallpox. Goitre, the enlargement of the thyroid gland in the neck, was common in our village of Lower Durshkhela and in our neighbouring village of Upper (*bara*) Durshkhela. Huge swellings in the neck were so widespread that a proverb came into being: 'Da Durshkhela ghorae de, lari eni, najde na eni' - he is from the village of Durshkhela, he can see the distance but cannot see near his feet. Oddly, villages south of the Durshkhelas and north of the Durshkhelas did not have a high prevalence of goitre. What were the reasons, I wondered? Later, I learned it was due to a deficiency in iodine.

As a child, I suffered from every sort of illness. I had a malarial fever that recurred every third day, when I would start shivering and suffer fits with foam coming out of my mouth. For relief, I went outside and lay down in the sun. This fever was believed to be caused by a djinn. Mullahs were brought in to perform *khpa wahala*, standing above me and moving their raised foot over my head down to my feet while reciting *dum* (incantations). They also wrote *taweez* that were said to ward off evil. In the village there was also a lady who could go into a trance and then say who the evil djinn was, whether it was Hindu, Sikh or fairy. She would announce that the sufferer had done a such and such a thing that was the reason for his or her illness.

I had another disease that I remember very clearly, which I contracted in one of my elbow joints and both my knee joints. Painful attacks lasted for months. In retrospect, I think this was a rheumatic fever. Rheumatic fever is supposed to 'lick the joints and bite the heart' but in my case it had the opposite effects. I also had a bad case of smallpox. One evening my mother took me in her lap and when I asked her, 'Is it raining?' I saw tears suddenly rolling down her cheeks, a rare occasion for a tough lady. Many years later I asked her about this episode. She explained that whenever a smallpox victim starts to talk about the rain, the smallpox affects the heart and the child never recovers.

Nonetheless, I did recover, and without the pockmarks that are such a common sight in Swat. My recovery was remarkable because in the village and in the whole valley, there were no qualified doctors, only the *hakims* (local healers) who made potions. During my serious illnesses, my father consulted with two hakims. One gave me 'sweet medicine,' which I liked, and one gave me 'bitter medicine,' which I hated. Lizards were supposed to be good for emaciated children and I was given boiled and roasted lizards, which I was told were birds. With this kind of medicine, only the strong survived. However, local cures sometimes did work. For example, some people, including my uncle, had large round scars near their wrists. These were the marks of the instillation of small pox scabs inserted into the skin, which gave immunity against smallpox. The Pukhtun knew about this kind of prophylactic vaccination before Edward Jenner discovered it.

I decided to apply to Medical College. My first choice was King Edward Medical College, Lahore, partly because of my uncle's experience. Expenses were again a problem, and there was no one to look to for guidance except my uncle, who was the only educated member of my family. In this situation, we went to visit Haji Roshan Tota in his crockery shop in Mingora. My uncles and my father often stopped there to have tea, talk politics, and partake of the famous Mashal Kabab. It was here that Tota suggested I seek the help of his son Bilal, who was already studying at King Edward Medical College. Bilal gave me application forms and taught me how to fill them in and send them. I also sought the guidance of another family friend, Haji Daud Seth, whose eldest son advised me to seek admission to Khyber Medical College in Peshawar, as it was nearer and cheaper. So I applied there rather than to King Edward.

Western medicine has quite a long history in Peshawar. The first hospital there was built by Christian missionaries who did good work in the medical field. When my grandfather Shahbaz Khan was shot in the thigh, he was operated on in Peshawar Mission Hospital. But despite their good deeds, the missionaries were spectacularly unsuccessful. One of them lamented to me that in his twenty years of medical and missionary work in the Pukhtun region, he could only convert two persons, and they were killed by their relatives. While in China, where he had also gone on missionary work, he was pleased to report that he had converted hundreds to Christianity. This reminds me of a story about a Hindu who converted to Islam. When he found out that if one leaves Islam and returns to his previous religion, his head has to be chopped off, the Hindu remarked, 'What a religion. When you want to join they chop off a part of your penis and when you want to leave, they chop off your head.'

My application forms for medical school had to be processed by the secretariat of the Ruler of Swat, which was a fair, transparent, and bureaucratically hurdle free procedure, unlike the corrupt inefficiency that was the norm after Swat State was amalgamated with the rest of Pakistan. Purdil Khan, the Ruler's private secretary, helped me with the application because of his close friendship with my uncle Nisar Khan. Purdil Khan was a soft-spoken, intelligent man who was always well dressed in coat, trousers and tie.

To facilitate my smooth entrance into medical college, my father accompanied me to Peshawar. We stayed with the family of Aslam Khan in the village of Upper Pishtakhera, where we were entertained in their hujra. Sharif Khan Baba, my father's adventurous uncle, had met Omar Khan Baba, Aslam Khan's father, during the Hajj when the journeys were long and travelling was by foot, mule and camel. The friendship continued as Omar Khan and his family came to Swat in summer to escape the heat of the city, and we visited Peshawar in the winter to shop, see the zoo, and enjoy the sights. Aslam Khan's sons, Faqir Mohammad Khan and Nisar Khan, were very pleased to see us, although we were unannounced guests.

Pishtakhera villages are famous for their clean drinking water, which is considered to be an aphrodisiac. The hygienic drinking water system facility was built by the British on the Bara River, which drains from the Tirah Mountains where the Afridi tribes live. The Tirah is a scenic area near Peshawar that has been a battleground for many years. It remains a hideout for renegades and Taliban fighters. Cannabis is grown there and *chars* - hashish - is manufactured and then smuggled out to the rest of Pakistan and elsewhere.

Our family friends in Pishtakhera village were Muslim Leaguers and were against Ghaffar Khan's Red Shirts or Khudai Khidmatgars, who had supported the Congress Party before Partition. My father also liked the Muslim League, not because he knew the manifesto of the party, but because of the name Muslim. The Congress Party was considered to be a Hindu Party and Ghaffar Khan was known to be a friend of non-Muslims. For these reasons, Ghaffar Khan's loyalty to Pakistan was questioned, and the work of the Red Shirts was forgotten.

One of the loyal servants of the Pishtakhera Khans told us a story about how the local Khans managed to win the elections during the time after partition when Chief Minister Abdul Qayum Khan of the Muslim League was in power. The servant, a confidant of the Pishtakhera Khans, was sent to the Chief Minister (CM) to tell him that his friend Aslam Khan of the Muslim League Party was going to lose the election. The CM ordered a police officer to put all the votes into Aslam Khan's election boxes. So rigging in elections started immediately after the creation of Pakistan. Winning at any cost is ingrained in our culture. There is also a saying: 'Zar wakhla che Khan she. Che Khan she zar der dee' - give gold to become a Khan. When you are Khan, then there is plenty of gold.

The Pishtakhera Khans said that I should stay with them while studying in Medical College because our grandfathers were friends, but Durveza Khan was already living in their hujra and receiving free boarding and lodging. Instead, I had to go into the University Hostel. Money for fees and other expenses was borrowed from well to do relatives or from other sources.

The admission process for Swati students went through the Peshawar Government Secretariat, which was originally built in the British era. I cannot forget the image of the secretariat. It was an impressive complex, featuring wide-open spaces and large flowerbeds. The building itself had an eastern look, with arches and spacious verandas decorated with flowerpots. Without delay, the servant ushered me in to see the Assistant Commissioner. This bureaucrat was very polite. He looked at the letter from the Chief Secretary of Swat and quickly assured me that I would be admitted into Khyber Medical College.

At that time, the Pakistan Government gave an annual subsidy to the rulers of autonomous states. In the case of Wali, this was kept with the Political Agent (PA) in Malakand for distribution as scholarships for deserving or well-connected students. My father asked Khan Bahadur Sultanat Khan to put in a word *(safarish)* with the Wali and he agreed. My father and I then went to see the ruler. When we entered his office, Khan Bahadur was sitting with him and mentioned the scholarship. I could see from the Wali's face that he was not inclined to grant this favour. But Khan Bahadur said, 'Qamar Khan (Khaista Dada) is loyal. The opposition to your kingdom comes from his brother and his uncle.' A scholarship was granted.

The next step was to go to Malakand, where the Political Agent had his offices. The Malakand pass is the gateway into Swat, Dir, Chitral, Kalash, Wakhan, the Hindu Kush (Hindu killer) mountains and the Pamir Plateau - the roof of the world. The British and before them the Mughals and Alexander the Great knew the strategic importance of this place. Alexander the Macedonian reached these mountains after fighting and conquering for eight years, travelling 18,000 kilometers from Greece. In Jalalabad, on what is now the Afghan side of the Pamirs, he divided his army. His lover Hephaestion marched through Khyber to be east. Alexander himself led the army to the north through the Kunar valley, subdued the tribes and crossed to Bajaur, going eastwards through Dir, Malakand and Swat. Alexander fought his way through and was injured in the leg. He married a local girl to gain an alliance. The Mughal King Babur also married a girl from this region to try to win support. The British did not follow the policy of intermarrying, and faced many uprisings in the region, as chronicled by Winston Churchill in his book, The Malakand Forces. He mentioned the 'mad fakir' from Swat, who organized and led his forces against the British in Malakand. I asked my uncle Khan Dada, just before he died at a very old age from Alzheimer's disease, whether he remembered this Swat Kheli - a mass uprising for a just cause. He said he was ten years old when he took part. The 'mad fakir' told his followers that his spiritual power made the big guns of the British unworkable. People were afraid of British artillery, but not of swords, rifles and hand-to-hand fighting. However, their bravery did not prevail. Many died, cut down by British gunfire, and the rebellion was unsuccessful.

One had to pass through the Olive Grove, the scene of heavy fighting between the tribes and British Indian troops, to reach the Political Agent's offices. The olive trees were in a cemetery and Pushtuns avoid cutting trees in a cemetery, so the spot was very beautiful. In fact, all over the region, the local graveyard was a place where shade could be found and picnics held. I still remember the stately chinar trees that cast shade in the graveyard in Durshkhela. However, today most of the graveyards in Swat have been denuded of their shade trees, which have been sold off to timber dealers by greedy village elders for tiny sums of money. This is another instance of the gradual degradation of the environment in Swat, where the woods everywhere have been chopped down and sold, even if they are in reserved areas. As is now typical, bribery overturns law. The people do realize that destroying the forest leads to flooding and disastrous soil erosion. But they say, 'If I don't cut and sell the trees, someone else will do it.'

To return to my story, in 1958, Pakistan was independent and the PA was a khan from Mardan. He followed an illustrious line of previous agents and other British officials, including men like Dundas, Cunningham and Olaf Caroe, who were excellent administrators and very knowledgeable about the Pukhtun. Her Majesty Queen Victoria's government had learned that to keep the peace they must send their top people to the North West Frontier. Since then things had changed for the worse, as I soon discovered. Unlike the officials in Peshawar, the Malakand PA was not accessible and there were difficulties in getting the stipend. Later that I came to know that official money meant for education of Swati students was embezzled in the Political Agent's office. Corruption, so rare in British times, had become routine.

Finally, after a great deal of effort spent getting letters of recommendation from people known to the PA, I received my stipend of eighty rupees per month. The stipend was sufficient during a time when a gram of gold was worth less than two hundred rupees. I was happy because I would be able to buy sharp clothes, flashy jackets and new brown shoes (chappels). More important, I was happy because I was going to study in a place where there were smart single girls.

CHAPTER EIGHT

MEDICAL STUDIES – PLEASURE AND PAIN

☪

In our class there were boys from the borderlands between Afghanistan and Pakistan, which was then called the 'tribal area'. It included the Mahsud, Wazirs, Dawars, Bhittanis, Burkis and some others. This designation was later changed to 'federally-administered tribal areas', FATA. The tribal people from the borderlands are religious and independent thinking but will go to any extent to help and oblige a friend. Betrayal in friendship is considered a sin. I sometimes ask my Waziri patients, 'Who is *nar* [strong] - you or Mahsud?' They always say Mahsud. For years, it was said that FATA was the area where Osama bin Laden was hidden, having been given refuge by the tribes, who were bound to follow their code of honour. Of course, we now know that he was in Abbotabad, very close to the military college there.

Some seats in the college were reserved for tribal students, but the literacy rate in the area was very low, so the college had only a few boys who actually came from Waziristan and the other frontier tribes. Instead, boys and girls were admitted from other areas by using fake domicile certificates and by bribing the officials. Material corruption such as bribery was uncommon among the tribal people, while smuggling was simply considered to be free trade. Both cannabis plants and opium poppies have been grown in this region for generations, and they consider it their right to control their own fields. Secular education for girls does not occur in the region. When I ask some of my patients from FATA about girls' education (*sabagh*), they assume I mean going to a religious seminary. This is partly because of lack of accessible schools for children and partly for economic reasons, because in religious seminaries, everything is free.

I became friendly with one student from Waziristan who became a radiologist. Years later, both of us attended a medical conference in Paris. On the street, we came across a lady selling tickets for a show. I asked what type of show and she said, 'a very hot show.' My Waziri friend asked me what was meant by 'hot.' I said I did not know, but suggested going, and so we went. It turned out to be a nude show, and he kept his eyes shut most of the time. When he opened his eyes, he looked at his watch and said, 'It is time for prayers. Which direction is Mecca?' In the meantime a girl reached our row and wanted her pants pulled down. I asked the Waziri and he did oblige, but with closed eyes.

Because of the lack of education for girls, there were no female students at the college from the tribal areas, but there were girls from other areas of Pakistan such as Rawalpindi, Lahore and Karachi. These girls from these urban areas did not wear a headscarf or burqa. They also mixed freely with boys. Christian girls were more open. There were two Christian girls, Iris and Barbara, in one of the higher classes. Iris was fair and shapely, while Barbara was dark and heavily built with prominent buttocks. The Pushtun boys admired them. '*Kwannati, anangi*' - buttock and cheeks - were engrained in the psyches of Pushtuns in general and Swatis in particular. However, with modern information technology and exposure to western media and literature, it seems breasts are now becoming more popular as topics of discussion and interest.

The Pukhtun girls would discourage the other girls from mixing and becoming free with the boys. One of our class fellows, a Khattak from the southern districts, was fond of a girl, but since a Pukhtun does not know how to build relations with the fair sex, he made a nuisance of himself and she slapped him in front of our class. She was interested in another boy, but he was too shy to talk to her.

Coming from Swat, where we did not have exposure to the opposite sex, I was very embarrassed with girls, but the boys from Peshawar and non-Pushto speaking areas were at ease. To overcome my excessive shyness, I started taking part in the college's annual staging of dramas. A Bengali was in charge of putting on dramas, skits and other shows. He was a talented person, as people from that country are often good at fine arts such as stage shows and dancing, both popular and classic. I remember one performance that was very much enjoyed by the Pukhtun boys. He showed the shadows of two persons behind a transparent curtain; one voice said, 'bend slightly, raise a little, slightly turn right and that is fine.' When the curtains were drawn, there were two people, one with a full sack on his back. I took part in a skit labeled 'Da Wache Khan' - the good-for-nothing Khan. I also played a Chitrali sitar accompanied by someone drumming on an earthenware pot covered with rubber. These simple instruments were popular in Swati villages where people entertained themselves at night in their hujras.

Barbara, Iris and another girl in the senior class named Shamim appreciated my sitar playing, but there were no comments from the girls in my own class. Playing musical instruments and singing was not considered respectable in Pukhtun society. I stored my sitar in my hostel room, but it had to be kept hidden from my parents and close elder relatives, otherwise I would be called '*dum*' - musician - which was a great shame. It was Ghani Khan, the poet, writer and sculptor son of Ghaffar Khan who had said 'Pushtuns like music, but look down upon musicians.' However, exposure to an audience did alleviate the perspiration on my forehead whenever I faced the girls in the class.

Anatomy, Physiology and Biochemistry were taught in the first and second year. Dr Fida Mohammad Khan (FDK), who was the Principal of the school, was a surgeon, but was made Professor of Anatomy because there were no other qualified teachers in that subject. He was not interested in teaching and most of the actual instruction was done by his juniors from Punjab and Bengal. FDK was from Hangu area in the southern districts of NWFP (now Khyber Pukhtunkhwa - KPK) Pakistan. Some of my classmates mentioned that he was 'Sunni' as opposed to another Professor of Medicine from the same area who was 'Shia.' This was the first time I heard of Shias and Sunnis, as there were no Shias in Swat and so no sectarian fighting. People were only known to belong to certain tribes such as Painda Khel, Mamat Khel or to castes such as carpenter, weaver and so on.

Fida Mohammad Khan made sure that all the girls wore a headscarf - *dupatta* - or a chadar and sat separately from boys. The workers as well as the junior teachers were afraid of him because he was born and bred a *sakh* (real) Pukhtun Khan and so was used to having his orders obeyed. He would not spare anyone who did not attend to his duties. The Pukhtun are known to be good administrators who get work done because they use harsh measures to punish failure.

The dissection hall, where dead bodies were kept, was clean and odour-free. Running water was available for hand washing. The dead bodies were dissected by one student among the group of three or four boys. One read the book and the rest of us observed. As an excuse to talk to the girls, sometimes boys went to the girls' table, supposedly to compare the nerves or arteries or the relations of the muscles to each other.

We found many of our teachers boring. They put no effort into making their subjects interesting, and their own formal training was usually lacking. The only primary research conducted in our first two years was undertaken by one of the junior teachers, who made us take vitamin C and asked us to collect our urine in flasks. The boys wondered how the girls could collect the urine, but a student from Peshawar city, who was older than the rest of us, said that the girls would use funnels for that purpose.

Students from the historical city of Peshawar were called *kharian* - city dwellers. The culture of Peshawarites differed from that of other Pukhtuns, as they are business oriented and their relations with others were also thought to be business oriented. This was a trait that was not liked by people from the tribal regions. The city of Peshawar has produced good doctors like Professor Qazi, Dr Saeed-ul-Majeed, Dr Sher Ahmad, Dr Amjad Hussain and others but also writers of international repute, and artists who have contributed in their fields. Some Bollywood actors from Peshawar, such as Yousuf Khan (Dilip Kumar), Raj Kapoor and Shah Rukh Khan, are internationally known.

Some of my cohort from Peshawar who became successful doctors emigrated to the USA and Canada. One, Dr Naseem Ashraf, was the president of APPNA - Association of Pakistan Physicians of North America. In Pakistan he became very close to the military ruler, General Musharaf, so much so that billions of rupees were placed at his disposal. Whether what Dr Ashraf was doing had any impact on the socioeconomic conditions of the people is not clear. But because of his close relations with some USA Senators and Congressmen, he was able to smooth relations with the USA whenever Musharaf was in 'hot water.' It was said that an airplane was always ready on the tarmac for Dr Ashraf to dash to the USA.

I went to Peshawar to see cinema films occasionally. Indian films were very popular and tickets for entry to the cinema hall were usually difficult to get. We bought them on the black market, which meant paying extra money. However, a son of our villager Bakhtak Mama was employed as gatekeeper and he sold me black market tickets without increasing the price. Bakhtak was popularly known in our village in Swat as '*Batak*' - literally meaning male duck.

Transport in the late fifties from the University to Peshawar consisted of *tongas* - horse drawn carriages - and government buses. People also used to walk or ride bicycles. There were very few privately-owned cars. One of the only private cars in the Medical College belonged to the Principal, Dr Fida Mohammad Khan. Some other teachers also had cars, but I remember his, because he had a special place reserved for parking. One day when another teacher parked a car in FDK's parking place, he was furious.

The first year of Medical College was interesting in the sense that there were girls in the class, and also because I met students not only from all parts of the North West Frontier Province (now changed to Khyber Pakhtun Khwa) but from all over Pakistan, including Campbellpur (later changed to Attock), Montgomery (changed to Sahiwal) and Layal pur (changed to Faisal Abad). The first year was also interesting since the subjects were completely new for me. The second year was stressful because I had to recall all the taught subjects of Anatomy, Physiology and Biochemistry. There was a sharp division between the basic sciences and the clinical sciences. The system of teaching and examination was inherited from the British era and no one thought of making the subjects more interesting by making the courses more clinically oriented. Learning was completely by rote and there was no concept of research.

The first year examination was internal and so simple that everyone passed, but the second year was tough because external examiners conducted the exams. I found physiology fascinating, partly because it related to the day-to-day working of the body, such as eating, breathing, urination, defecation and sexual functions, and partly due to the teachers, who were respected and who tried to make the subject more interesting. We read the chapter on sexual activity ahead of time, discussed it among ourselves and made jokes about it. Anatomy was made more interesting by the teacher's illustration of the actions of the muscles of the buttocks, because while describing the attachments, nerve supply and actions he gave the example of Brigitte Bardot.

Dr M.K. Afridi, a world-renowned malarialogist and the Vice Chancellor of the University, was interested in the development of quality medical education, but our college was not recognized by the centralized federal regulatory authority. General Burki, the Health Minister during the martial law regime, decided that he wanted to abolish and discontinue all 'below standard' medical diplomas and degrees, which included those granted by our administration. We students resisted and went on strike until the college was recognized. Pukhtuns are generally highly individualistic, but if there is a threat from outside, they unite. As I mentioned, the same thing happened when the Dir Nawab invaded Upper Swat as the opposing dullahs cooperated against him.

Going on strike was new to me as I was from Swat, where the Wali did not allow unions, demonstrations or strikes. So I was not surprised when after our strike there was talk of the termination of some student ringleaders. M.K. Afridi decided to address us, and we gathered in the Pathology Department. There was pin-drop silence as he entered, since we respected him because of his past track record and moreover because he belonged to the well-known and warlike Afridi Tribe from the Frontier region. I thought he was going to announce some harsh measures against us. Instead he congratulated us and said that we students had 'strengthened his hand.' We cheered and the strike ended. M.K. Afridi, being an intelligent and cosmopolitan man, knew how to handle young students and how to make the best use of the opportunity. Soon after that meeting he and the Principal went to see Health Minister Burki and President Ayub Khan and put forward the case for recognition of Khyber Medical College. He not only gained recognition for the Medical College, but even got more funds for development of the Institution. It was probably Einstein who said, 'In every difficulty, there is opportunity.'

The third year of medical studies was something I looked forward to as it is then that you start going to the wards and interacting with patients. In the first year and second year I only dissected dead bodies. Moreover, at that point one is called 'Doctor Saib' and begins carrying that marvellous invention, the stethoscope. Even to this day, a Pushtun patient, whether as in-patient or outpatient, is never satisfied unless the doctors make use of the stethoscope. Patients from Afghanistan, whether Pushtun, Tajiks, Uzbeks or Hazaras, also expect their blood pressure to be recorded and some other investigations to be performed. They especially like blood tests or imaging such as ultrasonography, which they call a TV examination. Even if these procedures are unnecessary, it is important to meet the expectations of the patients in order to maintain their confidence. I believe that communication with patients and their relatives is important on the part of health workers, no matter how many technological advances are made.

Pharmacology was the main subject taught in the third year. Our teacher, Inayat Khan, knew how to teach and how to make the subject interesting. He was a Pukhtun from Charsadda area of Pakhtunkhwa (PK) who had taken his PhD at Edinburgh University in Scotland. He told us about his meetings with Cunningham, the Pashto-speaking Governor of North West Frontier. A famous bridge in Upper Swat that was built in 1944 is known as Cunningham Bridge. In the recent devastating floods (2011), most of the bridges in Swat were washed away except this one. Inayat Khan settled in Geneva after his retirement, following his son who was a radiologist in Switzerland. In one of my travels to Geneva, I looked in the telephone directory, found his name and phoned him. He was pleased and wanted to know how I had found his name. I had to say that all the people, including the taxi drivers, knew of Professor Inayat Khan.

In the third year of Medical College, the students were supposed to attend the 'ward rounds'. The round consisted of a senior doctor, the junior doctors, the trainees' doctors and the nurse in charge of the ward, who was called Sister. In those days, the majority of the nursing staff were Christians, but there was one Muslim nurse who was from Hazara, a Hindko-speaking area. She was fair and pretty, knew her job and was popular among the teachers and senior students.

During rounds, all patients were asked how they were and encouraged to ask questions of the doctors. Our teachers were our role models for applying the human touch. I remember them all. They taught us well, gave us regular demonstrations, and were kind to the patients and their worried relatives. Professor Nasiruddin Azam Khan was one of our Professors of Clinical Medicine. Like the Muslim nurse, he was from the Hazara area and was Hindko speaking. He was short, always well dressed and a disciplinarian. He was punctual and expected everyone else to be on time as well. In Pukhtun society being on time was not highly valued, so this was a constant problem for us. However, there are reasons for our habitual lateness: no matter what, a Pukhtun has to attend to a guest first, that is, provide hospitality. A Pukhtun also has to be helpful to whomever seeks help or protection and is obliged to be generous and to provide sanctuary. These are fundamental principles of *Pukhtunwali*, the Pukhtun code of honour. Professor Nasir was brought up in the Hazara area, which is mainly non-Pashto speaking and where Pukhtunwali is not a central value. He also was educated as doctor in Britain and so did not really understand our customs. Nonetheless, his lectures were well attended and his teaching demonstrations in the wards were never missed because his knowledge and teaching skills were proverbial.

Our other Professor of Medicine was Raza Ali. He was a well-built, domineering Shi'a Pushtun from the same Hangu area as FDK. He later took over the job of principal from his countryman. It was whispered in the student circles that he had an extramarital relationship with a lady from a political family. In the late fifties doctors were officially allowed to start private practice in their residences and Raza Ali was one of the first to take advantage of this opportunity. His fee was sixteen rupees for consultation. This was later doubled.

To gain the goodwill of our teachers, some of us referred private patients to their clinics. This could lead to embarrassing incidents. For example, a schoolfellow of mine was a pilot in the Air Force stationed at the Peshawar Air Base. Although the armed forces had very good medical facilities in their Combined Military Hospital, my friend asked me to take him to a private eye specialist, since he was afraid of being grounded if any defect was found in his eyes. Whenever there were patients we knew from our villages or from school, we students helped them even at the cost of our studies. To a Pukhtun personal relationships are considered more important than work. Accordingly I took my friend to see Professor Qazi, who was my eye and ear, nose and throat teacher. Professor Qazi examined him and reassured him that his eyes were fine. Then he escorted us to the gate of his house, looking at our hands and pockets, but no money was forthcoming. The pilot was accustomed to free treatment from the military, I had no money, and Dr Qazi was too polite to ask for payment.

Other problems arose regarding the payment of fees. Once a surgeon acquaintance of mine examined a patient in his clinic for hydrocele - fluid in the testicular pouch (a common disorder in Pakistan) - and, without writing a prescription, told him to go to the hospital for further treatment. The patient refused to pay anything as no medicine had been given or prescription written. The surgeon replied: 'If you consent to fondle my balls, I'll pay you double my fee.'

However, usually doctors had no problem getting fees from private patients, since people soon learnt that they could get quicker admission into the hospital if they had seen the doctor in his private clinic. Touting, commissions and other unethical practices were bound to develop. At one time the Dabgari area in Peshawar, where many doctors' offices are now located, was known for its brothels. I heard someone say that the sex workers have been replaced by medical prostitutes. Greed is part of human nature and is present to a greater or lesser degree in everyone. Medicine is not immune, even though it is called the 'Noble Profession.'

Other vices were also practised by some of our doctors. One of them forced the male relatives of patients to have anal intercourse with him in the side room when he was on night duty. I later realized that there were also alcoholics and religious zealots in the profession. Although most doctors stick to their Hippocratic Oath and follow ethical practices, nonetheless, individual and collective regulations are needed to offset temptations for corruption.

It was no secret in the student circles that 'Raza saib', as Professor Raza Ali was known, and 'Nasir saib', as Professor Nasir was known, were not on good terms. Raza saib was a Shia Pushtun from a rugged area where sectarian problems are common. Nasir saib was from the Hazara area, where people are soft spoken and intertribal jealousies and sectarian violence are not present. Moreover Raza saib was senior to Nasir saib and was making a lot of money in his private practice; he did not want competition for his private patients from a competent person like Nasir saib. So among the classic three Z's (zar, zamin, zun), in this case it was zar (gold) that was the cause of discord. We students knew about the problematic relations between them and were careful not to take sides. For us, passing the final examination was our main objective and we all were afraid of being failed out of revenge.

I remember two happenings from the teaching rounds. Once Nasir saib ordered a drip of milk to be delivered through a stomach tube to a patient who was suffering from a stomach ulcer. Relatives of patients have to provide medicine and other stuff needed for care of their near and dear ones if they fall ill, so the man's son was responsible for getting the milk. When the drip was given, Nasir saib saw a greenish fluid flowing down the tubing. 'What is it?' he asked. The son of the patient said, 'Doctor saib, you had said to bring milk from the bazaar, but I got tea instead, because my father loves green tea.' In another incident, a wrestler from Peshawar was admitted to the ward. In English, Raza saib told the patient to eat vegetables. The patient did not understand and asked the younger doctor what was meant. He said, Raza saib has told you 'ghass kao' - eat grass.

People in general and Pukhtuns in particular like to be praised and to be well known and respected in the community. So I was very pleased when I topped the university examination in the third year, which was a surprise for everyone as the students expected a girl student, Jauhar Khatoon, or an older boy named Ismael Mahmudi to top the class. I was especially happy because I came to the attention of the girl students in our class as well as to Shamim, Barbara and Iris from the senior class. They congratulated me, but I was still too shy to exchange pleasantries.

The summer holidays stretched from June to September, so we students went back to our homes. The journey to Swat was long and tedious. I took a government transport bus, which was then called a GTS. The service from the university was regular and efficient in the early sixties - very different from today. The first stop on the way to Mingora was in Mardan and the next stop was in Batkhela, near Malakand. In Batkhela, the bus stopped near a hotel where the driver and conductor were given free meals. The front seats were reserved for ladies, and there were always one or two clad in shuttlecock burqas or long black chadars wrapped round the body, showing only the eyes. If a lady noticed that a man was gazing at her, then she would cover her face.

At Mingora I got off the bus and took another one north. This first stopped at Pir Kali, the village where Mir Qasim Baba, one of the commanders of Mahmud Ghaznavi's army, was buried after he died in battle. It was considered a holy site. On the third day of the Eid celebrations boys and girls attired in their new clothes gathered near his mausoleum to sing and dance This practice was recently discontinued after protests by religious zealots. After stopping in Pir Kali I used a tonga to get to Kuze Durushkhela village. When I got home, I was obliged to sleep in the hujra, as adults were no longer permitted to sleep in their parents' compound.

The local people expected me to treat their illnesses and give them medicine, usually without paying anything. Sometimes I made mistakes, though luckily none were fatal. The wife of my eldest uncle once asked me for medicine to stop her itching. I had read pharmacology and gave her an anti-allergic promethazine (Phenergan). She slept all night and woke up in the middle of the next day. I learnt many of my clinical skills in my village, including injection in the knee joints, by practising on my relatives. Malaria was common, but I was able to give effective treatment for it. Tuberculosis was also prevalent. It was imported from Karachi, because the Swatis who worked in the factories had not developed immunity. They often caught tuberculosis and then came back to the villages and infected others. Unfortunately, effective BCG vaccination was not generally available.

The subjects in the fourth year of medicine were Surgery, Medicine, Pathology, Hygiene and Forensic Medicine. One of the professors was religious and gave more marks to female students who wore the dupatta (head scarf), so the girls soon learnt to wear one whenever he was the examiner. They would take it off afterwards.

A story was circulated among the students about the elder brother of Professor Ifthikhar, who taught hygiene. His brother was a philosophy Professor at Islamia College. It was said that he carried a stick with him and at night would put his stick in the corner and then sleep in his bed. At times he was so deep in his thoughts that he would put the stick in his bed and stand himself in the corner of this bedroom.

In the higher classes in medical college, the students were sent to better and larger hostels. We were given places in hostel number two on the first floor. At night we gathered in Raunaq Zaman's room. He was good at writing and composing poetry, but did not take much interest in his medical studies. In his room we gossiped about the day's activities, mainly about which girl was seen with which boy. In the early sixties, there was no regular entertainment or activities in the hostels, so we used to plot how to disturb the sleep of the other students. One night Raunaq Zaman got hold of a stray dog, knotted used boot polish tins to a rope, tied the rope to its tail, and released the dog, which started barking and ran across the yard, the tins making a lot of noise. All the students woke up and came out of their rooms. They knew who had made the mischief but left it to the wardens to investigate. The Chief Warden was Maulana Abdul Qadir, a fine, cultured, soft spoken man, a fatherly figure who radiated an air of authority. The senior warden was Dr Abdul Matin, a well-dressed intelligent man and a disciplinarian. He later became Vice Chancellor of Peshawar University.

The second university hostel where I lived had accommodation for hundreds of students from many faculties. It was shaped like a rectangle and the first floor had one row of rooms with open space all around it, so that if a student came out of his room at night to make mischief, the rest of the students could hear him. There was one student nicknamed 'Maraz' - quail. One hosteller would start calling 'Maraz,

Maraz!' and the rest of us would join. Maraz would shout insults and fight with the other students, but to no avail. His reaction encouraged even more mockery, so much so that he eventually had to leave the hostel. This was the time when Russia had just sent Yuri Gagarin into space. Gul Rose, our class fellow, used to ascend to the roof to study. The hostellers started calling him Gagarin, but he laughed it off. That was the right reaction.

In the fourth year, we continued to go to Lady Reading Hospital to learn clinical skills. One of the teachers in surgery was Dr Feroz Shah, a soft-spoken, highly-skilled surgeon from the village of Achini near Peshawar. Once, when he was presiding over a clinical demonstration in a class, I put a question to our classmate who was presenting the patient. He happened to be from my 'opposite group' and probably thought I was trying to belittle him in front of the girls. Members of his group and mine got up from their seats and started to exchange hot words. Our Professor walked out of the room. Some neutral individuals then intervened and we did not come to blows. After this episode I was deeply ashamed and went to Dr Shah to apologize. The Pukhtun does not believe in making apologies; in fact there is no known original word in Pukhto for 'sorry.' Presumably the Pukhtun thinks he must suffer if he does anything wrong, or perhaps his pride means he can never admit to wrongdoing. Whatever the case, I had attended a British-run school where our English teachers taught us to say sorry. Dr Shah accepted my apology and said that in losing one's temper, one's pulse races, one's blood pressure rises and one does not gain anything. I have kept his words in mind ever since.

We watched from specially-built galleries when operations were performed. I remember some; one was the circumcision of an adult from Waziristan. Circumcision was not common during childhood in tribal areas in those days. Others were for peptic ulcers. Operations on volvulus have also stuck in my memory as the large intestine looked big and inflated. Volvulus is common in parts of the world where people eat a high fibre diet. On the medical ward, we saw patients with bloated abdomens because of cirrhosis of the liver. One could see a lot of cats and stray dogs lurking outside the hospital, as disposal of waste following surgical operation was not efficient.

The routine work for doctors in those days was so heavy that there was little time to collect data about diseases. However, this is no excuse for not doing original research. If teachers create a culture of research then research will be done, no matter how demanding the daily routine is. But I do not remember anyone presenting data about original research in my medical student days.

In our spare time we went to the coffee shop for tea and samosas. The shop was built on raised ground near a huge tree planted during British time. Even though it was named a 'coffee shop,' there was no coffee and I had no idea what coffee was. It was during one of these outings that a nude photo of a female was circulated among the male students. I had never seen or heard of nude photographs, but nowadays the children are exposed to pornography from young age. I am not certain what the consequences are.

In the fourth year of medicine, we were also taken to the water purification plant built by the British on Bara River to supply clean water to the cantonment and the Governor's house. This water purification plant still exists. The British served and ruled for a long time in the NWFP and did a lot of useful work in the areas of education, health, communication and agriculture water management. They built Islamia College, one of the best during that time. The wide roads with trees planted alongside them are also the legacy of the Anglo Saxons, as are the numerous agriculture canals. The hallmark of good governance in those days, and today, was that if you were given a task, you had to complete it regardless of where you were and whom you were working far.

In the third year annual examination I topped the class, but in the fourth year I failed in the subject of hygiene. In the oral examination the examiner, who was from Lahore, asked me about the various types of toilets and how these worked. I had read the book but had not grasped the mechanics of water closets, because I was born and bred in a village where, even in the early sixties, there was no proper modern water sanitation system. There were supplementary examinations after few weeks. I did pass the second time around and was promoted to the final year of Medical College.

The subjects in the final year were interesting, but there was a lot of hard work and cramming. I borrowed a monograph on diseases of the liver from the library and found it interesting. I became even more interested in the book because one of our pretty female classmates, who always kept herself reserved and came to the college clad in a burqa, asked me if I could let her have the book for few days. The author of that book, Prof. Sheila Sherlock, later became Dame Sheila Sherlock. Many years later, I had the good fortune of attending her much-sought-after lectures in London. Professor Sherlock's husband Dr Geraint James facilitated my becoming a fellow of the Royal College of Physicians. He had written an article about the Silk Route and I sent a letter to him outlining my views about certain diseases. He was gracious enough to write back and suggested that I should apply to become Fellow of the College. He also wrote to the Principal of Khyber Medical College, Prof. Nasir-ud-din Azam Khan, who was the only Fellow of the London Royal College of Physicians in the region. He guarded his position jealously, but I did become a Fellow of the College.

In the fourth year, male students were not allowed to enter the Zenanna (restricted to women) Hospital and see the patients who had gynaecological and obstetric problems, so for training in midwifery we had to go to either Karachi or Dacca in East Pakistan. I went to Karachi along with my classmates. We were supposed to travel in the second-class train compartments, but to save money we bought tickets for third class. The train service from Peshawar to Karachi in those days was still efficient, but overcrowded. In the 1930s the British-built railway stretching from Khyber to Karachi was intact, unlike the present time when the environmentally-friendly railway system is in the worst possible state. One of our professors saw us struggling to get places in the third class compartment and made sure that in future the students utilized the money given to them by the administration for the second-class berths.

The journey was a long one with frequent stops. One could hear different languages, see different costumes and eat different regional food as the train stopped in stations along the route. Although we only stayed a month in Karachi, the time was interesting, enjoyable and rewarding. One wishes that there were visits and exchanges at younger ages between people of different cultures and different ways of life nationally as well as internationally. Ignorance about other people's religion, customs and ways of life breeds prejudice.

In Karachi's Dow Medical College Hospital we went to the Delivery Room at night, when it seemed that most babies were born. Someone said that one of the reasons is that ova are fertilized at night following sexual intercourse. By putting on gowns that covered us from head to foot, we tried to make sure that the mothers did not know we were males. However, as I am a six-footer, whenever I entered the labour room the mother would recognize me and start shouting, in spite of her labour pains, 'Mard hain, mard hain!' - a man has entered, a man has entered! The staff nurse would then ask me to leave, so I did not have the chance to see a live delivery, how the vagina dilates or how the instruments are applied to bring out the child safely. I did once see a gynaecological operation at college, performed by the Professor from Bengal. He remarked that he was going to put in another stitch for 'tightening the vagina to make her husband happy.' That reminds me, in the eighties when I was in Multan, a reputedly very pious city in Pakistan, that I saw a long queue of men formed near a cinema hall and found out that they were waiting to see a film showing childbirth.

In Karachi we also attended some lectures given by a Swedish expert and I vividly remember him showing a clip of a film which illustrated the point that progress does not take place if there is uncontrolled population growth. The main image in the film was of a man who was running but did not make any forward progress. At the end of the lecture the Swedish expert asked us for comments and questions. I got up and said, 'Sir, we do not need family planning.' He was visibly upset and asked what I meant. I replied, 'Sir, raise the standard of living of our people and family planning will look after itself.' I had read that countries with high standards of living have low population growth.

In Karachi, even in the early sixties, one could still see the willing (or unwilling) immigrants from India living in squalor for lack of rehabilitation. When I came out for a walk at night-time I saw hundreds of people sleeping on the footpaths and keeping themselves warm by burning paper and other articles. There were plenty of rickshaws (three-wheeler taxis), mostly driven by Pukhtuns from Swat, Dir, tribal areas and the Hazara region. At that time Pukhtuns in Karachi lived in a place that came to be known as Pathan Colony. Some young people from my village, including my relatives from the Painda khel, had also migrated to Karachi to seek jobs. They invited me to visit their places in Pathan Colony. The place was a shanty town; houses consisted of mats or rusted corrugated iron sheets supported by bamboo poles that resting on dirt floors. They were living as bachelors, surviving from day to day, sending most of their money back to Swat to support their families. But despite their poverty, they were hospitable and generous. As I was leaving the hujra in Pathan colony after partaking of their meagre food, they put money in my pockets.

In the early sixties the Swatis in Karachi mostly worked in the cotton mills. I heard them talking about Valika Mills, etc. Like other Pukhtuns, some Swatis were also working in transport and construction work. Some younger boys earned their living by polishing shoes. When I saw some of the Pukhtun shoeshine boys in Karachi, it reminded me of my school days at Murree Hills in the early fifties. In the school we had to clean and polish our shoes. The boys from Karachi remark that 'Khan saib' (as they called me) was polishing shoes again, just as they had seen the Pukhtun shoeshine boys do in Karachi. Some men also worked in private houses as *chowkidari* - watchmen and guards.

Recalling the *chowkidari* reminds me of the late sixties when I was in the United Kingdom. The famous Pakistani religious leader Maulana Abdul Aala Maudoodi was visiting London and the Pukhtuns living there were asked provide him with guards. In a humorous tone, I told the organizers that in Karachi, we Pukhtuns do 'chowkidari'. 'Do you still expect us to do your security duties in London?' But one Pukhtun from Swat did volunteer to act as personal bodyguard for Maulana Maudoodi.

In the early sixties, the majority of immigrants from India after partition settled in Karachi. They were called 'Muhajirs' and were Urdu speaking. But Karachi, a port city, was already home to a thriving business community (Memons, Parsis) and to the native Sindhis. Economic migrants from up country also poured into Karachi after partition, so that there were people from all parts of Punjab, NWFP, tribal areas and Baluchistan living together in the city in harmony. There were neither sectarian nor ethnic disturbances. How different it is today! What are the causes of the riots and battles leading to the loss of precious lives in later years? Were these political, economical, environmental? We need research with a view to bringing peace and harmony to the biggest city in Pakistan.

At medical college, whenever I read about a disease, I thought I had it myself. When I learned about diseases of heart valves in which palpitation occurs, I thought I had narrowing of one of the valves because during childhood I had had a long illness affecting my joints. I would not consult a doctor for fear that I would be labelled as having a serious disease. But the fact is that palpitations are a common symptom and everybody gets them at various times, either for physiological reasons such as nervousness, or following exertion. When we studied appendicitis - inflammation of the appendix - the serious aspects of the disease such as rupture leading to complications were mentioned, and I thought I had appendicitis. I consulted my surgical teacher in a busy outpatient clinic, who advised X-rays. I went to the X-Ray Department, where I was told to get an enema first. The enema was to be performed in the Casualty Department. As there were no qualified nurses, a trained male worker was supposed to administer the enema. He handed me a long tube that had to be inserted in the rectum and soapy water run through it, not a very elegant procedure for a proud Pukhtun. I overheard some doctors gossiping about the doctor in charge, who was fond of drinking beer. Alcohol was easily and openly available in the fifties and sixties. One night the colleagues of the doctor in charge of the Casualty Department put urine in his beer bottle, which he drank and enjoyed.

After the enema, I got the X-ray of my abdomen, but after seeing it, the radiologist said it would have to be repeated following another enema. I was flabbergasted, but did not say anything.

Since then, medical care has improved a lot; disposable enemas are now available. There has also been a serious effort to make medical procedures painless for the patients, thanks to Western scientific innovations. I have learnt that it is a doctor's job to explain to the patient why the investigation needs to be done. Rudyard Kipling's Ws - why, which, what, when, where (and also how) - are helpful in dealing with patients' questions. The doctor should also have three As: ability, availability and affability.

After hearing that I needed a repeat enema I went to the casualty department in dejected mood. When I reached the department, which is now called the emergency department, I saw a crowd of people gathered there. A traffic accident had occurred on the road, and I was shocked to see two of my former teachers from Swat with blood splashed all over them. Although one of them only had a few scratches, the other, Mr. Danishmand Khan, needed an immediate blood transfusion. I volunteered to give blood. Ever afterwards, Danishmand Khan recalled that I had helped him in his time of need. Acts of help, especially during emergencies, are always remembered.

Some years later I had to undergo an operation in England to remove my appendix. I had pain periodically but was reluctant to have the operation; however, my colleagues at Christchurch Hospital forced me to be admitted and Dr Jessop, an experienced surgeon, successfully performed the operation. I agreed to be admitted on one condition: that Mr. Jessop would not give me the digital rectal examination, which he did not. I was given pethidine injections for pain and immediately felt very good. I have always wanted these injections to be repeated. No wonder people become addicted.

After the operation, I had a high temperature with shivering, which was thought to be malaria. After the nurse removed the stitches pus gushed out, and my fever and pain subsided. Wound infection was not suspected, since the conditions in the hospital were antiseptic; it was assumed that I was the victim of some exotic tropical disease. In developing countries we can only ensure antiseptic conditions by giving large doses of antibiotics before and after the operation.

Regarding the reluctance by Pukhtuns in general to examine the back passage, certain areas of NWFP (now KPK) and Afghanistan are known for homosexuality. This is especially so of the Bannu area in the southern districts and Kandahar in Afghanistan. A joke is that when the birds are flying over Kandahar and Bannu, they cover their back passages with their wings for fear of molestation.

Kandahar, the origin point of today's Taliban, is also a city that has produced great men like Ahmad Shah Abdali, who ruled Afghanistan and Northern India from 1747 to his death in 1773. In the book, *Later Mughal History of the Panjab* (Courtesy Salim Ansar of Islamabad) Hari Ram Gupta provided these observations concerning the great king's character.

"Alexander Dow painted the following picture of Ahmad Shah Abdali in 1768. 'This prince is brave and active, but he is now in the decline of life. His person is tall and robust, and beard very black, and his complexion moderately fair. His appearance, upon the whole, is majestic and expressive of an uncommon dignity and strength of mind. Though he is not so fierce and cruel as Nadir Shah, he supports his authority with no less rigour, and he is by no means less brave than that extraordinary monarch. He, in short, is the most likely person now in India to rescore the ancient power of the empire, should he assume the title of king of Delhi.

"Ahmad Shah Abdali was one of the greatest conquerors who have ever appeared in Asia.... His chief contribution lies in the fact that he was the creator of independent Afghanistan. He adopted a different policy regarding various parts of his kingdom. In his dealings with Afghans and Baluchis he pursued the principle of conciliation. He tried to please and win over the people first and the chiefs who could not be reconciled were reduced by force, and then treated kindly. He won over the people by giving equal consideration to the many tribes of Afghans, and several tribes of doubtful origin... Besides, he enforced many humane reforms in order to win their goodwill and co-operation. He stopped the form of punishment requiring the loss of limbs such as nose or ears, and forbade his successors to revive this cruel practice...

"The Sayyids and priests were granted the privilege of sitting in the presence of the king, and also of dining with him on Thursday. His troops were paid in his presence. He did not impose heavy taxes on his people, and the revenues of Afghanistan, properly so termed, never found their way into his private coffers.

"The chiefs were kept contented by giving them a share in the administration of the kingdom. He extended their powers, though they were made dependent on him. He formed a council composed of the leading chiefs of various tribes. They were consulted on almost all the important state affairs, and their advice was often adopted. His government in short resembled much more a federated republic of which he was the head, than an absolute monarchy. After a victory he always gave up a large part of the spoils of the enemy to his soldiers; he never adopted an arrogant tone of superiority with their chiefs, which could hurt the feelings of those with whom he had once been on equal terms, and who had elevated him to the sovereign power...

"In personal character he was simple, modest, affable, generous and cheerful.... in spite of his perfect dignity he assumed the manners of a fiqir and his extreme meekness, which was known everywhere, gained universal approbation. On state occasions, however, he maintained his dignity by displaying considerable courtly pomp and show. He was easy of access and administered justice on principles of equity and law of the land.

"Add to this that he was above the influence of the harem, a foe to drunkenness and renowned for his generosity and charity... amongst his own people he is regarded as the most glorious type of the nation and as the most finished model for its rulers."

Another King of India who belonged to this region (Afghanistan and North West Pakistan) was considered to be one of the 'greatest the world ever has produced and will produce', according to the Deputy Director of India Office Library of London. This was Sher Khan, who became Sher Shah Suri. Like Ahmad Shah, he was always concerned about making the lives of his subjects easier and better. He built the road stretching from Kolkata to the Khyber Pass, which was provided with all facilities for travellers such as wells for drinking water, caravanserais, and so on. He was also the architect of the communication system and the revenue system. He had two unfulfilled wishes: one was to bring his tribe from the mountainous and arid land to settle them in the plains of India, the other was to build a road from India to Mecca in Saudi Arabia.

The present political leaders in Afghanistan and the ISAF/NATO forces can and should emulate the character and habits of successful past rulers like Ahmad Shah Abdali and Sher Shah Suri, who put the welfare of their people first and acted without arrogance. Winning the hearts and minds of people in this region would be conducive to lasting peace, which in turn will lead to progress and prosperity.

In the final year of medical studies all the subjects, such as Eye, Ear, Nose and Throat, Medicine, Surgery, Gynaecology and Obstetrics were crammed together, so that in the annual examination one had to appear in all the subjects. When it got close to the examinations we read our books everywhere, even in the dining rooms and toilets. I could easily remember certain diseases, as I had those diseases during my childhood in the village in Swat. It was nice to know that conjunctivitis was due to infection rather than to the 'evil eye', as I had been told when I was a boy.

In Karachi we had seen childbirth and learnt about the stages of labour that a lady has to go through, so these were also easy to remember. Six weeks was given to prepare for the examination and we knew that previous years questions were often repeated so we were able to mug some of the answers. I passed all the subjects the first time, but did not get a top position. As expected, Jauhar Khatoon won the gold medal as she was not only a pretty face but also brainy.

CHAPTER NINE

INTERNSHIP AT
SAIDU HOSPITAL

☾

After spending five years in medical college one learns the theoretical aspect of the diseases, but for practical skills one had to do a one-year 'house job,' which is now called rotation or internship. I applied for a house job in surgery because surgical skills were important if one had to do independent medical practice in a rural setting. I was called for an interview, and was offered a job without salary. I was in a dilemma, as the scholarship from the Swat state was meant to last for only five years. My dilemma came to an end when I got a letter from Dr Rashid Ahmad of Swat saying that I should report to the Saidu Hospital in Swat, which I did. Saidu Hospital was the second biggest hospital in the state. The largest was called Central Hospital, also situated in the Capital of Saidu Sharif. Saidu Hospital had wards for indoor patients, an out-patient

My father with three of his twelve children, wearing gold threaded caps.

Teachers are role models for students. My teachers at Lower Topa School.

Pukhtuns are fond of guns and hunting. There is a dire
need for healthier sports.

Tariq Nishtar, a friend from the
Kaakar Tribe, with his father riding
on a stallion at an early age, but now
courageously struggling with illness in
ripe old age.

Our Lower Topa School
Headmaster, Mr F. Shaw, with his
wife Harriet and their children.

Pukhtun children like pets.

Mum and Dad with Inams.

Eating habits are developed in childhood, and bad habits may lead to obesity.

A baby's cap in the olden days in Swat.

Nationalist Leader Khan Lala in Piccadilly Circus, London.

A Pathan boy with his friends in Multan, with a cricket bat (made popular by Imran Khan) instead of a gun.

Children and grandchildren, with proud parents.

Visitors from Malaysia with their nearest and dearest.

Changing of traditions: love and marriage from the Khattak tribe by a nephew.

Pictures on the wall remind one of the good times.

Iranian food is usually healthy: salad, vegetables and fruit. Rice is staple with 'Teh deg', dough. Fermented sour milk is the favourite drink.

'Keep trees for everlasting greenery' - signpost in a park in Isfahan.

Grandchildren are adorable.

My grandchildren together (except Essa and Abdullah).

On the occasion of Persian New year and 'haftseen'.

Happy Swati UK children with their mother and uncle.

Some children have grown up, while others have left for good
(by courtesy of Cherry Lindholm).

Happy Masood
from the Wardag
tribe of Afghanistan.

Cyrus with his dad
(photo by Cherry Lindholm).

The top MBBS graduate and holder
of nine gold medals –
my daughter Mah Muneer Khan.

Charles and Cherry Lindholm.

Sucha with her daughter on her wedding day.

Dad was fond of falconry.

Hajj is one of the tenets of more than one billion people.

department (OPD), an operation theatre, a few private rooms, and a small X-ray department and laboratory. In the 1960s there were no trained technical staff and no nurses. Training was strictly on the job. It was at this early stage of my career that I learnt that a reasonable intelligent person without formal education or qualifications could do these technical tasks if properly mentored. So, a lack of formal education is no excuse for not doing the job.

The sick people of Swat were fortunate to have a remarkable person in charge of the hospital. This was Dr Najibullah, who had qualified in 1949 from King Edward Medical College. He was born, bred and educated in the Punjab and was a member of the prominent Chuhan family. Punjabis on the whole are polite, and think before they act, unlike the Pukhtuns, who act first and think afterwards. There is a story illustrating this: a king was warned that he would be assassinated by a person with three testicles. He ordered his bodyguard to search out this person. One man immediately went into hiding. His friend asked him: 'Why are you hiding? I know you only have two testicles.' The other replied, 'The King's bodyguard is a Pukhtun. He chops first and counts afterwards.'

Dr Najib came to Swat to join the State Health Services following the lead of his uncle, Alaullah Khan, popularly known as Wakil Sahib (lawyer sahib), whom I have already described. It was nice of Dr Najib to send me the following testimonial:

"Dr Sher Mohammad Khan joined service as a Medical Officer in the then Seat State in the early sixties of the last century. This state, though part of Pakistan, had its own Ruler, Maj. Gen. Miangul Abudl Haq Jehanzeb. The state was fully autonomous in its internal affairs. Its departments, Health, Education, Roads and Buildings etc, were well developed and rapidly developing further. This was all due to the personal interest of the Wali of

Swat (The Ruler). I myself was Director Health, senior physician and in charge of the fairly large Saidu Group of Hospitals (about 300 beds).

"When Sher reported for duty I was impressed by the tall, handsome doctor. Later, in the wards, I found him intelligent and eager to learn with his graceful manners and wit. He belonged to a well-respected influential family of Bar-Swat.

"Sher was one of the very few who learnt my dictum that medicine has to be scientific, logical and diagnosis-oriented, albeit adjustable to local social and economic circumstances. I am glad to say that he still follows it; few others do.

"He was with us for about a year and then proceeded to UK for higher studies. He passed his MSc in Nuclear Medicine, perhaps the only one to do this from this country. Later he proceeded to get his MRCP. Returned to Pakistan in 1974 he joined PAEC as a medical doctor in peaceful uses of Atomic Energy, in which he served well all over Pakistan. After retirement he joined Pakistan Rec Crescent Society NWFP chapter as its head (honorary) for a few years. At present he practises medicine with an interest in oncology at Rehman Medical Institute."

When I joined Saidu Hospital Dr Najib had gone to Edinburgh to take an examination for admission to the Royal College of Medicine, which he was awarded in a short time. The other doctor in the hospital was Rashid Ahmad from Mingora, who came from a business family. Both of his brothers were also medical doctors.

I worked late hours and came at night-time to see patients. My learning was without supervision until Dr Najib returned from Edinburgh. Soon after he asked me to remove fluid from the chest of a patient. I was anxious about doing this and so delayed. The next day, he took me and the patient aside and gave me a hands-on lesson on how to aspirate the chest. At the same time he delivered a good verbal dressing-down. That was when he told me that he had learnt all surgical procedures by reading books and then following the steps in an actual operation, since if a patient came with obstruction of intestine or some other problem, he had no choice but to operate. By this method, he had learned how to perform cataract operations, how to remove tonsils, and how to open up the abdomen, do an appendectomy and relieve torsion of the large intestine. He also taught himself how to diagnose blood diseases by using a microscope. I followed his example and learnt some of the operations, such as prostatectomy, by a combination of reading and practical experience. This method has greatly helped me in my career.

The Wali of Swat, Jehan Zeb, was very interested in the development of education, health care and infrastructure. He made sure that healthcare, especially for poor patients, was free, and he generally acceded to Dr Najib's requests to purchase new equipment. When a new X-ray machine was purchased, there was no one to operate it and give reports on the patients' X-rays. I could not refuse when Dr Najib asked me to manage the X-ray Department. He provided me with books on radiology, which I read, correlated with the clinical features of the patient, and used to write up my reports. Later on, in the seventies, this experience of self-learning helped me to start a programme in ultrasonography for the first time in the region and probably the first time in Pakistan.

My monthly salary when I began work in the hospital was 250 rupees. I was on the waiting list for an official residence, but in the meantime Dr Sherin Jan very generously accommodated me in his house. He was the first dental surgeon in Swat. His clinic was next to my examination room. After finishing seeing patients, I sometimes went into the dental room and learnt how to extract teeth. After finishing the day's work followed by an afternoon siesta in the summer, the two of us, accompanied by Dr Gul Roz, often went on evening walks along the roadside, because there were no public parks. We passed the Swat Club, where indoor and outdoor games such as badminton, tennis and squash were available, but these courts were mainly used by the government officials and lecturers from the Jehan Zeb College, the majority of whom were from the Punjab or Urdu speaking, and who had probably been taught these sports during childhood. Neither I nor any of my friends knew how to play any of these games.

Once, after returning from my walk, I heard a hissing sound upon entering my room. When I put the light on, I saw a big cobra, swaying half above the ground with its hood expanded and tongue flickering. The snake was beautiful, but it had to be killed. I also had another kind of encounter during my walk with my friends. One day in a narrow road in the middle of the Mingora Bazaar the Wali's car slowed down. He looked at us very keenly and then drove off. Sherin Jan and Gul Roz jokingly told me to get ready as the Wali likes tall, slim fair-looking boys in his entourage and one night he might call on me.

This reminds me of a story dating from the early 1960s when Queen Elizabeth and Prince Philip visited the Swat Valley. The Prince, who had a sense of humour, asked the Wali to give him one of his young smart bodyguards to take back to London. The Wali refused. During his visit the Prince hunted monal pheasant in the mountains. The monal pheasant is a beautiful bird that was commonly found in Swat when hunting and shooting were restricted. Now it is almost extinct. Riding through the valley on a sunny winter day, Prince Philip asked why people were simply basking in the sun. 'Don't they have any jobs to go to?' He did not realize that farming was and is the only source of employment in the valley. We were told that during this trip the Queen taped messages for her children and sent them to

Buckingham Palace. It would be interesting to hear these tapes of the visit to Swat when there was peace and tranquillity and people could sit outside without fear of bombs or Kalashnikovs.

One day I saw Dr Sherin Jan in his clinic, looking very happy. I asked him about the reason for his unusual joy. He said he had given dental treatment to the Wali of Swat, who was very satisfied and asked him what he needed for his dental department. As a result, the dental department was provided with all new equipment and a whole new facility was built in the hospital premises. The Wali often took a personal interest in such projects, and even decided which colour tiles should be used in the building. One of our colleagues, Dr Mohammad Khan of Matta, went every Friday to pay respect (*salaam*) to Wali Sahib. As a result, he was the first of us to get an independent posting in charge of a hospital. I had not learnt that in order to achieve success it was necessary to pay my respects to those in power on a regular basis.

The Wali was usually benevolent, but he also could be frightening. One day his secretary, Purdil Khan, told me that the ruler wanted to talk to me. I went to Purdil Khan's office, where I was told that Wali Saib wanted to see me because my brother, Durveza Khan, was writing derogatory pieces about him in the English daily the Khyber Mail, which was the only and probably the first independent English daily from Peshawar. I was afraid, because the Wali was known to order his guards to beat people who had offended him. Purdil Khan accompanied me to the audience. I was made to sit in a chair, but Purdil Khan remained standing. Also standing was the Wali's chief of bodyguards, who held a big club in his hand. The Wali asked Purdil Khan about me, and Purdil told him about Durveza Khan's inflammatory statements to the press. The Wali looked at the floor for a minute. Then he raised his head and said 'Purdil, Durveza levanae de' - Durveza is a mad man. I stood up and left quickly, greatly relieved.

Another incident led to a potentially more serious run-in with the authorities. I usually attended the outpatient department to see that the patients were treated on time. There were separate male and female waiting areas and the entrances to the examination rooms for males and females were also separate. Mohammad Sherin was the orderly in charge. He had no formal medical education, but, like Dr Najib, he was self-trained on the job. He was efficient and knew all about the patients. One of his tasks was to make sure that everyone entered the examination room in turn. One day Sherin burst in and said 'Wali Sahib Jamaadar mata kanzal okra' - the bodyguard of Wali Sahib insulted me. This was because the bodyguard was attempting to enter out of turn and Sherin had stopped him. I backed up the orderly. As a result, blows were exchanged and the bodyguard was beaten up.

I did not realize the seriousness of this act. My early education in the Murree Hills, where I was a school prefect, had taught me to be fair, transparent and a strict disciplinarian. I had not yet realized that there are separate rules and regulations for the poor and the rich. Nor did I know that there are separate rules for government office holders and ordinary citizens. The bodyguard complained to Dr Najib, the Chief of the hospital, who in turn politely called me to see him after I finished with the patients in OPD. I thought my days as a salaried person had come to an end and wondered what I was going to do if I was thrown out of my job. After seeing my patients, I went to Dr Najib's office. Without saying anything about the incident, he said that he had made separate arrangements for treating the bodyguards and officials of the Swat State in the OPD, as these people were in hurry because of their responsibilities and could not wait with the rest of the patients.

After a few weeks living with Dr Sherin Jan, I was given official housing meant for doctors. I had enjoyed the hospitality of Sherin Jan for weeks without paying anything. In Pushtun society, a guest or friend is not expected to pay or even share the expenses no matter how long he stays. Those who demand or expect to pay or share the expenses are considered beghairat - shameless, without honour.

My new official residence was next to that of Chand Bibi (Moon Bibi), the first qualified lady doctor in Swat. Chand Bibi was the daughter of a teacher, and had graduated from the medical college in Lahore. She provided much-needed medical attention for the women of Swat. Chand Bibi was unmarried and I was a bachelor. She did not know that I had been engaged to my first cousin ever since her birth. Perhaps she was thinking of marriage when she invited my mother and sisters to visit her whenever they came to see me from the village, but they did not disclose my engagement. Tragically, she later committed suicide by sprinkling kerosene oil on herself and setting fire to her clothes. Why did she do it? No one knew. Women rarely committed suicide in Swat, and if they did the method was usually drowning themselves in the river or eating the poison used for killing lice.

The hospital was within walking distance of my house, so I saw patients in the evening whether I was on duty or not. One night when I went to the ward, the relatives of a patient told me that the man's behaviour had suddenly changed and that he was talking incoherently, disorientated, and so on. When I went to his room he was quiet, but had a vacant look. I sent a message though a ward orderly to Dr Najib, who was kind enough to write back that I should give multivitamin injection to the patient, which I did. The next day the man was well and knew where he was. I realized for the first time that you could sometimes cure madness with multivitamin injections. The patient had pellagra, which is a vitamin deficiency disease consisting of three Ds - diarrhoea, dermatitis and dementia.

Degrees were handed out at Peshawar University during convocations that were held on a regular basis. In due course I received a letter about my class's convocation. I went to Peshawar to attend, met my class fellows, both males and females, and exchanged the latest news and gossip - especially about who was going to get married to whom. After we received our degrees there were photo sessions. Individual photos were taken of us all wearing our black gowns, caps and holding the degrees in our hands. Photos with friends were also taken, as were photographs of the whole class. Some of us who were interested in certain girls tried to stand near them. This was during the first martial law of General Ayub Khan, who later became Field Marshal and President of Pakistan. The Vice Chancellor of the University was Chaudhry Mohammad Ali, who had very little experience in education, but who came from Ayub Khan's area and was his political ally. He replaced the previous Vice Chancellor, Dr M.K. Afridi, who was, as I have mentioned, a world-renowned physician and educator. The Wali of Swat was invited by the Vice Chancellor to chair the Convocation. As I also mentioned before, the Wali's son was married to the daughter of President Ayub.

I had been informed that I would get the Gold Medal for scoring top marks among the students from the tribal and autonomous states, but this was changed at the last moment because another student claimed that he had higher marks. His domicile was actually not in the tribal area, but he had friends in the University and a relative who was high up in the bureaucracy. This was my first brush with the injustices of society. In my resume, I had to be content with writing 'President's Award proximet accessit,' a term which was suggested to me in later years by Dr McDonald who happened to be a colleague of Dr Nowsherawen Burki, cousin of Mr. Imran Khan, the famous cricketer turned politician who campaigns for a corruption free society in Pakistan. In 2011 people - especially young people - flocked to his meetings in thousands.

It was during the convocation days that one of my old classmates told me that he had applied for a voucher of employment exchange in order to go to the UK. He also told me that the person in charge of granting these vouchers happened to be one of the senior students from our days in Jehan Zeb College in Swat. To grant a voucher he did not require *safarish* - recommendations from influential people - or any greasing of his palm. He was a polite man who did his job honestly and efficiently. I went to his office but before I filled out the form, he entertained me with tea and sweets. This is a tradition in Pukhtun society. At times this custom is not only a burden but a waste of time for the host and the guest. On the one hand, a host has to be hospitable; otherwise he would be labelled a miser. On the other hand, a guest, no matter how busy, cannot refuse for fear of being called too proud. After I filled in the forms the official told me that I would get the voucher in a month, which I thought was too long, as I wanted to leave Pakistan as soon as possible to go to the country of my dreams.

There was another reason behind my rush to depart. The family of my first cousin wanted me to marry her as soon as possible and now I could no longer excuse myself on account of my studies. I considered my first cousin to be my sister and did not want to marry her, despite the arrangements my mother had made when she was born. Her family approached the Wali and asked him to intervene, but the Wali would not interfere in the personal affairs of his subjects. My refusal and my later marriage to a girl from Isfahan led to a serious rift in my family.

The doctor who introduced me to the man in charge of the employment exchange, was slim and fair, and had been very good in his studies both in Jehan Zeb college and Khyber Medical College. He eventually married an English woman and settled in the USA as a practising gynaecologist and obstetrician. Years later, when I was on a short-term trainee grant in Staten Island, New York, he invited me to Atlantic City. A woman working in his clinic also accompanied us. He told me that she was expert in 'blow jobs.' I hadn't the slightest idea what he meant. This was the first time I went into a big gambling palace, though the hujra I stayed in Qambar during my school days had operated as a kind of local casino. I had also once accompanied Prince Amir Zeb to a 'Bunny Club' in London where there was gambling. I did not gamble, but the Prince lost all his money and borrowed a hundred pounds sterling from me. He recovered his losses and won thousands of pounds more. Afterwards, he gave me my hundred pounds back, but I had been expecting a share in the booty he won.

In Delvare, I visited my obstetrician friend's lavish estate, which featured a heated swimming pool, expensive cars and a stable for his horses. I praised his luxurious style of living, but as a Pukhtun I was also jealous and wished that I had the same sort of advantages. Just as we were sitting down in his drawing room his young son came in and, without greeting me, demanded, 'Dad, give me a fag.' My host looked at me, shame-faced, and obliged his son by giving him a pack of cigarettes. Later, he remarked that even though he enjoyed his hard-won luxuries, he worried about his personal life. Would anyone in Peshawar allow his son to ask for a cigarette or disrespect a guest? The last I heard, he and his wife were divorced. I wonder how one can have a modern life style of living without losing traditional values, which are present in every culture, East, West and the Middle East.

After waiting a month, I received a letter from the employment exchange to say that my immigration voucher had come. I lost no time in going to Peshawar to collect it. The next day, after returning to Saidu Hospital, I went to see Dr Najib in his office, showed my permit and told him I wanted to leave for Great Britain to work and to pursue my postgraduate studies. To my surprise, he said that I would not be permitted to leave the service, because I was a scholarship holder and had to continue working in the hospital. I could not understand why he wanted me to stay rather than go abroad. I knew that it was not because of any shortage of medical doctors; there must have been other reasons. I became very emotional and began crying. He felt sorry for me, consoled me, and assured me that he would persuade the authorities to give me a 'no objection certificate' that would allow me to depart.

A lot of hurdles still had to be crossed before I could leave, even though the immigration voucher was sufficient for me to enter Great Britain. Money for the ticket had to be found, a passport had to be issued and warm suits had to be purchased. The ticket problem was unexpectedly solved when I received a letter from my childhood friend Fazli Ali, who had earlier immigrated to England, saying that he would not only send me the ticket, but also extend all help when I landed in London. While waiting for the tickets to arrive I continued my usual routine of going to the hospital, seeing patients in OPD and in the wards, writing reports on X-rays and at times helping in extraction of teeth. Walking on the roadside to Mingora was my main pastime in the late afternoon.

Passports were difficult to get and required a letter of recommendation from a person from a higher position in the government. I went to see Crown Prince Aurang Zeb, who was the son-in-law of President Ayub Khan. I requested his help and he agreed to give me a letter of recommendation, but first he had to ask permission from his father, the Wali. Influence on my behalf was also exercised by the Wali's wife, Begum Sahibe, who was sister of Prince Bahramand, who was a friend of my father, Khaista Dada. Eventually, the Crown Prince came back after consulting his father and issued a letter of recommendation to the passport officer in Peshawar. I was very pleased that my work was being accomplished without hindrances, and immediately went to Peshawar with the letter.

I called on the passport officer, who was a short, soft-spoken Punjabi who wore his black achkan coat buttoned to the neck. In the early sixties there were not many Pakhtun government officials in higher echelon. When the passport officer (PO) saw the letter from the son-in-law of President Ayub Khan, I was quickly called into his office and told to come after a day and the passport would be ready. This was no small feat, even in an era when the red-tapeism of today was in its initial stages.

That night I went to stay in a *serai* - a small hotel - in the back of Peshawar's famous Qissa Khwani (storyteller) Bazaar. The hotel was recommended by a colleague in Swat as it was run by his friend; moreover it was near a famous tikka kabab place. The next morning, when I left the hotel, I was not charged. In the Pukhtun tradition, friendly relationships were more important than monetary benefits.

I took a *tonga* - horse driven coach - and went to the passport office where I was called promptly and not required to pay the usual bribe to the *peon* or the assistant in the office, as had become the custom after the departure of the British. I was warmly greeted by the Passport Officer, who shook my hand; in return, I used both hands for clasping his, which is a mark of respect in a Pukhtun tradition. A bear hug is normal if you know the person very well.

The PO handed me my passport along with a sealed envelope. He insisted that I deliver it to the Crown Prince myself. I later discovered that the contents of the sealed envelope was a letter from the PO in which he asked to be promoted and posted to someplace other than Peshawar, since there was not enough shopping there to make his wife happy. Whether his wish was granted or not, I never knew. I was interested in more exciting things: my journey to England and a new life.

PART TWO
A Pukhtun In England

CHAPTER TEN

ENTERING THE PROMISED LAND

In the 1960s, air travel to other countries from Pakistan was mainly by Pakistan Air Lines (PIA). PIA was very well managed as it was headed by an Air Force officer, Nur Khan. Those were considered the golden days of PIA, because of timely arrivals and departures and courteous, smartly-dressed and attractive cabin crew.

The flight was from Karachi to London. The passports for valid visas were checked, but there were no other security checks. I was made to stay in a Karachi hotel overnight. When I went out at night-time, the scene in the street was the same as I had seen during my student life. I could see people sleeping on the footpaths; there were rickshaws (three wheelers), small British and German cars were used as taxis and *tongas* (horse-drawn vehicles) were also used for transport. The street dwellers were mainly Urdu speaking, while the transportation system was dominated by Pukhtuns, but there was perfect harmony between the two communities, unlike in later years.

A young Pukhtun taxi driver asked me whether I wanted a lift to see a film. When I said no, he asked me, 'balzai ta ze' - do you want to go to some other place? A Pushtun visitor was assumed to want either to see a film or visit a brothel. Some of the occupants of the brothels were also from up country areas such as Swat, Dir, Buner and Hazara, because the human traffickers bought and sold girls to a life of filth and misery because they were unhappy in married life or too poor to bear the burden of living.

It was during one of the pilgrimages (Haj) when my father had gone to Mecca that a woman was looking for a person from Swat. She met my father and related a sad story of forced marriage to an old man in Swat. She ran away from the house, met a man who took her to Karachi and sold her to a brothel. A Sindhi visitor to a brothel married her and took her to Saudi Arabia. The woman said to my father that she was living in a holy place and happily married, but had guilty feelings. She asked my father to ask them to forgive her and divorce her fully as she was still leading a life of 'sin' while living in a holy land. Khaista Dada was true to his promise, as Pushtuns used to be; he went to see the family of the lady, who were still living in poverty, and they were pleased to hear about their dear one living in the holy land, but there was no need for a divorce, since the ex-husband had died.

The first stop on the air journey to London was Beirut. As the aeroplane came nearer the airport, I could see the tall buildings interspersed among pine trees on the slopes. Lebanon was considered a tourist heaven and was peaceful in the sixties. At the airport, I was attracted to the perfume section because there were fair-skinned sales girls. A Pushtun born and bred in

Pushtun surroundings, has a preconceived notion of beauty - 'white is beautiful' and *sraanagi*, with pink cheeks, big eyes and big buttocks. The salesgirls had all the features except the big buttocks. One girl sprayed perfume on her hand/wrist and asked me to smell it. I reluctantly put my nose near her hand. She had long, tapering fingers and painted nails. I could neither compliment her because of shyness nor buy the perfume, as I had only ten pounds sterling in my pocket.

The next stop was in Egypt and there was also a third stop somewhere in Europe before a dash to Heathrow, London, but I do not remember where. I remembered Egypt and the Pharaohs from my childhood. In the village life one learns in the streets or in the hujra or Mosques.

Mosques are visited five times a day. The prayer leaders are full-time employees, but are respected and obeyed. They can sway the people to peace and humanitarian work but at the same time they can create hatred among different sects, sections and classes of society. Traditionally, the Khans controlled them, but as one of the religious party leader said in March of 2012 'Khanism is finished'. Another source of learning in the villages was playing in the streets and watching what others do, such as mating of dogs and other animals.

Pharaohs were mentioned in the mosques in a derogatory manner. In hujras, the beauty of - 'da Misar Khaze', ladies of Egypt - were talked about. So when we landed at Cairo Airport I remembered my childhood days of listening to the mullah in the mosque and overhearing the people in hujra chatting about the beautiful women of Egypt. As we were waiting to come down from the aeroplane to the tarmac, an air hostess standing beside me with an inviting look told me she was going to stay in London for a few days. She further enquired if I would be staying there too. I was too preoccupied to answer, as I was going to a strange new place. I had apprehensions about whether I would be welcomed by someone. I had no idea what the young attractive air hostess meant. All the way I was preoccupied with the thought and was praying that Fazli Ali, my friend and schoolmate, would receive me on arrival.

The passengers as they landed were welcomed by a manager of PIA, a tall, fair, moustached Pukhtun gentleman, along with a plump but well-dressed air hostess. We had to have chest X-rays done at that time for the detection of tuberculosis. When the nurse learned that I was a doctor, she was visibly pleased and introduced me to the doctor who greeted me and wished me an enjoyable and rewarding stay in Great Britain, but I was anxious and nervous.

As I came out, I saw Fazli Ali and my first prayer was answered. He was accompanied by his brother-in-law, known in Swat as Farid Khan, but he had changed his name to Khurshid Ahmad after the name of a student activist who became a Jumaat Islami, leader in later life.

Fazli Ali had bought a Mini car, popular in the sixties in England before Japanese cars flooded the market. Farid Khan was to drive the car from London to Southampton, where a sizeable community of Pukhtuns from Swat, Mardan and Swabi belonging to the Yusufzai tribe lived. Pukhtuns by and large are hardworking, especially when they are away from their villages and home towns. A lot of them worked in the ships stoking the fires of the coal-powered engines. Southampton, or as Pukhtuns called it 'South Tum Tum', being a seaport, was a convenient place to jump ship for a better life.

The journey to Southampton took us more than an hour, as the motorway was yet to be built in the south of England. It was night-time and the traffic was light. I was impressed by the lack of hooting by the car drivers, as I was used to much hooting and overtaking in Pakistan. Pushtuns are usually impatient in their work and dealings. Fazli Ali told me that he had recently bought the car specially on learning I was coming, so that we could travel and see places and friends together. He was known for his resourcefulness and helpfulness.

When we reached Southampton, he told me that Farid Khan lived in Shakespeare Avenue and also added that lords and rich people used to live there. I had never heard of a lord, but knew about Shakespeare from my schooldays, when our British teachers took the students to see educational films. Fazli Ali was also known for exaggeration

My first night in England was in FA's rented room in Farid Khan's house. The room was small, so I slept in his bed and he slept on the floor. Pukhtuns in the UK had yet to forget their hospitality and generosity.

The next morning Farid Khan invited me to breakfast, which consisted of eggs and buttered bread as Bakht Sarganda (prominent fortune) had learnt her cooking in the house of Qazi Saib, who entertained people and had lot of friends, not only in Swat but all over NWFP (North West Frontier Province, now Khyber Pukhtunkhwa). He was from a religious family but made sure that all his sons were properly educated. His daughters had no schooling.

Farid Khan often related his tough childhood story; he was born in a village called Barikot, where Alexander the Great travelled to the Indus River. His mother died and his father remarried. His stepmother was not kind to him and he ran away from the house and entered an orphanage in Punjab. The orphanage children went around to various places to collect donations, and one day a businessman noticed his fair colouring, went to the orphanage and adopted him as his son. He grew up there and had some education, but had to leave that house again to go to Karachi without informing his foster parents. Farid Khan took the secret to his grave; he never revealed to anyone why he had left the house of his foster parents. It was conjectured that it was because of some illicit relations with a girl. Because of 'honour killings', Pukhtuns have to keep their illicit relations very secret.

FK had a two-storey house, and he used to let the top floor. He had rented the upper portion to Sikhs, as he had lived in Punjab and was friendly with Punjabis, though he was not aware of the intricacies of Pushtun culture. The Pushtun people living in Southampton objected to Sikhs living with a married Pushtun family in the same house.

FK had one daughter and two sons born in Southampton. He wanted them to be well educated and brought up as Pukhtuns and good Muslims as he himself tried to live a clean life: no crookedness in his dealings and not betraying friends. The daughter started working in a bank, wearing the eastern 'shalwar' (baggy trousers) and a scarf on her head, but she used to change into a skirt at the bank. Her maternal uncle and mother married her to their nephew to enable him to immigrate to the UK. This marriage was against the wishes of FK, the father, who wanted my brother Abdullah Khan to marry her. The marriage ended in divorce in spite of two children. Divorce for Pukhtuns in the second generation is no longer a taboo. FK died of a 'broken heart' as they say, because his children did not behave the way he wanted them to behave with his friends and close relatives. Pukhtuns expect their children to act and behave the way they wanted them to behave even if their own characters are questionable. There is a proverb in Pushto, 'Mullah chesawaye, amalpekawa, chesakaye, amalpe ma kawa' - whatever Mullah says, act on it, but do not do what Mullah does - in other words, Mullah should not be your role model.

I continued to live in Fazli Ali's small rented bedroom, sharing his bed at night, as he had opted for night duty in the Pirelli Cable Factory; whether it was because he got more money or it was out of concern for me is not clear. It was winter and very cold, so I was surprised to see ladies walking in the nearby shopping centre bare-legged and without any head covering, as I did not know that ladies wear skin-coloured stockings and shapely legs as a sign of beauty. I was brought up in a society where ladies were fully covered and you hardly saw a woman in the shops.

I used to accompany FA to the grocery shops to buy food. Two pounds sterling was sufficient to last for a week for two people in the early sixties. There was only one shop owned by a Pukhtun, who sold halal meat, and it was expensive. The lamb was brought from Bradford in Yorkshire, where a sizeable community of immigrants from the sub-continent lived. Bradford is known as 'Little Pakistan' 'or 'Bradistan' because of the large number of immigrants. On one of my visits to the Pukhtun shop, which was later named Khyber Foods, I noticed a blonde, middle-aged woman and was told that she was nanny to the children of Ghani Khan, the owner of the business. Ghani Khan is not to be confused with another Ghani Khan, the poet, sculptor and intellectual, the son of Baacha Khan, popularly known as Frontier Gandhi.

I was looking for a job in a hospital and sent off applications after seeing advertisements in the British Medical Journal. Every application was answered with regrets. The problem was that I had never been taught how to write an application and what sort of jobs I should apply for. In my medical college days neither ethics nor the proper way of applying for jobs was taught. Weeks passed and I was still unemployed. I did not know any medical doctors to guide me and my hosts and other Pukhtuns who were working as bus conductors, drivers and factory workers knew nothing about hospital jobs, although they were kind to me and would put money in my pocket whenever they came to see me.

One day they came to Farid Khan's place and asked me to start working as a bus conductor, because they had seen very well qualified people coming from Pakistan doing all sorts of menial jobs. It was true, as one of my colleagues when I had started working for the British National Health Service had set up a sweetmeat shop in London which was very popular. He belonged to the family of a renowned sweetmeat businessman from Karachi, but the family wanted him to be a surgeon. One Pukhtun, not my host, took me to a social security office where I could get unemployment benefit. An attractive, polite, red-haired lady helped me fill in the forms and asked me to come once a week to collect my benefit. I was in a dilemma: on the one hand it would be nice to see the attractive lady once a week, on the other hand how could a person belonging to Khan family and a medical doctor accept free money without any work? I did not visit the place again. It was the first time I had heard about a 'welfare state'. I had heard in the sermons in my village as well as in Peshawar that a true Muslim country has to be a welfare state. My nephew Wali Mohammad Khan (WMK), who belonged to the *tableeghi* (group of preachers) recently joined his wife and children in London and told me that he was now entering the 'Muslim State' in a real sense because his wife and children, being British citizens, were given free accommodation in central London and other benefits.

During my stay in Southampton, a Labour Government was in power and Harold Wilson was the Prime Minister. It was during this time that the Home Secretary was asked in a BBC interview about the loss of millions of pounds sterling by the evasion of taxes by immigrants. His answer pleased and surprised me: he said that the immigrants were sending money back to their families, moreover he had to spend a more or less equal amount by employing more tax inspectors and so on.

I was getting frustrated and depressed and was thinking of becoming a bus conductor, a job which was easy to get, but my problem ended through a strange coincidence. Fazli Ali took me along with him to Heathrow Airport to meet a friend who was coming from Swat. At the airport we met two medical doctors both from Swat working in the NHS. After exchanging the usual long greetings, bear hugs and enquiring about the family I told them that I had been in England for the last three months. Dr Alam, who wanted to become a surgeon, discouraged me, while Dr Majid Khan, who was a Medical Registrar in Geriatrics with Dr Brocklehurst, took my details and promised to help me.

True to his promise, as Pukhtuns usually are (otherwise they are labelled as *beghairat*), Dr Majid Khan rang up to say that he had found a job for me for two weeks as a locum in Farnborough Hospital, Kent. Fazli Ali took me in his car. On our way the countryside, the farms on the roadside, the sheep and cows grazing in the fields reminded me of my home in Upper Swat and I wished I had not come, but a Pukhtun is supposed to continue struggling until he has achieved his target. In my case it was to pass the postgraduate medical exams leading to membership of one of the Royal Colleges. To think constructively was instilled in me since my childhood, but unfortunately, destructive thinking is also instilled in other young Pukhtuns at an impressionable age because of their circumstances, either born or imposed on them.

We reached Farnborough, famous for its annual international air show. It was in the afternoon and we went straight to the apartment of Dr Majid Khan outside the hospital. The surgeon whom we had met before in the airport greeted us and told us that Majid Khan was in his room taking a rest. After a little while Majid Khan joined us, along with a young girl who was introduced to us as a typist in the hospital and who was going to help me in completing the official formalities in the hospital. The image of the attractive girl still persists somewhere in my neurons, whether it is because of her selfless help or her pretty face is hard to decipher.

I asked Majid Khan about his friend, a non-medical person who had travelled on the same plane and was seen off on Peshawar Airport with great pomp and ceremony. He said his friend was working in a post office. He had had a friendship with a girl, who had broken it off, saying that the friend was becoming 'too serious', meaning that he wanted to marry her.

In the hospital, I knew about the routine clerking of patients, going round with the senior doctors and prescribing medicine, but the nurses were well trained and helpful and would guide me.

A seriously ill and unconscious patient was admitted one evening. I put up a drip of normal saline and gave her glucose in her vein. She was diabetic and on a long acting anti-diabetic drug called sulphonurea, which was available at that time. Bedside testing of estimation was not available at that time. The anti-diabetic medicine was known to cause low blood sugar, which is very dangerous to the brain cells. Giving glucose to the patient helped her and the next morning she was conscious and talking during the ward round, led by the consultant physician. The physician asked where I had received my medical education and training. He was impressed, which helped me in getting my next job.

I was attracted to one of the staff nurses, who had brown hair and was well built. One day she felt my keen gaze as she was distributing medicine. She looked at me, smiled and showed me her left hand with a ring on her finger.

I was given a room in a doctor's hostel and almost all junior doctors were local. We used to take meals together in the dining room. Fruit was also served. One day a junior doctor helped himself to a banana, asked me to help myself and then asked, 'Do you have bananas in your country?' I said, 'Yes, but you eat fruit on the dining table and we climb the trees and eat the fruit'. He said, 'really?' He took it seriously, rather than a joke. I was finding the English people reserved with a lack of humour, and not too much concerned with the outside world. In the sixties an average person in England did not know about Muslims or Islam; they had heard about India, but not Pakistan. They knew about the Khyber Pass only because of a TV comedy show called 'Up the Khyber Pass'.

My two weeks of hospital work was enjoyable and rewarding and I had one referee now, Dr Majid Khan, who belonged to a well-known Yousufzai family of Dir and was related to Omara Khan, a one-time ruler of Dir State - known as Napoleon of the Frontier by some quarters. Omara Khan had laid siege to the British Garrison stationed in Chitral Fort. Majid Khan's family had migrated from Dir and were given refuge in Swat by the then ruler of Swat. MK put in a word to the consultant geriatrician, and my referee helped me in getting a job at Orpington Hospital, Kent, for six months.

Orpington Hospital was in Orpington, Kent, considered to be a beautiful area of England, but the mind has to be free of stresses and strains to enjoy scenic surroundings. I was mainly concerned with a job and Membership of the Royal College. The hospital was on high ground and most of the sections of the hospital were separate, so that one had to walk through the grounds. It was a single-storey building, but I was also supposed to do duty in casualty, where emergency patients were dealt with, one half day a week. Doctors were supposed to give intravenous injections and stitch the wounds, as nurses were not allowed to do so by the General Medical Council (GMC), the UK regulatory body.

A road traffic accident victim was brought to the casualty when I was on duty. The well-trained staff nurse dealt with the wound, but it needed stitching and I did not know how to do it because I had not worked in surgical wards in England. The staff nurse, Barbara, volunteered to do the stitching and we became friendly, but it was platonic. Barbara had red hair and was plump and told me that her name was written on my back and none of the other girls would dare to come near me. It was true, as Barbara was senior and dominant and during the combed dancing parties of doctors when senior nurses were invited, the girls avoided me because I did not know how to dance. There is a Pushto proverb, 'Gadesa di khokwanaraquede di' - dancing is nothing but gyrating buttocks.

There was only one Indian doctor, an orthopaedic surgeon in the hospital; the rest were all locals. The hospital was attached to the world famous Guy's Hospital of London. Most of the doctors from overseas worked in hospitals in the north of England and Wales. My colleagues had lives of their own and English people would not interfere with your life or give you advice, or invite you to their houses, unlike the Pukhtuns, who, at times, would give you uncalled for advice or interfere with your life. So I was lonely, and went into London on Sundays, to Hyde Park Speakers' Corner. I had heard you can give speeches here on any topic without being prosecuted, though derogatory remarks about the Queen were prohibited. During the sixties, one black Jamaican speaker was very popular among the blacks and the coloured people who came to listen to his sarcastic speeches. He used to talk about the white man's domination of Africa and West Indies and racial prejudice in the UK. He would make his talk interesting by bringing humour and sex into it. He would come down from his rostrum and distribute leaflets, which were separate for blacks and whites. One day he was going to give me the leaflet for whites, but he changed his mind and gave me the leaflet meant for coloureds after I explained who I was. He said, 'Some people look white but their hearts are with the blacks'. Most of the immigrants, rightly or wrongly, felt they were discriminated against. As a result, the Labour Government had to create the Race Relations Board.

The hospital had major medical specialties, such as medicine, surgery and obstetrics. Geriatrics, or disease of old age, was a new specialty which was not popular with local doctors. There were no sub-specialties such as cardiology or diseases of the lungs. These patients were admitted to the medical ward. One had to spend six months in general medicine (house physician) and six months in surgery (house surgeon) before eligibility for registration and applying for a senior house officer (SHO) post, the duration of which was one year, followed by a registrar job, which was for two years. Before applying for a top consultant post, one had to spend four years as Senior Registrar, equivalent to Chief Resident in USA.

Before finishing one job, I had to start thinking of my next. All posts were advertised and awarded on merit, but 'putting in a word' did work, as in my case Dr Majid Khan had put in a word to a consultant geriatrician, who was a soft-spoken man and had served overseas as a doctor in the British Army. He told me to examine as many patients as I could, as in that way I would learn clinical medicine and pass my examination. The postgraduate education was not structured in the NHS like the United States system of healthcare education. As a junior doctor I was left on my own to work, study and try passing exams without formal guidance or coaching. Like other local doctors, I had to depend on the guidance of those who had got their membership of the Royal Colleges.

My immediate senior (SHO) was Dr Hill, who was married to a staff nurse in the hospital. He reminded me of my schoolteacher Mr. Hill, who was a disciplinarian, and we students at that time used to talk about how he punished us for spitting, which is a common habit in the villages and in the streets of Pakistani cities.

The registrar was a lady named Jennifer who was unmarried, gentle and kind to the patients and her subordinates. She would ask me to contact her even at night if I needed help with treatment of patients. Whenever I phoned her at night, she would pick up the phone promptly. I heard music playing in the background with singing. It transpired that she was a fan of Joan Baez, the famous American folk singer. Beatles and Rolling Stones songs were popular among the younger doctors. I liked watching the girl singers on television. Shirley Bassey was an American singer popular at that time. I liked Petula Clark's song 'Downtown', while 'Green Green Grass of Home' sung by Tom Jones reminded me of my lush green village of Swat. I often listened to songs which brought nostalgia, because I was homesick: I had been brought up in a Khan family, pampered and provided for without any effort with whatever was available, and had social status both as a doctor and member of my tribe, Painda khel. But in England, no one knew about my proud lineage.

Doctors were given four weeks' annual leave, when a locum doctor had to work in our place. An Australian lady doctor was appointed when Jennifer went on annual leave. She was elegant, well dressed and outspoken, unlike the other English lady doctors. She happened to be living in the same block of rooms as me. The rooms were simple, but painted elegantly, and because they were temporary structures one could hear the next-door neighbour if there was loud conversation. I used to contact the lady at night to make sure that patients received the correct treatment. Unlike Jennifer, she would take time to answer and then tell me to wait before giving me advice. I imagined that she slept naked and took time to put on clothes, as some of the women in my village used to sleep naked, because they had one set of clothes and they did not want them to get torn. I had never heard of or felt a woman's soft silken nightdress. Later on I discovered that my senior lady doctor would wear contact lenses which had to be removed at night, and that was the reason for the delay in answering my query about serious patients.

One evening there was unusual excitement among the male and female doctors during the dinner in the evening. I thought there was a dancing party in which some girls from other hospitals were invited. I was told that there was going to be a boxing match broadcast direct from America after midnight - the word 'live' was not common for direct broadcasts. They also said it was going to be the 'match of the century' - the sentence used by the master of publicity Cassius Clay, who changed his name to Mohammad Ali. His popular sayings, like 'float like a butterfly, sting like a bee' were mentioned. Some of us did not sleep, while others woke up early in the morning. There was excessive consumption of beer that night and I helped myself to a drink called Babycham, which was thought to be non-alcoholic, or at least I was told so. Ali's previous fights were shown, when Joe Frazier was called 'rabbit'. He never stopped shouting and hurling abuse at his opponent, Sonny Liston, who was called 'ugly' and 'big bear'. He never stopped saying, 'I am going to kill you, you big ugly scoundrel'. Seeing the features of Mohammed Ali, I was convinced that 'black can be beautiful' even though I had been brainwashed, like so many others, into believing that only white is beautiful. We all were waiting for a long boxing duel, but it turned out to be a short one. Sonny Liston, the world champion, was floored in the first round and he refused to fight on. He was demoralized by the verbal bombardment of Ali.

Visits to Southampton continued whenever there was a long weekend to see my friend and other Pakistanis. The underground rail journey to London was quicker from Orpington and from London to Southampton. I caught the surface train, which was always on time - something which I was not used to in Pakistan. People would sit quietly; they read newspapers or books and I would hardly hear any conversation except the occasional 'thank you' and 'sorry'. I was told before coming to the UK that I should make use of these words frequently in Britain. I was of the opinion that all the Western people were reserved, but in later life on a visit to the USA, when I was in a shuttle bus to a medical conference in Detroit, Michigan, a stranger sat next to me and said, 'Hi, my name is John, what is yours?' While travelling alone in the trains and not accustomed to reading either books or newspapers, I was attracted to sparsely-clad ladies with shapely buttocks. Interest in big busts and legs came at a later stage. Intimate kissing on railway platforms and in the parks were strange sights, but of keen interest.

One day as I reached Southampton, there was a lot of commotion among Pukhtuns. In the sixties during the debacle of India and Pakistan, it had been announced by India that they had captured Lahore, an important city in Punjab. A Sikh came to the Pukhtun shop owned by Ghani Khan and Siraj Khan and said 'Khan sahib, hum ne Lahore kofatahkardia' - Khan sahib, we have captured Lahore'. Ghani Khan, without asking any further clarification or deliberation, stabbed him with his big meat knife. He fell down, started bleeding and was taken to hospital where he was operated for injuries to the intestines. Police came, and Siraj Khan confessed instead of Ghani Khan. Siraj Khan spent three years in prison in Winchester. I asked him for the reason for this sacrifice, and his answer was that he was single, while his friend and partner was married with children. This episode shows how the Pukhtun will go to any lengths for his country without thinking and will even go to jail for years for the sake of his friend, as Siraj Khan did for his friend and partner.

Later on, another serious matter between two Pukhtuns was barely averted. Sherzada Khan (SK) and Nasir Khan (NK), were living in Farid Khan's house following the removal of Sikh tenants from his house. A girlfriend of SK had come to see him, but he was not present. His next-door neighbour invited her in. The girl told SK about it and he was furious and threatened to kill NK, who had to leave the house. On the explanation of NK and others that no sexual intercourse had taken place the matter was peacefully resolved, but they remained unfriendly to each other for the rest of their lives. Sectarian, ethnic 'honour' and religious matters are occasionally brought and fought in the adopted countries.

At this time, people, especially students, were very politically active in Europe and America because of the Vietnam war. On my visits to London, I would see demonstrations and hear young students make fiery speeches. Tariq Ali from Oxford University, who was elected President of Oxford Students' Union, used to give speeches in Trafalgar Square and I went to watch him as people had said that he was a Pathan from Pakistan. Ali became a successful author of many books and a broadcaster in later life. Pushtuns will flock around another Pushtun, especially away from their region, if there is some charisma. These days they gather round Shah Sayed in Karachi and Imran Khan, the cricketer turned politician, whenever he visits Pakhtun Khwa (North Western Pakistan). People, especially the young ones, attend the meetings of Imran Khan, founder of 'TehrikiInsaf' because he says he would bring corruption-free society to Pakistan; justice and employment to the masses, a Herculean task, but not impossible. In the seventies people flocked to Bhutto because his political slogan was 'Rotie, Kapra, Makan' (food, clothes and shelter). Young people in Swat also joined the Taliban because they had said that they would remove exploitation in society.

My first salary payment was about two hundred pounds sterling, and I was told to open an account at a bank. I went to the high street in Orpington, found a branch of Lloyds Bank and asked the gentleman on the counter about opening an account. He rightly wanted to know my credentials, but I thought he was belittling me because I was a foreigner from a third world country. There were hot words on my part and the young Englishman on the counter was visibly surprised and upset by my attitude. The British, during the heyday of their empire, learned about the cultural sensitivities of Pathans. They became successful rulers among the Pukhtuns when they started sending educated and trained British officers like Roos Keppel, Dundas, Robertson, Cunningham and Olaf Caroe. In later years the same bank held an enquiry against me because they suspected me of money laundering - they thought I was Dr A.Q. Khan of the Atomic Bomb project and the alleged proliferation of nuclear bomb technology.

The six-month full-time job at Orpington Hospital taught me a lot: the way the healthcare system works in hospitals; the free treatment without consideration of status; learning to stand on one's own feet when it comes to job seeking and passing medical exams. Patients, especially the elderly, are not to be left on their own when discharged from the hospital. It gave me some insight into the culture of English people, at least those working in the hospital or admitted as patients in hospital. Except for one, all my colleagues were local and there was hardly any discussion about the negative aspects of the people and the country. I went to all the wards to say farewell to the nursing sisters in charge of the wards, as they are the ones who are with the patients all the time.

I could not see the helpful Staff Nurse Barbara who did all the stitching of wounds in the Casualty Department for me and whose name was 'written on my back'. When I bade farewell to the nursing sister in one ward, she said 'goodbye, you have given me grey hair'. The sister was tall and aggressive and would drink whisky in the side room with her male friend working in the hospital, and I openly resented this. One day she called me to see a patient who was talking incoherently and suspected of stroke. I came to the ward, examined the patient and found that her dentures were not fitting. The patient was wearing someone else's dentures. I told off the nursing sister, which was unlike an English medical doctor, but I was brought up in a different environment.

Chapter Eleven

NEW EXPERIENCES: CHRISTCHURCH, ST. ANN'S AND BOSCOMBE

After working for six months in an NHS hospital, I learned how to apply for a job and how appointments are made. Now I had two referees in the UK, as I had made sure that I did my duties properly, especially writing up the history of the patient, sending requests for blood tests and other investigations, writing down in the medical record what my seniors had ordered and promptly seeing the patient if the ward sister called me. Once I was reprimanded and learned my lesson for not doing a blood test, as I thought there was no medical indication for it. My senior said, 'Sher, there are three indications for doing the tests: one is medical, the second is academic interest and the third is because some bloody fool has told you to do it'.

I started applying for senior house officer (SHO) posts and was called for interview. I got a post in Christchurch Hospital, Hampshire. There was not much competition, as working in geriatrics was not popular. I was not interested in acute medicine at that time, because I was scared of dealing with young acutely ill patients, just in case I made mistakes and would then have to face action from disciplinary authorities, and also my conscience would prick me. I had also heard that the General Medical Council had revoked the licence of one doctor from Swat. He was working as a house surgeon in a hospital when his senior consultant surgeon noticed money missing from his wallet. He suspected the only overseas junior house surgeon and reported him to the General Medical Council (GMC), who erased the suspected doctor's name from the Medical Register. Intervention by President Ayub Khan, the then Martial Law Administrator of Pakistan, could not restore the doctor to medical practice until he had finished the period of punishment. Lord Cohen of Birkenhead was the head of the GMC at that time.

The regulatory authorities, such as the hospital system at local level as well as at national level for accountability, were well in place and ran efficiently in the UK, unlike in Pakistan where you could 'get away with murder'. Like Orpington Hospital, Christchurch Hospital had open places with well-maintained lawns and evergreen trees. The wards for patients were long and wide but there were one or two side rooms attached to them. The building was also old and except for one ward, the rest were on the ground floor. Like the rest of the junior doctors, I was living in the hospital residences which had all the facilities for dining and relaxing. I started noticing my surroundings like a child growing up, as I did not have to struggle for a job at least for a year, but stresses and strains of different sorts had to be overcome.

Christchurch was a small clean place near the sea and had all the amenities. It was known for its architecturally-famous church. I had heard about churches from my school days, as one of my class fellows, Asher, was the son of a priest, and had wondered at that time how Christians say their prayers. I was also sorry for Asher, a soft-spoken, well-behaved slim boy who would not go to Heaven, as he was not among the chosen Muslims. This type of thinking for people belonging to other religions had also presumably made Durvza Khan, my stepbrother in the school, wrestle to the floor another Christian boy, Dennis. He had started beating him and kept on shouting, 'become Muslim!' Pukhtun brought up in their own surroundings think everything can be achieved with force.

I did go to church and found that there was music and singing of hymns. The church was full on Sundays, but one could hardly see anyone on other days. This reminded me of a Pukhtun who had converted his Christian friend who would regularly say prayers for a few weeks, but came back to the Pukhtun and said, 'Khan, I want to go back to my previous religion'. Khan said, 'Peter, you were better than us as you were coming to the mosque regularly'. Peter said, 'It is a full time job, I cannot do it any more'. It is not clear whether the Englishman was circumcised or not, but his chances of infection were less because of good healthcare, unlike the Hindu, who got infected following circumcision and who had said, 'Hum ghinlar, hum din lar' - I have lost my penis as well as my religion.

In Christchurch Hospital I was assigned to do medical duties in the children's ward when the house doctor was off duty. I had no experience in dealing with children's diseases, but the Registrar, an overseas doctor from Greece, was kind and always available on the phone even when he was on a weekend trip with his blonde girlfriend, a hairdresser. We all used to call the Greek doctor Theo, short for a long and difficult name to pronounce, even for the local doctors.

The ward sister was a slim lady with a shrill voice who was always shouting at the junior nurses, giving the impression that she was under stress. I was always on my guard when visiting the ward in case I provoked her. I asked Theo about her and he said 'she is unmarried, she has no boyfriend and looks after her old mother when she goes home. One can't blame her for her behaviour. She is liked by the consultant children's specialist who covers three hospitals because she is efficient and because she would report to him directly if there were deficiencies in the care of ill children'.

However, being brought up in a different culture, and being from a proud 'Khan family', I could not tolerate the rudeness of the Head Nurse, so I reported her to the hospital secretary, Mr. Guy - a soft spoken, fair-haired, middle aged man (the managers of the hospitals were called secretaries then). Mr Guy said there had been a lot of complaints against the nurse in charge and he was going to call her and the matron.

The matron was an unmarried elderly lady. She was kind and polite to everyone. Once I said to Theo, 'What a kind, elegant English lady'. He said, 'She is Jewish'. For the first time I learned that Jewish people can be good people, as the village preachers had drummed the negative aspects of Jews into people, and still do.

The hospital secretary called me to his office. The Head Nurse, Matron and some of his staff were already there when I entered. Mr. Guy talked about the value of politeness in dealing with people, using his typical British way. I once again had a taste of British justice. The first one was during my schooldays, when my headmaster Mr. F.H. Shaw, had taken action on my complaint and had not renewed the contract of a British teacher.

The Head Nurse never shouted again in the ward and was prevented from entering it. As they say, 'all's well that ends well'.

During my stay in Christchurch, I met a very nice person, an army engineer called Shujaat who had come to the south of England with his family for training. We used to go to the New Forest on picnics. It was good of him to send me his impressions when I told him that I was writing my life story. He wrote as follows:

"It is very difficult to describe Dr Sher Mohammad Khan, who combines in himself a multitude of attributes that manifest the intellectual, professional and spiritual dimensions of his life. I first had the good fortune of meeting him in 1969 when I was attached with MEXE in Christchurch in the UK, for getting experience in R&D. I was looking for a good doctor, located nearby, who could treat me for my stomach problems. He was then a medical registrar in Christchurch Hospital. I could not believe my eyes when I found a tall, handsome doctor from Pakistan who was known to be not only competent in his field but also enjoyed a good reputation in the community who could trust him with their lives. That showed the warm, caring and empathetic nature of his personality.

Thanks to his futuristic, innovative and fertile mind, he soon realized the importance of nuclear medicine, and did his Masters in this newly-emerging field, also obtaining membership of the Royal College London. He later came back to Pakistan at the invitation of Chairman, Pakistan Atomic Energy Commission, to raise and head nuclear medicine facilities for the first time in the then NWFP province of Pakistan for the benefit of people of that area.

Our contact and friendship continued over the next 46 years. I distinctly remember my visit to his outfit when I was Engineer-in-Chief, when I was highly impressed by his organizing abilities and professionalism. As a human being, I found him cool, calm, deliberate, warm-hearted and an excellent friend and head of his family, who should rightly be proud of him. May God bless him with health, happiness and long life."

Most of the junior doctors in the hospital were from overseas. There were doctors of Indian origin, Pakistan, Sri Lankan and East African. Diva, a lady doctor from Bengal, was an elegant, talented lady who was interested in classical Western music and regularly went to Bournemouth to attend the concerts. Shukla, a middle-aged Indian doctor, made sure that Diva was protected from the rest of the young doctors.

Das Gupta, another Bengali doctor, liked to relate stories about Pukhtuns. There is one funny story I still remember, probably because of its sexual connotations. Naked girls were paraded; males from different parts of India, including a Pukhtun, were made to watch and their erections were measured. The Pukhtun did not register any erection. The jury was surprised, but suddenly the Pukhtun registered an erection and when they looked at the girls, some of them had turned around and showed their buttocks. Pukhtuns are rightly or wrongly known for homosexuality. As a joke people say that in the Afghanistan War, the Nato forces wear their bullet-proof vests on the buttocks rather than on their chests.

It was in the south of England that I met my future wife Shahnaz, an Iranian. She had come to learn English in an English Language school in Bournemouth. I jokingly told her that I would teach her English and she should teach me Persian, as I was fond of two Persian books, Gulistan and Bostan by Saadi. The rest of the story is like a story in Pakistani or Indian films: a young man meets a young girl, they fall in love, but there are difficulties with the parents, and differences. Ultimately these are overcome and the young man and young girl are happily married and live together. In our case the marriage was solemnized in three different places: once in the local church, another time in the Iranian Embassy, where the official told me, 'we have given you a beautiful Iranian girl'. I answered, 'and you have got a handsome Pakistani boy'. The third time, a 'Nikah' ceremony was conducted by a visiting religious scholar from Pakistan, Maulana Abu AlaMaudoodi.

Unlike the head nurse from the children's ward, the other head nurses were polite. They made the other junior nurses work hard but had very little idea of good nursing care, because continual nursing education and medical education were not in vogue at that time. Sister Wright was a charming lady. She was polite and would always give me a cup of tea after the ward round. Once she said, 'what beautiful nails!' I did not know that a man's nails could be good looking. She said, 'you have a white crescent-shaped area at the root of the nail, which is rare'. I started realizing that people have different values in different cultures: good points were highlighted and appreciated, unlike the place where I was brought up. Questions are considered impolite, but I ventured and asked Sister Wright, 'How many children have you got?' She said, 'I was married to a doctor. He was good in his profession but was a bore. We divorced'. She also said that she had decided not to waste her life having children and bringing them up. I had felt sorry for her, but she was enjoying her life and playing guitar and singing in a pub at night time in the New Forest.

The New Forest, a beautiful place in the south of England, was of great interest to me, not because of the wild ponies, the rabbits, the greenery and the pleasant walking areas, but of some historical aspects; I was told that the trees across hundreds of acres of land were planted at the time of a benevolent King of England and it reminded me of Wali of Swat, who was also benevolent and did a lot for education, forests and health. I was also told that Lawrence of Arabia had his fatal accident while driving his motorbike in the New Forest.

I had also read a book in which it was mentioned that Lady Sale was buried in a chapel in the New Forest. During one of the Afghan Wars, she was taken hostage and lived in a village in the house of a tribal Pukhtun chief for almost two years. She was extended the traditional hospitality and protection. She was neither harmed nor molested, according to the Pukhtun honor code of Pukhtunwali, which does not allow women and children to be maltreated.

The New Forest had an abandoned airstrip where I learnt to drive in my small second-hand car. My friends told me that passing the driving test was more difficult than getting MRCP (Membership of the Royal College of Physicians) I passed the test at the third attempt by correctly doing the three-point turn, stopping in an emergency, starting uphill and knowing the Highway Code. In my country, a driving licence was easy if you paid for it.

Dancing and drinking parties were held periodically in the hospital, and girls from outside and some senior female staff were invited. Student nurses were not supposed to attend these parties in the doctors' residential quarters. Charity shows were also held in the hospital. A girl who won a world beauty contest was invited to one of these functions, as she came from a town near Christchurch Hospital. I was supposed to receive her and escort her to the dance floor, but to the disappointment of one lady organizer, I failed to attend the event. I regret it to this day but I had my reasons: I was supposed to wear a dark suit with a bow tie, which I did not have, and I did not know that one could borrow such things. I had not shed my shyness and I thought my Middle Eastern girlfriend would mind, because of the natural jealousy that we find in women in general and in Middle Eastern and Asian women in particular.

My one-year stint in Christchurch was coming to an end, which meant I had to start applying for another job. The stay in the area was rewarding and enjoyable. I had walked on the seaside, watched women in their bikinis lying on the sand and seen people fishing with rods. In my village, nets were used for catching fish. On a clear sunny day, I could see a distant island in the clear blue sea, which was unlike the Swat River, which was gushing and foaming because of fast flow and rocks. The walks in the New Forest watching the cows and ponies were exhilarating. There were concerts in Bournemouth, where a troupe from Dagestan, a central Asian state, have remained in my memory to this day because the dancers were clad in long, multi-coloured flowing dresses, which had reminded me of my part of the world.

I got a job in London, and before leaving I went around the hospital to say farewell. When I went to the Lady Almoner's place, she said she wanted to talk to me. The Almoner was a tall, well-built lady slightly on the obese side and had freckles on her face. I knew her well because we used to discuss the social aspects of the elderly ill patients - whether they were fit to be sent home or their relatives would take them home, or if they should be committed to the care of welfare state or government or private nursing homes. The Almoner said, 'You are professionally sound and take an interest in your patients, including their social aspects, but you are lacking one thing'. I impatiently asked her 'what is it, madam?' She said I was lacking 'salesmanship'. It was the first advice I had been given by a middle-aged English lady and I took it on board, but I have yet to develop salesmanship. My impression was that an English person never gives you advice, presumably because they want to avoid encroaching on the personal life of another person. In Pakistan, I was used to receiving uncalled-for advice and unnecessary interference in other people's personal, social and spiritual lives.

The Almoner also told me about the hijacking of one elderly lady suffering from pneumonia by the owner of the private nursing home. The sick lady was rich and did not have close relatives, and the owner of the nursing home wanted to defraud her by manipulating her will. Greed and crookedness are found everywhere, but to a lesser extent in some societies.

I was selected as Senior House Officer in St Ann's Hospital, in the infectious diseases unit. The unit was a prestigious one because the consultant in charge, Dr McKendrick contributed the section on infectious diseases in Price's text book of medicine. The infectious disease unit admitted patients suffering from malaria, typhoid fever, meningitis, diarrhoea in children, jaundice and other exotic and tropical diseases. I learnt the infectious and tropical diseases in that unit, which helped me later in my medical career. The Human Immunodeficiency Virus (HIV/Aids) was not known at that time, but poliovirus was known and the unit had two polio patients, one male and one female, for long-term care because of paralysis of breathing muscles. The lady was put into a breathing tank while the male was provided with facility of bed movement, using a whistle for up and down movements. It was a surprising and pleasant experience for me to see two disabled people looked after by dedicated nurses and doctors. As I write this section (2012), Pakistan is one of the three countries in the world where polio has yet to be eradicated because of inaccessibility (because of man-made disasters).

There was no room available in the residential quarters, so the Hospital Secretary suggested that I should rent a place near the hospital. He called a young man by the name of Peter, who said he had a vacant room in his flat, so I started sharing the flat with Peter. When the doctors and nurses heard that I was sharing the apartment with Peter, they would ask me with sarcastic look on their faces, 'Oh, you are living with Peter'. It was later that I found that Peter, a nice, polite and always a helpful person, was gay. He would be away all night and come home early in the morning over the weekends. I asked him once, 'Peter, where do you go at night?' His answer was, 'I go to the North Circular Road, where I enjoy myself'. The truck drivers used the circular road and parked their trucks at night prior to the building of the motorway. He also told me that on week nights he went to the public lavatories to look for contacts, using special signs for attraction. One day he woke me early in the morning and said, 'Dr Khan, can you help me please?' He showed me his back and there were marks of teeth. He said his client that night had been a foreigner and in climax had bit his back and said some foreign-sounding words. Same-sex marriages had yet to be legalized. After less than a month I moved to the residential quarter of the hospital, but I continued to see Peter in the hospital and would ask him for a room in his flat if I had a guest overnight.

The housemaid in the doctor's quarter was a Greek Cypriot, a plump and helpful lady, who spoke in broken English. I learned about pita bread from her, as it reminded me of my village where I used to love to eat bread baked in earthenware ovens. The area surrounding the hospital had a Greek and Turkish Cypriot community. Some of the patients in the hospital could not speak English. It was here that I learned about the genetic inherited disease thalassaemia, which was prevalent in Greek and Turkish Cypriots. This inherited disease is found all over the world, but much more common in the Mediterranean, Turkey, Iran, Afghanistan and Pakistan, right up to Swat. The Persians had fought their battles in the Mediterranean region and later the Greeks during Alexander's time fought their way up to India. The 'Silk Route' up to China also stretched from the Mediterranean through this long route. As I mentioned earlier, Dr Geraint James, the husband of Professor Dame Sheila Sherlock, the 'Liver Lady', had written an article regarding diseases and the Silk Route, and I had written to him asking him about certain points in his article. He recommended me to the Royal College of Physicians for Fellowship. The local fellows were guarding their unique fellowships of the Royal College of London jealously, but as I shall discuss later, I got the coveted fellowship of the Royal College.

Sometimes reputation, either good or bad, helps or goes against you because of the area where you come from originally. In St Ann's Hospital two doctors from the North West of Pakistan had worked in the hospital: one was Dr Siraj and another was Dr Tariq Nishtar. A physician with an interest in chest diseases spoke very highly of Dr Siraj's medical capabilities. I learned about him when I returned to Peshawar. He ultimately became a leading physician in the area and retired as Professor of Medicine of Khyber Medical College. Dr Brice, who was a consultant physician and was 'coloured', said that Dr Siraj was at consultant level, but was serving as medical registrar. Dr Brice had presumably also faced discrimination at a certain stage of his career.

The other doctor from Northern Pakistan was Dr Tariq Nishtar, who had served in the same unit of infectious diseases in the UK where I was working. A staff nurse knew him and told me that he was thin and had hardly any flesh on his body. I had not shed my Eastern shyness then and did not venture to ask her how she knew about the flesh on his body. The staff nurse was from Wales and in the hospital parties she would start singing loudly and swearing in Welsh after taking one or two alcoholic drinks. My consultant also told me that if I wanted a job in Pakistan, I should write to Dr Tariq Nishtar, who was well placed because of his family background and contacts in high places. My chief knew that in Pakistan merit comes low on the priority list for jobs.

I used to go and see other people who had come from Swat and kept shops near Finsbury Park, London. Sher Afzal Khan (SAK) and his elder brother were with their families, living in the same house. Amin-ul-Haq was also with them. He had married an English lady but had left her and was looking for a wife from his original place, Swat. Intermarriages were often unsuccessful because of different values and different backgrounds.

One day SAK told me that Maulana Maudoodi was visiting London and the organizer of their party, Jumaat Islami in London, wanted Pukhtun help. Maulana Abu Ala Mandoodi was given Pukhtun volunteers for guard duties. Jumaat Islami did not want trouble because of the backlash of Qadinis in London. Maulana Mandoodi had come to London for medical treatment. He was widely read and used to regularly read the weekly Time Magazine, Newsweek and the Jewish Journal. I asked him why he read the Jewish literature, and he said 'you have to know everything about your adversary'. Muslims would ask him about the observance of purdah among their women folk. He advised them that the Christian missionary's dress was sufficient.

I was with him when he was being admitted to a Harley Street clinic. As we entered his private hospital room, a female staff nurse was waiting. She greeted us and shook hands with us. MM asked for kosher food. He also had a good sense of humour and he wrote me a long letter which I have yet to trace, because his close party disciples kept and recorded everything he did during his stay in London, including the nurses' notes in the hospital. It was good of Sher Afzal Khan (SAK) to organize my Nikah ceremony by MM, who was pleased to do it. He did ask whether the girl was Shia or Sunni, but did not comment further. He wanted to write everything in detail with his own hand, solemnizing the Nikah, but I did not want to insist on it, which I still regret. Khurshid Ahmad also visited him and he asked him about the translation into English of his 'Tafseer' - commentary - on the Quran. His son Dr Farooq had also come from the USA. As MM was going to the hospital, he asked for his son because of his strong parental love. After recovery from his operation on the kidney and prostate, a dinner was given in the Dorchester Hotel, sponsored by Saudi Arabia. I was invited, but could not manage to be there because I had moved to Christchurch as a Medical Registrar.

Sher Afzal Khan from Swat was not only a hospitable person but always kept abreast of the politics back at his home region and also in the UK. He invited and entertained the visiting politicians, such as Baacha Khan and Qayum Khan. Dr Mehr Taj and Baristar Dilawer Shah were also his guests in London. They had recently married, and Dr Mehr Taj had brought her Pukhtun style gold jewellery with her, which she used to wear. My cousin Ihsan, son of my favourite maternal uncle, was also visiting London at that time. He was fond of guns and rifles as Pushtuns are, so we went to Piccadilly in London to see shotguns, especially those made by Holland and Holland and Churchill, the famous brands. He went inside the shop and I was waiting outside enjoying the scene in the street. Ihsan came out and said that the sales girls were not giving him attention. A person from 'Khan Family' expects and is accustomed to special attention, not knowing that values are different in different societies.

I thought of an idea for attracting the attention of the girl. As we entered the shop, I started reciting the Arabic prayers which every Muslim knows by heart, and I also said 'Ya Sheikh, Ya Sheikh'. The sales people noticed it and thought we were rich

Arabs, and gave us all their attention, showing us the guns and even offering to take us to the factory where special guns would be made for us. Profit motives in business probably override everything else.

Once again, I got a job in Christchurch Hospital after the usual process of application, short-listing and interview. The appointment was in general medicine as a medical registrar. I was now married and was given an apartment outside the hospital. It had two storeys and was surrounded by trees and green lawns. The apartment had all the facilities and I did not have to pay rent. The hospital management were also providing cleaning facilities, inside as well as outside. I started feeling the joy of being married and also felt a taste of some power in the hospital. Humans are happy when they are wanted at home and have some status in the social circle. But as they say 'life is not a bed of roses', and I had yet to pass my postgraduate medical examination to get membership of the Royal College, which was essential to get a senior post in UK or Pakistan in the sixties. Proper postgraduate education and training had yet to be streamlined, so one had to do the job and sit for examinations. Formal courses were also held but these were in a haphazard manner and one had to pay for attendance. As some of the overseas doctors used to say, 'half the money earned is spent on medical courses and the rest is spent on intercourse'. In my case, I had difficulty with the essay-type questions because of my non-English speaking background and failed in theory papers but passed in practicals and viva-voce. I remember enrolling in a correspondence course and when I sent the answer to one of the questions the comments were, 'this answer will not get you through MBBS, what about MRCP'. But I passed the exams the first time when the Royal Colleges changed the system to multiple choice questions.

The overseas doctors also learned about examination tricks and about the idiosyncrasies of the Royal College examiners. Papworth courses in London were popular among the overseas Indian and Pakistani doctors. There was one examiner who was a neurologist and was fond of asking the cause of rheumatic fever, and one had to answer 'virus infection', otherwise one would fail. Objective testing was not common.

In those days there was an editorial on overseas doctors in the British Medical Journal and I wrote a letter, which was published 46 years ago (1969) and is reproduced here in toto.

Doctors from Overseas

Sir, your leading article (22 March, p.729) is both timely and commendable. The policy makers can and should take the steps suggested by you, as it will avoid smear campaigns against these unfortunate doctors and a remote possibility of "back lash."

What should be done to thousands of immigrant doctors who are already here? Should they be treated as disposable objects— used and discarded? The majority of them want to return to their own country after obtaining a postgraduate diploma. Failure rates among them are very high in these higher competitive examinations because of their inadequate training. They do not and cannot compete for the best jobs. If the service needs are carried largely by overseas doctors as you mentions, then surely they deserve a few more training posts in good peripheral hospitals with sympathetic consultants. These properly trained doctors will then perpetuate and propagate British medicine in their own country.

May I add a few more suggestions? Follow the Scandinavian countries in not enticing away the doctors from underdeveloped countries. If this is done in the guise of an "aid" then these countries can be helped at the source. They should also be told that their present system of medical education produces doctors whose first wish is to leave the country. Some sort of "bureau" should be set up in the countries of origin of these doctors for selection of doctors, and they should be given some introductory lectures in the N.H.S. practical procedures and the art of communication before they take up an appointment.

"Free movement of doctors around the world is an essential and traditional feature of medicine" but at the moment it seems to be one-way traffic from the underdeveloped countries. Many Afro-Asian doctors are serving in developed countries, but the present prevailing attitude towards them in employment and training is considered by many in this as well as other countries "frank exploitation" and "neocolonialism".

Doctors from overseas, especially from underdeveloped countries, should remember that the poor people in their own countries may not be able to offer them material benefits, but a doctor is still held in high esteem there, and is highly respected in these communities. The present conditions in the countries of origin of these doctors should act as a challenge and not a deterrent. — I am, etc.

SHER M. KHAN
Christchurch, Hants.
British Medical Journal 19, April 1969

By publication of my letter in a leading journal as above which criticized the system in a polite way, I learned that in a democratic system opposing voices are also heard in a transparent manner, unlike my country. Since that time there has been great improvement in the NHS and postgraduate medical education in the UK.

I supervised the house physicians, who were all locals, and I was responsible and accountable for patients admitted by three consultants. The senior consultant was Dr Bentley, an elegant person who came to the hospital in his Bentley car. Once when we were having tea after the usual ward round, he said, 'Interesting times are coming, but I won't be here'. It was the time when man landed on the moon for the first time. Dr Bentley was nearing retirement at 65. The second consultant was interested in blood diseases; he diagnosed himself as suffering from leukaemia (blood cancer) by looking at his blood film himself when he had fever. He died, as the treatment of blood cancer was unsatisfactory at that time. The sad news of his death was passed on to the third consultant physician, Dr Clarke, when we were doing the ward round. I could visibly see the grief and the tears rolling down his clean-shaven face. It was the first time I witnessed emotions on an Englishman's face, as I had been brought up thinking that the English people are 'cold' and do not express their emotions in public. Ignorance about other people and cultures can breed all sorts of misunderstandings.

I also found that Dr Clarke was Welsh, as he had a soft spot for one elderly patient who only knew the Welsh language, which was another addition to my knowledge - that there could be local people who did not know English. Dr Clarke was married to a lady who had Armenian ancestry. One of his sons, in later years when I had left the UK, travelled to Afghanistan and Northern Pakistan when the Silk Route came to be known as the 'hashish route'.

The two senior consultant physicians were replaced by Dr McDonald and Dr Loehry. Dr McDonald had an interest in kidney diseases and was proud of being Scottish. One of his previous colleagues was Dr Nowsherawan Burki, the cousin of Imran Khan, the founder and leader of Pakistan TehrikeInsaf (PTI or Justice Party). Dr Loehry was a physician with an interest in gastroenterology. He was young and had an Irish background. At that time most of the younger doctors wanted to become general practitioners (family physicians). One young doctor, by the name of Dr Coffin, I remember very well because one day the ward sister called me to come to the ward as Dr Coffin was doing some sort of post-mortem on a dead body. When I went to the ward, I saw a chisel in Dr Coffin's hand and he was trying to remove a piece of brain by chiseling the skull for further examination. The patient was of Jewish background and the Jewish people would not allow post mortems on their dead relatives. There was another story being circulated among the doctors, that one doctor desperate to know the cause of the death for research purposes had to use the back passage of the dead body to have access to the kidney. Some researchers go to any extent to satisfy their curiosity,

However, religious sensitivities were usually taken into consideration in medical practice and hospitals. For example, Jehovah's witnesses were not forced to have blood transfusions. It was the rule to write the religion in the medical record of patients. Once an old coloured patient was admitted and the nurse could not write the name of his religion as they had never heard it. I asked the old blind patient, who said, 'Zoroastrian'. He went on to explain in his humorous way: 'Zoroastrianism was a religion of Persians until the Arabs invaded Persia. Some were converted and some fled to India like my ancestors. The Indians could not pronounce Zoroastrian, so they started calling us Parsi'. The patient used six-letter and four-letter words throughout his conversation, not knowing that one of his listeners, myself, was a Muslim. Parsis are well-respected business communities in India and Pakistan. Mohammad Ali Jinnah, the founder of Pakistan, was married to a Parsi lady whom he had married when he was a practising lawyer in Bombay, now Mumbai. Peshawar in Northern Pakistan also had a Parsi (Zoroastrian) burial ground. One wishes that different religious practices and different cultures would be introduced to the younger generation by unbiased teachers in schools, colleges and universities, but at the time of writing, militancy, bigotry and intolerance are greater than ever.

One day I received a telephone call and on the other end was a person who sounded very nervous. He introduced himself Ahmad Hilal, the younger brother of Dr Bilal, whom I knew and who was a family friend. Since I had gone through difficult times when I first came to UK I asked Dr Hilal to come to Christchurch, which he did. By that time I knew how to assist or help the new doctors from overseas. I had also not forgotten my background, yet I tried to help all those who needed it. A few months' attachment with a consultant physician would help a newly-arrived overseas doctor by steering him or her in the right direction.

Dr Hilal started working in Dr Tattersall's unit. Dr Tattersall was a known to be difficult to work for, but Ahmad Hilal recalls that the period of attachment with him helped him in later life. Sometimes experience teaches one a lot. As is expected in Pukhtun culture, other doctors from Swat, Dr Inayat and Dr Nisar Haq, had also contacted me to help them in finding jobs and I could not refuse or excuse myself because relations, even distant ones, are more important to a person brought up in a tribal or Pukhtun culture.

Since Southampton was not very far off, we periodically went there to continue our already established relations and contacts. I liked going to the seaside, watching the ships berthed in the docks and also watch people sailing off. Southampton was the place from which RMS Titanic sailed on its maiden tragic voyage, along with some five hundred Southampton people, over a hundred years ago.

Fazli Ali, SAK and other Swatis, Siraj Khan, Haroon Rashid Khan, Shamshad Khan and Haider Khan, continued to be hospitable and went out of the way to entertain guests in their houses despite their busy routine of life. One wondered whether the first and second generation would be the same or they would have different values and attitudes. I met one annual visitor to Southampton in FA's house and he was introduced as Maulana Rahat Gul (RG). RG corrected me and said he was Maulavi, which is of lower rank in religious order. Like other religious people, but unlike military personnel, RG showed humility. He also had a sense of humour and once, in later life, I said to him to help himself to halva, a sweet which Mullahs are known to like. He said, 'all of you like halva, but you people blame Mullahs for it'. RG was friendly with Ajmal Khattak, a poet, writer and nationalist, and very close to Baacha Khan, the Pukhtun leader. RG used to come to the UK for donations, and he spent the collected donations transparently on building a mosque and a school where children were taught religious plus modern education. The madrass (school) was run by RG's well-educated sons.

Our first child, Mah Muneer (MM) was born in Boscombe Hospital. She was two weeks post mature. Whether post maturity can make one 'brainy', as she turned out to be in her later life, is not known. Pukhtuns want male children and will continue to have children until they have a boy. Those who have no male child are called *mirat*, as they would not have anyone to inherit their property. Females are not supposed to inherit property, as in the case of my grandmother, who was the only child, so her share of the vast property was inherited by her cousins.

Shahnaz was admitted to hospital for delivery on April 1st, and I hoped the delivery would be delayed, otherwise people would call her newborn baby 'April Fool'. Mah Muneer was born after midnight and when I saw her in the cot, she had already started sucking her thumb, a habit which has already passed on to her children, Danish, Deena and Daneen (three Ds), our grandchildren.

Shahnaz loved children and always yearned to have them. The first child is difficult to bring up but is always precious for everyone. I had to examine MM almost every day, sometimes more than once, as Shahnaz wanted to make sure she was breathing normally and her heart was beating. If there was the flickering of an eyelid while MM was asleep, I had to make sure it was normal. If I did not examine the child on time, then MM was to be taken to the child specialist. In my case, when I was born in my village, I was given to my Nanny to be looked after. Whether it is the Iranian culture or natural for your parents/mother to love children, bring them up with excessive care, educate them and then try to put them on the right path to enter the wide world, is not clear to me. But judging by the level of literacy and standard of living and the relative peace, prosperity and progress compared to neighbouring countries like Afghanistan and Pakistan, it is probably due to the Iranian way of life.

MM, our first child, was growing as most children grow. Her mother took special care of her, feeding, cleaning, clothing and showering kisses on the baby. Special mixers for food were bought in in anticipation of ingestion of solid food. Baby foods were available in the shops, but Shahnaz preferred to make her own with fresh ingredients. I had very little role except occasional bottle feeding. I had only seen breast feeding. People in the villages still do not know how to look after children properly, including vaccination against childhood diseases. No wonder infant mortality was high in the fifties and sixties and even now in the nineties, especially in the north west of Pakistan and the borderlands with Afghanistan. For the first time I realized that education in general and education of females in particular is important. Shahnaz was not only educated, as girls in Iran have equal opportunities with boys, but had training in midwifery. I was brought up in a village where children were left to themselves to grow without any conscious effort to bring them up, educate and vaccinate them. I started wondering whether Iranian culture had this basic ingredient of love of children, or if it was natural in every mother. It was later in life, when I spent about two months in Burma, now Myanmar, that I realized that they also gave special attention to their children.

Once we had visitors: Colonel Shujaat Hussain (SH) and his wife, who had come from Pakistan. SH was surprised to see Mah Muneer sitting quietly in a round netted cage playing with her toys without crying. He was used to seeing babies crying and in my village it was common sight. This is probably due to neglect of children and other environmental factors. Once I heard the sound of something rolling down the stairs and when I went to the stairs, I saw MM standing at the bottom rubbing her eyes. No serious injury had occurred, but we made sure that the top of the stairs had a childproof gate. Accidents can easily occur if one is not careful in the house when young children are growing. Safety measures for children were unheard and the common remark was 'Allah ye lo yey - aw Khial ye sati' - God makes children grow and protects them. Some beliefs can be taken as excuses for neglect, perhaps due to deliberately wrong interpretations of religion, or ignorance.

The routine work of going to the hospital and attending the outpatients continued, but I was given an extra duty, which was to look after the sick nurses, for which I was paid a portion of the honorarium given to the consultant physician. Sometimes he forgot my share, but I did not dare to remind him because I depended on him for my future reference, which counted a lot in getting a job.

Once my senior consultant said that he would be going sailing over the weekend and I could contact so and so in case of a medical emergency. I began realising that there are other things in life besides your routine job. I had also not heard of people going on holidays to other places, but they planned holidays well in advance, sometimes to exotic places. So we also started going out on day trips at weekends. The south of England has some nice places to see. It was a pleasure to see farms with the hedges planted with rhododendrons. The flowers were multicoloured and I was told that the plant was from the Himalayas. I had seen the red flowers before, as young people from Swat used to go to the holy site of Pir Baba with their drums and sitars and return with red perfumed flowers of the wild rhododendron. The leaves were dried and then burnt to ward off evil spirits. Young people visited Pir Baba in Buner, and on the way back they used to sing and entertain themselves. Khaista Dada - handsome daddy - my father had also told me about one song which they used to sing - 'Larum pa karakar, reghlum pa Juwarni, Khudaya rake Begum Jan gharaghari' - I climbed up the Karakar mountains and came down Jware mountain, I wish I could get an attractive lady Begum Jan.

The sports, the entertainment, the outings without fear, singing and dancing during marriage ceremonies or during Eid festivals are no longer available for the younger generations, especially in the north west of Pakistan. Instead, they are encouraged to take arms and train in destructive methods, to themselves as well as others. The reasons for this kind of attitude need serious research on the part of social scientists in order to put the people, especially the younger generation, on a more constructive pathway for themselves, for society, for the region and the wider world, because people are now living in a 'global village'.

The museum of old cars at Beaulieu was a historical, educational and entertaining place to visit. I saw a painting of one of the relatives of Lord Montague and became interested when I read underneath his portrait that he was the person who had supervised the building of the railway in the difficult mountainous terrain of the Khyber Pass in the thirties. This was an engineering feat par excellence by the British. Two steam engines were used; one in front and one at the back. Alas the railways, an environmentally clean mode of transport, have been neglected because of poor governance and leadership.

The local doctors went on holiday to Europe. Spain and the Mediterranean islands were popular as holiday resorts. I used to do locums - part-time relief work - either in hospital or with general practitioners to make extra money during my earned leave.

During my annual summer leave, I went to Norwich in the eastern county of Norfolk. One of the partners in the general practice was also on leave. We all travelled in a car and our stay was arranged in a hotel, where I discovered the smoked herrings called 'kippers' which were served for breakfast. I was used to hospital practice and for the first few days I took a long time to see the patients, unlike the senior GP, who disposed of patients quickly. The GP was a soft-spoken and polite person. He told me over a cup of tea: 'Patients who are ill will come again and it is easier and quicker to prescribe medicine and dispose of them'. I took his advice and did not spend too much time in examining and investigating the patients.

One day as I was examining patients, the GP said that he was sorry to hear about some episode in a mosque in Jerusalem. He said that some people were crazy and did crazy acts, but it did not mean that all Christians or Jews were against the Muslim religion and their places of worship. I kept on listening, but did not have a clue what had happened. It was afterwards, when I got to the hotel, that I read how someone had set fire to the Agsa Mosque.

The two weeks' locum work in general practice was enjoyable and rewarding. At weekends we went to the Broads, lakes and canals dug in the marshy land which were now used for boating and leisure purposes.

CHAPTER TWELVE

SOUTHAMPTON AND NUCLEAR MEDICINE

I continued to study for the exams to get Membership of the Royal College. I tried my luck in London, Glasgow and Edinburgh, but failed the theory because of the long essays required. As already mentioned, I passed in the practicals and viva voce. My two years of medical registrarship were coming to an end and I wanted to get a postgraduate degree in medicine before I went back, because going back to the country where I was born and bred without getting any diploma or degree would mean shame for me since I was brought up in a Pukhtun family where one had to succeed at any cost.

I heard that a new department had been established at Southampton General Hospital and they needed a junior doctor. Dr Garnet, a very bright young consultant, had established the department, but as it was a new department for the use of radioisotopes in medicine, the future for younger doctors was unpredictable and the local doctors were reluctant to join the specialty of Nuclear Medicine. Radioisotopes in medicine were used by physicists and medically-qualified persons had yet to enter the specialty.

I also went to see Dr McCready at the Royal Marsden Hospital, Surrey, to find out more about the Master's Degree in Nuclear Medicine. Dr McCready was an intelligent and convincing doctor of short stature who had a strong Irish accent. He was one of the pioneers of nuclear medicine in the UK. He had a sense of humour and would say that Shakespeare had the same accent as his. As I was waiting in Dr McCready's secretary's office, I wished I could have a similar secretary - polite, smartly-dressed and shapely.

Dr McCready came out and took me into his office. During my village life in childhood I was not taught to receive guests in this way because hujras were open spaces. People would get up to receive guests and would make them to sit on *charpoys* - big chairs. They would always see guests off by saying goodbye, sometimes taking a long time. The Mullahs in the mosques, while talking about the seerat of Prophet Muhammad (PBUH) would talk about receiving and seeing off guests even if they belonged to other religions. They would also emphasize that it was this 'excellent' character and civility towards the other human being that made people to flock to Islam.

Dr McCready convinced me about the bright future of nuclear medicine, but I was only interested in a postgraduate medical degree. I applied for the job and got it without competition. When I joined the department as a junior doctor, Dr Garnet had already emigrated to Canada, which was inviting talented people. In his absence, part-time consultants from the Navy came two or three times a week. These consultants were in the nuclear submarine fleet in Hasler, Portsmouth. Surgeon commander Duncan Ackery was the senior consultant. The rest of my colleagues were basic scientists and engineers. I also learned that basic scientists have an important role in medicine. Richard Mardell was the chemist in charge of the 'wet tests' using radioactive substances. He was a short, bearded, intelligent man, interested in research as well as routine work. He got on well with his medical colleagues, unlike some others who bickered about territory. Dr Ray Pope was a physicist, a quiet gentleman married to an Australian lady, Patricia, whom he had met in the USA. Patricia was from a farming family from Australia and she talked openly about her background, unlike other local ladies whom I met socially as well as in the department. The department was a close-knit one and we shared our experiences and secrets. The secretary, who took dictation from Duncan Ackery, told me she wished she could sit in his lap while taking it, but he had a life of his own. He had a friend, Hamish, a nice young man from New Zealand. Hamish was a school teacher who became an artist. Both of them visited Peshawar and I took them to see Chitral, Kalash Valley and Swat Valley. They retired to Menorca, where they had a house. My wife and I visited them in Menorca and enjoyed their hospitality for a week. The last I heard from them was that Duncan had severe pain in the back and was operated upon. Hamish was faithfully looking after him.

Denise was a young technician. In the seventies only medically-qualified doctors were supposed to give intravenous (IV) injections and Denise used to call me to give them using a rectilinear scanner. A camera for taking pictures was invented later on. Denise would sometimes call me and say, 'Omar Sharif, the patient is ready for injection.' The film Dr Zhivago had been recently released and a lot of people had seen it. Denise thought I looked like Omar Sharif because of my moustache. The last I heard about her was that she had developed the crippling disease multiple sclerosis. I kept in touch with my colleagues after leaving the Nuclear Medicine Department. Was it because it was a small and close-knit department, was it due to my adulthood, or was it because my colleagues were unusually friendly - or the combination of all three? I could not tell.

In the early seventies the BBC started showing programmes about sex education in the late hours. We used to watch it at night and discuss it during tea time in the department. Once Ray Pope asked me, 'Do they teach sex education in Pakistan?' I said, 'We learn it in the streets by watching dogs and other animals'. I also said that children and adolescents learn it by swearing and abusing each other during fighting because of lack of healthy sports. I gave my colleagues some examples like 'jumping from the sky on top of someone's sister or mother'. Ray Pope, the physicist, remarked, 'What terrific acceleration during copulation'.

At Southampton General Hospital, Nuclear Medicine was a new department and I was the only junior doctor. The medical school had recently started when I joined the NMD. I remember a professor of medicine very well because his name was Jack Howell, and Evelyn Howell was mentioned by Olaf Caroe in his book The Pathans. EH translated Pushto poetry of Khushhal Khan in to English and Latin. One of his poems is reproduced below.

A Poem by Khushhal Khan Khatak (English translation by Sir Evelyn Howell)

Roses, wine, a friend to share -
Spring sans wine I will not bear,
Abstinence I do abhor,

Cup on cup, my Saqi, pour.
Hark! the lute and pipe! Give ear!
What says music to our cheer?
Time once flown returneth never,
Idle moments gone for ever,
 Wouldst recall them? Call in vain.
Life, our mortal life, hath sweetness,
As its sweetness, so its fleetness,
 Count it nothing, 'tis no again.
Doth time tarry for thy prizing,
Or make speed for thy despising?
 Time hath all young lovers slain,
Time is heedless, time is heartless -
Saqi, fill and fill again.

Jack Howell was the Professor of Medicine, and he was tall and intelligent. He did research and had many publications to his credit on diseases of the chest. For some reason he would make sure I attended lectures given by visiting lecturers. Once a lecture was delivered by a person who was half paralyzed due to hemiplegi and who used a blackboard. As he started cleaning the blackboard, I got up from my seat and tried to help him, but he would not let me do it. I learned that one can also be useful in a society if one is disabled and old.

I remember a cousin of my father whom we called 'Baz Dada', Falcon Dada. He had hemiplegia and was always lying in a charpoy. He developed bed sores and incontinence. His wife was looking after him, but there was neither proper care nor proper medical attention. Seeing a person with a hemiplegia giving lecture was a new experience and a lesson for me. This was I think Mr. Guyton, who has written a book on physiology.

On the advice of Duncan Ackery, my supervisor, I started

research on the use of radioisotopes in diseases of the lungs. The chest department was well staffed as it had Dr McLeod, internationally known for McLeod's syndrome, and Professor Howell. I started collecting patients but did not have any idea how research was done. In the Medical Colleges, one was supposed to mug books to reproduce the answers to the questions set in annual exams, but one has to have educated, research-minded teachers and seniors to inculcate the spirit of research in juniors. My scientific colleagues helped me and I worked hard as I had to get the MSc degree, otherwise I would not be able to show my face to the people in Swat.

Radioactive xenon gas was used for investigations and comparison was made with standard procedures. The medical records of patients were collected, but the research work had to be typed prior to submission. I asked the secretary, who typed a few pages, but I felt that she was reluctant to continue. By that time I had realised that English people are often too polite to say no, unlike in Pukhtun areas, where one can straight away refuse to do something.

I wished I had learnt how to type, because during my work in Saidu Hospital in Swat Prof Danishmand had persuaded me and Sherin Jan, the dental surgeon, to learn typing and we had attended few classes in Mingora, but had not continued it. Shahnaz came to my rescue as always. We bought a typewriter in London, which Shahnaz used for writing my applications for jobs. So she volunteered to do the job in spite of her schedule of looking after a child and other domestic chores. She did a very good job of it, including drawing the illustrations. The 'M' in MSc should be Shahnaz's. The dissertation was judged to be one of the best by Professor Edward Williams, but I failed in the physics part of the examination, because of my weak scientific learning background in the school and college. And I still had to take my exam in nuclear medicine.

Professor Edward Williams was a physicist in the Middlesex Hospital, London and later on completed a medical degree and was made head of the Nuclear Medicine Department. He was from Wales and was interested in mountaineering. In the early 1950s he had visited the northern areas of Pakistan, bordering Kashghar, and some areas of China. This is the biggest area of high mountains in the world. He had an uncle, Buster Goodwin, who served in the North West during the British occupation. Goodwin wrote a book about his time based on his dealing with Pushtuns. I had the good fortune of meeting him in Rawalpindi, when he was living at 303 Peshawar Road. Edward Williams told me about him and had said Goodwin did not want to leave the place in his old age as he was attached to the people. A Pushtun family was living with him and looking after Buster when I went to see him.

Dr McCready and Dr Ackery guided me in studying for examinations and recommended a book to study for physics. I liked the clinical lectures, but mathematics, physics and radio-pharmacy were difficult to understand. My classmates were all local and were already known in their fields, such as Dr Keith Britain and others. One day Duncan Ackery said, 'If you rub shoulders with some of your classmates, you will get something'. There is a Pushto proverb, 'Da Alim Sara chegarzina Alimba she' - if you keep the company of a learned person, then you will also become learned. I passed the examination at the next attempt and did not have to rewrite the dissertation because it was judged as one of the best.

Professor Williams was the chairman of the examiners. He was a kind man and had talked to me about his mountaineering trips and about his uncle. When I entered the examination room, he greeted me and after few clinical questions by the other examiners, which I answered correctly, I was allowed to leave. As I was leaving, ED got up and opened the door for me. It was a nice gesture on his part. I wondered if it was because he wanted to show the other examiners that he did not want to fail me this time, or perhaps it was because of his pleasant and kind gesture to a person who had come from an area where his uncle had served and because he had visited the region as a mountaineer? Human nature is the same everywhere. If one has fond memories of a place, then it is natural to be good to people coming from that area.

After getting my MSc from the London University, I had another shot at MRCP and passed. This was the time when one could have many attempts at membership of the Royal Colleges. The theory exam was multiple choice questions and on the morning of the examination, I had a fever, but Shahnaz forced me to take the exam. After a few days, a thick envelope came in the post instead of the usual thin envelope, so I knew I had passed before even opening the envelope.

Now I had two 'hats', and I was thinking that when I entered the Khyber Pass after crossing the Durand line, I would be boasting two postgraduate degrees in medicine and no one could prevent me from getting a job in Khyber Medical College. However I had not foreseen the difficulties and the medical politics.

The Nuclear Medicine Department was next to the Gastrointestinal Department in the hospital and I used to go through it. The middle-aged sister in charge used to greet me and took an unusual interest in me. She even asked Duncan Ackery whether I was married or not. She herself was married to a doctor working in another hospital. One day she invited me to tea in her friend's flat. We went together and had tea, but I excused myself as I had to pick up my child from school.

The next day I received a phone call from Dr Ahmad Hilal. After spending some time with Dr Tattersall in a holiday resort town in Bournemouth he had got a job in the north, but like a good friend he would always keep in touch. He said he dreamed that I had some domestic problem. 'Is everything all right?' he asked. I told him the story. He said, 'Did anything happen?' I replied, 'Nothing happened. I was a virgin when I got married and I continue to be a virgin'. He said, 'God help you'.

CHAPTER THIRTEEN

LIFE AND WORK
IN ENGLAND

Southampton is a seaport, and has all the amenities. One could enjoy the city life, go to the New Forest for a picnic and see its wild ponies. To the west of the New Forest is the seaside town of Bournemouth, where people flock during their summer holidays. London is not very far from Southampton. Winchester, the old capital of England, is also near, and its cathedrals and churches are worth seeing. Visiting some of these, I could see plaques in memory of men who had fought in the North West Frontier of the subcontinent of India.

Portsmouth was the naval base from where battleships at the time of Nelson and before used to sail with cheers of 'Rule Britannia, Britannia rules the waves'. Further to the east is Brighton, a sea town where the harbour had buildings of architectural marvel. We went and see these historically interesting places.

We lived in a house rented by the hospital authority on Westwood Road. The house was large with front and back gardens, and here Mah Muneer used to play, swing and sometimes run after stray cats in the garden. Two more families were living in the same house. One was an eye specialist who was married to a Swiss girl. She was dark, though I had always thought people from Switzerland were by and large blond and fair. Later she told us that she was adopted. The eye specialist was serious, both in his work as well as in his relations. He was also religious, unlike his wife, who was an extrovert. The last we heard about them was that they had separated. The other couple living in the same house were Mormons. I had never heard of Mormons. He would explain and preach to me about their faith, but once you are Muslim you are always a Muslim.

There was a sizeable immigrant community living in Southampton. There were Pukhtuns, Punjabis, Kashmiris, Sikhs, Hindus and Bengalis. The majority of the Pukhtuns worked in ships such as those of the P&O line and used to 'jump ship' and stay illegally until they got their nationality. They used to work in the factories as labourers, some as bus conductors and drivers. Some had started small businesses and prospered in later lives. The Muslims started a Welfare Society and I was made a position holder in it. There were some active members, including Bashir from Kashmir, Sher Afzal Khan, Haider Khan, Haroon Rashid, Ghani Khan, Shamshad Khan, Farid Khan and Siraj Khan. Fazli Ali, my schoolfellow and friend, was always interested in doing some good for the immigrant community. Fazli Ali's friend, Pir Moid, started as a businessman importing footballs from Sialkot, Pakistan, but he told me later on that he was disgusted by the fraud and corruption in Pakistan. He also became successful in the property business and later on built a mosque and became a PIR with a sizeable following in the UK and Pakistan. His son Anjum became a successful property businessman. Most of the immigrants lived in the Derby Road area of Southampton, because the property there was cheaper and they felt at home among their own people.

I used to go to the Derby Road area to buy meat, vegetables and imported foods. The shops owned by Pukhtuns and other Pakistanis were open seven days a week till late at night. One evening I noticed some burning red candles in the windows of some of the houses. I asked the shopkeeper what they meant. He said 'Don't you know?' I showed my ignorance, and he said that there were prostitutes in the houses. I had heard of 'red light' areas from returnees from Bombay in my hamlet and also from those who were working in Lahore, but did not know about the 'oldest profession' in this seaport.

As I was the President of the Pakistanis' Welfare Society, we started planning for a mosque and a community centre. The Sikh community had started a *gurdwara* in an unused church, as there were many abandoned churches in the seventies in England. We found a house not very far from the homes where I had seen the red candles, but proper permission had to be obtained from the council in Southampton. The application was rejected on the grounds that they had already given permission for one and the neighbours had complained about the 'singing' and playing of the harmonium. It turned out that they meant the Sikhs' religious place where 'Bajan' was played. In the early seventies, people in England did not know about Islam. Some members of the council were invited to see how Muslims offered prayers. They were impressed with the ablution and the discipline during the prayers, and permission for a mosque was granted. In a democratic system, minorities are not ignored, as was the case of Muslims in England.

Steyning is a village in Sussex, not very far from Southampton. Professor Maulana Abdul Qadir, the Director of the Pushto

Academy in Peshawar, who was visiting the UK, had told me about visiting Sir Olaf Caroe. He told me that Sir Olaf had put Pukhtuns on the world map by writing a book, 'The Pathans', in 1957. The then Director and Pioneer of the Pushto Academy could not have imagined that Pukhtuns in Afghanistan and North West Pakistan would be on the front pages of the newspapers, television news and internet in the 21st century because of the natural and manmade disasters which were imposed on them by devastating external and internal factors.

Hardly a day passes now when Swat and the Mahsuds and Wazir of Waziristan are not in the news. As I write this piece, news has been broadcast regarding the killing of Pakistani soldiers in Miran Shah, and also about drone attacks. More than a hundred years ago Sir Evelyn Howell wrote about the murder of a British political agent and commandant in a journal. Has the world not yet learnt how to deal with Pukhtuns? Force and military solutions have never succeeded in the past. It is high time for fresh thinking and a new approach to be adopted. There is no dearth of scholars in the world.

Coming back to the story of Sir Olaf Caroe, I had heard and read about the myths - real or imagined - about the origins of Pukhtuns. Bani Israel was mentioned in the hujras and *shajaras*, the written tables of tribes. Semitic and Aryan origins were discussed. In the sixties I wondered whether blood tests, especially blood groups and haemoglobin, could help in the elucidation of the mystery, so I found the telephone number of Sir Olaf and phoned his house. Lady Olaf picked up the phone and said that Sir Olaf was sleeping and he would phone me, but I said I would phone again. I talked to him and told him I was interested in the medical side of investigations into the origin of Pukhtuns. He suggested Dr Qazi, a general practitioner living in the north of England. He also asked me about my tribe. I said it was the Painda khel from Swat and he said there were Painda

Khels in Dir. He asked me about my home address in Southampton and I said '*melmastia*', hospitality, and gave him the full address. A few days later, I received a letter and on the envelope was written 'melmastia' in English, but in brackets it was written in the Pushto alphabet. Alas, the letter has been misplaced, but I am going to search for it. Shahnaz is my custodian and as usual a Pukhtun blames his wife if anything worth keeping is missing.

I could not get hold of Dr Qazi in the north of England, but I did contact an expert in haemoglobinopathy at Cambridge University whose laboratory was a reference lab for the World Health Organization (WHO) for blood diseases affecting haemoglobin. As I write I am still interested in solving the dilemma; it should be easier now because of modern methodology and technology, but the latest I heard was that a lady doctor by the name of Shahnaz (not my wife of course) has gone to work on it in Israel regarding one of the 'lost tribes of Israel'.

Shahnaz had always wanted us to have our own house. I was not interested because I wanted to go back to my place of birth, but women are usually better when it comes to matters of finances and shopping. We found a house in Chandlers Ford and paid the down payment and the rest was on a mortgage. The price of the house, which was detached, was £7000. Our neighbourhood was occupied by English people. Our next-door neighbour had an American wife who worked in my hospital, and I used to give her a lift to the hospital in my car. She said she would pay for regular daily lifts, but I was not used to accepting or expecting payments. One of the doctors in the hospital, seeing me with a blonde lady in a car, told me to accept her offer of payment, otherwise she would think I expected something else, which could never be thought in the case of a neighbour's wife.

One day the neighbour's dog was taken by the police because another neighbour had complained of disturbance through excessive barking. It was not me, because I was fond of dogs and was accustomed to all sorts howling in my village, but I did appreciate that neighbours have rights and police do take action about genuine complaints.

I used to take Mah Muneer to park to play with other children, but I did not know the requirements of toys for children or teaching or reading stories to them. Her mother knew about the day-to-day care because of her urban Iranian background. Shahnaz also made sure MM was admitted to a proper school. Some people are lucky to have responsible wives because mothers are most important in bringing up children. I did not know about MM's high intelligence until we wanted a school-leaving certificate from the Headmistress and she insisted that we should not take MM to Pakistan because she was very intelligent. Shahnaz had to say that Pakistan also needed intelligent people.

Our second child, Mujgan, ('Long Eyelashes'), was born when we were in Southampton. It was bright sunshine, unusual in the month of November in England, when I went to the hospital to see the new arrival. Shahnaz looked in a pensive mood and the baby was asleep. The rays of sun coming through the window made her look very pretty. Ultrasonography was not advanced enough to detect the gender of the foetus, as in later years. Ultrasonography is a painless procedure for the patients, but it has made abortions more prevalent because In Middle Eastern, Iranian, and Pukhtun society, for some reason, male children are much preferred. We were happy to have a child, whether male or female, and Shahnaz, being a loving mother, told me not to disclose whether we were unhappy in any way for not yet producing a male child. And when my parents heard we had had a girl they wrote to me not to worry as sometimes daughters are better and 'God would be kind enough to give us a son one day'. My parents were right. We did have a son one day, and Mujgan proved to be a wonderful daughter. In later life when she was a happily married doctor living in Al-Ain, United Arab Emirates (UAE), which I call the land of plenty as against Pakistan which some people call 'the land of pure', Mujgan called her mother daily to enquire about our wellbeing and provide us with 'five star' facilities whenever we visited them.

Since both Shahnaz and I were working, at times we needed babysitters, and there were two ladies in the neighbourhood, one from Finland, a young blonde lady, and a Greek lady, plump but polite. They used to babysit on payment. The Finnish lady was learning to be an opera singer and sometimes one could hear her voice singing in operatic style.

In England, we did not have to make any special preparations for the arrival of the child. During antenatal care the doctor made sure that the mother visited the facility regularly, thanks to the excellent health care system of the United Kingdom. The British National Health Service (NHS), which is envy of the entire civilized world, was started in the 1940s by a Labour Health Minister, Aneurin Bevan. Sometimes a good idea started by one person is further encouraged by other likeminded people and is sustained, leading to common good. In our case, the British welfare state provided milk daily and some money on a weekly basis without us asking for it. Healthcare was also free. There has always been discussion regarding the system of government, whether socialist or capitalist. Every system has its advantages and drawbacks, but in our case as immigrants and minority, the socialist Labour government was preferred.

Emotions run very high when there is some catastrophe in an immigrant's country of birth. When the serious riots started in the then East Pakistan, Bengalis and West Pakistanis also started demonstrations in their adopted country, the UK. In Southampton, there were not many Bengalis. Since I was one of the active members of the Pakistan Welfare Society, people expected that our society would play a positive role. One Bengali came to me and asked me, 'how about starting a group and naming it WE - W for West Pakistan and E for East Pakistan?' He also told me about the atrocities committed in East Pakistan and the stepmotherly attitude of the Pakistani Mission in London. The Embassy in London was not giving a passport to a Bengali, so he set the embassy on fire. The language issue was the start of the troubles in East Pakistan. Bangla, their language was being replaced by Urdu, a minority language. The rulers of West Pakistan had also removed a popular Governor, Azam Khan, a Pukhtun who had done a lot for East Pakistan and wanted their rightful share for development. Pakistan had earned considerable foreign exchange during the Korean War because of the jute of East Pakistan, but very little was spent in that part of Pakistan. The last straw on the camel's back appeared when the West Pakistanis refused to accept their popular leader Mujib-ur-Rehman and imprisoned him in Durgai fort, not very far from Churchill's picket in Malakand, North West Pakistan. Bangladesh had to come into existence because of the policies of military and civilian leaders. It was emotionally traumatic to see people being hacked to death on television, and to see General 'Tiger' Niazi stripped of his military stars on his shoulder and the spectacle of the abandoned boots of soldiers in the battlefield. It is hoped that one day someone must pay for these cruel injustices.

Southampton University was comparatively new, and the Medical School was newly established in the South of England when I was working in the Nuclear Medicine Department in the 1970s. The founding fathers of the Medical School had made it sure to design the teaching methodologies and curriculum in such a way that the future health givers are taught to cope with the changing world. The teaching was also made more interesting for the students by introducing them to patietnts in the first year of their studies.

The students were introduced to the family physicians' health care work in the community in the first year. The clinical teachers were also involved in teaching the first and second year students, unlike in the past when the basic sciences of Anatomy and Physiology were taught by non-clinical teachers. Southampton University had made sure that they should attract bright people with track record of publication and vision. Professor Acheson and Professor Jack Howell were the two medical professors I remember well. Professor Akhtar, born in Pakistan, was also a teacher and supervisor of PhD students.

One day JC had come to NMD to collect some scans for his inaugural lecture, 'A Breath of Fresh Air', and I overheard him talking to Duncan Ackery saying that two people had applied for a job of professorship, and that one was Wrong and one was Wright. Professor Ralph Wright had accepted the job. JC had a sense of humour, which is thought to be essential if one is supposed to remain humble in dealings with others.

Professor Akhtar, a Pakistani-born scientist, was head of the Biochemistry Department. He supervised many PhD students, many of whom were of Pakistani or Indian origin. He was married to an attractive German lady, Monica, who had learnt how to cook the Indian and Pakistani dishes. Shahnaz and I had the pleasure of trying her delicious dishes in their home not very far from where we lived in Chandlers Ford.

I noticed that Akhtar helped himself to one dish at a time, unlike the rest of us, who mix all the dishes in a plate and then ate it. Once I asked him the reason and he said, 'I want to enjoy the taste of each dish separately because by mixing, the taste of the food changes'. He was of course a biochemist. He was also awarded a Fellowship of the Royal Society (FRS) because of his achievements. Professor Salaam, the Nobel Laureate, was another one at that time who had the distinction of being an FRS. Both these scientists always tried to help Pakistan and other developing countries in their development of science and technology. Professor Salaam died broken-hearted because his country of birth had labelled him a 'Non-Muslim'. This occurred in the late 1960s at time when a secular, intelligent but ambitious and arrogant man was at the helm of affairs in Pakistan. Self-interest and survival played a dominant role in the decision-making of certain people who were at the helm of affairs. Wrong decisions focusing on self-interest and survival and not on merit can cause havoc and even death by hanging, as was the case with the Late Zulfiqar Bhutto, Prime Minister of Pakistan. He had ignored a deserving Pukhtun Army General and appointed General Zia-ul-Haq, whom he thought to be weak and malleable. Another PM, Nawaz Sharif, had to pay with imprisonment and asylum when he had ignored a deserving senior Army general, Ali Kuli Khan, and appointed General Musharaf.

There are a few things which I would like to record for general interest regarding Southampton University and some of the personalities working there. Professor Akhtar held functions in the university on Pakistan Day, the anniversary of the day when Pakistan came into existence. Some dignitaries were invited, and there were no objections from the University authorities, nor did these functions, which could be called parochial events, reflect adversely on the Pakistani students or Dr Akhtar. In Southampton healthy educational activities were encouraged and directed. Once I heard that a person by the name of Dehlavi had been invited and I thought, how could they invite a person from Delhi, which was the capital of India? Being born and educated in schools and colleges in Pakistan, I had been brainwashed like others that India and Indians were enemies. It turned out that Mr. Dehlavi was the High Commissioner of Pakistan in Great Britain. Young children exposed to 'hatred material' in books and schools carry their perceptions into adolescence and adulthood.

Prof. Akhtar told me that he had once been invited to a dinner by one of his relatives who belonged to a religious party in Pakistan. After dinner, his host led the evening prayers, but he did not take part in them. The kindergarten-going child of his relative came to him and said 'Uncle, you did not say prayers'. Dr Akhtar told him, 'Son, I do not say prayers'. The child started crying and went to his father and said, 'Uncle will be going to hell'.

The question of proper education to children arises, but then what is the definition of 'proper education' in terms of peace, progress and prosperity at regional, national and international level? MA had refused to accept an award when Zia-ul-Haq was the martial law Administrator and President of Pakistan, because he said he had executed Mr Bhutto, an elected Prime Minister of Pakistan. Once MA asked me, 'Do you know who has done the greatest harm to your country?' I said 'Pakistan is also your country'. He replied, 'My country is Britain'. I thought of politicians' external foreign agencies and government, as I and others were led to believe by the controlled print and electronic media in Pakistan, but he said, 'The dictators. He did not give reasons and I did not pursue it. I mentioned such a role of the dictators to my friends in the Armed Forces without mentioning whose opinion it was regarding the harm done by the Army, but they would always say that the armed forces had tendered a lot of sacrifices. They believed that service in the armed forces makes one loyal. If one considers European history, countries such as Greece, Portugal and Spain in Western Europe are economically worse off, because of the dictatorial military system of government.

I had been thinking about the factors which make countries less developed. It is probably the suppressive governments and society and weak leadership. One economist, a Nobel Laureate, mentioned that countries which had a free press never suffered from famine. Empowerment of people at grass root level also makes things better. Decentralization has also proved better for a country and its people, but one wonders why these proven methods are not adopted.

After spending some time in the Nuclear Medicine specialty and getting a postgraduate degree from London University, I wanted to go back to the specialty of general medicine, as it was called in the 1970s in the UK, and internal medicine in the USA. The nomenclature has changed since that time; now we have specialties, sub-specialties and super-specialties. A job was advertised which was a training post, especially for those overseas graduates who wanted to go back to their country of birth. This suited me well, so I applied for the job. Dr McDonald gave me a good reference and Dr Royds, a Scot, selected me. I continued to live near Southampton and was commuting to Ashford Hospital, Middlesex, near Heathrow Airport. During the process of selection for the Senior Registrar job I also learnt how to write a recommendation letter from Dr McDonald. He also taught me how to write a report for a lawyer in a legal case; the longer the text, the higher the fee.

Since Heathrow Airport was near the hospital, every six months a rehearsal was held for coping with a major air disaster. The hospital was a big one catering for all the medical specialties except cardiovascular surgery, cases of which were referred to Harefield Hospital in North London, where internationally-renowned cardiac surgeon Magdi Yaquob worked. Part of my duties was to go there once a week to get training in the medical aspects of cardiovascular diseases. During that time consultants were educated to cope with all sorts of diseases to make them 'generalists'. Later this was changed to put the emphasis on narrow fields. In the health care system there is always a need for generalists who need to sort out where to send patients. I am told that 'hospitalists' in the USA play this role.

Ashford Hospital was attached to St. George's Medical School, from which the junior doctors were selected, so all the junior doctors for whom I was responsible were local. They were all efficient, knew their jobs and were intelligent. I do not remember a single instance where I had to tell them that they had not done the tests for patients or had not followed any protocol. Responsibilities and ethics were inculcated in the medical student. There were no formalities.

Many of these doctors had a sense of humour. Once I asked one of the Senior House Officers to prepare one patient for sigmoidoscopy, a procedure for looking through the back passage, which was neither elegant nor painless at that time. The SHO (I forget whether his name was Bob, Peter, Steve or John) said, 'Sher, do you want him to face Mecca or Jerusalem?' He meant the knee/elbow position. I said, 'I would prefer him to face Rome', meaning the lateral position. These rare exchanges about patients were never mentioned in front of them.

One of the SHOs, Bob Milstead, along with his wife Jill and their friend Steve Schey and his girlfriend, visited us later on when I had returned to Peshawar. They took the Silk Route and travelled by road through Afghanistan, crossed the Khyber Pass and reached Peshawar. It was a great pleasure to see them and be their host in Peshawar. Bob and Jill have always been helpful and good friends. While I was writing this I asked them for some pictures of when they had visited Swat about thirty years ago, and they kindly sent me pictures of their visit.

The medical department in Ashford also took part in the initial experiments in CAT scanning (Computerized Axial

Tomography); the name was later changed to CT scanning, which has persisted. EMI's laboratories were near the hospital at that time and were involved in initial experiments. The physicist got a Nobel Prize for his invention, which has made life easier for patients, especially for those suffering from brain disorders. I used to look after the neurology patients and inject air and other material for investigations of brain diseases, and the patients complained of severe pain; we had to keep them lying in bed for twenty-four hours. Thanks to the scientists, especially Western scientists, life for these patients has become easier. I say Western scientists because over the last 900 years there has been no contribution from the Muslims in terms of scientific or technological inventions for humanity at large, as there were in contributions to mathematics, optics, astronomy and so on. The reasons need to be investigated, because there is no dearth of money in the Muslim countries.

My other responsibility was to look after the few beds reserved for neurology patients. The consultant was a tall, elegant physician who was also practising in the world-famous Harley Street in London. His name was Alan Bonham Carter, and he arrived in his Rolls Royce with the plate ABC1. My primary consultant was also a physician nearing retirement who had an interest in rheumatology but was a general physician. He would at times call me to look after his outpatient clinic because he had a 'bad night'. I learned that he had coronary artery disease and sometimes at night he injected himself with a diuretic to ease his shortness of breath. He had a devoted wife and a young secretary. He told me that he had trained her young secretary in everything: how to take dictation, typing and sending letters to the family physicians. I wondered whether he had also trained her in other aspects of biological life, as in those days a sitting government minister had resigned because his secretary had accused him of making her pregnant.

Most of the junior doctors were locals, but in certain specialties, such as anaesthesia, ear, nose and throat and the casualty department (later the name was changed to accident and emergency) were manned by overseas doctors. Dr Jamila Khattak, Dr Shuhrat and Dr Rafiq were from Pakistan. Jamila married Dr Hazrat Bilal and it was in this hospital that they met each other. A photograph of her brother Abbas Khattak, who became Air Chief Marshal of the Pakistan Air Force, was always in her room. When I told Abbas that his picture adorned the desk of his sister, he said, 'it depends on our relations at the time, because sometimes the pictures is put away in the drawer'. The Khattaks belong to a well-known tribe of Pukhtuns and there have been a lot of famous people belonging to this tribe. The warrior Pukhtun poet Khushal Khan belonged to it. Begum Saifullah Khan, sister of Aslam Khattak, was widowed when her children were young, but through her efforts she educated them to become successful businessmen, politicians and doctors. Pukhtun ladies, if educated and not suppressed, can play a positive role in bringing up their own families and contribute in making society as a whole better. Wali Khan, son of Baacha Khan, the preacher of nonviolence among Pukhtuns, said once that he was Pukhtun first and then Muslim. He meant that Pukhtun had been in existence for thousands of years, while Islam came later. However this was exploited by official and non-official elements, leading to deleterious effects on the nonviolence movement among Pukhtuns.

In Ashford Hospital, I was given a room in doctors' quarters where I stayed when I was on night duty. Besides the local British national doctors, there were Arab, Iranian, Indian and Pakistani doctors. As is natural, they listened to their own songs and music. Once a local doctor told me, 'I hear melancholy voices coming from the room of doctor so-and-so'. If one is not used to Arab, Turkish and Iranian music, the classical songs sound as if someone is crying. Western classical music is soft and melodious and those were the days of pop and rock music. The Beatles were at the top. Shirley Bassey, Petula Clark and Dusty Springfield were popular and famous.

While on emergency duty, I was told that our gynaecologist had suffered severe pains in the chest on his way to the hospital and was driving himself there. We were waiting in the casualty department and when he reached it he collapsed, but he was resuscitated because we were all trained in resuscitation. I asked the Senior Nurse to give me lignocaine for injection, as it was the standard treatment for heart irregularity. After injection he started fitting, but he recovered. It turned out that the dose of lignocaine was ten times more than recommended. I had forgotten an important lesson, which was to check the medicine before injecting the patient. One learns from one's mistakes, but doctors' and nurses' mistakes are sometimes too costly.

Another serious episode occurred when I was on emergency duty. A young dental nurse who was pregnant was admitted to the hospital for control of diabetes mellitus. Insulin injections were started and the next day she lost consciousness. We thought it was because of very low sugar - hypoglycemia - which can cause brain damage permanently, but in spite of glucose administration the patient did not recover. Sudden or unexpected deaths had to be investigated by a Coroner's post mortem. My senior consultant, Dr Royds, told me that he would accompany me to the pathologist's examination room because the pathologist was usually not polite to doctors who were junior to him. When the patient's skull was opened during post mortem examination, the veins and major vessels were all affected by thrombosis, which is a very rare complication of pregnancy. I have been talking about Pakhtun culture - 'panah' or protection - but in British culture, and I suppose other cultures, your senior will also come to your rescue.

Ward rounds were led by consultants and each patient was discussed. Most of the patients were elderly. I still recall one elderly lady who was suffering from pneumonia, which is known in medical circles as the 'old man's friend'. She said, 'Please leave me to die. I want to join my husband'. Her husband had recently died. The consultant said that sometimes the wishes of patients had to be considered. Euthanasia has been controversial and will remain so, but the doctor's job is to give life, not to take it.

After the ward round, we all sat in the office and the sister in charge gave us tea or coffee. Politics would be a topic of discussion at times. We had a Labour Government and Wilson was Prime Minister. The senior doctors usually favoured the Conservatives and the consultant used to say 'Labour is ruining the country', but one outspoken younger doctor who happened to have a long red beard favoured the Labour government. I was too much concerned with my future and politics never crossed my mind, but most of the immigrants were in favour of the Labour party. Only recently (2009) a young lady belonging to an immigrant family from Pakistan, Miss Warsi, was chosen as Chairperson of the Conservative Party. The party hierarchy would always be at the side of the young and handsome Prime Minister of the UK on overseas visits, especially to Pakistan.

CHAPTER FOURTEEN

TRAVELS THROUGH EUROPE, TURKEY AND IRAN

As I shall discuss in more detail later, I became more determined to go back to the place where I was born and where I was needed more. I wanted to go by road and was told that the car had to be 'tropicalized', which meant special electrical wiring, double capacity of the water tank, sturdy tyres and a special plate to protect the sump had to be provided. I made enquiries and was told that everything had been standardized and they were not making special measures any more as they used to do in the past.

The Automobile Association (AA) was contacted and they sent me detailed maps, an itinerary and instructions about the dos and don'ts. I was told that in Turkey, Iran and Afghanistan, children might throw stones, but I was to smile and wave at them instead of stopping and scolding them. Shahnaz and I wanted to see the European countries on the way and then spend some time in Iran with Shahnaz's parents in Isfahan. The journey was interesting. We also took Mah Muneer and Mujgan with us. MM was four years old, while Mujgan was not yet two.

The car was ferried from Dover to Calais, as the Channel Tunnel had yet to be built. We had to go by road from France to Belgium. It was a long but interesting journey. I had been under the impression that everyone in Europe could speak English, but to my surprise, very few people knew English and at times we had to face some difficulties because of the language, but people were polite and helpful in general. It took me some time to get used to driving on the right. It was a pleasure to drive on the Autobahn in Germany, because of the wide, smooth multiple lanes. I started the journey in March, when it was still cold in Germany. In Cologne, I saw people wearing shorts at night. I asked one gentleman for directions; he was thinly dressed and could not understand me. It turned out that a festival was held in Cologne in March and people had come out at night dressed in fancy clothes.

I nearly had an accident in Munich because I took the wrong turning, but the busy traffic stopped and I was told to take the correct course. The road from Germany to Austria through the mountains was picturesque and it reminded me of the zigzag roads of Swat. Salzburg was the next stop, where we stayed for the night. It was the skiing season and we could see people travelling in their cars with skiing equipment.

It was in later years that I met a German doctor, Professor Gregor Prindull, in a medical meeting and since that time we have been in contact by phone and letter and periodically meet during conferences. The letter he sent me recently when he learned about my autobiography reads as follows:

Sher is a good friend of mine. Over the years we have met at numerous occasions, mostly in connection with medical conferences. I also met his family and had a delicious dinner at his home.

Sher is a devout Moslem who, a few years ago, went on Hadsh, where I, unfortunately, could not accompany him.

The first time I remember meeting Sher was at a medical conference in Karachi at an evening get-together. Next morning we went on a trip to Mohenjo-daro to be introduced to the ancient Indian culture. I remember Sher being highly interested with a considerable background knowledge.

Another occasion was at a congress in Peshawar, where he had invited me to give a talk. The congress was well organized and all the speakers spent a lovely evening at a historical hotel. I think it also was at that occasion that we made an excursion to the Khyber Pass through which, over the centuries, several western armies had passed on their way to India, with high fatality rates.

Also during that congress, Sher took me to his estate in the Swat Valley. We went by car and on the way visited several of his friends and relatives, including a wedding party.

His estate is located in a beautiful mountainous region. It consists of a small comfortable villa to which a school for children from the neighbourhood is attached. Here I learnt about Sher's social commitments and interest in educating and promoting children and preparing them for a successful life by giving them the necessary basic information including reading, writing, mathematics, and some knowledge of English. I understand that on the basis of this training, a number of them acquired higher education at renowned institutions including universities.

I also visited him at the University Medical School of Peshawar, where he was head of the Department of Clinical Oncology and Radiology. Sher has always had good connections to Western medical institutions and professionals and tried to implement their standards to the treatment of his patients whithin the regional limitations. He also sees numerous patients free of charge and has helped in natural catastrophes such as earthquakes.

We also met twice in Germany. On one occasion, he was invited by the German Red Cross with whom he collaborated. We spent an interesting tourist excursion when we saw the Pergamon Altar in a museum and I again could profit from Sher's excellent knowledge in Indian history, telling interesting stories about different emperors, including Akbar and Ashoka.

The second occasion was an international congress on environmental medicine in Potsdam, where Sher expressed his concerns about environmental hazards in developing countries, especially through the import of western industrial products and achievements of technologies.

In Lucerne, Switzerland, Sher participated in an ESPHI (European Society of Paediatric Haematology/Immunology) congress and, together with his wife, we made an excursion into the beautiful surrounding mountains.

It is good to have permanent friends, especially at an advancing age. *Erhalte Deine vielen Interessen weiterhin und bleib ein so offener, an allem interessierter Freund, wie Du es bist!"*

Border security was not tight in any of the countries up to Austria. No questions were asked regarding why we were travelling, where we were going and which place we were going to stay overnight. When we entered Yugoslavia, which was all one country in the seventies, people appeared different to me from the people in the countries we had crossed so far, both in their facial features as well as their attire. The night was spent in Zagreb. It was a quiet place and the people were friendly. I started noticing uniformed officials in the streets and roads. It was peaceful times in Yugoslavia, which was under Russian influence in the Eastern Bloc during the Cold War. Since I had heard and read about the suppression in the Eastern Bloc, rightly or wrongly, I had become biased and felt suffocated, which made me more careful in my driving on the roads.

As usual, we started early in the morning on our journey from Zagreb. The roads were well built but were single carriageway and had to pass through mountains. On the way we were stopped by a policeman. He personally checked the car lights and brakes and opened the glove compartment. He could not find any fault, but said that we were speeding and wanted the fine in dollars. I did not have any dollars. At this juncture, Mujgan woke up in the back seat and started crying loudly. The police took pity on us but demanded a packet of cigarettes before they finally let us go. The rest of the Journey to Bulgaria was uneventful, but at the border, many questions were asked and our luggage was thoroughly searched for saleable items and for propaganda literature.

Sofia, the capital of Bulgaria, was our next stop for the night. The city was beautiful and clean with wide roads and a combination of old and new buildings. People were friendly but tried to avoid talking to strangers. We spent the night in a nice hotel, where we also met some guests from East Germany. One introduced himself as German. I said, 'East German?' and he laughed.

The next day we reached the Turkish border at Istanbul. For the first time we were welcomed when they saw the green passport. Turkey was the only country in the world where Pakistanis were welcomed. Similarly, while visiting China in later years, I found that Chinese also treated Pakistanis well. Self-made notoriety was probably the reason for the maltreatment of citizens of certain countries. The historical city of Istanbul was not only welcoming, but also looked like home. The historical places such as mosques, churches, palaces, museums and gardens had to wait for our next visit as we were in hurry to reach our first destination Isfahan - Nisfejehan, or half of the world.

On our way to Ankara we crossed the Bosphorus Bridge on the Sea of Marmara. I stopped at the other end of the bridge and looked at the sea and Istanbul. It was a majestic view under a clear sky. The bridge connected the East with the West. I had read that the Turkish Ottoman Empire extended up to Vienna. In later years, when I took a conducted tour of Vienna up the River Danube, a pretty guide took us to an old church. She explained the various paintings on the walls, described the roof and pointed to a painting of Christ. I noticed that in the painting Christ was depicted wearing a turban. I asked 'How come Christ is wearing a turban?' The lady said that the painting had been done during the Turkish time.

On the roads in Turkey, bullock carts, donkey carts, mules and donkeys laden with loads were frequent sights, which added to the feelings of being at home. To reach Iran, we had to cross the Tahir Pass. I did not realize how high it would be. The road had many potholes and it was late in the evening, but we continued our journey up the Tahir Pass and spent the night at a small roadside hotel where the barbecued meat was delicious. The border formalities on the Iranian side were thorough. Reza Shah's portraits were everywhere. I had been warned that they might send a policeman with me to make sure I did not sell the car on the journey to the next border, but the custom authorities stamped my passport with a picture of a motorcar only.

I tried to speak Persian with people, but it was a mixture of Pashtu and Urdu words. The first victim of my half-baked Persian was a person in a petrol station where I wanted to check the air in the tyres. 'Agha hawadari?' I asked him. The man looked at me but did not say anything. I had in fact asked whether the man had gas in his stomach for expulsion through his back passage!

We were in the Azerbaijan region, where people speak Turkish, but in Reza Shah's time the language was discouraged. We spent the night in the capital of Azerbaijan province. Shahnaz took over the language part of our dealings in Iran, as I had already burnt my fingers, so to speak, by saying impolite words to polite people. We headed towards Tehran, where we were to be received by a family whom we had met in England.

The roads in Iran were well paved and we hardly saw any bullock carts and donkeys on the main roads. The image of the 'Shahanshah' - the King of Kings - was everywhere, with portraits and check posts on the highway. We also saw a display of damaged vehicles on the roads, warning drivers not to speed. I also saw for the first time ladies neatly clad in black chadars driving vehicles. A lady's face surrounded by a black scarf looks very attractive, as if it is a framed picture. Some of the ladies were clad in hijabs and looked delicate and attractive. Since I was coming from the West and used to the Western dress of the women, I wished I could see more, and there was lot for the imagination to ponder.

When we reached Tehran we had some difficulty in finding the house of our host, but like Pukhtuns, Iranians would go out of their way to give you directions for your destination and sometimes they would accompany you. Our host Dr Dalil had come out to the main road to receive us. He was an anaesthetist who had come to the UK for training a few years before. He had come to England when one still had to put money in the meters for gas, electricity and to use public toilets. He asked me once, 'Do I have to pay money even to breathe?'

Once we were invited to a restaurant in Southampton and we took him along. When the bill for the food was received everyone started paying their share and he was surprised, because in the Middle East and the East sharing the bill for the food was not done.

DD took us to his home, where greetings were exchanged. Kissing of both cheeks and the hands took place and there was a long exchange of greetings by Shahnaz with the host wife asking about the near and dear ones and even the distant ones. I could only understand the frequent exchange 'fidatshum and Qurbane Shuma'. Persians are used to long exchanges of greetings, even on the telephone, before coming to the point. I was anglicized after spending ten years in England and was used to short sharp greetings and coming to the point.

I noticed a small pond in the courtyard, surrounded by roses. The pond had a fountain. No wonder in Omar Khayyam's poetry one finds red roses sitting near the free-flowing water while sipping wine. Some selected Persian Rubaiyat has been translated by Arbab Hidayatullah, a Ghoria Khel Momand Pukhtun, who handed out the book for free. AH is nearing his nineties and is a retired police officer who reached the top of his rank. When I picked the book up in a bookshop and was about to pay, the sales boy (In Pukhtun Khwa there are no sales girls) said, 'It is free' and I was surprised. Is it age which makes the author generous, or is it his career in the police department, or is it that the Momand Pukhtuns are generous on the whole? There are two types of behavior which I found characteristic of Momands during my medical career. If one Momand falls ill, there are many who would come to help, and Momands do not beg. Some of Omar Khayam's poetry translated by AH is reproduced here:

Look here Mufthee of the town and be the judge
Whether we intoxicated with the cup of wine
Are not better humans, more sensible because
You suck the blood of peasants and we sip wine

I value the cup of wine more than the company of pious men
A gulp of it, indeed, excels in value the kingdom of China
You can find nothing better than wine on this planet
Its bitterness has made thousands of persons sweet

A respectable-looking man addressing
A woman of dubious character said to her,
'What a shame to give up the right path for the wrong one.'
She said, 'I am what I look. Tell me, are you what you look?'

The days and nights as they pass measure your life
Do not throw them away as if you never lived them
Spend them in merriment and enjoy every moment
For days and nights will be there but you will not be

It is the quality of wine to expel conceit from head
It is also its quality to help unravel knotty problems
With a cup of wine Iblees would also have acted wisely
And bowed before Adam and pleased his God.

Coming back to our story of our host in Tehran, in his house I noticed beautiful hand-knotted carpets in the corridor, on the walls and in the rooms. Dr Dalil asked me to make myself comfortable by taking my shoes off, but I was afraid that my shoes and feet might smell because of the long journey. Later on I learned that Iranians take their shoes off inside houses. They also sit on the floor covered by carpets with cushions and take food sitting on the floor, but this habit is fast changing, both in Iran and in Afghanistan. Our host also made us sleep in their bedroom and had moved to a smaller room.

When I woke up the next morning, I noticed a provocative picture of a woman on the wall. Breakfast was served with tea without milk, with cheese, *rehan* and home-cooked bread baked in an earthenware oven. During breakfast I mentioned the nice photograph to Dalil. He immediately told his wife to give the painting to us. Showing admiration for an object is thought to mean that the person wants the object. I remember once a manager of hotel in Peshawar saying how beautiful the turquoise ring his guest from Iran was wearing, and the Iranian removed the gold ring from his finger and handed it to the manager. The Pakistani manager never returned the golden ring. I was careful not to use words of admiration such as 'how charming your wife is', in case the Iranian says '*shumashud*' - all yours.

In informal discussion in England, I often came across the word 'possessive' when there was gossip about girlfriends, wives or husbands. Since I had been brought up in the Pukhtun culture, I wondered how one could tolerate someone talking about one's girlfriend or wife in a sensual or derogatory way.

Spending a few days in Tehran was not only enjoyable but rewarding. Tehran is a modern city with high-rise buildings which give it a superb view of the snow-covered Alborz mountain in the background in the winter. We went to the museum in Tehran, where there were many pieces of ancient and modern interest to see, but I kept on looking at two objects: one was the jewel-studded Peacock Throne and the other was a crown containing one of the largest diamonds in the world. The story goes that when Nadir Shah was returning after his successful campaigns from India, the then king of India, who was Mughal and wearing a regal crown, came out to say good bye to him. Nadir Shah, seeing the ruby and diamond-studded crown, said that one of the traditions of Iranian Kings was to exchange headgear. He took off his headgear, gave it to the King of Delhi and took his crown and put it on his head. That is how the crown has pride of place in the Tehran Museum.

The museum also had rare pieces of the handmade silk carpets which once adorned the palaces of kings and other nobles. Some antique carpets were from the mosques. The restaurants in Tehran had Persian cuisines as well as European. I liked the delicious kebab prepared Iranian style. Pulao Zerishk was also new for me and the different types of bread were not only good to look at but tasty. Fruit and aromatic herbs and vegetables were served before the main meal in the houses, which is medically sound as I did not see many obese people on my first visit. Watermelon was the favourite fruit. The Iranians use the watermelon and other melons to the full and do not waste any part of the fruit. The edible part is eaten, the seeds are dried and then roasted for munching at leisure and the skin is used for feeding the animals, so there is minimum degradation of the environment.

Some Iranian girls were wearing skirts and blouses, while others were neatly clad in black chadars. On a visit to one restaurant, I noticed some young European travellers next to our table. They were sipping *abe jo* - locally-made beer - and some were taking *abe ali*, bottled sour milk with dried wild mint. In the early seventies, alcoholic drinks were freely available and were made in Iran. I also found that Iran was well ahead of the countries of the Middle East in terms of the production of consumer goods. Cars and coaches were manufactured and exported. I found that the standard of living and the quality of life were ahead of the surrounding countries in the Middle East. Was it the emphasis on education and the money well spent by the government, or due to peace and stability? Savak, the intelligence service, was dreaded. Since I was used to the freedom of the West, my host had stop me when I started criticizing the government or the Shah openly. They would say, 'in Iran every second person is a member of Savak'. I did not hear 'loose talk' among the people whom I met in Tehran. Was it because of the strict control of the regime of Shah or the Iranian culture or both? I could not discern. Among Pukhtuns, slanders, negative aspects of a person, family and groups, always come under discussion. 'Ghaibat' - backbiting - is known to be sinful, but only in theory.

I found many young European tourists in Iran, which was the first staging post on their way to Afghanistan, Pakistan, India and Nepal. Someone coined the word Hashish Route for the same route, while more than eight hundred years ago it was called the Silk Route. The route was used for commerce and trade and silk and spices were exchanged for goods made in the West. Travel was not easy, but must have been interesting. People were adventurous and there were no manmade disasters in countries stretching from Italy to India and onward to China.

The Silk Route is known for a remarkable family from Italy who took this route from Italy to China. Marco Polo, a remarkable young Venetian from Italy who travelled in this region when he was in the service of Kublai Khan, the Chinese Emperor, earned a place in the history of the world. He wrote about the people and fauna of the region which is known as the North West Frontier and is now Pakhtunkhwa, when he was in the service of Kublai Khan, King of China. The Marco Polo sheep is named after him.

Marco Polo also mentioned that the ladies in the mountainous region, probably Swat, Dir, Chitral and Gilgit, had big facial features and broad posteriors (buttocks) which the men liked. This is probably the first time that goitre - enlargement of the thyroid gland - was noticed by a keen observer. Iodine deficiency and pollution of drinking water is and was responsible for this disfiguring malady. McCarrison in the nineteenth century, while serving in Gilgit as British doctor, did original studies on the causes of goitre in this region. The village of Koza (lower) Durshkhela, where I was born, is also known for 'Durshkhela Ghawryan' - village of goitre. The story goes that once a newly-married young lad went to sleep with his bride on the third night after their wedding. He had not seen his wife before, as was the custom, and is still is in some cases in the 21st century among the Pukhtuns. As he nervously reached the bed he found his wife lying flat and covered by a quilt. He pulled the quilt off, palpated her face and exclaimed, 'Khkwele, ghatpossmakh de' - what a big, soft face. The answer came 'da me khoghwar de, makh me la bal de' - this is my goitre, my face is different.

In Iran, our destination was Isfahan, which is known as 'Nisfe Jehan' - half of the world. My in-laws lived there and I had not met them before. The journey by road from Tehran was through sparsely-populated dry land, but some hamlets were near the road and I could also see some villages. Unlike the houses in the villages of Swat, these houses had dome-shaped mud roofs. Persians are good at innovation and the roofs minimized the heat in the summer. In some places I saw tall mud-built rounded single structures with multiple holes and thought they were the minarets of mosques. Shahnaz told me they were pigeon houses, built by farmers to collect pigeon droppings for manure for the growing of melons. I also learned about the ancient Persian method of underground water channels, *qanat*, which was used for irrigation purposes.

After driving through the dry and sun-scorched land for some hours, I saw greenery, mountains and turquoise-coloured domes and minarets. It was Isfahan - nisfe Jehan. I could see the smile on Shahnaz's face. I asked her, 'is that Isfahan in the distance?' 'Yes, my Isfahan' she said, and the tears rolled down her face. Isfahan was the birthplace of her mother, who was born in a small village called Saeed Abad near the Zainda Rud - Zainda River. Her name was Ashraful Saadat Qurani and she was proud to be in the long line of descendants from Fatima, daughter of Prophet Muhammad (PBUH). They had a handwritten Koran in the family, written in Kofi script. My father in law, Nasrullah Nasseri, was from the south of Iran, Kuzhistan. He knew fluent Arabic, as do most of the Iranians living in the south. He also knew fluent English, unlike the other Iranians, who preferred French to English, but he worked in the Anglo-Iranian Company and had close formal as well as informal relations with his British colleagues. How did he become 'Nasseri'? He told me that the Shah wanted every family to have a surname. 'I chose Kazarooni, but it was taken by someone else and I had to settle for Nasseri,' he said.

Nasrullah Nasseri was polite, easy-going, frank and free with me; he did not mind sharing with me his relations with girls prior to and after marriage. My mother-in-law was an elegant lady, always well dressed, soft spoken but with an air of authority. When she was young NN used to ask her to stand on his hand and he would lift her up. He was a bodybuilder and wrestler. Persians have been fond of wrestling since ancient times. Rustam and Suhrab wrestlers are mentioned in the epic book Shahnama by Firdoosi. Since the epic book has been translated to many languages including, Pushtu, my father Khaista Dada knew about it and called our son Cyrus, Rustam Khel - belonging to the Rustam tribe.

Driving into Isfahan was exhilarating: it had wide, well-paved roads with trees, flower beds, a river with blue water, old bridges with arches and mountains in the background, making you feel as if you were looking at a painting. I could not wait to see all the places, but the usual formalities of meeting the extended family of Shahnaz and accepting their lavish hospitality had to be dealt with first.

I parked my car in a garage and walked to NN's house in Sheikh Bhai. As I entered the house, I saw a pond, surrounded by rose bushes. The roses were in bloom and were of different colours and shapes. NN was fond of growing roses and was a member of the British Rose Society. He noticed that I took interest in them and quickly named some: Queen Elizabeth, Princess Margaret, Farah and so on. I also heard of the world-famous Persian poet, astronomer and mathematician, Omar Khayyam, in whose poetry roses and wine are frequently mentioned. I had forgotten my oriental etiquette, so I started extending one hand for greetings, but my mother-in-law grabbed me, kissed me on both my cheeks and asked me in Farsi how I had been, how my parents were, how my sisters and brothers were and how were the neighbours. Shahnaz was translating, but I could only understand the frequently-mentioned word *fidutshum*. There is no exact English meaning for it, but the nearest is 'I sacrifice myself for you'.

After the preliminary greetings, I was ushered into a sitting room. The room had Isfahani carpets on the floor and silk carpets on the walls. Once again I forgot to take my shoes off. I noticed that my chair was bigger and higher than the rest. My mother-in-law kept on looking at me very keenly and so did my brother-in-law Dr Hushang Abdali (HA). Later I learned that they had thought I would be dark like the rest of the Indians and Pakistanis they had come across, but they were surprised to find me fair with brown hair and tall with blue eyes. My mother-in-law and brother-in-law had opposed my marriage, but my father-in-law was in favour and completed all the formalities including documentation. Shahnaz had made sure that an attached bathroom was built with the bedroom as Iranians used the public baths where there were elaborate arrangements for male and female sections.

The old religion of Persia was Zoroastrian. Hashmat Furghani was the nephew of my mother-in-law and married to her daughter Shaista, meaning refined lady. He wanted to show me Ateshgah, a burial mound used by the Zoroastrians. We went to see it, climbed the mound and saw the place where dead bodies were left for birds to eat. It was a place for keeping a fire burning for religious purposes. Isfahan has a sizeable population of Armenians living in a separate quarter called Julfa. They were living peacefully and practising their religion without disturbance. Shah Abbas, in whose time Isfahan was the capital, had brought them to that place to build the palaces, mosques and other places, as they were expert in architecture, especially mosaic work.

I was taken to Maiden Shah by NN, who spoke English fluently. In ancient times the place was open. Ali Qapu was chosen as a seat where the king used to sit along with his entourage and watch *chogan* - polo - which originated in Iran and was introduced to India by Mughals. Polo is still played in the northern region of Pakistan, in Gilgit and Chitral. More than a hundred years ago when Lord Curzon visited this area and the Pamir Mountains, he wrote about people playing polo.

Masjid Shah - Mosque of the King - was built during the golden period of Shah Abbas. Blue mosaic tiles decorated the minarets and the multiple domes. The recitations of the prayer leader could be heard in far-off corners of the mosque because of reverberation caused by multiple cupolas. Another mosque in the same area, Masjid Lutfullah, had a single large dome. There were also shops in the large rectangular open space. The shops were selling paintings, handmade silver, metal and wooden artefacts. Next to Maidan Shah was a covered bazaar where foodstuffs, herbs, dried vegetables and some exotic edibles were sold.

In Iran, different regions have cuisines of their own. In Isfahan, Biryani, Gaz and Polao Zerishk there are some specialties. Gaz is a sweet in which there is special gum collected from trees found around Isfahan. NN told me that Gaz is an aphrodisiac. Polaki, another sweet containing zafran, is also supposed to have aphrodisiac properties. I could not tell my father-in-law NN that I did not need an aphrodisiac. I could not prescribe Viagra for NN as it was thirty years earlier before sildenafil, the darling of the people, was discovered.

Isfahanis were fond of picnics and eating food in the parks on the banks of the river. While walking in the park with NN and Hashmat Furghani, we often came across families sitting in the park enjoying kebabs, Palao and dogh - sour milk - and they would say 'be farmayed' - come and join us. I wished at that time that I could go and sit with them on their carpets and partake of their delicious, aromatic and colourful food.

Chahar Bagh (four gardens) was a pleasure, because I could see people sitting on benches munching pistachios, roasted pumpkin and melon seeds. There were four lanes: two were for traffic and the middle two, which had flower beds and benches, were for pedestrians.

In the old quarter of the city there was a large mosque, almost a hundred years old and made of mud bricks. The windows had thin white marble panels for light; there were also basements with thin marble. I wanted to say prayers, but NN said that I had to pray like the shias, otherwise people would mind. Most Iranians belonged to the Shia Muslim sect, but there were also Sunnis, Bhais, Christians and Jews. There was also a church not very far from where we were staying. Dr Pont was a missionary doctor whom I had previously met and who was friendly with my father-in-law.

We stayed in Isfahan for a few days which was most enjoyable as I met courteous people, the food was delicious and the historical and religious sites were breathtaking. There were also lots of European Asian tourists. The few days' stay in Isfahan gave Mah Muneer and Mujgan ample time for orientation, as we had to leave them in Isfahan in the good care of the Ashraful Saadaat Qurani and Nasmullh Nasseri.

The rest of the historical and picturesque places near Isfahan included Persepolis, the tomb of Cyrus the Great. We planned to see the burial places of sages like Sheikh Saadi and Hafiz Sherazi on our next visit. We embarked on our journey towards Afghanistan, but a lot of mountainous areas had to be covered before reaching the border. The Automobile Association had supplied me with all the details regarding the route, as well as what to expect on the road and at the borders. We travelled in a Ford Cortina towards Tehran, up a zigzag road through the Alborz mountains and then descended to the plains on the other side. Our aim was to reach the religious city of Mashhad, where I wanted to see the Mausoleum of Imam Raza.

On the way to Mashhad, we spent our first night in a small town somewhere as we descended the Alborz Mountains. I do not remember the name, but it was probably Abe Ali. We reached Mashhad the following night. I had heard the name of Mashhad, as it was famous for its religious significance. It is the holy city for the Shia sect. The literal meaning of Mashhad is martyrdom. The eighth Imam, Imam Raza, has a shrine which is visited by millions of Muslims each year. In the morning I went to see it. Near the shrine is a large well-built mosque, Masjid Goharshad. It was built by the wife of Shah Rukh, king at one time. There were lots of people from all parts of the Muslim world. The shrine had a gold-coloured protective fence all around. Shahnaz told me it was pure gold. There were guards surrounding the shrine to prevent the devotees from touching and kissing it. The devotees were crying as they were going round the shrine. I stood, watched and also talked to some Pukhtuns, as Pukhtuns can easily be recognized by their dress, headgear and style of conversation. The ones I talked to were from Parachinar on the North West Frontier of Pakistan.

Mashhad has also been the capital of Persia in the past, during the time of King Nadir Shah Afshar and a King from the Abbasid period. A Pukhtun, Ahmad Shah Durrani (Abdali), also ruled over it for a brief time. Mashhad also boasts some great people, writers, poets, scientists and physicians who were either born or buried there. Imam Ghazali lived there and Sufism is said to have started and thrived there. I did not have the time to visit the library containing old manuscripts. In Afghanistan and India books were written in Persian. In my birthplace, Swat, Persian was taught in the schools. Letters and legal documents were written in Persian.

After spending a day in Mashhad, we started travelling towards the border. For the Iranians, the formalities of leaving the country were tough at that time. Reza Shah had strict internal control due to his well-organized and dreaded intelligence service, Savak. Dictators depend on and give absolute powers to the 'intelligence services' and they become untouchables, especially in third-world countries. The border police would scrutinize the Iranians leaving the country. They had to submit their passports in Tehran before departure, which were to be given to them at the border. Shahnaz's passport was delayed and we had to wait for another 24 hours. The night was spent in the border town. Iran had places for guests to stay even in the villages, which were clean and tidy as cleanliness and tidiness are instilled in Iranians from childhood. Fortunately the passport was delivered when we went to see the immigration officer. The customs made sure that we were travelling in the same car we had entered Iran in. After crossing 'no man's land' we entered the Islam Qila of Afghanistan.

CHAPTER FIFTEEN

AFGHANISTAN

The immigration personnel on the Afghan side treated us courteously: they stamped the passports and let us enter without searching the car or our luggage. As we finished the usual formalities, I noticed a collection of chappals - shoes - with opened soles. These were shoes which had been used by the smugglers of heroine, hashish and opium. No wonder the route was called the 'Hashish Route' in the seventies. The smugglers of contraband items invent and discover ingenious ways of smuggling and making a quick buck. On my return journey to London by road, the doors and seats of my car were also stripped at the Turkish Bulgarian border to make sure that I was not hiding hashish or heroin in the car's compartments.

As we drove out of the customs area, we were greeted by Haroon Khan, my maternal uncle (stepbrother of my mother) and my younger brother Shad Mohammad Khan, whose name I had changed from Shada Nosh. Haroon Khan quickly distributed money among the people who were standing nearby. The Pukhtun custom is to give away alms in the form of coins or notes, either by throwing them over or twirling them around the head. The practice of putting money on the head to be taken by someone has persisted to this day. This is usually more common in marriage ceremonies, where money is put on a man's face by his friend and a gyrating female dancer comes and takes away the money, at times pinching or slapping the cheek. The person pinched becomes happy because the custom does not allow him to join the dancing girl. A pinch or slap is as close as he can get to her.

As we drove towards Herat town, I found the roads well paved and saw graceful camels carrying loads and also bearded Afghanis and their ladies and children wearing multi-coloured dresses with metal coins sewn to them. I was struck by the similarity between Herat and Isfahan. Like Isfahan the roads were well maintained with rows of trees on the roadside. I could also see blue minarets and domes. Later I learned that Herat had been a part of Persia from the time of the first Persian Empire in the world during the rule of Cyrus the Great. Herat was fought over by different dynasties because it was strategically placed militarily and politically and was a trade route to Middle East, Europe, Russia, Central Asian States, China and India. It was also called the Jewel of Khurasan. The important developments in terms of building, arts and religious places were during the Saffavid times of Shah Abbas the Great. The city was finally annexed to the Durrani Kingdom of Afghanistan by a benevolent Pukhtun King Ahmad Shah Durrani (Abdali), and remains so to this day. In the spoken languages, I discerned traces of the Persian language in the seventies. The majority in the suburbs of Mashhad spoke a dialect of Persian. Household goods were imported from Iran and the food was also similar. I expected to find many people speaking Pashto. I did not find this, but I did find people with Chinese faces. Most of the people were Tajiks. Among the minorities were Pushtuns, Hazaras, Uzbeks and Turkomans. Sunni Muslims were in the majority, but there was also a church in Herat and the relics of the Zoroastrians' fire temple.

We stayed in a hotel which was clean, and the service was reasonable. The workers were all Persian or Dari speaking, as it was called in Afghanistan. Pukhtuns are generally not good workers when it involves cleaning, cooking and serving. They are good at hard work such as construction work and security work as they can be trusted and dependable in these occupations. I asked for a typical Herati speciality for food and they served rice in a large dish with ghee and cream of milk, dried and powdered cheese and some brown-coloured powdered herbs. The food was delicious. In the morning, breakfast was served with fresh baked bread, cheese, fresh fruit and tea without milk. In Iran and Dari-speaking areas of Afghanistan, tea is served without milk unless one asks for it.

In the morning in Herat I made sure that the petrol tank was full and I had some additional petrol in a jerry can. AA had given us instructions that petrol stations were only found in the towns and cities. The other written instructions were that we were not to stop on the road in sparsely-populated areas of Afghanistan.

The road towards Kandahar was wide and paved, but the colour looked different: it was cement coloured rather than tan coloured. I learned that the road from Herat to Kabul was built by the Russians. They had made concrete slabs which were transported to Afghanistan. They were then joined and spread on the roads. One could see the joints between the slabs on the road. In the sixties and seventies, Russia, the USA, Europe and other countries like Japan wanted to have influence over Afghanistan. Students would study in Russia and armed forces personnel were usually sent for training. The universities in

Kabul were infiltrated by the so-called right wing and left wing groups. The superpowers' rivalries and infiltration by the secret service groups of the neighbouring countries, as well as the superpowers, had devastating effects on Afghanistan and its people in later years.

While travelling on the roads one hardly saw motor vehicles, but camels, ponies, mules and donkeys could be seen, along with sheep on their way to summer pastures. The Ahmadzai tribe travel with their possessions, lock, stock and barrel. There were some checkpoints, but they only asked for 'vaccination' and we had been instructed what to do: all one had to do was to show a vaccination certificate. They would accept it because they could not read English.

The journey was smooth until we got near Kandahar, when we were stopped at the checkpoint. They wanted to search the car, and there were delaying tactics. An army Jeep stopped, from which a sturdy officer stepped out, and seeing us being unnecessarily detained, he told off the persons manning the checkpoint and told us not to worry as they were stupid Afghanis. I was surprised at him calling another Afghan stupid. He actually meant Pushtuns. It was later that I learned that Dari-speaking Tajiks were literate, while the literacy rate in Pushtuns was very low. There was also rivalry between Tajiks and Pushtuns.

Short of Kandahar City, I stopped near the river, which, unlike the Swat River, was flowing quietly. The water was bluish and clean, not muddy as I had expected. I was told that a big international airport was to be built in Farah Province near Kandahar. The USA was building an airport, while the Russians were engaged in building the infrastructure north of Kandahar.

As we got nearer to Kandahar, I started noticing people wearing turbans; they looked tall and the majority were bearded.

They were chatting in a familiar language to my ears - Pushto - but in a different dialect. The western Pukhtuns speak the softer dialect of Pashto, while the eastern Pukhtuns speak the harder dialect, but standard written Pashto is supposed to be Yusufzai Pukhto.

When we reached Kandahar, we went straight to a Government-run hotel which had all the facilities, including alcoholic drinks. At night time we were told to go to a restaurant called Gulgula, which was supposed to serve Afghani food. There were young male and female foreigners there in a happy mood. They were smoking and I could smell the aroma of hashish. The food consisted of Kabuli Palao, tikka and kebaabs. Fresh pomegranate juice was also served. Kandahar is famous for fruits such as pomegranates, apricots and melons. The fruits are tasty as well as colourful, especially the apricots, which are probably the best in the world for colour and taste. The pomegranate groves surrounding Kandahar city served as shelter for the Mujaheed during the Russian period and the NATO-led battles in later years. Kandahar (or Qandahar) has many historical places, but I was interested in two sites; one was the mausoleum of Ahmad Shah Durrani (Abdali) and the another was Ashoka. According to archaeologists, the city and surrounding area is seven thousand years old and has been described by N. Dupree as follows:

'Early peasant farming villages came into existence in Afghanistan ca. 5000 B.C., or 7000 years ago. Deh Morasi Ghundai, the first prehistoric site to be excavated in Afghanistan, lies 27 km (17 m.) southwest of Kandahar (Dupree, 1951). Another Bronze Age village mound site with multi-roomed mud-brick buildings dating from the same period sits nearby at Said Qala (J. Shaffer, 1970). Second millennium B.C. Bronze Age pottery, copper and bronze horse trappings and stone seals were found in the lowermost levels in the nearby cave called Shamshir Ghar (Dupree, 1950). In the Seistan, southwest of these Kandahar sites, two teams of American archaeologists discovered sites relating to the 2nd millennium B.C. (G. Dales, University Museum, University of Pennsylvania, 1969, 1971; W, Trousdale, Smithsonian Institution, 1971 - 76). Stylistically the finds from Deh Morasi and Said Qala tie in with those of pre-Indus Valley sites and with those of comparable age on the Iranian Plateau and in Central Asia, indicating cultural contacts during this very early age.'

The word Kandahar, according to various sources, is derived from the Persian words 'Kand' meaning candy and 'Har' meaning necklace. Others say it is akin to Gandahara, which was a civilization stretching from the Hindu Kush to Suleiman Mountains where the majority of Pukhtuns or Pushtuns were settled. The Pactya, which was a Persian tribe during the time of Cyrus the Great, settled here. The Pukhtun word and the Pukhtun ancestry are probably derived from the Pactye tribe. Alexander called the city Alexandria and it remained the capital of successive dynasties. The region was ruled by the Iranian Saffavid dynasty until Mirwais, the chief of the Ghalji Pushtun tribe, defeated them and extended his kingdom right up to Isfahan. Mirwais Ghalji, or Hotak, is known as the George Washington of Afghanis. Kandahar was also a seat of power during the Kingdom of Ahmad Shah Durrani (Abdali), whose kingdom extended from India to Iran. Some people who belong to the Bakhtiari tribe, living in the mountains (Loristan) near Isfahan, still call themselves Khans and Abdalis. They are fond of guns and horses like Pushtuns and are freedom-loving people.

We went to see the Ahmad Shah Durrani Mausoleum, an impressive place with arches, domes and minarets. Blue tiles with floral patterns decorated the inside as well as the walls and pillars. Quranic verses were written on the walls in the building.

There were some European visitors, and I also met Qazi Hussain Ahmad (QHA) who was travelling with Khanzada, a tall handsome person who had studied in Jehanzeb college, Swat, and belonged to a well-to-do family from the Attock Area in Punjab. I found QHA a soft-spoken man with a beard. He reminded me of Maulana Maudoodi, whom I had met in London in 1968 through a friend, Sher Afzal Khan. I did not know that QHA belonged to Jumaat Islami (JI), but he became Amir (Head JI), and an effective one, in later years.

Later I realized that religious people can also have a sense of humour. QHA was in hospital because of his heart problem when he was being wheeled out after discharge, and I went to him and said 'Qazi Sahib gunahgarstataposkare de' - The sinner (I) had also been asking about your health. His answer was 'da gonahgaranodua hum gableegi' - the prayers of sinners are also granted.

Next to the Mausoleum was a Friday mosque, where the King and other government functionaries used to offer their Friday prayers. During Taliban rule Kandahar was also the capital. My younger brother, Kamal Khan Paindakhel, was popularly known as Maulana Kamal because of his religious education in Rawind, and later, as a prayer leader in Dewsbury, England. He owned a madrassa in Nottingham and Manchester and went to Kandahar during Mullah Umar's time. He was invited to address the Friday congregation, which he did. Mullah Umar then invited him to join the Taliban in their work for the people and Islam. Probably the reason was that Kamal had lived in the UK and was also well versed in Islamic education, and would be able to convince Westerners that the Taliban were not so bad as they were presented by the media.

When I was in charge of a 'hospital' in Peshawar, the Taliban Health Minister used to visit the hospital and send patients. He was a soft-spoken, polite man who did not expect any special protocol. He mentioned that they were going to import machinery for agriculture. I handed him a plan for building facilities through the International Atomic Energy Agency (IAEA) in Vienna, but he expressed his doubts about the acceptance of the project because of the adverse propaganda in the West.

In later years when CNN was making a documentary called 'In The Shadow', I learned that Osama bin Laden either used to live or have an office opposite our house in the university town. Medical people are usually, like myself, too immersed in their routine day work to take notice of other people. However, the patients tell them their secrets, due to the nature of their job, medical and others, which people of my profession are not supposed to divulge. But greed and jealousy are common human passions and healthcare personnel have been used by the spy agencies to gather information, as occurred in the hunt for Bin Laden, where vaccination against polio was used as a ruse to find him. This later led to retribution against innocent health workers. Similarly, during the siege of Chitral in 1895, McNair acted as a medical doctor, travelling up the Malakand pass through Dir State to figure out the route through which relief could be sent. McNair's description of the prevalence of diseases and observations during that period are interesting.

In Kandahar, I also wanted to see the Ashoka Relic. Kandahar had been important politically, commercially and strategically through the ages. Not only had Buddhism spread to South East Asia through Afghanistan, but the Buddhist Maurian Emperor Ashoka had built a monument with inscriptions in Greek and Armiac which is present to this day. Even in 21st century it is an important base for NATO and ISAF forces. The Taliban have their adherents in the city as well as the surrounding Pushtun areas. They occasionally make their presence felt by assassinations and suicide bombings.

It was during the reign of Emperor Ahmad Shah Durrani that relative peace and stability had come to the region and his capital Kandahar. He made a nation of Pushtuns and Afghanistan by conciliation and skilful consultation. Revenge jealousy is built into the psyche of Pushtuns, but at the same time nanawate - conciliation - and jirga - consultation - are also built into the culture of Pushtuns. Unfortunately, vested interests in Afghanistan from internal as well as external countries have used 'divide and rule', and favored revenge over conciliation, leading to devastating effects in Afghanistan.

On my journey towards the East, I came across many interesting cities, among which Esfahan had special significance as I am emotionally attached to it; it is also considered 'Nisfe Jehan' - half of the word. The other city was Kandahar, where I saw people attired in familiar dress. They were tall, well-built and handsome people speaking in my mother tongue.

Germany and Turkey were the countries where I felt happiest during my short journey by car. I had heard since my childhood sitting in a hujra that Germans are brave people and are related to Pukhtuns. Without knowing the pros and cons of the Second World War, the people sitting in the hujra in my village would celebrate any victory by the Germans. We were greeted by the Turkish immigration people and they treated us well for the first time during our journey from London to Istanbul.

From Kandahar, our next stop was Kabul. When we reached the city, I found it a busy place. I could see ladies wearing skirts and some were wearing 'hot pants'. There were also ladies with black burqas (veil) and 'shuttlecock' burqas in white and blue. The men were wearing all sorts of clothes, from pants to baggy trousers. Turbans and Karakul caps were the headgears of adults, while the younger ones were bare headed, some with long hair and some with crew cuts.

We stayed in the Kabul Hotel, where the rooms were spacious, the service was efficient and the food was delicious. There was live music in the dining room and the Rubab, the string instrument of Pushtuns, and the harmonium were being played. The songs were in Dari and Pashto. The Dari songs were from Iran, sung by Gugush and Haida. The Pasto songs depicted the valour of Afghans and the nomadic life, such as 'Bibi Sherini' which also became popular in neighbouring countries later on. Foreign guests from Europe, Iran and the USA would start dancing on the floor to the faster music. I heard the word *loyshae*, a Pashto word meaning 'may you live long'. Alcoholic drinks were freely available.

Historically, Kabul was a part of the Persian Empire. The Macedonian Alexander also passed through this area, but like Kandahar, which was named after Alexander, Kabul has not been mentioned by the historian; probably it was a small place in 330 BC. The son of Ahmad Shah Abdali made it the capital and it has remained so to the present day. Zahir Shah was the king. One could see development in the city and there was peace. I do not remember, when we stayed in Kabul in the seventies, people carrying guns or the sound of gunshots at night. People could walk at night without fear of being molested, and we walked in the streets late at night.

We were told to see the Babur gardens before leaving Kabul. They were well planned, with shady trees, flowers and rose gardens. People were picnicking and there was an atmosphere of harmony and peace. We went to see the Babur grave and offered *dua*. Babur established the Mogul empire and Kabul as its capital before the Delhi Sultanate. He had written a lot about Kabul, the tribes living there, the languages spoken and the natural beauty. He wanted to be buried in Kabul and his wife made sure that his remains were brought there from Agra, India.

After spending some time in Kabul, which was enjoyable

because of the food, the familiar language and the people dressed in familiar clothes, we embarked on our journey towards Peshawar through Jalalabad and the Khyber Pass.

The road was well paved and I was told that it had been built by the Japanese. In the 1970s some foreign governments wanted to help the people in a peaceful way without giving them the feeling that they were occupying forces. The road passed through mountains and lush green fields, and the yellow flowers of mustard were seen everywhere. We stopped in Jalalabad for lunch and found that everyone spoke Pashto. I could also see turban wearing Sikhs in some of the shops and streets. The Sikhs spoke fluent Pashto, but some also spoke Urdu. Most of the population of Jalalabad are Sunni Muslims, and later I learned that Ahmad Shah Abdali made Jalalabad his base for conquests. He consolidated his empire some 200 years ago before the division of India and birth of Pakistan.

In the restaurants, there were tourists sitting and smoking and they were in a happy mood. I asked a worker in the hotel whether there were places worth seeing, and he mentioned the mausoleums of Amanullah Khan and Wazir Akbar Khan. Amanullah Khan wanted the development of Afghanistan when he took over as Amir in 1919. He wanted to establish railways, electricity, education and the emancipation of women. Germany and France were interested in his plans, but he did not succeed because of internal jealousies and external vested interests.

Wazir Akbar Khan belonged to the Momand tribe. During his time in government he sent families from Nangarhar province, gave them government land and settled them in other parts of Afghanistan, so one can find Pushtun families in Herat, Balkh, Mazar-e-Sharif and other parts.

In the 70s Kabul and the border areas were peaceful, but in the 19th century, during the three Anglo-Afghan wars, the region saw atrocities, hand-to-hand fighting and massacres. In the second Afghan war thousands of British and Indian forces were slain, and only one medical doctor survived to tell the story. Paintings show him riding a horse and crossing to British India. It was in later years when I was practising medicine that a patient by the name of Zareshk Momand came to see me from Afghanistan. On his follow-up visit I learned that he was a Pashto poet, and he presented me a page of his poetry.

د مخلوق خدمت کښې ښته د خدای رضا
په اخلاص سره خدمت کړې د هر چا

هر بیمار سره په ورونر تندې غېږ بوي
خنده روپا ترې پینشته کړې بیا بیا

دیر په غور معاینات د هر بیمار کړې
په نسخه يې نه ماتیږي د چا ملا

ټول صفات د داکټری په تا کښې وینم
خدای دې مه، بدر نکوه تر ابدا

صفت نه، کرم حقیقت والیم دروغ نا
اې داکټر شیر محمد خانا حق کښې ستا

کامیاب او آباد اوسې اخلاص منده
ستا دارو دې هر بیمار ناشي شفا

د برخورد نه، دې راضي زیرک شاعر دې
دا رحمان هسپتال ښه، ښکارې په تا

شاعر: زیرک (بر خور افغانستان)

God is pleased if you help people,
If patients are addressed with smiling face,
If every patient is investigated thoroughly,
If your prescriptions are not "back breaking"- not expensive
In you I see all the qualities of a good doctor.
Oh God keep him away from "bad time".
I am not praising him, I am saying the facts and not telling lies.
I wish you success, o selfless man.
I wish your medicine to cure every patient
From "Bar Khurd" Zeerak poet is satisfied with you.
The hospital where you are working should be proud of you.

CHAPTER SIXTEEN

RETURN TO PAKISTAN

☪

Sightseeing in Jalalabad had to wait for the next time, as we were in a hurry to reach the border before nightfall. The border formalities were neither strict nor thorough. In some countries you have to use contacts to get things done or grease palms, but in my case Dr Hazrat Bilal, the elder brother of Dr Ahmad Hilal and a resourceful person, had facilitated the customs and immigration formalities. Hospitality and green tea were offered to us by the officials. I had to make sure that my foreign wife was made to feel at home at every stage. Leaving her job in the UK, a country which is a welfare state and where our two children were born, was a big undertaking on the part of Shahnaz, but sacrifice is built into the culture of Persians.

In the 1970s the borders were geared to tourism. We found a small hotel where we were greeted by a smart manager, Mohammad Ali, from Parachinar. We found the place clean and tidy. The service was efficient, and I had to tell my wife that we

Pakistanis are not that bad if we try. Near the hotel and on the roadside, people were asking if we wanted to exchange foreign money for rupees. One pound sterling was equivalent to 16 rupees, and a dollar was worth nine rupees at that time. After taking tea and resting, we embarked on the route through which Alexander the Great, Mahmud Gaznavi, Babar and Ahmad Shah Abdali had gone to India with their armies on horseback, with camels, mules and donkeys and on foot. Most of the invasions had been from Afghanistan to India, but Buddhism had spread from the opposite side, from India to Southeast Asia through the Khyber Pass. At one time the 'Hippy trail' from Europe to India and Nepal was through the Khyber Pass.

The Khyber Pass and the surrounding area were in the control of Ranjith Singh until the British defeated them and took over the region, which witnessed three Afghan wars. In later years the pass was used to transport materials for NATO and ISAF forces stationed in Afghanistan. In the late 1960s there was a television comedy series in the UK called 'Up the Khyber Pass'. There were some derogatory clips, and some English people who had served on the North West frontier objected to it, so the series was discontinued. Our journey was of course not 'up the Khyber Pass' but down it. On the roadside, there were the insignia of the British Indian forces and in some places concrete boulders remained as obstacles to Russian tanks during the 'Great Game Time'. In the 1930s the British had built the railway for quick transportation through the mountains by multiple tunnels, a marvellous feat of engineering. The railway track and the tunnels are still intact, but they are not used because of mismanagement by the Railway Ministry of Pakistan.

I had seen the multi-coloured paintings and decorations on buses and trucks by Pushtuns before I went to England, but in England people talked about the arts, holidays, good food and visits to art galleries. During my childhood when I saw air guns, rifles and fights between both humans and animals, I started thinking that there was more to living than working, studying, passing examinations and copulation. So my aesthetic sense started developing when I was in Great Britain. I saw that the trucks and buses from Kabul to Peshawar through the Khyber Pass had colourful paintings depicting forest scenes, rivers, birds, fountains and so on, and paintings of Indian film stars and Pakistani film actresses such as Madhu Bala, Meena Kumari, Noorjehan and Sabiha. The pictures showed only busts; buttocks were not shown. The Sufi poetry of Rehman Baba, Khushal Khan, Tappes and sometimes humorous writings were also written on the buses. Some are reproduced below:

Kar da gulu ka che seema de gulzar shi
Azghi ma kara pa khpu ke bade khar she.
"Sow flowers that your surroundings become a garden
Don't sow thorns, for they will prick your own feet".

Translation by Robert Sampson and Momin Khan from Rahman Baba's poetry. Rahman Baba's themes were romantic, spiritual, and goodness toward all mankind.

Che llzzat ye da sro shoondo uee moundale
Nore meene da sharabo pa jam na ke
"How wonderful the taste of lips so tender and so fine
It banishes all craving for the sparkle of red wine".

Be la deedana ba rogh na sham
Ka pa dalo dalo de rashi kaghazoone
"Your message after message, your letter after letter.
Is nothing to compare with a moment spent together".

Translation of tappas by Arbab Hidayatullah, A Pakhtun Khan over ninety years old, who is a fine retired Police Officer still active mentally and physically.

Pre me salaam de, Jurgi che pendi she.
"I salute those who assemble for together for consultation – Pukhtun Jirga".

Da Afghan pa nang me watrale tora
Nangiale da zamane khushal khattak yum.
"I fought with sword in my hand for protecting the honour and dignity of Afghans.
I am Khushal Khattak, the Nangyal (hero) of the era".
Khushal Khan Khattak.

Translation by Ghani Khan Khattak.

Las pa walare rechaper ka,
Tar kenasto gora sa pekhweena.
"Embrace me while I am standing.
I do not know what is going to happen while I start sitting".

Khudaya be nanga zoa rona kre,
ka pa deedan pase ye rande pa stargo shama
"I do not wish to see a son who has no honour,
even if I lose my sight wishing to see him".

Tappas translated by Salma Shaheen PhD, Former Director of Pushto Academy.

Khpale Khula Wahali Shparus
"Their mouths have destroyed sixteen people."

The explanation by Leonard N. Bartlotti is as follows:

This reminds one of the saying "careless talk costs lives", first used on posters in World War I as an admonition against talking too freely in a time of war, lest a spy was listening who could gain information that would cost lives. A similar American saying was popular during World War II, "Loose lips sink ships". In Pashtun culture, where men live and die for honour, lies, gossip and malicious rumours can destroy reputations and lead to unending and costly blood feuds.

Khattak ba zaredo na ka
dabal ghamona ye na kaweli.
"Khattak would never have become old
Had he not been worrying about the problems of others".

From the book "Rohi Mataluna" by Mohammad Nawaz Tair and Thomas C. Edwards.

Pa "overtake" (using the English word) me khafa na she.
Nawakhta keegi da jana deeden la zama.
"Do not be angry if I overtake you on the road.
I am going to see my beloved and it is getting late".

Anonymous.

We reached the Rural Academy at Peshawar in the evening, passing through Ali Masjid, the narrowest part of the Khyber Pass, Jamrud Fort and Islamia College, which was started by the British and had some fine educationalists from Great Britain. Some of the names are still on the hostels and in the college and have not been erased, as in other places. Pushtuns do remember people who have done collective good for them.

A place was reserved for us in the guestrooms in the Rural Academy by the resourceful brother of my friend Dr Hilal Ahmed. I wanted to make sure that my wife was made comfortable and was introduced to the good parts of Pukhtun life. The Director of the Rural Academy was Shoab Sultan Khan, who was born, bred and educated in India but had migrated to Pakistan. He was a fine, quiet, intelligent and cultured person whom I remembered from my college days in Swat. The then principal of Jehanzeb College, Hafiz Usman, brought in bright lecturerers, and he was one of them. The principal, an educationalist and the teacher of the Wali of Swat, was given a free hand to hire intelligent and educated teachers and he recruited from all over the country.

The Rural Academy was meant for the development of the rural areas, because in resource-poor countries, the majority of people live in these areas. The idea was that the development of rural areas would alleviate poverty and the literacy rate would increase. Environmental degradation would be halted. Akhtar Khan was the person who convinced the rulers of Pakistan at that time of the desirability of these rural academies in Pakistan. Ayub Khan was at the helm of affairs. He was a military dictator but had the welfare of the common man close to his heart. He also had some good people in his close circle, and there was economic development. Relations with our powerful neighbour China were initiated, improved and cemented.

Pakistan has always been under the influence of the USA and Western camp, and relations between the USA and China were partly facilitated through the efforts of Pakistan when Henry Kissinger travelled to Beijing from Islamabad. The founder of the Rural Academy, Akhtar Khan (Akhtar means the Eid festival when people are happy and hearty and gifts are exchanged as at Christmas), wanted the rural populations to be prosperous. He had an idea, but ideas do not work unless and until one learns how to implement them, which means a lot of effort and patience. Judging by the work he did in what was then East Pakistan and West Pakistan, Akhtar Khan had altruism, was successful and is remembered. The impact of this work had been good for the people, but sustainability in every work is important, as all good projects in developing countries initiated by Europe, the USA and even Japan and China fizzle out after a while because little attention is paid to sustainability.

After spending the night in a well-run guest house in the Rural Academy, I went to the medical college to find out about the availability of jobs. i thought i was well qualified and experienced, and they would welcome me with open arms. I was accustomed to the British system, where merit was considered first by and large, but they had also subtle ways of rejecting people if they wanted to. I had written to the college, but there was no answer. I had written to Prof. Gardezy, who was married to an English woman, and I thought he would be helpful. One of my consultants in the UK knew Prof. Tariq Nishtar, and I had also written to him. What I had not realized was that contacts, political pressure, gifts, friendship, relations and 'greasing the palm' matter more than merit. My request for a job fell on deaf ears.

When I met Tariq Nishtar, he remembered that I had written to him. A nurse working in St Ann's Hospital had once asked me where I was from and I had told her. She said Tariq also came from that area. 'He was nice but skinny', she said. I was dejected because I had to get a job, since I had to support my wife and two children, who would not be able to live in a remote village in Upper Swat where there were no proper educational facilities.

Then as I was coming out of the medical college, two things happened. One was that I saw my name on a board meant for all those who had topped the exams in various years, which made me happy because of my achievement. The second was that I met Dr Shams, an intelligent doctor, a bearded man who could speak Pashto with a Hazara accent. He greeted me warmly and sensed that I was unhappy. I told him the story of my hunt for a job. He told me to go to see the chairman of the Pakistan Atomic Energy Commission (PAEC) in Islamabad, as they were going to build an atomic energy medical centre next to the medical college. I also met Dr Amjad Hussain, who was working in the surgical department. He told me not to return and spoke about the stepmotherly attitude in the college towards qualified, experienced doctors. He was bitter about his seniors, Dr Feroz Shah and Dr Kabir in the surgical department. They had lucrative private practices and probably did not want competition. In my case on the medical side, the established doctors probably also did not want rivals in private practice. It was said that Dr Shah had done his own vasectomy when he was in England. He eventually was married to a fine lady, Dr Mussarat from the city of Peshawar, but did not have children. Dr Mussarat, who was younger than he was, looked after him very well in his old age.

Dr Kabir was an intelligent and clever doctor who succeeded in establishing a lucrative practice for himself; he established the first medical college in Peshawar and then a university in the private sector. Local connections (political and business) in Peshawar, national connections such as in Karachi where he he was able to make use of his medical education, cleverness and futuristic thinking without confronting the powers that were; all these factors enabled him to achieve what he wanted for the benefit of his own family and other people.

Dr Amjad Hussain had very good intentions when he returned to Peshawar along with his American wife. He wanted to contribute to his profession of cardiovascular surgery, to medical education and to the welfare of the people in general.

A combination of adverse circumstances and frustration with his working environment made him leave for 'the country of opportunity', the USA. It is said that if you have talent, then the sky is the limit there. Dr Hussain achieved what he wanted to do in terms of professional excellence in Toledo, Ohio, in social status and in his appetite for writing, since he writes a regular column for the local newspaper and has published books. He has of course not forgotten the place where he was born and bred. His regular annual visits to Peshawar, his lectures in his alma mater and his meetings with dignitaries are given prominence in the print and electronic media.

I knew him from our college football days. I was the goalkeeper and he was the defender. When he could not prevent the ball getting past him he would shout at me 'stop the ball, stop the ball!' but there would invariably be a goal. With a tinge of arrogance he would say it was the goalkeeper's fault. As they say, Pushtuns are generous but jealous. So it was probably his ambition, straightforwardness and lack of humility of which his seniors in the surgical department at Lady Reading Hospital had become jealous.

In 1972 Bhutto had called a meeting in Multan of the scientists of the Pakistan Atomic Energy Commission (PAEC) vis-à-vis nuclear weapons and other uses of atomic energy. Some of the scientists were only in favour of military uses, but common sense had prevailed and then Chairman Munir was in favour of peaceful uses. It was at this time that some of the Pakistan Atomic Energy Commission's medical and agricultural centres were established and expanded in terms of hardware and software.

On the advice of Dr Shams I proceeded to Islamabad to see the Chairman of the PAEC. I stayed in the Intercontinental Hotel at a discounted rate, because I knew the accounts officer from his days in England when he was doing chartered accountancy. The next day I went to the offices of the PAEC, which were in a rented building. The security guard took me to the director of the establishment, Qureshi, who was a retired army major. He was generous and told me that they were looking for a person like me as they were going to establish a nuclear medical centre in Peshawar. He called the security person and said 'Sahib ko secretary ke pass le jawo' - take Sahib to the secretary's office. I followed him up the stairs and he kept on saying 'come, come' in English. As I was following him, I took a wrong turning and lost sight of my guide. As I was inquiring about the office of the secretary the security guard rushed and started saying 'no no!' He picked up the phone and said to his senior 'Angrez urdu bhi bolta hai' - the visiting Englishman also speaks Urdu.

Security in the PAEC was very tight, and was the responsibility of retired army personnel. The security guard who accompanied me was a Pushtun, as Pushtuns are preferred for guard duties because of their physical and mental abilities. I was ushered into secretary Khan's office. His complexion was light and as his name was Khan I started talking to him in a mixture of English and Pashto, but he said his ancestors had forgotten the Pashto language in India. How long does it take to forget the language of one's ancestors and adopt a new language? The PAEC secretary asked me whether I was married to a foreigner. I said yes, but so was the Prime Minister, Zulfikar Ali Bhutto. The meeting was not satisfactory and later on I learned that the secretary was senior in the Pakistan Atomic Energy Commission and wanted the job of the Chairman, but Prime Minister Bhutto had appointed a nuclear engineer, Munir Ahmad Khan, who had been serving in the International Atomic Energy Agency (IAEA) in Vienna Austria and was married to a fine German woman.

I went again to Director Qureshi's office, but he sensed that

I did not have satisfactory answers about the job. He made an appointment for me to see the chairman of the PAEC. The following day I went to see Chairman Munir Khan. I had been thinking that since he had worked in Europe I would see smartly-dressed young women in his office, but there were none. Women are by nature polite and are better at office work, and this is probably one of the reasons why such work is done properly in the West, unlike in developing countries. PAEC was supposed to be a secret organization, and women and people belonging to certain religions and family connections in India were weeded out.

Munir Khan greeted me when I entered his office and served tea and biscuits. He said he wanted to establish institutions so that scientists, engineers and medical people working or studying abroad would have places to come back to. The people in his office used to make fun of his excessive eagerness to entice scientists to return to the country by saying that they had been 'trapped'. But he had not forgotten the traditional hospitality of his ancestors from Afghanistan. His son, Omar Khan, told me that his father had preserved some old stuff belonging to his ancestors in a box but they (the younger ones) would make fun of it. Feelings and values change from generation to generation. The elders sometimes expect their juniors to behave the way they want them to, but inheritance or genetic makeup play an important role.

I was offered a job, but I had to fill in a long security form. I had to state the party my father belonged to and wrote 'Muslim League Party at the time of writing' because people kept on changing their political parties in Pakistan. For my mother's party I wrote 'women's liberation front'. I handed over the forms to Major Qureshi, who told me to change the details about the political parties because the PAEC security personnel wore army 'strait jackets' and if I was rejected even the chairman would not be able to do anything. I left the office happy that my job hunting had been successful, not knowing the future bureaucratic hurdles I would face. I returned to Peshawar on the Grand Trunk Road first built by Sher Shah Suri from Calcutta to Khyber Pass.

We started early in the morning for Swat, taking the shorter route through the Hashtnagar area, whose people had rendered sacrifices for independence during British India. We crossed the bridges over the Kabul River and the Swat River, reaching Takht Bhai, where there are archaeological sites from the Buddhist period. We travelled up the Malakand Mountains, the site of many battles during the British era, and stopped at the top to take rest and have green tea. I showed Shahnaz the olive grove where there was hand-to-hand fighting between the British troops and the Swatis some hundred years before the recent Taliban uprising.

We descended from Malakand top on a zig zag road that led into a picturesque valley. When we reached Chakdara I pointed the fort on the bank of Swat River and also pointed the watch tower perched on the top of the hill, where the Churchill Picket was commemorated. This was the place where Sir Winston Churchill stayed in 1897 when there was uprising by the Pukhtun people who were led by a "Pir" (a holy man) from Swat called "Sar Tor Fakir" and "Mulla Mastan". Churchill called him "mad fakir" and "mad mulla" in his first book, *The Story of the Malakand Field Force*.

I mentioned the Churchill picket to Shahnaz, but she was not interested. She was constantly thinking of her children left behind in Isfahan and her future life in a strange place where she did not have relatives and did not know the language and customs. The love of people and children are more important; the rest is secondary.

When we reached Chakdara, the bridge built during the British time linking Dir and Chitral looked striking with its red colour. In the devastating floods of 2010, most of the bridges on the Swat River were washed away, except the two bridges built during the British time, which were the Chakdara Bridge and the Cunningham Bridge in Upper Swat, constructed in 1944.

We bypassed Thana, where a school was established at the turn of the 20th century and where my maternal uncle Nisar Khan had his education. The people of Thana, which was a part of Swat, are by and large educated because of the school. I remembered Tahir Khan, the writer and poet who became director of the Pashto Academy. The area has produced some good people who have contributed towards the development of society because of their proper education. The founder of Yusufzai Tribe, Malak Ahmad Baba, is buried in the cemetery near Thana.

When we reached the first checkpoint before entering the previously autonomous Swat State, I noticed that the police manning it were dressed in a different uniform from the one I was used to before I left for England. I felt sorry that Swat, which had been run efficiently, had to be amalgamated with the rest of the North West Frontier Province (NWFP).

Lundaake was the name of a place on the border of Swat State. My friends belonging to Punjab and Karachi used to make fun of some of the names, such as Lundaake itself, because the word 'lund' means penis in the Urdu language. A story was also related to a me by a humorous teacher from Saidu Sharif, the capital of Swat State. A Pukhtun family from Swat visited Lahore every year to buy cloth and make clothes from a particular tailor named Chaudhry. The clothes were tried on first before the family returned to Swat. The tailor asked whether the shirt fitted well. The Swati answered 'Thora sa lund hain' - in Pashto 'lund' means small. The Pushtun suddenly realized his mistake and then said 'I'm sorry Chaudhry sahib, because the word I used means small in Pashto'. Chaudhry answered, 'Do not worry Khan sahib, we also call a small penis 'lund'. For a bigger penis we use 'Lawra' in Punjabi'.

CHAPTER SEVENTEEN

BACK TO SWAT

☾⋆

The checkpoint at the border with Swat was mainly used to prevent grain produced in Swat from being sold outside the state so that prices were controlled, and also to prevent human trafficking. Swat girls were sought after in the brothels of the big cities because of their fair colouring and good looks. Predators were always on the prowl, and some would marry these girls and then sell them to those who controlled the world's oldest profession as sex workers. The Wali made sure that this practice was prevented and would use his influence to bring the girls back and hand them over to their families.

After passing through the checkpoint we headed towards Barikot, which was called Bazira during Alexander the Great's time. It reminded me of my childhood, when I used to come and stay at Qazi Sahib's house, the father of my childhood friend Fazli Ali. Qazi was an intelligent, religious man but not a bigot. He practised 'unani' medicine, Greek medicine, and was famous for treating the ailments of children. The children and parents liked his medicine because they were not bitter and did not have side effects.

When we reached Hodigram village I remembered that people used to say that Mahmud Ghaznavi's army commander died some thousand years ago during the battle with the local population, who were Buddhists at the time. The shrine, surrounded by evergreen trees, is still visited by devotees. I also saw the Gira mountain peak where the chief Gira had his castle and water was supposed to be lifted from the Swat River to the peak by some ancient system. Hodigram village also rang bells because Shad Mohammad Khan (SMK), an English teacher who had always praised my maternal uncle because he helped him to get out of the Pakistan Air Force, where he was serving as an airman. He would always remember the help extended to him but at the same time was always on the lookout for revenge if he was slighted in any way. SMK was from a 'Khan family' and he resented having to take a lower job in the Air Force. 'Forgive and forget' is taught in the mosques right from childhood, but at the same time stories of revenge are circulated, talked about and encouraged in Pukhtun society.

Ayub Bridge on the Swat River had to be crossed before reaching the Shamizai area where my village was. People crossed the river on rafts made from inflated animal skins, called 'shanazoona'. Every village on both sides of the river had people who were given land for their upkeep by the village community to do the job. These people were called 'jalawanan'. The Swat ruler built wooden bridges. A special relationship with President Ayub Khan in the late 1950s facilitated the construction of the proper bridge, which was named the Ayub Bridge but was washed away by devastating floods in later years. One wonders why the bridges on the Thames in London and the Hudson

River in New York have been intact for hundreds of years, but the ones mentioned do not last long.

Regarding Ayub Khan, a story related to me by a doctor is worth mentioning: the doctor happened to be present when Iskandar Mirza and Ayub Khan, the Chief of the Army of Pakistan, were visiting the then Governor General of Pakistan, Ghulam Mohammad, who was unconscious because he had a serious disease affecting the brain. Ayub Khan came nearer to the Governor General and said in a loud voice, 'Sir, we will miss you'. The Governor General opened his eyes and Ayub Khan said to Iskandar Mirza, 'the bastard is still alive'.

Pakistan has been ruled by some physically and mentally sick people in the past. The question arises: should top decision-makers who are found to be physically and mentally ill and who make decisions affecting people in their own countries or other countries be exposed by doctors or other close people? I put this to a British Cabinet Minister during a medical conference in the Royal College of Physicians in London at the end of his talk on 'global health'. He said that he had raised this question in the United Nations. The world is witness to the catastrophic effects of the top decision-makers of the superpowers in the 20th century and even the 21st century. The hasty division of India was partly due to the physical illness of the leaders of undivided India. For example, Lord Moran, Personal Physician to Winston Churchill, wrote about decisions Churchill made while unwell. The dictators and despots in Third World countries also need to be exposed regarding their medical history, so that the world becomes a more peaceful place to live in.

We crossed the longest bridge over the Swat River and entering the Nekpikhel area, which had powerful khans who controled the area by the traditional ways of the Pukhtuns; they helped those in need and came to the rescue of people who were the victims of injustice, collectively making sure that the preachers of religion and bigots did not incite people. In the 1970s as we were on the road home, there was peace and people were doing their day-to-day jobs, grazing cattle in the fields and cultivating their land. However, the roads were not in as good shape as they were in the Wali's time.

The Nekpikhel area was the centre of the Taliban movement in recent years. The Taliban leader, Mullah Faz-ul-ullah, had his headquarters in Imam Dheri in the Nekpikhel area. People would flock to his place. He used FM radio to broadcast sermons, incitements and news favourable to the Taliban..

Ningwali village was on the boundary between the Nekpikhel and Shamizai area. The village was known for its good quality of rice and ranja, used by the women for beautifying their eyes. When I was practising in my village at weekends in the 1970s, a child diagnosed with cancer was brought to me by his father from this village,. The child's name was Minhaas. I asked the father why he had named him so, as Minhaas was an Air Force pilot who had shot down many enemy planes. He said he had named him because he wanted his son to be a great man when he grew up, but now the boy had cancer and with tears in his eyes he said 'Da cancer na sok na joreegi' - no one can be cured of cancer. It was gratifying to see him and Minhaas again ten years later; Minhaas had been cured of his disease and was studying in the 10th class. Cancer is not an incurable disease, and thanks to the scientists of the West and Japan, research is continuing and cancer cells are being 'targeted'. At the time of writing, bullets 'targeting' human beings does occur from Khyber to Karachi in Pakistan, which literally means 'land of the pure'. Intelligence, skills, power and talent can be used for destructive purposes or constructive purposes.

As we rounded a bend on the road towards Shamizai area to the north, I stopped and pointed out to Shahnaz the blue water of the undulating Swat River and the snow-covered mountains of Mankial and Falaksair, a beautiful scenic spot in the wide and concave valley. There was hardly any comment from her. I was trying to impress her with the scenic beauty of Swat, which was known as the Switzerland of Swat, not knowing about the future turmoil to take place in this scenic valley, lasting for years, when a barrier was set up in this area by the Taliban.

The 'Shamizai' also came to prominence during the era of the Taliban in Afghanistan. Maulana Nizam-ud-din Shamizai (MNS) belonged to a village not very from far from the village where I was born. He was a teacher of Mullah Omar when Mullah Omar was a student in a religious seminary in Karachi. The Home Minister of Pakistan, Moin Haider, who has a sense of humour and is an intelligent and well-meaning person, took MNS along with others to ask Mullah Omar to hand over Osama bin Laden. Mullah Omar could not be convinced, because in Pukhtunwali, *panah*, or protection to a stranger or guest, is built in. When anyone seeks panah, questions about are not asked about whether the person is an assassin or a mass murderer.

As one crosses the bend near Ningwal village, the view to the north is superb, but Pukhtuns have always been interested in feuds and fights, individually or collectively. Those Pukhtun leaders who tried to put them on the right path towards peace, progress and the good things in life either failed themselves or were forcibly made to abandon their struggle.

This reminds me of a meeting with Ghani Khan (GK), a poet, philosopher and sculptor who was admitted to the Bolton Block at Lady Reading Hospital. Omar Khan, son of the late Munir Khan, Chairman of the Pakistan Atomic Energy Commission, wanted to interview GK, who later on started a website, harrapa.com. GK said that when Pakistan came into being, Baba (Baacha Khan) was a peaceful man who wanted to devote the rest of his life to the welfare of human beings and the new country. So he wrote a letter to Jinnah and gave it to GK to be delivered. GK was stopped on the right bank of the Indus River near the Attock Bridge. The letter was confiscated and he was sent to prison. The history of Pakistan, tarnished by military coups, assassinations, dismemberment, insurgency, targeted killings, corruption and power shortages, would have been different if these two great leaders of the sub-continent, Jinnah and Khan Abdul Ghaffar Khan, had come together in their pursuit of uplift of the people and the region.

When we reached Sher Palam, a village where Khan Bahadur Sultanat Khan (KBSK) lived, I remembered my childhood, when my maternal uncle Nisar Khan always went on the side road to pay his respects. He resented it, but the upper Swat people were all scared of KBSK. On the roadside, he had planted walnut trees and no one dared to pluck the walnuts. It is said that fear of human beings, individually or collectively, dominates much of our social life.

The next place on the road to home was Pir Kali, where there was a shrine to Mir Oasim Baba. The legend says that it was the grave of a commander of the Mahmud Ghaznavi forces who died during a battle with the Swatis, who were Buddhists at that time. On the third day of the Eid festivities (after the end of the fasting month of Ramadan), young people, both boys and girls, used to come to Pir Kali, in separate groups, to sing, play music and dance wearing new clothes.

We crossed the bridge towards Matta, where I had attended school before going to public school in the Murree Hills. The places reminded me of the times when I used to walk or request a lift on a bicycle from classmates or go by tanga (horse-driven carriage). We would get down near the grave of another saint known as 'Sheikh Farid', about whom a proverb in Pashto says, 'Sheikh Farida, Khula Chappa Behtari da' - it is better to keep one's mouth shut at times and listen. Recently I saw and bought a book written by Sir Richard Branson entitled "The Virgin way. How to Listen, Learn and Lead" which reminded me of the saying of the Pukhtun saint.

Chalgazae, a graveyard on the road near Baidara village, was the scene of the ambush of Afzal Khan, a Mamet Khel political leader, by the Taliban. He and his nephew were seriously wounded and his guard died. A Painda khel, Mohammad Rahim Khan, took timely action by coming to the rescue, so further tragedy was prevented.

As we approached my mother's village, I saw a large crowd waiting to greet us. Jehan Sher Khan (JSK), my younger maternal uncle, was prominent among the crowd, as he was a tall, handsome man. We had lived together when I was in primary school in Saidu. JSK lived a full life, entertaining his friends to good food and drink and not taking part in active politics. At night he was be surrounded by people who wanted free homemade alcoholic drinks without the fear of police, as alcohol was banned. Some of them used to get drunk. Once a mother of one of them complained to JSK that her son said all sorts of things when he came home, but last night he had said, 'Tagh kum zai de, agae achum' - where is the place where hens lay eggs, because I want to lay an egg.

JSK had a colourful life, with two wives As well as many mistresses, whom he kept in the houses of his servants or his sister. The question arises - should someone from a Khan family think of himself all the time by indulging in merrymaking or also look out for the welfare of people in his surroundings, as Khans are supposed to do?

His elder wife was selected by his mother from her own Mamet Khel tribe and the younger was from an Afghan family. Both of them were nice in their own way. The elder had one daughter, an intelligent, blue-eyed pretty girl who would always regret that she had been prevented from going to school. JSK had two boys from his first marriage and tried his best to educate them - one was sent to Japan - but for some reason, probably 'Khanism' instilled in them by their environment, they did not come up to the standard he wanted. There were six daughters from the Afghani lady, a fine woman, who made sure that her daughters were educated and brought up well in the Pukhtun environment. Educated mothers, especially in Pukhtun society, are important.

JSK had faith in my medical advice. He would always consult me first and follow my medical advice, except during his last serious illness, which I learned about later on when he was in Agha Khan Hospital in Karachi. Because of internal rivalries between the sisters and wives, the serious illness was kept secret, as one side wrongly thought I was favouring the other side over the stepsisters and brother. Disputes on division of properties among brothers, sisters and cousins are cause of serious conflicts in Pukhtun families. Sisters are ignored in the division of property. Writing proper wills should solve some of the problems. I also stopped near the family graveyard where my maternal uncle, grandfather and grandmother were buried, and offered dua.

I have already written about the eldest maternal uncle, Nisar Khan, who had altruistic qualities. He had inherited his intelligence from his father and a quick temper from his mother, who happened to be Mamat Khel. The combination of both genes probably made him support and help not only his near ones but also unrelated people. He also had the jealousy and vengefulness of a Pukhtun. He confronted courageously and made a dent in the powers of all powerful Khans in upper Swat, which others had tried before him but had to face assassinations, confiscation of property or expulsion.

Jehan Sher Khan (JSK) was Nisar Khan's younger brother. He also had four stepbrothers. JSK shared only one quality with his elder brother, and that was the love of women. They shared this characteristic with my maternal grandfather, Falaqus Khan (Philip), who had three wives that he kept in three separate houses, knowing very well that they would fight among themselves if kept in one place. I usually stayed in the same room in my maternal grandfather's hujra whenever I was on a visit to my mother's village. When he had his first arranged marriage, he went to the house to be with his bride on the third night of the festivities, as was the Pukhtun custom. He came back to his room in the hujra where I was sleeping. He could not sleep the rest of the night, as he was restless. It reminded me of a young lad who had come to me for consultation, as I knew his family. He was in distress and wanted help, as the coming night was the third night of his marriage and he was going to sleep with his bride. He pulled out a pistol and said that if he was not successful in the sexual act, he would shoot himself. I asked why he was thinking in that way. He said that people say that one cannot get an erection if one is used to 'hand practice' as he was; he had also tried to have sex with a 'girls' guide' but could not get an erection. I reassured him and gave him tablets in an unlabelled bottle and told him to take one tablet before attempting sexual intercourse. The tablets were simple multivitamins, as Viagra was not available at that time. The next day he was happy and told me that he had had sexual intercourse three times and the fourth time, the bride had refused, because she felt sore. There are psychological reasons for impotence and sexual weakness. Quacks know about it and thrive on it.

After going through my mother's village, I reached a village called Chaghwar. Later on the name was changed to Sahib Abad, a village of the Sahibzadgan Syeds. Masoom Jan, my classmate, lived there, and during my childhood I went their house and sometimes stayed there when Fazli Ali came. Masoom Jan helped his younger brother Roidad to become educated and he became a doctor, went to the USA, got a postgraduate qualification and settled in West Virginia. Dr Roidad in turn supported his relatives financially and they were educated and are doing well. My father told me that they used to respect Sahibzadgaan Syeds and also trust them, so much so that they left their womenfolk in their houses if they had to attend to intertribal skirmishes. Trust is said to be a two-way process.

Chapter Eighteen

HOME AGAIN

☪

When I reached my home village many people came out to greet us. There were children, boys and girls, elderly people with white flowing beards, my father, uncles and brothers. We had to walk to the house along the streets, as there was no road for the car. Shahnaz was wearing a chadar and she had to walk with my sisters to the house. The welcoming of the people of the village was spontaneous, as I had been neutral in the sense that I had not taken part in village politics.

When I reached my house there were bursts of gunfire, which was a tradition to welcome a guest. The streets were decorated with multi-coloured papers and the walls were temporarily whitewashed. Normally cow dung cakes are put on the street walls to dry for use as a fuel for cooking. Later on when my daughters, who were born and bred in the UK, noticed these cow dung cakes stuck on the wall they had asked their mother, 'Mom, what are these?' Their mother replied, 'They are cow dung.' 'But how can cows climb up the walls?' they asked.

When I entered the house, there was drum beating, dancing and singing. My sisters were throwing money and children were collecting it. Since foreign travel and staying for a long time were less frequent in those days, people used to celebrate the homecomings of their dear and near ones. In my case women and children had gathered to see how my wife looked. They would sit near her and keep looking at her. Some would take her hand to see whether her hands were the same as theirs. Shahnaz said, 'Am I a museum piece?' I said, 'You are lucky that people give you so much attention.'

I also recognized some of the women with whom I used to play hide and seek in the evening when we were young. One reminded me by saying, 'Za Mahal yum' - I am Mahal. She was a pretty girl, fair with brown hair. She would come to the door of her house and I would kiss her on her rosy cheeks, as Pukhtuns were used to doing. I learned kissing on the lips in England.

The street decoration and arrangements were made by my stepbrother Zaman, who was good at organizing things. He was also thankful to me because I had sent him four thousand rupees at a time when a 'tola'of gold was a hundred rupees, as he wanted to go to Beirut to study in the American school, but he never went there.

After an emotional meeting with my mother, sisters and other relatives, I went to the hujra (men's house). The streets leading there were the same, with children playing, animals being taken out for grazing dogs, cats and chickens. The water in the village canal looked clean, unlike in later years when people started throwing refuse into it and built houses and encroachments over the free-flowing water. I used to swim in it along with other children of the village.

When I entered the hujra, there were a lot of people to greet me. The hujra was the same as others I had seen, with three rooms and a big veranda. The wooden pillars with elaborate fine handiwork were intact, but there was one person missing from the hujra: my youngest uncle, who had no children and who lived and looked after the place, had passed away. Charles Lindholm, who was on a visit to Swat as a guest of Zaman, had sent me a letter informing me of my uncle's death. Those were the days when young people from Europe and the USA wanted to seek enlightenment in the Orient and try hashish and LSD. Hari Krishna was popular in the West and some young people would go to India to find gurus for enlightenment. According to the biography of the CEO of Apple, Steve Jobs, he also went to India to seek enlightenment. Some of these young people did well in their future careers; Charles Lindholm became a Professor of Social Anthropology, an expert in anthropological research in the Middle East, Afghanistan and North West Pakistan and the author of several books and articles. One of his teachers, Dr Abraham Rosman, told me one should not have favourites in one's children and students, but Charles was his favourite student. Since Charles, who was called 'Charlus' by the villagers, did his field study for his doctorate in Swat, he always had fond memories of his stay in the village, which he called, 'Shin Bagh', and kept an interest in the progress of Pukhtuns in general and Swatis in particular. He and I later collaborated on some interview, which I will reproduce later in this book.

I went to the village cemetery and offered dua to Uncle Tra Dada and others. The cemetery was described by Charles as one of the most beautiful places in the village, because it had large evergreen trees of olives, mulberrys and chinar trees - oriental planes. Zargaishun, my nanny, who had looked after me during my childhood, also came to greet us. She kissed me on both cheeks, and I avoided it because she would open her mouth wide and then rub her tongue over my face, so saliva would be all over my face. I prevented her from kissing Shahnaz, but she did not like this and said in Pashto that she must kiss her daughter-in-law. Zargaishun had married again for the fifth time. She had only one daughter, who was given to a professional musician Omra Yar (friend for life), who trained her as dancer and singer. She later married a hairdresser in Mingora and would come to see me at times when I was doing private medical practice in the village. She called me 'Rora' - brother - and I would call her 'Bachia', a word in Pashto used for younger people. Professional musicians with female dancers were free to practise their profession, because they entertained people in the marriage ceremonies and circumcision festivities and they had the protection of Khans in Swat. These people, especially the female dancers, went through difficult times during the time of the Taliban.

We stayed for a few days in the village. Relatives from the extended family came and extended their generosity and hospitality. Shahnaz was confined to the house, in the way you cage a pretty bird and feed it well. When I went to England, our house in the village did not have bathroom or toilet (WC) facilities. I had written to my father to ask him to build a room with an attached bathroom, which he had graciously done, but the ceiling was leaking.

Shahnaz was fond of my sisters, especially Sucha - pure - as she had brown hair and blue eyes, was fun-loving, and knew how to please guests. I had also told her how Sucha had sold her earrings to give me the money for my travel to Great Britain. In later years whenever I heard the song 'Walaye ma khar sawa' - do not sell your earrings - I remembered my sister, who died so unnecessarily during the time of the Taliban. The Pashto version of the song with my translation is as follows:

Song

"Zama greewan chi somara shleegi domra shleegi ba kho.
Ta da ghwagono walai ma kharsawa.

Kher de ku ze da dunya stargo ki azghi shama kho.
Da gul rukhsaar nemgarri ne khwakhawom.

Kher de tol jwand rala zrre daghasi parkhar predawa.
Pa zankadan ki kho mi khpal zangon ta sar predawa.

Za ba de khpal watan da har zalim greenwan ranesam.
Sta da waalo ba te pokhtana kaom.

Ze ba da khawri jabir khan ranesam.
Sta de jamo ba te pokhtana kaom.

Da kho jwandon de lwage tandi di teregi ba kho.
Ta da ghwagono walai ma kharsawa".

Translation:
I do not care about my difficulties
but you should not sell your earrings.

Do not worry if people think I am a thorn in their eyes,
but I do not like your beautiful face to be without earrings.

Let me suffer because of my tough life,
but I wish my head to be in your lap when I am dying.

I will get hold of all the cruel people of my country on my return
and make them explain why you had to sell your earrings.

I also wanted to know about the people whom I knew and with whom I had played during childhood and shared secrets with during adolescence. One was Awal Khan (first khan), who used to sleep on the veranda of the hujra, where unmarried young slept. They told me that Awal Khan had been banished from the village by his elder brother because he was caught sleeping with a married girl. He then went to Karachi for work.

Before 1947, people from our village and upper Swat went to Bombay, Ahmad Abad, Bengal and Delhi. Recently my schoolfriend from Dacca, Bangladesh, wrote to me from Australia to say that his grandfather had come from a village called Bama Khela in Upper Swat. The sons and grandsons who migrated from Swat have done well in India in many fields, including sports, such as the cricketer Arif Pathan, whose father hailed from upper Swat. After the partition of India, people started going to Karachi to seek jobs. Sher Zada Khan, who lived near our apricot, plum and mulberry orchard, had also gone to Karachi, where he established himself financially and politically. In the seventies people started looking for jobs in Saudi Arabia, Kuwait and United Arab Emirates. They do the tough jobs, such as transport and construction work. This reminds me of a song in Pashto:

The Pashto verses and translation are as follows:

Song

The following is a duet between the wife (beloved) and a husband (lover) who is working in Dubai.

Pa jara me starge sreshue, Janan kala ba raze.
(My eyes have become sore and red because of crying. O my lover (husband) when are you going to come back.)

Musafar yum dar zama, Ta kala herawum.
(I am a stranger in this country and will be coming, but I can never forget you.)

Ta musafar shwe pa Dubai, Za wahuma salgai.
(You are in Dubai and I am here alone sobbing.)
(I am coming soon because I love my country and I can never forget you my love.)

On Friday, which is a holy day for Muslims as Sunday is for Christians and Saturday is for Jews, I went to the mosque. I noticed some changes. As I stepped inside barefoot, I saw that the place of ablution (washing of certain body parts, including the reproductive organs) was cemented, unlike the big stones on the floor to which I was accustomed before I went to England. I heard an argument between two people about the proper washing of the bottom: three times from the right side, three times from the left side and three times from the back. One was saying that unless you do this, your prayers will not be accepted.

Strict adherence to certain rituals which may seem trivial are sometimes hotly argued. I remember once when I was saying prayers in Dewsbury, England, where there is a Tableeghi Centre, a person standing next to me during prayers would bring his foot to touch my foot; I would try to leave a gap, but he would bring his foot nearer again. At the end of the prayers, I asked him why. He said, 'Satan ghus jata hai' - if you leave a gap then Satan enters the row.

Once in London when I was sitting with Maulana Maudoodi, who was well read, a scholar and founder of Jumaat Islami (JI), I found that there was not too much strictness in ablution - Islam is a religion of peace, harmony and liberal views in relation to how one lives and relations with other human beings, including minorities and their religious places. But as is well known, ignorance breeds misunderstanding.

In the mosque I was offered a place in the front row during prayers, where my father and uncles were sitting. The sermon was conducted by the son of our traditional Mullah. His father was an intelligent man, but was restrained in what he was saying during Friday sermons. The tone of his son in his sermon was fiery and free. He was talking about the threat to Islam from Westernization and Western education. He also mentioned the *ghairat* - honour - of '*zamung khanan*' (our khans) and related a story of a person from another village who had illicit relations with a girl of our village. The person was caught, dragged away and shot in the fields by a khan. The police, who were efficient in Wali's time, did not intervene when there was 'honour' involved. I remembered the episode, as I was of school age. The person belonged to my mother's village and she was very upset and would say 'Zulam shawey de' - height of cruelty.

When I left for England, there were no schools in the village, but now a primary government school had been started and girls had also started going to the schools. There were no formal religious seminaries, but children were given religious education in the mosques. As I was coming out of the mosque, I noticed teeth stuck in the walls of the mosque. People used to put their decayed teeth above the ground in mud walls of the mosque, and this was still persisting.

After saying Friday prayers I listened to the Imam's Friday sermon, in which I noticed that there were some hints of 'freedom of speech' rather than the strict adherence to what the khan wished him to say in my childhood days. The mosque plays one of the dominant roles in a Pukhtun life, with people coming to the mosque five times a day for prayers for the people of the 'tul' (neighborhood) and collective decisions by the community.

In winter, people used to sit around a fire in an open hearth prior to and after the prayers led by the Imam. Wood was collected from every individual who owned property in a tul. The wood was primarily oak, because the fire lasted longer. Darr was the Pashto word used for collection of wood for heating purposes in both mosque and hujra. The mosques were built by the community and our mosque had a large veranda which was used for saying prayers in summer. There was a big hall that was used for saying prayers in winter. The pillars were wooden and carved with intricate flowery patterns. The doors were also carved and made of cedar wood. In the fifties and sixties, the water from the well was drawn by a *dengray* - a long sturdy log usually of olive wood, which is strong and does not rot if exposed to all sorts of weather in the open. To one end of the dengray was tied a heavy stone, while to the other end was attached a rope and a container for drawing water from the well. There were no bathrooms inside the houses for men in the fifties and sixties so there was only the room in the hujera for taking baths. This room was usually crowded in the morning because one has to take a bath after sexual intercourse or any type of orgasm, whether nocturnal emission or masturbation. I never heard anything negative about indulging in masturbation, either in sermons or in the hujra. In contrast, in the USA I heard that many years masturbation was considered to be both debilitating and sinful. It is also said to have brought harsh punishment in Germany.

As I stepped out of the mosque and was walking towards the hujra, I met a woman who said, 'Khana Pa Khair Raghle' - welcome, Khan. She embraced me and said, 'Begum saib dera khwale da' - your wife is very beautiful. Women do not embrace in public and people in Pukhtun culture do not talk about other people's wives in public, but she was older than me, knew me from my childhood and was our *kasabgara* - a person who helps in taking errands and does hairdressing. Younger people in a Khan family were taught to respect servants and other household workers by calling them 'Mama', 'Kaka' or 'Tror' instead of their proper names. Female kasabgars and other workers are not restricted to wearing burqas or confined to the houses as they have to in the village or other villages. Women from Gujar families also brought milk and wild fruit such as berries and figs to sell in the villages. As in most of the human cultures that have ever existed, there is male fear of women and a wish to subjugate them. Similarly in the Pukhtun culture, women sometimes receive unkind treatment.

The hujra was always next to a mosque. As I entered, people had gathered from other tuls to greet me. In our village there were be two main tuls and hujras, but when the population increased, the cousins of Khans, who at times are called 'Tarburs' - a derogatory name - had started their own hujras, so there were six when I left for Britain for further medical studies. When I returned to the village, smaller places nearer the houses by individuals were built and these were called 'Baituk' and used for guests and also by the younger generation to get together for music and entertainment. The jealousy of 'tarburs', 'cousins' or 'tarburwali' - jealousy among cousins - was also used by some powerful Khans in Swat and the Wali - ruler - of Swat and even in the British time, 'to divide and rule'. 'Tarburwali' or 'Trabgani' is ingrained in the psyche of Pukhtuns and the tribe, clan or Khel.

The hujra is another place that plays a pivotal role in Pukhtun or Pashtun life. As a growing child a boy learns from the elders about etiquette - how to behave, how to greet people and how to entertain guests. When he grows, he sleeps in the hujra and at times also uses it for his sexual activities (male or female) late at night when older people have dispersed to their houses. The place is also used for music and entertainment during marriage ceremonies. 'Jirgas' - gatherings of elders - are also held in a hujra and political decisions made. Joint decisions were made, negotiations and reconciliations took place in the community centre. Women were not invited to the hujra, but they did have a role in decision-making in Pukhtun life. The result was that there was once relative peace and tranquility in a village and in Pukhtun life. The question arises: is it because of the erosion of traditional life of Pukhtun, which has caused militancy internally and which is being exported externally, even to the West? The second question is how to reverse the trend in short term, medium term and long term for peace in the 'Global Village'.

In our hujra people asked me about the Western way of life and how people eat, dress and marry. Some even asked me whether the hair of the women was golden and whether they wore the chadar. Pukhtuns like white and rosy colours. The rosy cheeks, the red lips and long tresses of the shapely-built girls are the subjects of their poetry, as in Persian poetry. In my few days in the village, people even asked me about 'ghairat' - honour - in Western society. In the seventies people from Europe and the USA used to visit the East for enlightenment and to have a taste of churs - hashish. So Swatis had started seeing some visitors from the West and they were curious to know about Westerners. I was the only person from the village in the seventies who had gone to the West and lived in England. In the forties Pukhtuns went to India, mainly to Bombay and Ahmad Abad, and on their return, the villagers asked them about life in India. They would even ask about the brothels where you could 'buy sex'.

Our hujra was on high ground and one could see the mountains and trees, as the view was unobstructed. In the evening one could see the birds flying towards the tall trees in the cemetery. The atmosphere in the hujra was always jovial, as the men would talk about all sorts of topics, even the sexual misadventures of people when the khan and elderly people were not present.

Falcons perched on the walls and hunting dogs, mainly pointers, roamed freely in our hujra and courtyard. Fighting quails were in the cages. I greatly missed the presence of my youngest uncle, Sher Azam Khan, whom we called Tra Dada. He was the pivot of the hujra and the only person who could read and write in the village. When I heard of his death I was very sad and cried. Tra Dada was kind to children, but did not have any of his own. People gathered in his room on winter nights and he would read the 'Shah Nama' of Firdausi to them in his melodious voice. He was friendly with Mamet Khels and once I heard Afzal Khan Lala saying 'Sher Azim Khan Khog De' - Sher Azam Khan is a sweet person.

Swat, because of its scenic beauty and access through passes to the north south, east and west, has always been of interest to travellers, historical adventurers, conquerors and young people from Western countries seeking enlightenment. Buddhists had their monasteries in Swat because of the peace and tranquility. Alexander the Great fought his way towards the Indus River through Swat and it is said he married a local girl to seal a treaty with the tribes. Swat also had its fair share of tribal warfare when the Yusufzai tribe settled here, but they had a strict code of conduct when there were skirmishes between the tribes, which were not to harm children and females. It was well known in Swati culture that someone would be 'baigharat' - have no honour - if he considered himself 'zorawar' - powerful - towards women and children. Things are changing and one hopes that the codes of conduct and ethics of Pukhtunwali are not completely lost.

On my brief stay in the village, I noticed that the traditional power of the 'Khan', who would take an interest in the welfare of the people in his 'tul' and make sure that people were not incited in the mosque and hujra, was gradually but surely being eroded, but elders were still respected. In my case, people were coming from the surrounding villages for pakhair - welcome - which is an age-old custom in Swat. The womenfolk of landowners still kept to their houses except when there were marriage ceremonies or circumcision ceremonies, when the women would dress up and visit other houses and other villages. Women coming from working families, such as carpenters, hairdressers, leather workers and tenants of landowners, could walk freely in the streets and exchange greetings with men known to them and at times crack jokes. Boys played in the streets and still had their slingshots around their necks. I noticed all this during my few days' stay in the village before retracing my route to the West.

Chapter Nineteen

RETRACING OUR STEPS: OVERLAND THROUGH AFGHANISTAN

☪

On the day of departure, as before people gathered to see us off, but this time the atmosphere was not sad, because I had told my near and dear ones that I would be coming back. One person was missing, my beloved youngest uncle, Tra Dada, who had bid farewell to me the last time with tears in his eyes and put some money in my pocket. My father, who had a sense of humour, would say he was with 'hurrahs' in heaven. Women also came out to say farewell to Shahnaz, who was happy because she was on the way to see her daughter Mah Muneer, who was in the care of my in-laws in Isfahan.

On the way back, the first night was spent in the Rural Academy in Peshawar, courtesy of Shuaib Sultan Khan, a well-groomed, educated and ethical practising bureaucrat, and Dr

Hazrat Bilal (HB). HB handed me a heavy, solid package wrapped in a brown cloth to be given to a British doctor in England. He himself put it under the seats and said he would accompany me to the border so that the customs people, whom he knew very well, would not open the package. The contents were not revealed to me and I dared not ask him because of his hospitality during my stay. A Pukhtun once obliged will always try not to displease his benefactor or mentor.

I took the road, once built by one of the greatest Pathan kings of India who did a lot for the common man from Calcutta (now Kolkata) to Khyber, Sher Khan (Shah) Suri. Crossing the Khyber Pass gateway to India was easy and traffic free, unlike the later years when the only route to Afghanistan would be jam-packed with long trailers carrying fuel and food for the NATO forces during the Afghan War.

After crossing the narrowest part of the pass near Ali Masjid, I stopped and took a picture of an interesting signpost. On it was a picture of a camel pointing to one track and a picture of a car pointing towards the main road. One could also see young tribal women wearing multicoloured embroidered baggy clothes patched with metal coins crossing the road carrying wood, oblivious of the passing vehicles and the camels.

After a smooth journey by car through the Khyber Pass, we reached the border with Afghanistan. The border was demarcated by Durand during the British rule. When Pakistan came into being, the first Governor, General Mohammad Ali Jinnah, made sure he visited the border. He shook hands with the border police of Afghanistan, extending 'the hand of peace' to his neighbours in Afghanistan and ordered troops to be withdrawn from the tribal areas. Both Gandhi and Jinnah were peaceful people and wanted progress, prosperity and peace for the people. One cannot say the same for the people surrounding both Gandhi and Jinnah at that time. Gandhi was assassinated. Jinnah died in Balochistan on his way to hospital in an ambulance that broke down before reaching it. Both were peace-loving people who died in the early days of the births of their countries, resulting in warfare, death, destruction, fundamentalism and state-sponsored terrorism due to follies of successive governments and dictatorships. The borderlands had to bear the brunt of the man-made disasters. The region was used for training militants and launching of attacks, not only both sides of the border but all over the globe in later years.

As we were crossing the border in the early seventies, there was peace and goodwill on both sides and we had no fear of being shot or kidnapped on the roads or from above in the mountains or the air, and we reached Jalalabad, the first historical border town on the Afghanistan side. At that time, the Shinwari Tribe, the Momand and other tribes living on both sides were free to cross the border without restrictions and without greasing the palms of the border officials or having their money forcibly taken from them by the 'law enforcing' authorities on their way to Peshawar or Jalalabad.

When thinking about the 'warlike' Pukhtun, it is worth recalling that Europe was not peaceful until 1945, when the Second World War ended, and swhen ense prevailed because of the quality of the leader. An era of peace, progress and prosperity was then ushered into Europe. The firestorm that brewed up in Afghanistan in the 1980s and beyond was due not solely to the warlike tendencies of the local people, but to the follies of so-called leaders and the vested interests of the imperialists.

We reached Kabul in the evening. The area from Jalalabad to Kabul was peaceful in the seventies and the roads were well paved. Men wearing the typical Pukhtun dress of baggy trousers and shalwar could be seen walking with their cattle and camels. The women were wearing bright-coloured clothes with chadars on their heads. They would only cover their faces when they became conscious of men looking at them.

Kabul was also peaceful. It was Zahir Shah's time, and there were no checkpoints, nor could one see soldiers with their bulletproof vests. Young people from Europe and other countries could be seen in the bazaars and restaurants, eating barbecued meat and listening to live music played by Afghans.

After spending the night in a Kabul hotel which was well run and had all the facilities for tourists including courteous staff, clean rooms and hygienic food services, we set off for Ghazni and Kandahar early in the morning. There was not much traffic on the roads. Camel caravans could still be seen, with some Pukhtun women and children dressed in their typical attire on their way to the summer pastures. Some Pushtun tribes such as Ahmad Zai's and Niazis spent their summers in cooler places in Afghanistan along with their kith and kin and flocks of hundreds of fatty-tailed sheep.

On reaching Ghazni, I stopped to see the monument erected to the memory of Sultan Mahmud. Shahnaz was not interested, as she wanted to reach Isfahan as soon as possible to see Mah Muneer. Ghazni was a small village, but it rose to prominence during Sultan Mahmud's time. His father was Turkish and his mother was a Pushtun from Zabul. He learned Persian and spoke Turkish with the slaves from Central Asia. Sultan Mahmud invaded India several times and brought booty of precious stones, gold and silver. It is said that a visitor to his durbar could see precious stones of 'pomegranate size'. In one of his seventeen invasions, he wanted to stay in the area near the Somanath temple because of the beautifully-designed gardens, but his soldiers were homesick and wanted to go back with their booty.

Sultan Mahmud is known as a *butshikan* - destroyer of idols - but during his time Islam did not take root and spread. This was during the time of Muhammad Ghauri, another Afghan Pukhtun, that Islam was spread to India and took root because of his policies. In later years, I joked with my friends from Punjab and Karachi that if there were no Pukhtuns, there would not be a Pakistan and they would have Hindu and Sikh names, and my name would be Sher Singh instead of Khan. In response, they would give the example of Muhammad Bin Qasim, but he had confined himself to Sind only. Mahmud Sultan Ghaznavi also invaded Swat, which had been Buddhist at that time for a thousand years. He fought the Ruler at Udegram and it is said that he went right up to upper Swat, where my village, Durshkhela, is situated. My father's uncle, Sharif Khan Baba, who lived for more than a hundred years, said that the word 'Durshkhela' is derived from 'martyrs' from the days of Mahmud Ghaznavi, because hundreds of people died in the fighting, including Ghaznavi's son and a commander of his army.

In Udegram, lower Swat, one of the graves in the cemetery is thought to be the grave of one of his commanders. In upper Swat Ma Qasam Baba's *ziarat* - grave - in Pir Kali is thought to be the son of Sultan Mahmud Ghaznavi. Sharif Khan Baba used to say that Swat would always have *fassad* - turmoil - because Sultan Mahmud had cursed it. 'Swat duck da fassad' - Swat full of turmoil - is also mentioned in a lighter vein. Buddhism is thought to be the religion of peace, but Buddhist Swatis fought and were converted to Islam, and some of the statues of Buddha were destroyed, while the heads of others were cut off. Some of the statues had to wait for another thousand years to be destroyed, at the time of the Taliban. There are presently no Buddhists in Swat but Hindus and Sikhs do still live in Swat and Buner running their businesses and practising their religions in temples and gurdwaras. Two of my classmates, Ratan Laal and Rogh Nath, were Hindus and my colleague Sri Ram was Hindu. Alberuni, the Persian philosopher, astronomer, scientist and mathematician, lived in Ghazni during Sultan Mahmud's time

We reached Kandahar at night and stayed in a Government hotel. In Zahir Shah's time the government had built hotels in all the big cities with facilities for foreign tourists. He knew that tourism can play a dominant role in the economy and bring valuable foreign exchange.

Before setting off for Heart, the border town with Iran, we went to see the mausoleum of one of the greatest kings of India and Afghanistan, Ahmad Shah Abdali. Shahnaz read and translated the couplet written in Persian on the walls decorated with blue mosaic tiles in a flowery pattern. Ashoka was another place we saw again. One loves to see certain objects again, and Kandahar was neither overcrowded with blaring traffic nor were there army personnel. Everyone was busy in their routine work without fear of being shot at or kidnapped. Bomb blasts from the ground or the air were unheard of.

The Pukhtun region is 'man's land', but women do play roles behind the scenes and some have led Afghans from the front, like Malalai of Maiwand, who is considered the Joan of Arc of Afghanistan. Malai Joya is another lady who fought for the political rights of women. In later years Malala of Swat, a fourteen-year-old girl who spoke openly about girls and education during difficult times in picturesque, historical Swat, was injured by gunshots. Great Britain came to her rescue and she was treated in Birmingham Hospital in England and recovered to become famous for her bravery.

On the way to Herat, we learned that an international airport was going to be built to serve all parts of the world, like Dubai. The thinking of the leaders in Afghanistan in the seventies was peace, progress and prosperity, and moreover the external vested interests had not started their destructive role in response to the terrorist activities emanating from the region. In Herat, I asked for typical Herati food in the hotel and they served us delicious well-cooked rice mixed with lentils and served with pure ghee and fresh cream. At that time I was not thinking of my cholesterol levels, but in later years whenever I had cream and ghee, I would say, 'not to worry I will take two antilipid tablets instead of one'. International Pharma are always on the lookout for new medicines, not only to counteract our excessive indulgence in matters of food and drinks but also to remedy man's flagging sexual desires, either manmade following certain operations on the body or natural, due to advancing age.

People in Herat were speaking Persian, unlike Jalalabad and Kandahar, where they spoke Pushto. Shahnaz said there were many differences in their spoken Persian. She was born and brought up in the time of Raza Shah Pahlavi, when the thinking was that Iranians were superior in the region and had to play a dominant role rather than cooperation, coexistence and helping others. Their 4000 years of Persian civilization was drummed into the public with pictures of the Shah everywhere. In certain respects Iran was ahead of other countries in education, health and tourism.

CHAPTER TWENTY

IRAN ONCE MORE

☪

On the Iranian side of the border, we were searched for opium, heroin and marijuana. We were given two capsules of tetracycline to take before entry to Iran to make sure that we did not carry any germs. HIV and AIDS was unknown at that time. I had no problem with clearance by immigration on the Iranian side, but Shahnaz, being an Iranian citizen, had to go through rigorous questioning: it was Raza Shah's time and his intelligence organization, the dreaded SAVAK, was very strong, moreover some Iranian girls both inside and outside the Kingdom were active secretly in bringing the democratic system to Iran. We had to stay overnight in the nearest town to the border for clearance from Tehran.

The next day we reached the holy city of Mashhad, and since I had heard a lot about it, I wanted to see the mausoleum of the Eighth Imam of Shias Imam Raza. The mosque is one of the largest in the Muslim world and was built by the wife of one of the kings of Iran. The courtyard was big, and one could see the pilgrims sitting with their womenfolk and children in groups. I overheard some speaking in Pushto and asked them where they were from. They were from Parachinar in Pakistan. Thousands of people from Pakistan and Afghanistan visit the holy city of Mashhad and millions of pilgrims visit annually from all over the world.

Temporary marriages also take place in Mashhad, and this is exploited as a form of prostitution. The grave of the Imam was protected by guards as the devotees go round, some crying and others wanting to kiss the grave. 'Akhuns' - shia mullahs - dressed in flowing robes and wearing dark green turbans were standing and chanting and expecting the devotees to hand them some money. The scene near the *mazar* (grave) was very interesting for me to watch because as a Sunni I had never come across so much devotion from Shias in a religious place: the devotees were chanting 'Ya Allah, Ya Ali Mudud' and trying to get nearer the golden protective barrier around the Ziarat of Imam Raza.

I learned during the visit that Mashhad was not only a holy city but had been an educational and cultural centre and a seat of power. Some famous scientists, philosophers and poets were born here. Ibn Batuta, the world traveller from North Africa, had visited the city in 1333.

The winding road to Tehran from Mashhad was well paved as it passed through villages and towns. There was greenery all around. The traffic on the roads was more like Afghanistan. The Shah's government had made sure that speeding was controlled by traffic police. One could also see the broken vehicles involved in accidents displayed on the roadside as a lesson to speeding and irresponsible drivers. British, French and German car makers had established their businesses in Iran in the seventies, but Japanese and South Korean firms had yet to arrive.

We had to go up the zigzag road up Damavind Mountain and then descend to reach the modern city of Tehran. Dr Dalil and his hospitable wife were waiting for us in Tehran, where we spent the night. Their house was near an English-speaking school run by the Pakistan. Some Iranians who were very fond of learning English studied it in school.

We got up early in the morning, as we were in a hurry to reach Isfahan to see Mah Muneer. Before starting the journey Shahnaz and I took a stroll down the road soon after 'Azaan' - call to prayers. There was a pleasant aroma of cooking emanating from one of the shops. We entered the shop and tried *kali pachae* - deliciously prepared head and legs of lamb, cooked all night on a slow fire and served in the morning for breakfast. Iranians are fond of *sri paae* (kali pachae) and they are expert in preparation and cooking.

Before sitting off for Isfahan, Dr Dalil Altujar made sure that my petrol tank was full, the tyre pressures were right and the brakes were in good condition. His wife made sure that we had pistachios, almonds and *tukhm* - dried roasted pumpkins and sunflower seeds - for munching on our long journey. Iranian hosts always make sure that their guests are well stocked with dry fruit on their long journey.

The family of our host (adults and children) all came out of their house and walked with us towards the car. There was kissing on both cheeks and they said '*ba salamat*' (goodbye) and '*salaam be rasaneed*' (say salaam to your parents), before we started our journey. Urbanization had taken place in the seventies and the government of the day was vigorously encouraging so-called modernization and alien culture, to the annoyance and bitterness of religious and older people, but Iranians had not forgotten their hospitality, easy-going politeness and sense of humour.

The traffic in Tehran was busy and at times chaotic because there were so many vehicles. It was estimated that there were more cars in Tehran than in all Pakistan. It was pleasant to see the pretty faces of women driving cars and taking their children to school after driving through Pakistan and Afghanistan, where female drivers were unheard of. We had to pass through another holy city, Qum, on the way. Qum had a religious seminary unlike other seminaries in the Muslim world, where languages, social studies, science and studies in comparative religions were taught. It was said that hatred against other people and religions was never mentioned in Muslim sermons or books. Peace, universal brotherhood and peaceful coexistence were taught. So anyone educated in Qum not only knew about Islam but also other religious matters and some aspects of the world at large. The emphasis of the studies in the Qum seminary was on preparing students for their role in the 'global village', but at the same time to be loyal to the Shah and the monarchy.

After Qum, the road became straight and the terrain looked brownish because of the desert, but there were no mounds of sand; instead one could see greenery periodically following irrigation through the *qanats*, the irrigation system which the Persians used for hundreds of years. One could also see abandoned dwellings made of mud with rounded cupola-style roofs. The Persians also knew how to beat the heat of the desert. Innovation was built into the psyche of Persians, as can be seen from the architecture, the old bridges over the rivers in Isfahan, the carpets and the intricate work on the silverware and on wood. There were also roadside tea houses with toilet facilities. The Iranian way of using sugar in tea was to put a lump in the mouth and drink tea brewed on a *samwar*. I liked *polaki zaafrani* - small pieces of sugar mixed with safran (saffron), which is thought to be an aphrodisiac.

As we got nearer Isfahan, the scenery changed and one could see greenery, high ground and mountains. Who could have predicted that barely thirty years later, the area near Isfahan and Isfahan itself would be threatened with bombardment because of real or perceived nuclear installations? Pakistan and North Korea would be blamed for nuclear proliferation.

The journey by car to our destination was uneventful. As we entered Shahnaz's parents house she ran to Mah Muneer, picked her up, kissed her and tears of joy rolled down her rosy cheeks. I noticed water dribbling down the skirt of the child, the urine of joy. The urine of a child before the antibiotic era in Swat was thought to be helpful in conjunctivitis, and a child's urine was instilled in my eyes for eye infection during my childhood. Children are liked by everyone, but in my limited experience, Iranians and Burmese love them the most.

We also spent a few days in Isfahan. There was a lot to be seen: the historical palace of Shah Abbas The Great, the mosque where the windows in the basement were made of thin white marble because glass was not available, the Pule Khwaju Bridge over the Zainda Rud River and the burial sites of the Zoroastrians, the old religion of Persia. Shahnaz spent the few days in Isfahan visiting the members of her extended family of aunts and cousins. One elderly aunt was an elegant lady who was addicted to opium smoking. I had seen and knew of people who were addicted to opium eating and smoking cannabis resin - churs - but not opium smoking. Inhalation is a quicker way of getting a kick out of narcotics. It was Raza Shah's time and narcotics were strictly controlled, but human beings find ingenious ways of overcoming the obstacles. Iranians do everything in special fashion and style; the aunt was on a Persian carpet with an embroidered cushion at her back. The long smoking pipe was made of porcelain. One end had an aperture for opium and the mouth and a gold-coloured lining. It was called *wafoor*.

We were in no hurry to reach our destination of England and I wanted to see as much I could. The surroundings on the roads towards Azerbaijan were pleasant. Historically Azerbaijan was a vast country and people spoke Turkish. To reach Turkey one has to travel through the Iranian part of Azerbaijan.

We stayed in Tabriz, a large city with hotels catering for tourists. The food was delicious and the service in hotels and restaurants was efficient. People would speak to each other reluctantly in their own mother tongues, because minority languages were discouraged at that time. I had heard about Tabriz during my childhood because in the Pukhtun hujras people used to talk about Shams Tabriz and how he had thrown the books of Maulana Rumi into a pond when he had visited Rumi's madrassa in Tabriz. Pukhtuns in general revere Sufis and regularly visited saints and their *mazars* (graves), such as Saidu Baba and Pir Baba in Swat and Ajmer Sharif in India. The desecration of religious places or graves was unheard of in Swat. However, at one time in Swat, the word was spread that some of the prominent graves contained treasures, so people dug the graves up at night, but no silver or gold coins were found.

Chapter Twenty One

TURKEY AND EUROPE

We made sure to reach the border with Turkey early because we had to cross the Tahir Pass, a mountainous region separating Iran from Turkey. The Iranian customs officials made sure that we were taking our car out of the country, as they had stamped it in my passport at the entry point. The immigration officials also made certain that permission from Savak had arrived before Shahnaz could leave the country. There were no strict formalities on the Turkish side. Out of all the countries that we crossed on our car journey, Turkey was the only one which did not look at the green passport with suspicion; in other countries they would thoroughly check the luggage and every compartment of our vehicle.

The road over the Tahir Pass was very steep, with many potholes because of the heavy snow in winter. The road had hairpin bends. It was springtime and there was slush on the roads, which made the travelling dangerous, but we continued

On the way to Shimshal Valley near the border with China to conduct a
Medical Camp - courtesy of Aga Khan Rural Support Programme.

Happy Malaysian visitors.

Exchange of gifts with happy colleagues.

On the way to the Khyber Pass with guests. The goats
seem to enjoy the peaceful times.

PAEC chairman Munir Ahmed Khan in a happy mood.

Prof Zakia Minhas (far right). Her contribution towards women healthcare
and health education is unforgettable.

General Ghaffor visiting IRNUM to donate funds for equipment
and the construction of a unit.

Survey for disease prevalence in rural setup in a developing country.

Visit to Serendip (Sri Lanka).

With Canadian visitors in the Khyber Pass. Zig zag road and railway tunnel up the pass. This feat of engineering was supervised by Lord Beaulieu's father in the 1930s but neglected by successive railway ministries.

With visitors from Canada. Visiting the gateway to the Khyber Pass (ancient gateway to India) in peaceful times. In the picture goats are lying peacefully.

German Professor Gregor Prindal visiting labs.

Pirs (Sufi leaders) shut their eyes when among pretty girls.
Some keep looking but say 'astaghfirullah' later on!

President Faruqui of CPSP admiring books in library.

Governor Janjua with Dr. Ashfaq, Chairman, showing peaceful
uses of atomic energy.

Myanmar (Burma) with staff of the Nuclear Medicine department.

With spiritual and political leader Pir Sabir Shah and visitors from overseas.

Iranian Consul General and Hassan Jafary, a victim of extremism.

The visit of a Kohistani friend, Maulana Baqi, to Multan.

Chief Minister Pir Sabir Shah in happy mood. Only water in the glasses!

With Governor Kursheed after a conference on the prevention of cancer.

Staff of the IRNUM hospital.

'Medicine is a science through which one knows the states of the human body, whether healthy or not, in order to preserve good health when it exists and restore it when it is lacking.'

Definition of medicine by Avicenna (courtesy RCP London). There has been very little contribution by Muslims to science and medicine for almost a thousand years. Why? 'The closing of Muslim minds.'

Nurses are a vital component of the healthcare system.

Food and drink after a session of training in Japan.

As representative of doctors from developing countries to Japan.

Question and answer session.

German visitor Gregor in the hospital.

With the schoolchildren and their prizes.

Press conference on the killer plant tobacco, and smoking
and tobacco dipping (naswar).

With medical students on World Thyroid Day.

First strike of the shovel in digging the foundations for a
multi-storey medical block in Multan.

Visit of the Nobel Laureate Professor Salaam to Multan Medical Centre.

Medical college alumni.

Waiting for the President.

Environmentally friendly wooden tiller replaced by noisy farm tractors (courtesy Cherry Lindholm).

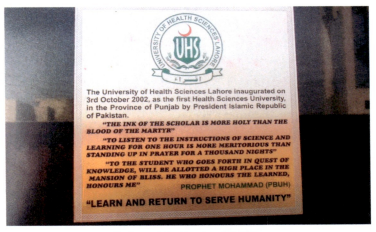

Sayings of the Prophet (PBUH).

The writing on the wall about smoking.

Asian-American Marjan visiting Shin Bagh School.

Durveza Khan with Jalat Mama and Dilbar in the Hujra.

'I will help humanity', the motto of Shinbagh School.

A bright school student of Shin Bagh welcoming
Dr. Hilal from New York State.

Visitors to Shin Bagh school from the UK and Bengal.

With Dr. Inam and Engineer Yousaf of PIEAS University.

Shin Bagh school with a background of the scenic Swat valley.

During a prize-giving at school.

Happy prizewinners at Shin Bagh school.

With Malala and her family.

This American Pukhtun named his house Khyber House - Pukhtuns
rarely forget their roots.

This was thick forests at one time

on our journey until we reached Erzurum on the other side of the mountain, thanks to the Automobile Association (AA), who had mentioned all the details of the route. Whenever people on the road or in the villages heard that we were Pakistani and Iranian, they would welcome us. Since the birth of Pakistan, relations with Turkey and China have always been friendly. Relations with Iran despite so many commonalities, have been ambivalent. In the case of border-sharing neighbours such as India and Afghanistan, the attitude of the successive rulers has been negative. As a result, the meagre resources which could have been spent on raising the standard of living of were spent on non-development projects.

The road to Ankara, the modern capital of Turkey, had fewer potholes. When we reached Ankara, I asked where Koni, the 'whirling dervishes' place was, but it was in another town where Rumi was buried. My father had worn a 'Rumi Topi', a long red soft cap with black hanging strings, which probably had its origin in Turkey in the time of the Ottoman Empire.

Ankara, a modern city, had well-paved roads and in the 1970s it gained high-rise buildings. It had less traffic than Tehran, but the traffic was more organized as I could see a lot of well-dressed police officers in the intersections, directing the traffic. The women were not wearing the headscarf and one could see smart, pretty girls in skirts and hot pants. I did not know much about what to see in Ankara, so we did not spent time sightseeing.

The drive to Istanbul we found exhilarating, because the road did not have potholes, and it had a separate lane for bicycles and bullock carts. The scene reminded me of my birthplace, Swat. The people also looked like the people living between the Indus and Oxus rivers, and when I stopped on the roads, one could find kebab, barbecued meat and nan (special unleavened bread). It was a sunny day and the bridge over the

Bosphorus linking the East with the West towards Istanbul, looked magnificent, as this was our first sighting of the calm blue sea. We stayed in Istanbul as there was much to see. Like Isfahan, one can never get tired of Istanbul. I learned that Istanbul was called Constantinople until the name was changed during the empire of the Turkish people.

After seeing the magnificent architecture, the museums, the churches, mosques and the treasures I got interested in the history of the Ottoman Empire, which lasted for more than six hundred years and extended from Eastern Europe to the west of Asia and the north of Africa. The conquest of Constantinople is said to be the pivotal point in its Eurasian character, because it was the gateway to the West. The reasons for its rise and fall, or for that matter the rise and fall of other empires such as the Persian Empire in ancient times and the British Empire in recent times, must be very interesting to know. I suppose there must be both internal as well as external causes.

Travelling is also education, and it was in Turkey that I learned the true meanings of 'sultan', 'pasha', 'Turkish caps' and 'harems', where a king would keep many women and only eunuchs were allowed to enter the women's quarter. I had heard a story in my childhood days about a Pukhtun who had gone to Turkey: on his return people asked him about the country he had visited. He is said to have reported that the country was a strange one: 'people looked like Pukhtuns, but I could only hear 'azaan' - call to prayers - in Pushto and the dogs were also barking in Pushto.'

Working in a hospital in the north of London, I used to come across Turkish patients with the genetic blood diseases which are prevalent along the Mediterranean and also right across the Silk Route. I was wondering about the Turkish and Greek immigrants, and it became clear to me that Southern Europe was a part of the Turkish Empire in the past and Cyprus was a part of British Empire. So invasions and occupations of peoples and countries not only lead to massacres, cruelty and rape but are the sources of certain diseases like thalassaemia and syphilis. Modern travel is also the source of some exotic and infectious diseases from Asia and Africa. So the world has become a 'global village' and disease prevalence has to be dealt with globally.

After spending the night and seeing belly-dancing in the historic city of Istanbul, we embarked on our journey very early to make sure that we would cross Bulgaria well in time towards Yugoslavia. At the Bulgarian border, there was a thorough search of our luggage and car. The car was taken to a garage, the engine was looked into, the panels of the doors were opened and spaces underneath the seats were searched. The Bulgarian customs people were looking for narcotics, especially hashish. In the seventies Bulgaria was in the orbit of Communist Russia and they had to toe the Russian line.

After spending hours at the border, we headed for Sofia. The name Sofia not only sounded romantic but pleasant, especially following a severe grilling by the Bulgarian immigration officials because I happened to be a Pakistani. It is said that 'one rotten fish spoils the whole pond' and the bad reputation in the sixties and seventies of Pakistanis has continued into recent decades all over the world, except Turkey and China, as already mentioned in these pages.

Sofia was a pleasant city and the people were pleasant, but as they say 'first impression is the last impression', and I was bitter, not realizing that the officials and the government do not represent the general public. In Sofia I crossed a red traffic light because of my mental state. The policeman whistled but did not stop me - he pointed to his eyes, meaning to look attentively while driving, but the eyes are controlled by the brain. It was in later years when my sight was damaged because of an eye surgeon's mistake that I remembered the Persian sage Sheikh Saadi's saying. He was asked, 'Is there anything worse than losing one's sight?' He replied, 'Yes, vision'.

Crossing the Bulgarian-Yugoslavian border was relatively easy. It was Marshall Tito's time and with his firm and disciplined rule he had kept all the nationalities living in Yugoslavia in harmony with each other. Democracy, which is supposed to have originated in Greece, is thought to be the best form of government, but some dictators and despots have done a lot for their countries and for the public good. Except in rare circumstances, monarchies have also been good for their people.

Budapest was like any city with bustling traffic and people always on the go. The people looked different to me in their demeanour; I had not realized at that time that there were many different people with ethnic, linguist, and religious backgrounds. To me they all looked harmonious and homogenous. Who could have predicted that in twenty years' time the whole country and the region would be in turmoil with neighbours killing neighbours, ethnic cleansing, massacres and division of the country? The basic human instincts of violence on different grounds can easily be aroused by troublemakers individually and collectively at different levels. History is replete with it. Humanity has yet to learn how to prevent manmade and natural disasters.

The road from Budapest to Zagreb passed through a rural area, and I enjoyed the scene as the ladies wearing baggy clothes working in the fields and some grazing their animals reminded me of Swat. I did not know that Yugoslavia had a multi-ethnic and multi-religious society living in peace because of the good policies of the leaders and non-interference by external factors. The road near Zagreb was zigzag and picturesque. The name Zagreb sounded to me Middle Eastern, like 'Meghreb', but it has nothing to do with it. Zagreb, as is well known, has a long history and became the capital of an independent state, Croatia.

Crossing into Austria was no problem from the immigration and customs points of view as Austria has always welcomed tourists and Vienna, its capital, is home to some United Nations organizations such as the Atomic Energy Agency. We stayed in Salzburg, a beautiful city. I looked at a tourist brochure and there was mention of art galleries, museums and music shows, but we neither had the time nor the patience to appreciate the so called 'good things' in life; I was brought up in a tough environment.

Our next destination was Munich in what was then West Germany. Germany's name was familiar to me since childhood because Pukhtun people for some reason associate themselves with Germans. If someone does a better job of some kind, they say, 'Da Germany Zuae De' - he is like a German. I also heard that of the tribes from the Steppes or the Central Asian Region who migrated, some went to Europe while others settled in Persia, Afghanistan and India. Munich also sounded familiar, as I had heard and read about it from my school and college days. Because the journey through Germany was along an autobahn, the first motorway through Europe, it was fast but monotonous. I thought I was driving very fast, but the German cars would easily overtake me. I had also not realized at that time that the faster you drive the more fuel you consume, but petrol was cheaper then.

In the seventies, few people could speak English in Germany, but in Belgium, I found it easier to communicate. In France, they were reluctant to speak English. The European Union has changed all this in terms of languages, travel and so on for the common man. One wishes that the countries of the Middle East, Asia and Africa could learn from Europe for the benefit of their own people and the world at large.

The last time I had driven through Munich, I had taken a wrong turning and made the traffic stop at the roundabout, but the drivers and the police were all polite and I was shown the right lane. The rest of the journey through Belgium and France was uneventful. We had to take the boat from Calais to Dover to cross the English Channel, but modern technology and the futuristic thinking of the leaders on both sides of English Channel has now created the Channel Tunnel. I felt at home when I reached Dover, but was in a hurry to reach Chandler's Ford in Hampshire, where I had bought a house for £7000.

The long and interesting journey by road through many countries with different cultures and different forms of governments varying from dictatorship to communism, monarchy and democracy finally ended, as so many things have to come to a stop. For many days my colleagues in the hospital would ask me about my journey. My younger colleagues asked me about the girls in different countries and whether they were pretty and easy-going. My senior, Duncan Ackery, who never married and had no children, was surprised that I travelled with a child for so many days, but Mah Muneer was a good baby and I do not remember her ever causing us any trouble on our journey. Moreover Shahnaz had always been a good mother, a good wife and very understanding and supportive to my extended family. Whether I have been a good life partner or like a Pukhtun who always think that ghairat (honour) is associated with their females, I do not know.

PART THREE

RETURN TO THE NATIONAL HEALTH SERVICE

CHAPTER TWENTY TWO

ENGLAND AND REPATRIATION TO PAKISTAN

☾

After returning from a long journey on the Silk Route, I had to resume my medical work at Ashford hospital near Heathrow Airport. I travelled daily by car from Southampton and make sure that I was on time for the ward rounds or outpatient clinics.

My job as Senior Registrar in Medicine was primarily meant for overseas doctors who would ultimately go back to their country of birth. My Chief, Dr Royds, a Scot by birth, was a general physician and used to look after patients suffering from all sorts of diseases, as narrow specialties were not firmly established in the late sixties and early seventies, but the trend had started for physicians to have an interest in certain diseases.

I was also responsible for looking after the patients of Dr Holditch, who had an interest in gastrointestinal diseases, and

Dr Alan Bonham Carter, whom I mentioned earlier. He was an elegant man. Whether the celebrity actress Helena Bonham Carter has any blood relationship with him, I am not sure. He would only see patients with neurological diseases. Thanks to modern technology and Western medicine, investigations of brain diseases with CT and MRI scans have become easy and painless.

Our hospital also took part in early experiments in CAT scanning (Computerised Axial Tomography). The young doctors for early training - house physicians - were sent from St. George's Medical School, London, and as a senior, I did not have any problem regarding their medical work of clerking and attending to the patients. Whether it was due to good undergraduate education or the British culture of attending to your duties, or both, I still do not know. As I mentioned earlier it is said that a good medical doctor should have three As under his belt - ability, availability and affability. Some, like Bob Milstead and Stephen Schey, one of the pioneers of bone marrow transplantation, became lifelong friends. They came by car to Peshawar through the Silk Route and the Khyber Pass on their onward journey to India and Australia.

As my training period neared its end, my chief politely and diplomatically told me that my chances of getting to the top level in the NHS, a consultant post, were not high. He would also give me the examples of his previous trainees who had struggled to get these jobs. I did apply for a job and was shortlisted. I went to Bradford, because there are so many Pakistanis settled there. I was supposed to go the day before to attend an evening dinner to which all the shortlisted candidates were invited, but I failed to go, which was a mistake on my part as I had not made plans or preparation for the interview. As they say, 'if you do not plan, you are planning for failure'. Since a consultant post was the highest post in NHS, they wanted to make sure that a proper person was recruited.

There were seven interviewers, including one woman. They were sitting in a semicircle and I was facing them. One person asked me many technical questions, which were difficult but relevant. He was a short person and not very impressive, unlike the others. I was told later that he wanted the job to go to his own candidate, who had been groomed for the job, but they had to go through the whole process in a transparent manner and according to the set rules and regulations.

I was made to sit and wait in a separate room. After some time, a gentleman came and told me politely that they were sorry that they could not select me. I was sad but not disappointed. The failure made me more determined to go back to the country where I was needed more.

Before returning to Hampshire, I went to see the streets and shopping centre of Bradford where the Pakistanis lived. The atmosphere was like any city in Pakistan: the shops were selling sarees, kameez, shalwars, earrings and necklaces as one sees in Pakistan. The aroma of spices was very obvious. Samosas, kebabs, tandoori chicken and pulao were available in the restaurants. I started photographs and the salesmen got suspicious that I was an Englishman taking pictures for ulterior motives, but they were satisfied when they learned who I was.

More than twenty percent of Bradford's populations are of Pakistani ethnic origin. The majority are Kashmiris from Mirpur, but Punjabis, Sindhis and Pushtuns also live there. In the 1950s immigration had started because of displacement as a result of the Mangla Dam scheme, and Britain needed labour for its textile mills in Yorkshire and Lancashire. Doctors from Pakistan started working in the UK in the 1960s, and I was one of those who came in the early sixties to work in the NHS and study for postgraduate qualifications. The earliest immigrants were sailors who settled in the port cities such as Southampton, Liverpool and London.

This reminds me of the 1980s, when I had gone to the USA to attend a medical conference, courtesy of the International Atomic Energy Agency (IAEA). I met an elderly Pukhtun, Hassan Khan from Mardan, through Dr Jan in Detroit Michigan. Hassan had come to the west coast of America as a sailor in the 1920s. Dr Jan was free with him and was joking that he had wives in every city of America and the latest one was in Detroit. Hassan was well respected in the American community in Detroit. His son wanted to poison himself because his girlfriend did not want to marry him, and Dr Jan said how naive he was to do such a thing in the USA. I had to say that Hassan's son had the genes of a proud Pukhtun, but the environment or nurture had mellowed his pushtunwali (code of behaviour).

I was offered a job with the Pakistan Atomic Energy Commission (PAEC), thanks to the Chairman, Munir Ahmad Khan, who told me that he wanted to build institutions so that qualified and trained people working or studying abroad would have places to come to. Another thing which he mentioned in the early seventies was that he wanted to build nuclear reactors for power generation, as Pakistan was short of electricity. He succeeded in the expansion of peaceful atomic energy by establishing medical and agricultural institutions from Khyber to Karachi, but he did not succeed in his second mission because the government of the day was more interested in the atomic bomb.

I also had to persuade my wife and children to come back to my birthplace. Mujgan was too young to understand the implications, while Mah Muneer was too polite to resist, even though it meant leaving her friends Sarah, Angela and others at her school. Shahnaz had seen my house with leaking ceilings and my village with narrow muddy streets with children walking barefoot and half naked, but she had also noticed and felt the unconditional love of my relatives and the people in general. She also knew her Persian culture and her parents had inculcated in her the need to stay with the family at any cost. I had also told her that she would study in medical college and there would be a lot of people to help her in the household chores, so there was something to look forward to.

Mah Muneers's school-leaving certificate had to be obtained. The headmistress of the school told us not to take her to Pakistan because she was too intelligent. 'Pakistan also needs intelligent people', was the curt answer we gave. For the first time I realized that children are assessed in Western schools and groomed and helped in their careers according to their aptitudes. This all depends on properly educated and trained teachers.

We opted for keeping the house, just in case we had to come back. It was a good decision, because later on we sold it for twenty times more than we had paid for it. A friend told me later on that there are three things which will be profitable in the medium and long term: investment in property, gold and raw precious stones.

We bought a second-hand Ford van to send our household goods by road. I also wanted the van to be used for taxi purposes in Peshawar to earn some extra money rather than depending on my low salary. This gave me problems in Pakistan, including threats of imprisonment, but that interesting episode, from which lessons had to be learnt, will be described later.

The contribution I had made towards a pension was reclaimed, which was a mistake, but I needed the money. We bought a new Japanese Nissan as I was told that spare parts were easily available. We made ourselves ready for the long journey, which was not new for us as we had done it twice before along the same route travelled by that remarkable family from Italy, the Marco Polos, some centuries ago for trade from East to

West. One wishes that trade and commerce could be established on this route in both directions for the benefit of people who in some countries are facing disaster because of militancy.

CHAPTER TWENTY THREE

MORE TRAVEL ADVENTURES

☪

We sailed across the English Channel, as the Channel Tunnel had not yet been built. Britain is and was called the British Isles because it is surrounded by sea, but the water all around had not prevented invaders like the Vikings. The journey through Europe was easy and I had no worries, but Eastern Europe was under communist governments and the worry started as we entered Yugoslavia as I did not want to give any excuse to the powerful police and intelligence agencies to fine me or even imprison me. In those days Pakistanis were known for drug smuggling, as at the time of writing, rightly or wrongly, they are known for terrorism.

Crossing the Bulgarian border, we were welcomed by the Turkish immigration and custom officials. Pakistan has always had good relations with Turkey and there has always been mutual respect. I wonder why.

The car had started giving us problems in Bulgaria, but I was afraid to show it to the mechanics. We stopped in Istanbul, a beautiful city and full of attractive and polite people, to repair it. The engine had to be overhauled, but the mechanic was confident of doing the job.

As we all left the car to go to the hotel, Mujgan was crying and screaming; she was scared of the flies, which she had not seen before. Man-made and natural environmental degradation has changed everything since that time and nowadays flies are no strangers in the UK. We saw a group of young travellers to Nepal in a van, and one of the girls was retching and depressed. Istanbul, or the gateway to the East or to the West, depending on how you look at it, had given her culture shock. There are many historical places to see there, but we went to the beach at the Sea of Marmara.

After the engine had been repaired we had to go slowly over the mountainous region, which had hairpin bends, and cross the Tahir Pass to reach the border with Iran. In Ankara, I saw a signpost for Maulana Rumi's place and again wanted to see the 'whirling dervishes', but the wish remained unfulfilled.

The Iranian border officials were not as harsh as the Bulgarian ones and not so polite as the Turkish. They stamped the passport showing a car, but did not let a customs official go with us to the border as they did in some cases. I noticed that one Pakistani, while handing in his passport, put some money in it, but the official, who happened to be a well-dressed woman speaking fluent English with an accent, returned the money. Pakistanis are used to thinking that unless you 'grease the palms' of officials things do not get done. Improving governance goes a long way in minimizing corruption. Putting the fair sex in charge of certain departments should also remove material corruption in the developing countries.

After spending the night in Tabriz, a Turkish-speaking town in Iran, we headed for Tehran, as Dr Dalil and his family were eagerly waiting for us. It was easy to find his house in the north of Tehran as it was near the Pakistani Iranian School, where the medium of instruction was English and Iranians were fond of educating their children in English. On my previous visits I had learnt to take my shoes off, as even the verandas had hand-made carpets.

We stayed the night, as before, in the master's bedroom, which was vacated for us. After taking a breakfast consisting of tea served in glass cups, cheese, special Iranian bread, fruit and basil leaves, we set off for Isfahan. I once again mentioned the nude painting and Dalil said 'peshkash, qabil n darad' - it is a gift from us, take it.

My father-in-law, Nasrullah Nasseri, who spoke fluent English, was waiting for us in his car in a pre-arranged place outside Isfahan. He was very pleased to see his grandchildren, as grandparents usually are. Agha Furghani, who was married to Shayesta, meaning beautiful and refined, which fitted her very well, had invited us to dinner and a show in a local hotel. The dinner was typical Persian cuisine: chilo kabab, salad mixed with herbs and fruit. The 'floor show' was a mixture of Middle Eastern - belly dancing - and western - rock and roll and cha cha cha. As we came out, Nasrulllah said Furghani should not have brought us there because there was some nudity and sexual innuendo in the floor show, but his son-in-law was a secular person and also had a sense of humour.

I once asked him the names of all the Imams and he related them, but said 'kazib' in one case. I did not know the real name, nor the meaning, of 'kazib'.

After visiting Shahnaz's extended family and going to the ancestral village Saeed Abad, a scenic village perched on high ground near the river Zainda Rud, and also seeing the hundred-year-old Quran in the family written in Kofi script, we embarked on our return journey to Tehran, Mashhad, Herat, Kandahar and Kabul. We stayed in Mashhad to pay our respects to Imam Raza, and in the huge mosque people of all ethnic groups could be recognized from their features and dress: central Asian states, the Middle East, Afghanistan,

India and Pakistan. On the way to Kabul, we also stayed in Kandahar, a typical Pushtun city where the mausoleum of one of the great kings of India and Afghanistan, Ahmad Shah Abdali, is situated. In later years during the Taliban era, they wanted to develop Kandahar further.

The atmosphere in Kabul in the seventies was different from the rest of Afghanistan: one could see girls wearing skirts and foreign tourists sitting in restaurants having drinks and smoking hashish. Women clad in shuttlecock burqas could also be seen. There were also men wearing suits along with traditional tribal gear, but the atmosphere was not suffocating and people could move around at any time of the day or night without fearing bomb blasts or Kalashnikovs, as in later years.

After spending the night in the Hotel Kabul and phoning friends in Peshawar to facilitate our smooth transit through the border, we drove the last leg of our journey, crossing the Durand Line, the Pakistan-Afghanistan border, towards Khyber Pass. At the border Dr Ilyas, a cardiologist, and Barrister Baacha were waiting for us. I knew Dr Ilyas from our days in England, when both of us were preparing for membership of the Royal College of Physicians. Barrister Baacha was well known in the society as he had been president of the Khyber Union and would take a stand and raise his voice fearlessly if there was any injustice in society. Baacha was also known for giving typical Pushto names to his children: Batoor, Tatara Guloona, Zara Sanga, Meena Gabeena and Sandara. I had the good fortune of looking after his mother medically, as she would only take treatment if I had prescribed the medicine for her. She was a fine lady who had helped in educating her children, who became useful members of the society.

Dr Ilyas took us to his house in Nishtar Abad, which was big and well maintained. We were put in an upstairs room and were very well looked after by his mother and sister. They were all very kind and made us comfortable. The house was opposite the mansion belonging to Zafar Ali Shah and his brother; they were a religious political family who had made their mark not only in business but in politics. The family knew how to play their cards and had learnt not to swim against the tide. The family had joined the Pakistan People's Party (PPP) in later years and Benazir Bhutto stayed in their house during her visits to Peshawar.

After enjoying the hospitality of Dr Ilyas and his family, we found a house for rent in University Town on a road named after a Pan-Islamist Persian or Afghani, Jamal Uddin. The house belonged to Engineer Majeed Khan, who belonged to a well-known tribe of Pukhtuns, the Momand tribe. The people of this tribe live on both sides of the Durand Line and have preserved the Pukhtun characteristics of hospitality, helping others in time of crises such as illness and dependence on one's own earnings rather than on charity. As the sage Sheikh Saadi has said:

Daste khud ra kus be kun
Minate her kus na kun
- tighten or use your hand for work and do not beg others.

Some people with a raw sense of humour use this saying in a different sense.

Our rented house had to be furnished. Instead of buying furniture in shops, I got walnut logs from Swat and called in the carpenters from our village, who had been with us for generations and were fine craftsmen. Walayat Bibi (England Bibi), my aunt, gave us her large fridge, which was rarely used in Swat because of the cold weather and intermitant electricity. My youngest sister, Jamala, came to live with us and was very helpful in looking after Mah Muneer and Mujgan.

Since there was no girls' school in our village, Jamala was uneducated in the formal sense. Shahnaz not only started teaching her household skills such as cooking but bought books for her to be taught at home. Shahnaz also tried to find a good match for her and succeeded in doing so by arranging a marriage to a fine, hard-working, educated man who became a doctor with a specialty in a largest organ in the body, the skin. At the time of writing Jamala and Inam have two daughters, Saadia and Huda, and two sons, Sheraz and Riaz.

One attraction of coming to Pakistan for my wife, whom Charles Lindholm labelled in later years the 'guardian angel', was to be admitted to a medical college. Another was that she would have home help, but the overwhelming desire was for us to be together as a family, as Iranians girls were taught the sanctity of family togetherness. Shahnaz's qualifications for admission were right, but they had to be translated and authenticated by the Foreign Office. 'Putting in a word' at a proper time by a proper person also helped: Begum Kulsoom Saifullah, an intelligent and pretty Pushtun woman, was close to the wife of the Iranian Council General in her official capacity as chairperson of the Iran Pakistan friendship organization, and she managed to put in a word to the Principal, Raza Ali, who had a soft spot for Iran because he was from the Shia sect. The bureaucratic process of using the 'proper channels' had to be overcome, but issues of governance and fair play were not so bad in the seventies as in the later years in Pakistan (the supposed 'land of the pure'.

Shuaib Sultan Khan, one of the finest and ablest in the bureaucracy, came to the rescue in a transparent manner, as his student working in the Foreign Office was contacted. When I went to see the gentleman in the Foreign Office, he was so impressed with his teacher and one-time chief that he said, 'if it is possible, I will make it probable and if it is probable, it will be done.' I learned that if one is a good role model to students or subordinates, then one will be remembered all the time. To the utter delight of NN and my mother-in-law Qurani, Shahnaz was admitted to the first year and also gained a scholarship from the Iranian Government, thanks to Fatah Nabavian and Mr. Samimi.

Shahnaz established a good rapport with the girl students, who were all younger than her. Some, such as Naseem Mustajab and Sheema Mirza, became lifelong friends. Some boys called her 'mother', and when she entered the class with other girl students they would say, 'Lona da moor sara raghla' - daughters are coming with their mother.

Shahnaz learnt Pushto easily and in a short time, because most of my female relatives were uneducated in the modern sense and she was interested not only in the education of the children, especially the girls, but in the overall standard of living of her husband's relatives. Learning a foreign language can be tricky sometimes. Once, while introducing my male cousin, she said, 'Daa de Sher tror de' - This is Sher's auntie. Once this also happened to Mrs. Sanae, the wife of the Iranian Consul General, who was learning Urdu. She complained that the house worker did not come to do the work when called, but she was using the word 'Jawoo' - go - instead of 'Aajaw' - come here.

Some of the female teachers, such as Professor Minhas, were also kind to Shahnaz. She was not only a good teacher and a skilled gynaecologist and obstetrician but a very good administrator. During her time as administrator of Khyber

Teaching Hospital, a lot of development had taken place, not only in terms of building and equipment but also in the teaching and care of patients. Improvement does take place if the top person has knowledge and managerial skills, but much more important is to have a 'heart' for the place and profession.

Annual examinations were very stressful, not only for Shahnaz but for me, because she would resist going in on the morning of the examination as she would say she was going to fail. I learnt to persuade her by asking her friends to encourage her, as well as to tell her to attempt the questions and try to fill in the paper with what she knew and not to think of passing or failing. She passed the exams at the first attempt and later became a self-trained sonologist, so much so that ladies from all over Khyber Pukhtunkhwa, Afghanistan and even Islamabad come to her for ultrasonography. If there is doubt about the diagnosis or some malformation of the foetus, women are sent to Shahnaz for a second opinion.

Once a well-to-do family from Mardan had an ultrasound scan done during the first pregnancy. They wanted to know the sex of the child, and Shahnaz told them it was a boy. Some of the rich patients want their children to be born in the USA or UK for nationality purposes, so this couple, along with their in-laws, travelled to the USA. There they were told by a sonologist that the foetus was a girl. The mother became very depressed and had to be admitted to hospital. The family phoned me and complained about the cost of the travel and living in USA, so I told Shahnaz to be careful with categorical diagnoses. There is at least a one percent uncertainty, but she said she would stick to her original diagnosis. Anyway, when the child was delivered, it was a boy. The family had employed a special nanny from Thailand for him. Whether the nanny did some special extra work for the husband is not clear. Later on, whenever I met the father with his son, I asked him, 'is this the girl who changed into a boy?' The last I heard about the couple they had separated, but Pukhtuns do not talk about separation or divorce as it is still taboo in their society. People still say in a derogatory manner that such and such a person is *talaqi* - a divorcee.

Pukhtuns always want sons, for various reasons: to help the father in his day-to-day work, such as farming, to be on his side if there is a feud and to inherit the property after the demise of the father. The family is considered incomplete if there is no son. Shahnaz knew about this, but the technology was not advanced and ultrasonography could not predict the sex of the child accurately. Being pregnant and attending classes in a medical college was a tough job, but not for Shahnaz.

One evening she told me that she needed emergency admission because of bleeding, otherwise she was going to lose the baby. I rushed to Prof. Minhas' house, which was opposite our rented house. Seeing me in panic with my baggy trousers, she calmed me down and reassured me that everything would be all right.

Our friends and near and dear ones heard about the emergency. It was nice of Dr Jamil-ur-Rehman and his Spanish wife Pakeeta, a very kind lady, to come to the hospital. Engineer Ihtesham and Dr Ikram volunteered to give blood. Dr Mehr Taj, an efficient doctor and teacher and later on a politician, stayed in the operating theatre until the baby was born and resuscitated the baby. The arrival of the baby was difficult, but our friends and relatives were all there to give a helping hand and Dr Parkash, who was a registrar in the children's unit, stayed all night to look after the baby.

Later on when Cyrus was grown up, we used to joke with him that he had arrived with great ceremony and he would not breathe for two minutes, so he had to be careful, but he turned out to have a sense of humour even during childhood. During General Zia's time, on admission to Primary School, Cyrus was required to answer some religious questions: his mother took him to one of the Army schools in Multan and the teacher asked him 'who is your prophet?' he looked at his mother and said, 'Sher Mohammad Khan'. The next question was, 'Kalma shahadat parho' - recite Kalma. Once againe looked at his mother, who intervened and said, 'His father does not know it, how can you expect a four-year-old child to know it?'

Child and mother mortality in Pakistan is very high. We were lucky in having friends and relatives in the medical fraternity, but what about the majority who have no access to quality healthcare? We did not have any problem with our two other children, Mah Muneer and Mujgan, because they were born in the British welfare state where the leaders had done and are doing everything to make the lives of ordinary people easy and comfortable. Pukhtuns in general and people in developing countries in particular have many children, as already mentioned in these pages, for obvious reasons: a low standard of living, low literacy rate and lack of facilities for family planning. My patients from Afghanistan usually have from half a dozen to more than a dozen children. When I ask them about it they say 'Allah Rakae' - Allah gives us - and they also say, 'Allah is rizaqrassan' - Allah provides food - which is true, but as I mentioned earlier, my tough mother used to say 'Rizaq spoo la hum pa deran milaweegi' - stray dogs get their food in trash pits.

This reminds me of a story attributed to a famous poet of India named Ghalib, who was fond of alcohol. Once, when he got his official stipend, he spent it on bottles of alcohol. His wife, who was religious, told him that they had to pay the debt they had incurred in buying food and asked them what they were going to do, because the money had been spent on alcohol. Ghalib is said to have told his wife 'Allah is *riziq rassan* - provider of food - but has not promised alcohol. But it is also said in the Quran that everyone has to work to get food.

CHAPTER TWENTY FOUR

THE PAKISTAN ATOMIC ENERGY COMMISSION

☪

In Peshawar at that time new department for the peaceful uses of atomic energy in medicine - nuclear medicine - was being set up. The hospital was built and the foundation stone was laid by Zulfiqar Bhutto. Chairman Usmani of PAEC had it sanctioned in the famous Multan meeting when there was heated emotional discussion about diverting resources to making the 'Bomb' because Pakistan's arch rival, India, had made the Bomb. Dr Gul Rehman, who was a properly-qualified radiotherapist, had made efforts to sanction the hospital. He also took a building contractor with him to be introduced to the chairman of the PAEC. Whether proper measures regarding the architectural drawings, discussion and vetting the plans about the hospital, open tenders etc. were arranged is not clear. I was not sure as I was a novice. As a user of the building for healthcare, I found many flaws in the building, including leaking ceilings, cracks in the walls and uneven floors, but as with so many things in developing countries, bribery, corruption, misuse of power and poor governance are rampant and buildings for healthcare are no exception.

The hospital building was unlike the other properly-constructed buildings of the PAEC, so extra measures for radiation protection for the staff and patients had to be taken. Nuclear medicine had been established for the first time in the province in the early seventies, but radiotherapy already existed at Lady Reading Hospital. Dr Abdul Hakeem Khan had started radiology and radiotherapy there. Lady Reading, the benevolent wife of the then Viceroy of India, had established the hospital in 1916. The name has not been changed so far, as in the case of Cunningham Park next door. There was a machine for the treatment of skin cancer, which is relatively common in Pukhtuns because of their fair skin and outdoor farming work. Some radioactive needles with a very long half-life were also present at LRH. The machine was shifted to the new building of Institute of Radiotherapy and Nuclear Medicine (IRNUM), as the new Director of IRNUM did not want competition. The radium needles were used for the treatment of cancer and could potentially cause cancer because of excessive radiation if not handled properly, but what happened to them is not known.

Lady Reading Hospital had another illustrious doctor by the name of Dr Abdul Hakeem Khan, who would treat patients to the best of his ability during the days when there were no narrow specialties in medical practice. My teacher, Dr Najibullah Khan of Swat, would give examples from Dr Khan and encourage the younger doctors to learn to try to handle all the emergencies and to innovate and extend treatment to the patients, even if there was a lack of healthcare facilities.

When I took over as Head of the Nuclear Medicine Division, I remembered these doctors' advice and took it upon myself to educate and train the technicians and medical doctors. As is well known, treating matters as challenges improves things. As I have mentioned, thyroid problems were common, as the region is iodine deficient and enlargement of the thyroid gland (goitre) was noted centuries ago by Marco Polo. Thyroid treatment with radioactive iodine was started by me for the first time in the province now known as Khyber Pukhtunkhwa.

Patients also bring personal problems to doctors. One of my patients, an elderly, soft-spoken woman from Peshawar, complained that her daughter, who was working in the administration department of the hospital, had a lot of bluish patches on her buttocks and thighs. Would I see her? I was reluctant, because the girl was working in the Hospital Director's office and I was not on very good terms with him, and the Director wanted the rest of us to keep away from his favourite girls. I suspected him of foul play, but it turned out that the superintendent in the office was involved. The superintendent had a long grey beard and led prayers in his village. It turned out that he liked to hold her thighs and buttocks with both hands, hence the bluish discolouration on the body. I found for the first time, but not the last, that long beards and marks on the forehead because of prayers are no guarantee of good behaviour towards the fair sex.

Confirmation of over-activity or under-activity - hyperthyroidism and hypothyroidism - by blood tests used to take a long time because biological methods were used for measurement of the hormones. Peaceful uses of atomic methods made these measurements quicker and easy, thanks to pioneers like Berson, Yallow and Ekins. Yallow got a Nobel Prize. Ekins, from the Middlesex Hospital, London, had also expected it; he was not only disappointed but was depressed for three months.

It is said that politics to some extent also plays a part in the granting of these high awards. Professor Ekins' secretary, an elegant Italian woman, told me about the political element. I had the good fortune of knowing Ekins. In the early seventies Peshawar was second to none anywhere in the world where thyroid maladies were concerned in terms of investigations and treatment using radioisotopes. It would not have been possible for me without the PAEC and the support of the Chairman, Munir Ahmad Khan, and his team of brilliant scientists.

One scientist, Dr Abdullah Sadiq, who is a theoretical physicist like the Nobel Laureate Salaam, had been very helpful in PAEC. Dr Inan-ur-Rehman was another person in PAEC who had been very kind like so many other and the space does not allow me to mention all of them, But Dr Abdullah sent me a piece which is reproduced below:

"I have known Dr Sher Mohammad Khan since the early 1970s. We first met soon after my return from the States. He had also then recently returned from the UK. The first time we met was in the hostel room of our mutual friend Mian Ifthekhar Hussain, then a student of medicine. Evidently it was early spring. I was dressed in my usual traditional dress with a warm Chitrali cap covering my longish hair. He later told me that he took me for a radical revolutionary! But for our conversations in our mother tongue Pashto and his traditional dress, with his tall handsome stature and very fair colour, I would have taken him for a European gentleman.

"It was a pleasant surprise to learn that we both worked in the same organization, the Pakistan Atomic Energy Commission (PAEC). He was then posted to the Institute of Radiation and Nuclear Medicine (IRNUM), Peshawar while I was working in the Pakistan Institute of Nuclear Sciences and Technology (PINSTECH), Islamabad. Our professional and personal association since then has grown and deepened with time.

"As an expert in Nuclear Medicine and Radio Therapy he had been greatly instrumental in launching the degree programmes in these areas in the then Centre of Nuclear Sciences (CNS) of PAEC. With his charm and skills of persuasion he persuaded the Academic Council of Quid-I-Azam University, with which CNS was then affiliated, to accept this programme, equivalent to its M Phil degree programme. Later on he helped CNS to persuade the Pakistan College of Physicians and Surgeons to accept this programme equivalent to part one of its Fellowships. This happened after CNS was granted degree award status by the Government as the Pakistan Institute of Engineering and Applied Sciences (PIEAS) and I was its Rector.

"Besides helping CNS/PIEAS in crucial ways mentioned above, Dr Khan strived to ensure that these programmes met international standards. He himself gives lectures there and identifies experts in relevant fields within and outside Pakistan for this purpose. He also examines students at the end of their course and clinical work and helps identify leading experts within and outside Pakistan and persuades them to act as external examiners. I recall Dr Ali Nawaz Khan, a leading radiologist of UK, and Dr McQueen, a leading Canadian oncologist, visiting CNS/PIEAS for teaching and examination during my stay there.

"One reason for our close association over such a long time is our common interest in social welfare, especially education. During our meetings we invariably discussed the plight of common people and the need for their education as a possible panacea for their problems. It was during one such discussion that he suggested that as an educationalist myself, I ought to establish a school for the children of my village. It was with his help and encouragement that in 1991 I started my school, Rextin Kore in Shaheen Town, Peshawar, just outside my village of Gharibabad. Dr Sher also helped me to raise funds, himself contributing, for the support of a significant number of needy students. He also used to regularly visit Rextin Kore, talk to the children and encourage them in their studies. After my resignation as the Rector of the Ghulam Ishaq Khan Institute of Engineering Sciences and Technology (GIKI) in 2007 I couldn't afford to run my school and had to close it in 2008 with a very heavy heart.

"Around the same time that I established my school in Peshawar, Dr Sher started a free weekend clinic in his home town, Koza Drushkhela in Swat. This entailed his driving for 7-8 hours after work on Fridays and undertaking the same long and arduous trip back to Peshawar on Sundays. Eventually he also established his own school, Sheen Bagh, in his hujra there. I had the pleasure of meeting the bright and smart students of Sheen Bagh when I stayed at his house along with my family during my visit to the enchanting Swat valley. Later on he very kindly invited me as the Chief Guest at the annual day of Sheen Bagh. Dr Sher gave me the same respect and protocol as he gave to the provincial education minister, whom he had also invited at that time. Needless to say he strives to provide the best available teachers, as well as the best possible facilities to the students of Sheen Bagh.

"Dr Sher is an exemplary Puxtun and an embodiment of Puxtunwali code. He is hospitable, he is generous and above all he is a friend in need. I have personally greatly enjoyed his generous hospitality a number of times, not only in his home town in Swat but at his University Town residence in Peshawar.

"The circumstances that led to my resignation as Rector of the Gik-Institute in September 2007 were greatly depressing for me. Instead of returning to Islamabad from Topi I decided to go to my hometown in Peshawar to fully devote myself to my school. The condition of the school at that time was far below my expectations. I was also finding it increasingly difficult to muster the financial resources to sustain it. This led to much deeper depression. It was during this most difficult time of my life that Dr Sher came to my help. He would frequently call me, visit me and take me out with him to the Peshawar golf course."

Some gaps did remain in the testing of the thyroid, which anatomically has a butterfly appearance in the neck. One of these was how to tell whether the swelling was innocent or due to cancer. A visiting expert from the Karolinksa Medical Institute in Sweden helped me; he said that all I had to do was to use a small needle and aspirate the material for examination under a microscope. The method came to be known as Fine Needle Aspiration (FNA) and Fine Needle Aspiration Cytology (FNAC), a painless and simple procedure in comparison with biopsy. FNAC is widely used for investigations of lumps and bumps in the body, but as in so many cases the interpreter has to be experienced. This butterfly-like organ under the skin in the upper body can mimic 59 different diseases, from psychiatric problems to changes in weight and infertility, which in a Pukhtun family can be the cause of more than one marriage (polygamy), but not divorce because divorce is taboo in the Pukhtun culture.

Gena Lee Nolin, one of the stars of the soap opera 'Baywatch', had undiagnosed underactivity of thyroid for many years, even in the technologically and economically advanced USA. This elegant, shapely woman took a positive approach when she was treated for her Hashimoto's thyroid disease and started a blog called 'Thyroid Sexy', a forum where problems of the thyroid are discussed in simple, non-jargon terms. I wrote to her to send a message on 'World Thyroid Day'. Her letter, which should be read and reread by medical professionals, is reproduced here:

Dear Doctor

You may or may not know who I am, so, allow me to introduce myself. My name is Gena Lee Nolin, and I was 'Barker beauty' in the show 'The Price is Right'. I then worked on a show called 'Baywatch'. I also had my own show, 'Sheena', among various acting and modeling endeavors. I have launched a campaign to raise awareness about thyroid disease. I have written a book about my story and my struggle with this disease. It was published by Simon and Schuster in October 2013. For many years I was very ill and suffered from severe fatigue, depression, weight gain, anxiety, hair loss, dry skin and a myriad other symptoms that we all go through when we have this disease. It was debilitating. I went to many doctors before I finally found one who discovered I had Hashimoto's thyroiditis /hypothyroid.

Words truly cannot convey how negatively this undiagnosed illness impacted my life for so many years. I was told to exercise, I was told to eat less. I was put on antidepressants, I was put an anxiety medicine. None of it helped.

I had a very bad experience when I was pregnant with my third child. I went to A fib and was almost cardioverted in my seventh month. It was due to undiagnosed thyroid disease. As you can imagine, it was terrifying for me.

I ask you to 'think outside of the box' in terms of the diagnosis and treatment of your patients. We as a patient community have found that while the TSH test can be a useful diagnostic test, it is not without its drawbacks. Too many of us fall through the cracks and remain ill when diagnosis and treatment are based solely on this test. The reference range is too broad and it seems there is continual controversy over what the reference range should actually be. I ask that you please test for Hashimoto's and Graves antibodies. I also ask that you test Free T3 and Free T4 levels, the actual circulating hormones, to give a more comprehensive view of your patient's thyroid status. In addition reverse T3 and a Thyroid Ultrasound, as my blood work did not show Hashimoto's antibodies. I was diagnosed via ultrasound.

I ask that you please consider the use of T3 medication in addition to T4 medication if your patient is not doing well on T4 medication alone. So many of us have problems converting T4 to T3 adequately, I was one of them. I was on Symthroid for a year and it did not help me. I continued to become more debilitated with each passing day.

I ask that you please consider the use of desiccated thyroid. Contrary to popular belief, it is not antiquated medication. It has been used successful for years, is still used today and many patients, including myself, have finally found the road back to wellness on it. I take natural desiccated thyroid. I was prescribed Armour Thyroid in Jan of 2011 and there are other brands available. There was a study published from the Endo 2013 conference status that desiccated thyroid is a safe alternative to Leothyroid, if you would be kind enough to look that up.

I ask that you look at cortisol level along with Vitamin D, Vitamin B12, iron and ferritin levels. My iron and cortisol were so low at one point that I had a difficult time with hormone replacement. Once I got them in a good range, I was able to tolerate the thyroid hormone and my body was better able to utilize it.

Most importantly, I ask that you please listen to your patient and look at their clinical presentation when they tell you their symptoms and how they are feeling. They know their body better than anyone.

Thank you for taking time to read this. On behalf of your patient, it is my hope that you will take it into consideration.

Their health and wellbeing depend on it.

Kind regards,
GENA LEE NOLIN

CHAPTER TWENTY FIVE

NEW DIFFICULTIES, SERENDIPITOUS TRAVELS AND EXILE TO MULTAN

☾*

We were living in rented houses and had to move depending on the wish of the owner, because there were no rules and regulations regarding the rights of tenants as in the United Kingdom or in the days of 'Khilafat' during the glorious days of Islam. During my childhood living in a village, people lived in either their own houses or in the houses owned by the Khan, in return for work whenever it was needed, either in the agricultural fields or in the Khan's houses. The Khan would at times marry the young, pretty daughter of the tenant as one of his four wives, or keep her in a separate house as his mistress.

The concept of buying an already-built house was not common in the sixties and early seventies, so we had to purchase a piece of land and build a house on it. My only experience was in the medical field and I did not know how to acquire or manipulate the system to get a plot of land in government-run schemes, but a family of Bara Khan Khels from Mardan came to my rescue; there was a plot of land opposite their house primarily meant for building a police station, but they did not want a police station opposite their house. But powerful and strong political families can easily make changes to the system. The better half of the land (two Kanals) was given to a retired bureaucrat, who sold it for a very high price, and the other two Kanals of land remained, which was disputed with the people of the neighbouring village. I was helped by Ghulam Nabi Khan and his elder brother GM Khan, a soft-spoken, intelligent man. A straightforward, well-groomed and well-trained bureaucrat from the Burki family facilitated the allocation of the plot to me. But serious problems remained; one was the dispute with the villagers and another was payment. One was solved by my experience as one of the chiefs of my tribe in Swat:- the use of strong-arm tactics. Another problem was solved by what I had learned in England: I had borrowed money from the bank.

A minor problem also arose in the hospital where I was working. My chief in the hospital had also applied for the piece of land, and he became furious when he heard through Dean Sahib, a religious scholar who was a member of the 'University Town' committee for sanctioning the plot, because he had himself applied for it. Dean Sahib, a religious scholar educated in the world famous Al-Azhar University, thought my boss would be pleased because someone from his hospital had got the plot, but it made things worse for me because of already existing simmering jealousy.

As is well-known, Pukhtuns are generous, and a lot has been written about this by outsiders. It is a part of the culture, but whether it will be passed on to the younger generations is uncertain, because it is not known whether this quality is because of nature or nurture. However, it has been postulated that there is a centre in the brain which deals with altruistic activity.

In my case, my senior and director of the hospital had shown generosity in the sense that he had encouraged me to apply for the job; whether it was because of selfish interest on his part as there was no one educated in the field of nuclear medicine in the region, or whether it was because of generosity, is hard to decipher. Jealousy goes hand in hand with generosity in Pukhtun culture. As I have mentioned, paternal first cousins are called *tarbur* - a person who can become an enemy if the opportunity arises. This characteristic has been exploited by rulers in the past in the Swat and Dir regions by chiefs of the tribes, and by the British. It is still being used and misused by the intelligence agencies and other vested interests.

I was subjected to indignities by the head of the hospital; for example a Naib Qasid- a person who runs errands - would come and say, 'sahib bulla ta hain' - sahib is calling you. I had yet to learn to please the boss at any cost and could not leave work in the middle and run to attend to his errands. I was also supposed not to shake hands with the peons and other so-called non-officers. My stint in the UK National Health Service had taught me to respect all the workers, whatever their status or job. Also, my father had taught me to respect our workers, whom we children addressed as if they were our relatives. A fair-skinned girl working in the laboratory used to stay after working hours and had sexual relations with the boss, which was no secret. The boss was told that I had shown interest in the girl. Family background also played its part in his jealousy. Professional jealousy, especially in private practice, was also rampant, not only in our hospital but also in the medical college among the senior professors.

Corruption in the purchase of equipment was also high and I was made to sign the documents, which at times I resisted. The combination of all these factors brought things to boiling point and I was officially forced to leave Peshawar and sent to a place where in British times people were sent as punishment. (In undivided India, people were sent to the Andaman Islands, which Pukhtuns called 'Tore Obe', Black Water. It was here that a Pukhtun stabbed Lord Minto, the Viceroy of India. It was said that 'Char Cheez Tohfae Multan/Garde, Gada, Garma, wa, gooristan', which means 'Multan is famous for four things, dust, beggars, heat and cemeteries'.)

I resisted for months, in vain. However I did utilize the time by visiting the Northern Areas, which has the largest conglomeration of high mountains in the world. The break in service also caused me a loss of lakhs of rupees when I was retired, as I was not told the rules and regulations by the officials, nor I had bothered to know these, being habituated to the Western system, where they try to deal with official matters in a transparent manner.

Some people are extroverts and can make friends easily and have friends everywhere and at all levels. Dr Ilyas, the cardiologist, was one of these. He arranged a trip to the Northern Region bordering China and asked his friends to join; one was a classical music lover from Karachi. One was a urologist from a Pukhtun family in Lahore, a cousin of Imran Khan, the cricketer turned politician, and there were other young men. I was asked, would I go? I said I would love to. I had heard about the high mountains and the scenic beauty of the Northern Region, at one time a part of Kashmir and a part of the Silk Route, from Professor Edward Williams, a relative of Buster Goodwin, a one-time commissioner in British times on the North West Frontier. Professor Williams was a mountaineer as well as having an interest in the thyroid gland. He had visited the region in the early fifties when there was peace and tranquility there, and he told me that he had even discovered and named some of the peaks.

All the arrangements and logistics were made by Dr Ilyas, a meticulous planner. We set out for the Karakoram Highway (KKH) to reach our ultimate destination of the Shimshal Valley bordering China. The KKH was built in the late fifties when Ayub Khan was at the helm of affairs. Ayub Khan was a Pukhtun belonging to a famous tribe, the Tareens. His ancestors had settled in the Hazara region and like many Pukhtuns when they settle in a new area, he had adopted the language of the new place. He had rightly extended the hand of friendship to China, demarcating the northern border area, and the KKH was built, a joint project in which many Chinese as well as Army Engineers personnel lost their lives because of the construction of the road in difficult terrain. Some international people have suggested that the Highway should be called the Eighth Wonder of the World.

Besham, a small town, was our first stop on the right bank of the mighty Indus River. We stopped on the bridge linking the two banks of the Indus, which was called Sinduh in the Rigveda some thousand years ago. Looking north one could see the majestic snow-covered mountains and the backdrop of blue water. It was the mountains of the south and west of this area that Alexander the Great had reached before tracing his route back and onwards to confront King Porus of India. The peak of the mountain is called Aoronos – Pir Sar - on the right bank, mentioned by Ptolemy, the Greek historian.

Dassu was the next place where we stayed on KKH. I went to a nearby middle school in Pattan village and examined the schoolchildren for the prevalence of thyroid enlargement. Kohistan, or the land of mountains, was a part of the princely state of Swat and the Wali Jehan Zeb was fond of education and had built schools in even the remotest parts. Pattan became well known in later years because an antique necklace of pure gold was found by a shepherd in the mountains. Some of the ringleaders from Swat during the Taliban era had also taken refuge in the mountains of Pattan and the Palus area.

People on the right bank of the Indus River are called Kohistanis. My father always told me to respect them and not to charge medical fees, because they were our *mamagan* - relatives on the maternal side. People on the left bank are Pukhtuns who migrated from Swat. Pukhtuns and Gujars have always been at loggerheads because of land disputes. The people of Kohistan are Sunni Muslims and are religious because they have studied in religious seminaries in Swat and have established their own seminaries. They have always been with the religious parties.

On KKH we stopped to see the rock carvings on the left bank of the Indus. Professor Dani, a world-famous archaeologist, had drawn attention to these rock carvings, which are hundreds of years old. I went near the river to see some of them. There were carvings of animals and humans with erect penises. These carvings can be seen on the rocks on the banks of the Indus up to Gilgit and beyond.

On the way to Gilgit we stopped to see Nanga Parbat, which means 'the naked mountain'. In local language it is called Diamir, the king of mountains. It is a majestic, snow-covered mountain which has always been a challenge for mountaineers. We took pictures before continuing and stayed the night in Gilgit, which has been the main town in the Northern Region. At one time the region was part of the Durrani Empire of Ahmad Shah Durrani. Ahmad Shah Durrani's empire was the biggest Muslim Pukhtun empire after the Ottoman Empire. The empire covered present-day Afghanistan, part of Iran, the central Asian states, Kashmir, present-day Pakistan and parts of India.

The predominant religion was Sunni Muslim. After the breakup of this empire following the death of Ahmad Shah Abdali, when internal squabbles started and the tribes did not have allegiance because of rivalries and jealousies, the northern areas also became under the sway of Mughals. Sufism started and Shi'ism became the predominant Muslim religion in the northern areas. Sikhs also ruled over the northern region, as it was part of Kashmir.

Travelling north on KKH, the scenery is fabulous, but when one reaches the valley near Nanga Parbat it widens and the scene with its snow-covered mountains becomes awe-inspiring. A German expedition was the first to attempt the summit of Nanga Parbat in the early 1930s, and the person who led the expedition was called Merkel; whether he has any relationship with Chancellor Angela Merkel is not known to me. Many lost their lives while conquering the peaks because of storms and avalanches. Among those who have climbed this difficult 8000-metre high mountain have been several women.

Gilgit is one of the main towns in the Northern Region, and it was here that Dr McCarrison, working in the British Medical Corps with meagre resources, did his original research on the enlargement of the thyroid gland in the nineteenth century and published his results in a medical journal, the Lancet, in 1916.

The offices of the Aga Khan Ruler Support Programme (AKRSP) for Northern Areas are also located in Gilgit. We went to the office and to my surprise met Shuaib Sultan Khan (SSK), who was the brain behind the whole programme. SSK was my English teacher in Jehanzeb College in Swat in the late nineteen fifties. He greeted us and showed us a film about the Aga Khan programme about education, poverty alleviation and health care. The literacy rate in females in Chitral and the Northern Areas is comparatively high because of the Aga Khan programme.

Thanks to SSK and the AKRSP, two helicopters were arranged to take us to Shimshal, as there was no road then connecting Shimshal from KKH towards the Khunjrab Pass, the last post before crossing to the Chinese territory of Sinkiang province. We also went to see the Batura Glacier, the largest glacier outside the polar region.

The Aga Khan's helicopters airlifted the medical team to Shimshal village. The team consisted of a cardiologist, a surgeon, a physician and some junior doctors. A young lady from the AKRSP also accompanied us. The short journey was comfortable because it was a sunny day and one could see the snow-covered mountains under a clear sky. The villagers and children, dressed in multi-coloured clothes and wearing hand-woven caps, greeted us, and we were taken to a place built by the AKRSP. The Aga Khan organization had reasonable facilities in remote areas.

The local school was used for medical examination. I saw one young girl who had hemiplegia (paralysis of half the body). On further enquiry, it turned out that the cause was injury to the head from a falling stone from the mountain. The village was situated at ten thousand feet and certain diseases such as polycythemia and hypertension are relatively common, as the body has to adjust to the environment. Enlargement of the thyroid was not so common as in Swat or Chitral.

The houses were all more or less the same: the door would open into a separate covered place and then you would enter the house. This was to prevent draughts. There were no locks on the doors to the houses. I asked one of our hosts, the only one who was working in the outside world, whether there was a need for policemen. He said, 'Don't suggest police for God's sake!'

Music was arranged for us at night time and we joined them in dancing to drums in styles of our own, as we represented all areas of Pakistan: Karachi, Punjab and Peshawar. As they say in Pushto, 'gada hiss nada kho kwana laqawal dee', meaning 'dancing is easy because it only involves moving the buttocks'.

I saw a yak for the first time, a graceful animal which is used for all sorts of purposes: milk, a beast of burden and tilling of the land, while the hair is used for garments. Six months of the year people live in the village, while in summer they go up to the mountains at 15,000 feet to graze their livestock. We had gone there in spring and the apricots, a common fruit, were in full blossom. There was also a place for saying prayers in the village called 'Jumaat Jumaat Khana' - a mosque. All the people were Ismaelis and they would go to the prayer place regularly.

The short visit was most enjoyable, because of the hospitality of the Ismailis, the scenic beauty of the place and the good company, but it had to end, as nothing lasts forever. We were seen off by men, women and children dressed in their simple but attractive multi-coloured clothes.

After weeks of procrastination when I did not want to go to Multan, because I thought I was being sent as a punishment, I decided I was obliged to go to there as head of the Nuclear Medicine Centre. The Chairman, Munir Ahmad Khan, had told me I would be sent back to Peshawar after a time. I took the PIA flight from Peshawar to D.I. Khan and then onwards to Multan. This was the time when PIA was efficient, on time and regular because of good top management. When the pilot announced that we were descending to land, I looked down through the window expecting brown desert, but to my surprise, I saw a lot of greenery due to mango plantations.

I was greeted by Zafarullah, the Administrative Officer, and taken to the medical centre. Once again I was pleasantly surprised by the wide metalled roads and the disciplined traffic, unlike in Peshawar. The medical centre consisted of old buildings, but the director's office was well furnished by the previous director, who presumably had good aesthetic sense. I was introduced to the staff, who were all polite. As I had not brought my family with me, a bed was arranged for me in the centre, which happened to be an unused operating theatre next to the director's office.

Early the next morning, I was woken by a loud knock on the door and I heard, 'Sir, jee namaz Ka time hogia hai' - sir, it is time to say prayers. This continued for the next few days until I stopped the night security person and told him that I did say prayers, but would make my own arrangements for waking up. The word had spread before my arrival that I was a very religious person. The centre had more than its share of 'Hafizes' - people who learn the Holy Quran by heart. In a smaller centre in Multan they had six or seven Hafizes, but in a bigger medical centre in Peshawar, they had none. In the 1980s the religious seminaries had not yet mushroomed on the North West Frontier, while Multan in Punjab, having been a spiritual city for decades, had special madrassas for learning the Quran by heart. During the Afghan war students (Taliban) were recruited from seminaries for the 'jihad' in Afghanistan. Multan and the surrounding areas had sizeable populations of Shias, but except for verbal diatribes in Jhang town, there were no incidents of sectarian violence and people lived in peace and had respect and tolerance for each other beliefs.

The Nuclear Medical Centre was in Nishtar Estate, where the medical college, nursing college and teaching hospital were situated. The place was named after Nishtar, the first Governor of the largest province of Pakistan. He belonged to the Kakar tribe of Baluchistan and was a loyal and dependable Pukhtun of the founder of Pakistan. His son, Dr Tariq, told me that there was a question of where to set up a new medical college after the King Edward Medical College in Lahore, and his father had said that any part of Punjab which donated towards setting up the health care facility would get the facility with government help. Multan people, who are known for charitable work, were the first to rise to the occasion.

Within the first few days I went to see the Principal of the Medical College, Dr Zafar Hayat, who said, 'Jo Multan ata hai, rota ha. Leykin jo jata hai, wo phir bhi rota ha' - Anyone who comes to Multan is unhappy and cries. But when he goes back he cries again. His elder wife was living with him in Multan, while the younger was living in Lahore.

I also met the son of past Principal of the Medical College, who had done a lot for the medical profession. Dr Ali, a psychiatrist from Swat whom I had known, had told me an interesting story. During Ali's entrance examination to the Medical College, one applicant was short and physically unimpressive, though mentally robust, but he had dentures at an early age. The principal asked him why. He said, 'I went on a hunting expedition for snow leopards in Swat and one leopard pounced on me. During the ensuing fight, I lost my teeth.' Ali did not get the reserve seat in the college meant for students from Swat, as the Swat Ruler, who was fond of education, had managed to reserve seats for Swatis in every medical college.

When I settled down in my new place in Multan, I got to know the people working in the hospital, from the lower ranks to technical personnel, scientists, doctors, managers and administrators and outsiders who I met socially or professionally. I found that people in my new workplace were different from Peshawar, where I had been working before. The people were polite and would do their duties and obey orders without unnecessary argument. It was natural for me to be depressed and resentful, as I had left my family and was posted in Multan as punishment, because I could not get on well with my Director. I do not know whether it was my fault, being accustomed to fair play, transparency and relatively clean financial dealings in Britain, or the fault lay in my chief, who had worked in various departments from lower ones until he became a doctor.

When my teacher, Professor Nasir of Peshawar, heard that I was being transferred, he asked Professor Siraj to go and ask the Director to reverse the order, but he was shown a thick file showing evidence of my disobedience, incompetence and refusal to sign documents for the purchase of equipment. For the first time, I realized that in Pakistan as in other countries, people can collect false evidence to implicate you in serious crime.

In my new place, I had a choice: whether to continue being resentful, or be positive and forget about the recent past. The attitude of the people in my workplace and outside (social and professional contacts) helped me to be positive and get on with the work. I had realized that the Medical Centre needed a lot of effort in terms of medical, scientific and technical upgrading. The existing building was not sufficient, so a new centre would have to be built, either outside the Nishtar Estate or near to the teaching hospital, or next to the existing building. The task looked gigantic, but as they say, 'where there is a will, there is a way'.

One also has to know who the top decision makers are and who holds the 'purse strings'. The Chairman, Munir Ahmad Khan, who was educated in USA and worked in Austria in an international organization, was all for development in Pakistan. His wife was a fine and attractive German woman. I am saying this because the right life partner can be of great help in discharging one's duties and responsibilities outside the home; the internal home environment works in tandem with the external environment.

The development and expansion of the medical facilities were in the interests of vulnerable people, and nature somehow helps if one tries to do something for the collective benefit. Dr Salaam, the Nobel Laureate, had relatives in and around Multan. He used to visit his relatives whenever he was in his homeland. I was told to receive him and facilitate his visit. Pukhtuns are taught from childhood to be hospitable, and I was happy to welcome him. Later I learned that our Administrator, Zafar, also belonged to his community of Qadianis, Ahmadis or Lahoris.

Professor Salaam was greeted at Multan Airport. It was prayer time, and he performed afternoon prayers the same way any Muslim would. I found him unusually quiet. When he came to the Medical Centre I showed him around and talked about the facilities. He suddenly cheered up and started taking an interest when I said that my idea was to take these nuclear medicine facilities to the doorsteps of people living in rural areas. I also mentioned that I wished we had light mobile units as peaceful uses of atomic energy. He suggested that farm tractors could be used to facilitate the transport of heavy equipment.

After being shown around the facilities he was offered light refreshment, but he did not touch anything, even the green tea. Was it because he wanted to avoid some sort of poisoning by one of the Pukhtuns, who are known for their religiosity and extremism? He probably did not know that a Pukhtun will go to any extent to protect a guest. I had learnt during my childhood that 'outlaws' from down country, such as Mardan, Charsadda Utmanzai, used to stay in our hujra.

This reminds me of a story. A Hindu was a guest of a Pukhtun people in a village and saw the local people gathered around the hujra. The Hindu thought some sinister plan was being hatched to kill him. He told the Pukhtun that he was going to hide somewhere, as the people had gathered to harm him. The Pukhtun host replied, 'Ma yerega, haghaba ta mar ki. Zaba the haghomelma mar kum' - do not worry, they kill you and I will kill their guest.

Salaam asked me to let him know if there was need for some upgrading in the Medical Centre. 'I will tell Munir' were his words. It was Salaam who had suggested to the late Mr. Bhutto that he should appoint Munir Ahmad Khan as Chairman of the Pakistan Atomic Energy Commission. As they say, 'strike when the iron is hot', so I took the opportunity and wrote the details up about graduation of the centre in terms of equipment, regular funds, human resources and building. However bureaucratic and political hurdles had to be overcome. The Medical College's Department of Radiotherapy considered us their rivals, and when we started digging the foundation, we were stopped by the college authorities and the government construction department, known for their corruption, came out in force. The Pukhtun usually cannot be cowed, and I would not budge. .

The Principal, Hayat Zafar, was not only intelligent but knew how to resolve the disputes. We continued the development work and a fine building was erected with facilities for in-patient care and prayer rooms and facilities for ablution. I knew building material such as bricks can be substandard, so I took measures to test the iron and bricks. I learnt that there are facilities available, but they can be manipulated and a favourable report can be obtained. The contractor got fed up with my interference and Engineer Shakir, who was a fine man, one day said, 'You are a doctor. When you make mistakes they are buried underground, while the mistakes of our construction engineers are above ground for everyone to see.'

Another card I had used which impressed the finance member was that the region earns a lot of foreign exchange for the country because of the export of cotton and delicious mangoes, and at least some of the hard-earned money could be spent on badly-needed health facilities.

This is how the facilities were upgraded in the Multan Centre, which was named MINAR - Multan Institute of Nuclear Medicine and Radiotherapy - at my suggestion, keeping in view the spiritual nature of the famous city of Multan, where one of the greatest kings of India, Ahmad Shah Abdali, was brought up, though he was buried in Kandahar, Afghanistan, the place of his ancestors. Prof Ashiq Durrani, one-time vice chancellor of Multan University, had written a book about Multan, 'Afghans in Multan' As they say, 'all's well that ends well'.

Serendip is the old name of Sri Lanka, and the word 'serendipity' comes from it. A medical laboratory course was arranged in the early eighties by the International Atomic Energy Agency (IAEA) based in Vienna in Sri Lanka. I was one of the attendees from Asia and Africa. There were also women from Bangkok and Bombay (now Mumbai). Dr Sheti from Mumbay invited me to visit Bombay and said she would arrange a meeting with Dilip Kumar, icon of Bollywood, who was a family friend. India and Pakistan have always been at loggerheads for many reasons and it was next to impossible to visit Bombay, the place about which I had heard during my childhood, in the days when travelling and seeking jobs in the sub-continent of India was unrestricted and people from my village used to go there to work. On their return relate the love stories depicted on film and told us about the different religions of people in India.

The six-week stay in Sri Lanka was enjoyable and rewarding. There was greenery everywhere and the Sri Lankan organizers, headed by Dr Piyasenna, had made excellent arrangements. I asked a question at the end of a lecture during the visit to tea gardens, whether putting milk first in a cup and then pouring tea over it or vice versa would make any difference to the taste. To my surprise, the chemistry lecturer said yes, the taste depended upon water ingredients, brewing and the quality of tea leaves. He also said that Middle Eastern people like strong tea and they export different tea leaves to them to meet their demand.

The visit was also rewarding in that I learnt the scientific basis of radioimmunoassay, a powerful tool in the investigation of diseases, for which a Nobel Prize was awarded, and one of the contenders, Professor Ekins, along with his Italian secretary and girlfriend, also came to Sri Lanka. A lecturer on fever had said that germs (viral, bacterial or parasitic) can be easily dealt with by the defence mechanism in the body if the temperature is high. This lecturer, who happened to be from Israel, would not accompany us to sightseeing places or cultural musical shows for security reasons, as there were Arabs among us.

Near the end of the world programme photos were taken and we wrote comments on the back. It was nice of Dr Sheti to write, 'the handsome man of the group' on the picture. My thanks to Dr Munir Siddiqui of Sindh, who introduced me to Muslim friends in Colombo; through him I learned that Sri Lanka is probably the only country where the Muslim minority are rich because of their business in precious stones and spices. I also learned that people had employed Pukhtuns to protect their lands in the jungles from elephants. A tourist place on the sea coast called Serendip was also visited, courtesy of Munir Siddiqui, a resourceful Sindhi. On the way back we sampled fresh coconut juice and saw breadfruit trees. In those days there were no tensions between Sinhalese and Tamils and one could visit any remote area of the beautiful island. The English word 'serendipity' was coined by Horace Walpole (1754) to denote 'the faculty of making unexpected and delightful discoveries by accident'. It was taken from the title of a fairy story, 'The Three Princes of Serendip', for the princes were always making discoveries by accident. John Adair, 'One of the foremost thinkers of leadership' according to Sir John Harvey-Jones, wrote in his book 'The Art of Creative Thinking' that one should practise serendipity.

CHAPTER TWENTY SIX

PEOPLE OF SOME IMPORTANCE

One may come across people of some importance anywhere or everywhere, but I was lucky in coming across some who had contributed to society or the region in a positive way. People can also contribute in a negative way, locally, nationally or internationally. In Pakistan, Qureshis and Gillanis were considered spiritual families and were respected. Also respected were Pushtun familes had migrated from the Suleman Mountains some hundred years ago and settled in vast plains where water was abundant because of the rivers. They had introduced productive farming methods such as mango orchards. The delicious mangoes of Multan are probably the best in the world in terms of taste. Durranis, Tareens, Babars and Sadozais were among the big farmers.

Azeem Khan Sadozai became a close friend, as he had not

forgotten his hospitality, and he knew the history of the people living in Multan and surrounding areas. Once he gave advice which averted a tragedy: a student of dental surgery hailing from Takht Bhai - a spiritual place during Buddhist times in Gandhara, now KP - was engaged to a girl whose mother was Pushtun. I was a part of the ceremony, in which there was music and dancing. The girl started learning the Quran from the son of a local preacher and after some time the 'Maulvi', who in later life was involved in corruption during the haj (pilgrimage) season, proposed to her and persuaded her mother, who was an ambitious lady, to break the engagement. For a Pukhtun living west of the Indus River it was a matter of ghairat (honour). One day the dental student came to me saying that his father had sent a group of people to kidnap the girl, as a Pukhtun would go to any extent to preserve his honour if his ego was hurt. Azeem, an elderly man, told the student to forget and forgive, as it was not unusual to break the engagement and he should forget his Pushtunwali - next to impossible for a young Pushtun.

AKS had also told me about the Tareens, and said that if I travelled by train I would see their never-ending mango orchards on both sides of the track. Mr. Tareen was an elderly, well-spoken gentleman who shared my interest in dogs. He had a Ridgeback guard dog, and told me that these dogs were better than Doberman and German Shepherd guard dogs, because in South Africa they were used to ward off lions from farmland. I was interested in retrievers and he suggested that I should get one from Allahyar of Khanewal, who was fond of animals and birds. I went to see his private mini-zoo. He would not let his golden retriever male dog service a bitch unless a sample was taken from the vagina and tested for infection first - a true animal lover and carer.

Multan was also a garrison town of some importance, and as it happened Major Dr Inam, my first cousin, was posted there. He was not happy in his work. I asked him the reason and he told me that his senior expected him to say 'sir, sir' all the time. It is sometimes difficult for a person coming from a 'khan' family to adjust himself to his working environment where you are expected to perform undue formalities. I told him to say 'sir' but think of 'da ghaun sir' - penis head. He was happy after that. I told a brigadier, a nuclear medicine colleague, about it and when he became a two-star general, I said 'now we have to call you sir'. He said, 'please, please don't call me sir!'

Another fine professional soldier I met during my stay in Multan was Hameed Gul, whose ancestors were pukhtuns but had settled in Punjab. He carried the Pukhtun 'genes' of stubbornness and the discipline of the army even after retirement. He was supposed to be the architect of the efficient, if dreaded, intelligence setup called ISI (Inter-Services Intelligence). I had attended the marriage ceremony of his daughter, which was attended by the President and Prime Minister at that time. That day had happened to be a Friday and after the prayers a gentleman, tall and well-built, got up and said in broken Urdu to President Zia that he posed as a staunch Muslim but the security guards did not join the Friday prayers; I learned that the person happened to be a Pukhtun visiting his son who was a major in the army.

Before I leave this topic, I ought to mention Dr Khurshid Pasha, a Yusufzai from Swabi who became a family friend. A well-respected physician by the name of Dr Rauf and Sher Muhammad Durrani (SMD) will always be remembered because of one episode. We were sitting in SMD's medicine shop when a gentleman came and SMD greeted him and entertained him. When he left Dr Rauf asked him who he was and SMD said the gentleman was his friend and a police officer. Dr Rauf married the daughter of Abdul Qayum Khan, one-time Chief Minister of NWFP, who said categorically, 'police officers cannot be anybody's friend'. I did not believe him, but was proved wrong in later life in Peshawar.

I went to Peshawar periodically as PIA was still functioning well, and I would take the route from Multan to Zhob, DI Khan and Peshawar on a Fokker aircraft. I had rented my house to the Canadian International Development Agency (CIDA) and often saw the Canadian Country Representative. He was new to the country and had yet to learn the culture of the people, especially the Pukhtuns. On one of the visits, I asked him about his work. He came straight to the point (unlike us Pukhtuns, who start with our own problems and then come to the point). He said, 'A strange thing happened yesterday. When I got to the office, there was no one there on time. I thought they had gone on strike without my information, but then they started coming to the office one by one. I asked why and they said they had gone to a *janaza* - a funeral.

The gatekeeper of my rented house did not know who I was, and on one of my visits to the house to see the CIDA representative he told me an interesting and strange story: the owner of the house was a doctor who could not face the people and went away from 'Pukhtano mulk' (Pukhtunland) because his wife had left him and the reason was that he had brought an American lady to live in the house. Of course, that doctor was me. This was half true, because Christine, a girl from New York of Jewish origin, was living with us and our children (MM, Mujgan and Cyrus) have fond memories of her. Divorce and separation are considered taboo in culture, but scandals and fabrication of stories are not uncommon among the Pukhtuns in spite of the fact that in religion backbiting is considered a sin.

Munir Ahmad Khan (MAK), the Chairman of the Pakistan Atomic Energy Commission, was true to his word when he had said that he would send me back to where I had started my work. MAK's forefathers had come from Afghanistan and like any Pukhtun he could not forget his promise. At an opportune moment, I was sent back to Peshawar as Head of the Medical Centre At my farewell party the staff were visibly unhappy that I was leaving, and some had tears in their eyes. I made sure to say goodbye to all those I knew. Multan has all the well-known families, like Gilanis, Qureshis, Durranis, Sadozai, Gardezis, Tareens, Babars and so on who have played their part in the politics and welfare of the people. It is almost twenty years since my stint in Multan ended, but people from the Seraiki belt still send me boxes of delicious mangoes every year.

Multanis always try to remember you if you have made any contribution towards their area. I was happy that the medical facilities in terms of in-patient care and laboratory facilities were increased and that scientists like Hafiz Ghulam Abbas, the medical doctor, Dr Dure Sabih and Dr Zahida had started taking interest in research work. We visited various parts of the surrounding areas for surveys of the prevalence of diseases. Sometimes we went outside Multan to see dog fights and fights between dogs and domesticated bears.

Before I end my reminiscences about Multan, its people and the Seraiki Belt, let me mention that many years later, the Director of the Medicine Centre, Dr Dur-e-Sabih, and the staff invited me to a celebration which was called 'Dr Sher M. Khan day'. The Chairman of the PAEC and former pioneer and rector of PIEAS University were also invited. I did not deserve the celebration, but it was nice of the director and the staff to remember me after so many years. He also gave me the task of speaking on 'Nuclear medicine in Pakistan: the way forward'. It was a great pleasure to see my previous colleagues in the Centre, the Nishtar Medical College and the city. I went to call on some members of the Qureshi, Gilani, Durrani, Sadozi and Babar families.

After the customary beginning of the presentation, I showed pictures of Nishtar, who had started Nishtar Medical College, and of Ahmad Shah Abdali, who was born and bred in Multan and established the Afghan Empire. Tributes were paid to the founding fathers of peaceful uses of nuclear energy in Pakistan, such as Usmani, MAK and others who were no longer alive. The English saying 'out of sight out of mind' can aptly be applied in some countries, especially Pakistan.

The father of nuclear energy in medicine is thought to be George von Hevesy (1859-1906). The joint approach to solving medical problems by involving scientists and engineers is exemplified by Dr Hamilton (1937), who complained to his nuclear scientist colleague about the need for a radioisotope of iodine with a longer half-life. 'How long do you want?' asked the scientist. The answer was 'one week'. This is how radioactive iodine with a one-week half-life was made. It has benefited thousands, if not millions, all over the world.

The question was also posed: 'Why does any specialty of medicine improve or progress, and for that matter anything else in terms of progress, prosperity, peace and quality?' The answer was obvious: leadership.

Since most patients are poor and material poverty in our society is common, I also mentioned to them a quotation of Virchow (1821-1902): 'Since disease so often results from poverty, the physicians are the natural attorneys of the poor and social problems should largely be solved by them.'

I was no longer in active service, so I could say what I thought was appropriate for the benefit of the staff working in the organization. I described the way forward: human resource development, quality education and training, no unnecessary dislocation of the staff, purchase and maintenance of equipment and above all, the consumers (patients) have to be the centrepiece.

Taking part in a village Jirga.

Children and adults in posing for photos in a hujra
(courtesy of Cherry Lindholm).

Children are fond of modern gadgets, but so are adults.
Picture of Sahovics playing with Cyrus' son.

Picture of the Sea of Marmara taken during the long journey to Swat;
the road was the Silk Road.

Rocket launchers were for showing to guests only.

Visit to Menorca, to the cottage of my boss (Duncan) and his friend Hamish.

Demonstrating an AK 47 in an Afridi Hujra to visitors from the USA,
UK and Australia during peaceful times.

Consul General of Iran in Peshawar. Picture also shows Hassan Jafry, victim of the never-ending sectarianism.

Dr Inayat Khan coming to the stage to take part in Pukhtun "Athan" (folk dancing).

Neglected historical and archaeological sites.

VC Qasim Jan receiving a shield during a conference.

Chuck and Cherry in their summerhouse.

'Haftseen' on a Persian 'Norouz'.

Visitors from UK and Bengal to Shin Bagh in peaceful times.

Picture taken in the 1970s of a whirlwind on the road from Kabul to Herat. Nature is today replaced by bomb blasts from air and ground.

. With Vice-Chancellor Ajmal Khan after his safe homecoming following his capture by the Taliban.

With friends in the Malakand area. In the background mountain peaks can be seen where Sir Winston Churchill stayed and sent dispatches to a London newspaper.

Laying a wreath on a plaque in a church in Peshawar in memory of Lady Mallam, humanitarian worker in NWFP.

Book-launching ceremony during the centenary celebrations of Islamia College; a pictograph of the college by Shakeel Ahmad Khan.

Get-together with old friends.

Peace is essential for prosperity.

The gift of a book is always memorable.

Architect Wasey Wardaq at work on restoration in the Babar Garden in Kabul, through the Aga Khan Foundation.

Love affair on social media: marriage of a Tabrizi Iranian girl to a Pakistani lad.

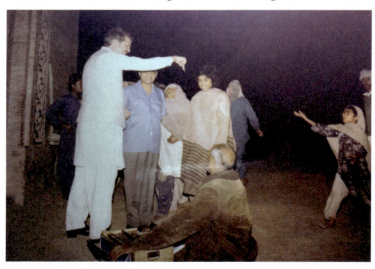

Poverty still persists in the 'Land of the Pure'.

Oath-taking ceremony, Upper Swat journalists' union.

Family friends Ray Pope, Pat Pope and their family.

Wild boar hunting in Multan.

Enjoying the hospitality of Corine and Aka Sultan in Paris.

A friend in need is a friend indeed: Entezam and Catherine Sahovic.

British Pukhtuns in London.

Remembering the founding father Malak Ahmad Khan Baba of Pukhtunkhwa.

Happy schoolchildren with their trophies.

Prof Siraj, Principal of the Medical College, applauding his bright student Mah Muneer.

Imran Khan, cricketer turned politician, does listen to good suggestions at times.

Prayers for Lady Mallam and others who had rendered humanitarian services to the former NWFP.

I was interrupted many times to make me shorten my presentation, presumably so that I should not say anything that would upset the overall organization controlling the PAEC. In the end I dedicated my presentation 'to all those who suffered/died of preventable diseases as well as because of the non-availability of nuclear, medical and other facilities'.

CHAPTER TWENTY SEVEN

RETURN TO MY CONTENTIOUS HOMELAND, AND A VISIT TO JAPAN

☪

My farewell to Multan was on a grand scale, but as I left the Seraiki land with a heavy heart, I was wondering whether I would be welcomed in the land west of the Indus River. Jealousy is built into the Pukhtun culture. As I have written before, it is no wonder a first cousin is sometimes called *tarbur*, a derogatory word in Pushto. Vengeance is also practised in the community. My predecessor, who had caused me so much trouble, was unhappy leaving Peshawar for Quetta. He was in the Medical Institute right from the start and thought and acted as if the place was his personal fiefdom, bypassing merit and appointing people who would be loyal to him, and doing so many other corrupt things which were the rule rather than the exception in government departments at the time. For example, purchases in the departments were made according to the highest rate of commission rather than the lowest bidder. As in other hospitals, patients were only entertained if they had seen the doctors in their private clinics. Printed addresses were given to the patients for visits to the private clinics.

There is a saying in Pushto or Pukhto that no matter how you try to avoid the courts, one of these days you have to face the music, so to speak. In our hospital, a woman doctor who was not brought up in the Pushtun culture was appointed to work in the hospital and given a room to stay there. I was told that a boy was visiting her every evening and would leave very late at night. She was warned to stop this practice, because of the sanctity of the hospital and because it did not match the norms of the Pushtun culture. She did not heed this advice, so she was told to vacate the room. She was stubborn and her luggage had to be removed and the door locked. She went to court saying that her diamond ring and jewellery had been taken away. She knew a female lawyer who became a judge of the High Court later on and was also friendly with the wife of a leading lawyer.

I had to attend court many times, and once faced the then Chief Justice Ibn Ali, who was the brother of my medicine teacher, Professor Raza Ali. He told us that if we doctors fought with each other, who would treat the ill people? That was the last hearing, but it was not the first time I had a brush with the law. On previous occasions, I had had to go to Rawalpindi to face Judge Tiwan in a smuggling case. This was the time when Zia was collecting evidence to prosecute an elected Prime Minster, Zulfiqar Ali Bhutto. At that time a Pukhtun judge of the Supreme Court resigned as he did not want to be a part of the manipulated judgment against Bhutto, in spite of the fact that Bhutto had showed his high-handedness to the Judge by superseding him in promotion.

One April in the late 1980s, Shahnaz and I were invited by Jamshed and his charming wife Nancy to their house to meet two 'legends' of the sub-continent of India who had come all the way from Bombay (now Mumbai). April is usually pleasant in Peshawar; the fruit trees are in blossom as the city is surrounded by orchards and was at one time called the 'city of gardens'. We had no difficulty in finding the house where we were to meet Yusuf Khan and Saira Bano, as the streets and roads were not crowded. Yusuf Khan, whose film industry name was Dilip Kumar, was proud to be Pathan and he mentioned the Pathan's character, dress and nature several times in his autobiography when describing his father, 'Aghaji', mother and grandmother. They had gone to Bombay and settled there but had not forgotten their roots in Peshawar. Jamshed and Nancy were his close relatives and besides Dilip Kumar, the family had produced other people who had made names for themselves in their fields. One was Rahim, an orthopaedic surgeon in Karachi whose surgical expertise was the best at the time.

In one of the early visits to Karachi I went to see Surgeon Rahim's wards and found them clean, tidy and well-staffed, and the patients were looked after well. Whether Pukhtuns are at their best when they are away from their place of birth, as in the case of Dilip Kumar and Rahim Khan, is not clear, but the question of 'nature and nurture' arises. I had known Nancy's father, Colonel Dastagir, a fine person who had great sense of humour. We used to go together for hunting and shooting, and I also knew the family through mutual Iranian friends at the time when there were no political or social restrictions on meeting foreigners.

I found Dilip Kumar courteous, quiet and very soft spoken, with no aura of superiority in any way. I did not have the good fortune of meeting the pretty Saira Bano, who was his fan and devoted life partner. Jamshed made sure to follow the tradition of Pukhtuns of entertaining the ladies and male guests separately.

The Pakistan Atomic Energy Commission (PAEC) was one of the few organizations in Pakistan which adhered to the rules and regulations, including fair play, as far as its employees were concerned. This was probably because the majority were scientists and engineers, and moreover the successive heads of the organization were all out to improve its internal workings without greed or amassing wealth in the wrong way, as was prevalent at the time. Munir Ahmad Khan was especially on the lookout for opportunities to send personnel on short training visits or long educational visits to developed countries. When my turn came I was sent to Japan. One of my colleagues, who had stopped in Bangkok on the way to Tokyo, told me about the girls and the massage parlours in Bangkok, in case I wanted to stop over there. I did stop and liked the food and fruit, especially mangostine and pineapples, which were relatively cheap. The flight with Nippon Airways was comfortable and the air hostesses were efficient and courteous. At Tokyo Airport I was received by a JICA representative, a lady with a broad smile who dealt with all the immigration formalities, but there were no security formalities. I was introduced to the other doctors in the lounge, who had arrived a short time earlier. One was a woman from Argentina and another was a doctor from Brazil who had brought his guitar with him.

We were taken through the busy streets of Tokyo to a hostel. The traffic was busy but disciplined and I did not hear any hooting on the road. The hostel was a multi-storey building with all facilities. I was shown my room, which was compact and had a small bathroom and rounded tub in which one could only sit. The instructions were not to drain off the water because the next person could use it. The doctors, about ten of us, were from the developing countries and we were supposed to attend lectures as well as practical lessons on cancer medicine.

In the first week a government official gave us a lecture on how the government functions in Japan. I was told that the Japanese bureaucracy is well educated, efficient and incorruptible. Since Japan has a history of earthquakes, an official from the Police Department gave us a lecture about the steps to be taken and which places to go to for shelter in case of an earthquake.

For the first time I learned how to access our allowances from the banks using pin numbers which were given to us. The daily allowance per person was enough for food and we bought noodles, as these were relatively cheap. Since the televisions in the rooms were pay sets, three or four of us used to gather in one room to watch pornographic films. The Malaysian doctor complained to our Japanese teacher that the allowance should be increased as it was not enough for watching TV.

The doctor from Malaysia also made daily phone his wife at 11 pm. Once he could not talk to her, and since he had a good sense of humour, we joked with him that she must have gone somewhere else. He was a nice, jolly man and would tell us about his home life. Once he told us that sometimes when they went to bed to make love, his wife wore a Gina Lollobrigida mask while he wore a Rock Hudson mask.

The hospitals in Japan were well equipped. The medicine dispensation places had two counters, one for traditional Japanese medicine and the other for allopathic medicine. The doctors were trained in prescribing both types.

The incidence of breast cancer was lower in Japanese women than in Afghanistan and North West Pakistan. I asked the reason, but the male Japanese doctor, who was polite like many other Japanese, did not answer me at that time because there were young nurses and female doctors present. Later on he told me that Japanese women have small breasts, but I did not have the chance nor the desire to see breasts in Tokyo.

I had heard much about Japanese cuisine, specially sushi, but did not know what it was, as I was using noodles, which were not only economical but only needed mixing with hot water to be ready to enjoy eating, thanks to the late Mr Fuko, who innovated the preparation of noodles for mass consumption. He died at the ripe old age of ninety-six; most of the good people live long lives. The billionaire Momofuko was famous for saying 'peace will come when people have food', and 'eating wisely will enhance beauty and health'.

To find out more about Japanese food, I went to a restaurant. Outside, the food items were displayed, along with the numbers and prices. I had to remember the numbers for what I wanted. I learned that sushi is pieces of fish served with special sauce and found it delicious.

Unlike the West, there were hardly any women present at the food tables with groups of men, so we Pushtuns are not the only one who think that a 'woman's place is in the home'. Unlike the West but like the Pukhtuns, I noticed that Japanese women walk behind men. The best meat I ever had, or will ever have, was Kobe meat in Japan. My thanks to Fuji Films, whose representative took me to a restaurant on top of a multi-storey building from which one could see the panorama of the lights of Tokyo at night time.

Teaching classes were regularly held in the morning and there were also Japanese doctors attending them. I found that no questions were asked by these doctors, unlike the West, where you are trained from childhood to be inquisitive. I asked why, and the Japanese told me that it was disrespectful to question a teacher and an elder, even if you think he or she is wrong. This was also prevalent in Pukhtun culture, but it is gradually but surely being eroded, for better or worse.

Our programme was well planned and well organized, as Japanese do, unlike Pukhtuns. We were taken to a Shinto shrine in Tokyo. The shrine was surrounded by a large park, and we saw a marriage ceremony in which the bride and bridegroom were led by priests towards the shrine. We were told that the original religion of Japan was Shinto. Buddhism spread from China and the Korean peninsula and was the second largest religion practised in Japan. Some Japanese converted to Islam during the Second World War and one *tableeghi* (preacher) who happened to be a Pukhtun from Swat visited us in the hostel along with a young Japanese convert.

After the visit to the shrine, we were entertained to a typical Japanese meal consisting of rice served in bowls, noodles, sushi and a drink called sake, made from rice. This was different from the West, where you help yourself from a common food dish. We were told to visit our embassies before returning to our countries. Since I did not know how to get to the embassy, I hired a taxi. The driver lost his way and I noticed that he stopped the meter. After half an hour of driving in the busy streets of Tokyo, we reached the Pakistani Embassy, but to my disappointment, the embassy was closed and the taxi had to take me back to the hostel.

On the way I asked the driver about his children. He said his wife lived in the north of the country and he had not been to see her for three years, so there was something in common between a Pukhtun and a Japanese. Pukhtuns work in the Middle East, but do not take their wives with them. The taxi driver did not accept a tip. I had noticed in the restaurants that the waiters would also not accept tips.

We were shown the Japanese Parliament, which is called the Diet, and the monarchy was explained to us. Their parliament has two houses, the Upper House and the House of Representatives. The judiciary is independent in the constitution. The system is more or less the same as in Britain. I asked whether the constitution had ever been abrogated or amended. The answer was that amendments or improvements are occasionally made, but he did not know about the abrogation.

Our Japanese teacher, who was middle-aged and very polite, would smile, but I had not seen him laughing out loud. He told us that we would be taken for a 'Chengiz Khan Lunch' on the Saturday. We went to an open space where plates of iron were arranged on open fires. Meat and vegetables were cooked and we helped ourselves. I was wondering whether we in Swat had learnt from Mongols: in the houses, *tabakhai* (iron plates) are put in an open hearth. Meat and vegetables are cooked on them and the family gathers round and help themselves.

I was working in the PAEC on the medical side and knew about the destructive uses of nuclear energy in a general way, but I did not know the secrets of making the atomic bomb. Japan had been on the receiving end of the destructive uses of atomic energy and we were taken to Hiroshima. We travelled by 'bullet train', accompanied by two Japanese ladies who were well versed in English. The train was clean. The passengers entered without jumping the queue or pushing and pulling and would sit or stand quietly. This was like Britain, but unlike some other countries, including my own. We reached Hiroshima at nighttime, and the Tunisian physicist and the South American lady made sure their rooms were next to each other. Both had been educated in France and knew French very well. At breakfast time I mentioned to the Tunisian scientist that I could hear screeching above my ceiling, followed after a while by splashing from the wash basin. He only smiled and said 'Alhamdulillah' after helping himself to an egg.

We were shown the remnants of the buildings devastated by the nuclear bombs and were taken to the museum, where some organs of the body were preserved and photographs were displayed on the walls. The Japanese did not tell us the causes or cause leading to the detonating of the bomb in 1945 which ended the war, nor did we venture to ask about the many deaths following the nuclear holocaust.

Japan was the second largest economic power after the USA, though it has been overtaken by China at the time of writing. Japan had tried to be a world military power, but it failed, suffering devastation to its land. A lesson can be learnt from this by the other countries, which is not to try and be a military power but an economic power.

We were taken to the Toyota Company, where the lady guide told us to select a person who would thank the Toyota management after they had shown us around and entertained us, which is a Japanese tradition. My name was mentioned, but the Indian doctor from Delhi objected to it. The problem was solved democratically and I got maximum votes. There is always unnecessarily rivalry even at individual level between these two neighbouring countries whose people had lived together for generations until 1947.

The Toyota people explained their style of management, and I learned that a worker on the shop floor can become the President of the Toyota Company, if he or she is talented. Loyalty is also important and members of the same family work in the same factory for generations. In some Western countries one is considered 'locked' into the job if one does not change jobs, but in Japan it is the opposite.

One can find Japanese cars in every country. One day on a short visit to the United Arab Emirates, which I call the 'land of plenty' because of petrodollars, I was looking out of a 'window' with a view to the six-lane motorway with green grass pavements lined by date trees. I counted hundred of cars, buses and vans and saw that most were of Japanese make, followed by German and British.

My six-week stay in Japan was not only rewarding but most enjoyable. I met people from South America, North Africa, India, Singapore and Malaysia and learned some aspects of their culture, religion and politics. JICA had planned the educational visit well.

It was time to buy some gifts for my wife and children, and I went to an electronics place called 'Aki Bara'. The name 'Bara' was familiar because we had a place in Afridi Tribal place where electronic goods were sold. People called these smuggled goods, but I called it a 'free trade area'. Pukhtuns can be good entrepreneurs and there are Pukhtuns in South Korea, Japan, Singapore and China engaged in trade without even knowing how to sign their names. I bought a genuine pearl necklace for my wife, but in later years it was lost to the chemical reaction of vinegar, used as a cleaning agent by none other than its owner.

CHAPTER TWENTY EIGHT

PREVENTION IS BETTER THAN CURE

There is an old adage 'prevention is better than cure', but it is not only better, it is cheaper, especially in resource-poor countries. IRNUM was the only institution west of the Indus River which was supposed to look after patients suffering from cancer. It was well equipped thanks to the PAEC, who were at the helm of affairs at the time. Maintenance and after-sales service of sophisticated equipment is difficult in poor countries, but there are ways to get around it and I had tried these, sometimes unsuccessfully, because of vested interests.

Patients came not only from far-flung areas but across the Durand line, the border with Afghanistan. Patients were usually accompanied by relatives and sometimes by neighbours because of extended families and lack of government facilities such as ambulances for transportation and poor governing. In the West and some countries in the East, health and education come on the top of the priority list, but these were neglected in Pakistan at the time of writing. The result was that while the IRNUM hospital had patients in the advanced stages of malignant diseases, the available resources had to be used judicially. Medical doctors are by and large poor managers, because they are not taught management skills during their undergraduate studies. On the other hand they are also averse to being controlled by non-medical personnel because of their egos.

Regarding research, I thought the best thing would be to find out the most common tumours between the Indus and Oxus rivers. In other words, an epidemiological study based in hospital, as population studies require time, money and political will. Decisions are usually made on impressions, but the correct decisions have to be evidence based, especially in medical management. Analysis is also important.

Oral cancer was found to be common in Pukhtuns, especially in the southern districts. This was because of using *naswar*, in which the main ingredient is tobacco, which is a known agent for causation not only of cancer of the month but of other organs in the body. Among the Pukhtuns, it is also known that 'be Nashe Sar da Kaddu yee' - anyone who does not take anything to make him 'high' is like a pumpkin.

Breast cancer was common in women, as in the West, but in our case, these patients presented in the late stages because of ignorance and lack of facilities. While presenting my data in a medical meeting, I said that I did not know why it was more common in the left breast than the right. A surgeon remarked that the majority of men were right handed, but there is no evidence that handling breasts causes cancer.

The hospital where I was working and in charge was primarily meant for diagnostic purposes, using radioactive substances, and the treatment of diseases using radiation. But if one wants to do justice to the field of medicine, then one has to either provide facilities under one roof or seek the cooperation of one's colleagues in other hospitals. As in other professions and sports, teamwork is important. A multidisciplinary approach is probably the best to manage a medical problem, but I found that most of the doctors wanted to work in isolation. We had to continue as best we could to cope with difficult problems of neoplastic diseases.

Oesophageal (food pipe) cancer was relatively common in the Afghans and Pukhtuns living in the borderlands. Muslim doctors had done a lot of work on this problem during the Golden Age of Islam. Among them was Abuzuhar or Aven Zuhr, as he is known in the European literature. He described the malady in which patients have difficulties in swallowing the food and used silver boogies for enlarging the gullet and milk enemas for nutrition. The disease is known in the Caspian Sea Belt, Iran, Afghanistan, Khyber, Pukhtunkhwa and northern China. The root causes could be lifestyle, environmental or infection, but at the time of writing no definite cause has been found. A great deal of research is going on, so scientists will hopefully find the cause and increase early detection and prevention. Treatment of course varies, from surgery, medicine, radiation or a combination of all three.

The Golden Age of Islam made great contributions to medicine as well as science. The books of Abu Ali Cenna, The Canons of Medicine (980-1037), were translated into European languages. Abu Mansoor's books on anatomy were taught in the universities. Al Razi's methods of diagnosis were followed and Al Nafis' treatment was followed.

Abu Ali Cenna also mentioned the signs and symptoms of 'love illness'- *ishq*. Previously from the time of Galen (Jalenoos), 'humour theory' was popular, but when Abuzuhar discovered the bug of skin disease, scabies, people in the medical field started thinking differently.

Those were the golden days of Muslims as far as science and medicine were concerned. Since that time they have made very few contributions to science, technology and medicine. I have been asking why this should be partly for my own knowledge and partly to impart awareness among the younger generation, but no satisfactory answers have been propounded. Once on a Fokker flight to Multan, I asked a barrister, Akram Sheikh, who later became Public Prosecutor in the case of General Musharaf. When I was living in Multan, his house was at the back of the house where I was living and at times the children threw stones into our backyard. Pukhtuns cannot stop retaliating, but the stone-throwing stopped when a brick was thrown across the wall.

In the early 1970s, a friend who was interested in heart diseases would always underline it if there was a Muslim name in the medical literature, but one could see very few contributions from the Muslim world compared to hundreds of years ago. It is probably because those who were at the helm of affairs after the Golden Age did not encourage research in science, medicine and technology, or that the emphasis was more on the fundamental aspects of religion. In the past there have been 'Asharites' on one had as well as 'Mutazilites' on the other side. People have interpreted Islam and Hadith in their own way and have formed groups, sects and even political parties. There have also been real or imagined threats from people belonging to other religions and countries. All this has probably led to the decline of the emphasis on medicine as it was during the Golden Age of Islam.

In the award-winning book by Sidhhartha Mukherjee the 'Emperor of all Maladies, a Biography of Cancer', breast cancer is called 'the queen of all cancers', as it is the most common cancer in females all over the world. As is well known, if you have to solve a problem, you must do some analysis that requires various steps, such as the collection of data. Breast cancer was a common problem in women in the region between Oxus and Indus. Data was collected and analyzed. As in the West, breast cancer was found to be the most common problem, but there were differences between our patients and the West: most of our patients did not seek advice until the disease was advanced because of the low literacy rate, non-availability of facilities and for Pukhtun cultural reasons. In Western books, it is mentioned that fertility in some ways is protective, but some poor patients had more than a dozen children.

Thanks to Western science and technology, the genes involved in breast cancer have now been identified. It has been proved beyond any doubt that breast cancer can be detected early by self-examination, and once detected early can be cured. Taking pictures of breasts using special X-ray machines (mammography) can detect cancer at an early stage. I procured such a machine, thanks to the PAEC decision makers, headed by Chairman Munir Khan and his efficient team led by Ashfaq Ahmad. They were always amenable to suggestions for improvement and advances in health care. There was no trained or educated radiologist, so I self-trained myself by reading books and then trained female staff in mammography. Once again it was the first facility between the Indus and Oxus Rivers. I had not forgotten the advice of Dr Najibullah Khan of Swat to self-train and educate yourself if experts in the field are not available. Later on a pretty female doctor, Dr Safoora Shahid, was sent to Paris to get training in imaging of the female breasts Dr Safoora continued to take an interest in breast imaging when she had become Director of IRNUM, and she set up a facility in her own private clinic after retirement.

Of course, diseases of various kinds have been present from time immemorial. They may be due to germs, inheritance, degenerative effects or lifestyle. Humans have always tried to find treatment for these maladies. Thanks to modern science, some of them can be prevented, while others can easily be treated. During my childhood, vaccination was not available in the village and I had to go through all the infectious diseases such as whooping cough, measles and smallpox. In my primary school days, every year I contracted malaria and lie in the sun whenever I got that episodic shivering. *Taveez* (charms) and *dum darood* was recited to ward off the 'evil eye' and the spirits.

The hospital (IRNUM) where I was working and was head was known as a cancer hospital and advertised as such by my predecessor. Cancer was and is still often thought to be an incurable disease. I had set up diagnostic tests using radioactive substances for non-cancer diseases such as thyroid diseases for the first time in the region and also for treatment purposes such as the use of radioactive iodine for an overactive thyroid gland (thyrotoxicosis, or Grave's disease). But people were reluctant to make use of it because they thought they had cancer. So measures had to be taken to allay the anxieties of the people by public education. On the discharge slips of the patients and the laboratory request for MS we wrote 'Cancer is not an incurable disease' and stated that the hospital had facilities for diagnostic and therapeutic facilities for other diseases besides cancer. It is the duty of a medical, nursing and allied staff to educate the public.

Surviving a disease depends upon several factors. The human body has a built-in mechanism to defend itself from external and internal threats. The well-known adage 'prevention is better than cure' still holds true and in poor countries, prevention is not only better but cheaper. Lifestyle is important in the prevention of diseases.

Even in developed countries, a diagnosis of cancer was a death sentence, but because of public education and effective treatment, a malignant disease is no longer considered incurable. This reminds me of a patient of mine belonging to the well-known Shinwari tribe, who straddle the borderland between Pakistan and Afghanistan and the Tora Bora mountains, which are well known because of the late Osama bin Laden. The patient told me that he was so scared of the hospital that whenever he got near it he would look at the other side, but as luck would have it, he was being treated in the same hospital. The patient had successful treatment and is now a lawyer in Kohat, KP.

Another patient, a child, had an operation in Rawalpindi. The abdomen was opened, a biopsy was taken and the abdomen was closed. The grandfather was told by the doctors, one of whom happened to be known to the family, that very little could be done for the child, who should be taken home. The grandfather was in the food business, owning a restaurant serving delicious tikka kabab, and he came to the hospital for consultation with tears in his eyes as grandfathers and grandmothers are usually very fond of their grandchildren. The child was successfully treated and has migrated to Canada with her parents. I took guests to the restaurant because of the quality food and once I took a specialist from the world-famous MD Anderson Hospital, Houston Texas, for lunch. The grandfather of the patient was relating the story of the successful treatment of his granddaughter and said 'Allah cured her', which was true because of our belief. The specialist, a world-renowned breast cancer specialist from Multan who had settled in the USA, said, 'Haji Sahib, apke nawasy ka Bhagwan Dr Sher Mohammad Khan tha Bhagwan (name of God in Hindu religions) of your granddaughter was Dr Sher Mohammad Khan'.

These instances are mentioned to illustrate that cancer is no longer a 'death sentence', thanks to the scientific advances of the West, Japan and Korea. Muslims also made great contributions towards medicine and science more than nine hundred years ago, but nowadays question are asked about the lack of contributions in the scientific field by the Islamic world. Cancer survival is always being debated.

However, the idea of 'survival of the fittest' has been around for many years and my biology teacher in Swat, a remarkable Pukhtun khan, used to talk about it. 'Survival of the fittest' means that those species best adapted to their surroundings continue to survive and reproduce, whereas those that are less adapted are doomed to disappear. As in 'evolutionary fitness', cancer survivorship depends on several factors such as the stage of the disease, overall fitness, the response of the medicine administered, the care of the family and the health care facilities.

Survival also depends on avoiding known causes of disease. Not to do so is inciting disaster. One does not have to look up the meaning of 'disaster' in a dictionary in our region, for it is a part of life: we witness it, we are the victims or the perpetrators or a party to it. To borrow a modern Western saying, 'we live it'. Manmade disasters are self-inflicted, either through internal forces or due to the connivance of external forces. Natural disasters are also thought to be partially manmade, according to environmentalists.

Similarly tobacco use and cultivation is a disaster. This reminds me of the early seventies, when a well-known politician who had been a student at Islamia College was visiting the USA on the 'Farmers to Farmers' exchange programme. The people of the USA have always tried to encourage people-to-people exchange programmes. I say 'well-known' politician because he is a rare commodity. Undemocratic forces, for their own self-interest, blame the politicians for corruption, being 'lotas', whatever that means, and for mismanagement, which in some cases is true. But this politician cannot be blamed. In fact, I once asked the nephew of the Governor of KPK, who was the politician's personal secretary, about the Minister. He praised him for his hospitality but then added that in three years neither the minister nor he himself had done anything for anyone. This is very unusual. Patronage and kinships work in Pakistan, rather than merit.

Regarding the history of tobacco, I asked him about the native 'Red Indians' (Native Americans). He told me that his Jewish farmer host was a very good man and showed him around the entire place, and at his request also took him, reluctantly, to a 'Red Indian Reservation'. When they went to the reservation there was an argument between the host and the Native Americans over why he had brought a foreigner to see their 'miserable' condition. The Native Americans told the Pakistan visitor that the white man had given them a miserable life, but they had also introduced them to tobacco, and so the white men were dying in hundreds.

Tobacco has been used by the natives of America for generations. Columbus is thought to have brought this plant to Europe. Sir Walter Raleigh brought tobacco to United Kingdom and it was introduced to the colonies of Africa and Asia. 'The killer plant', as it is known now, was introduced and cultivated in the rich fertile land west of the Indus River. The rich tobacco companies had persuaded the farmers to grow it by giving them incentives. Farmers started growing it instead of fruit orchards and wheat, and the result is that KPK has become deficient in wheat grains. On the health side, there is hardly any organ in the body which is not affected by using tobacco: cigarettes, 'chillum', 'hubble bubble', *shisha* and naswar. As I mentioned, naswar use causes head and neck cancer, which is most common in KPK.

It is high time that farmers were persuaded to grow wheat and fruit instead of the 'killer plant' which was introduced by the profit-making multinational companies. Like so many disasters, the tobacco disaster is preventable, but this as well as other self-inflicted disasters need individual and collective efforts. To control the use of tobacco, a society was formed called the Pakistan Anti-Smoking Society (PASS), and the active members were Aamir Bilal and Mukhtar Zaman, as reported in The Frontier Post of May 30, 1999.

Call to ban sale of cigarettes to teenagers

F.P. Report

PESHAWAR - The Pakistan Anti-Smoking Society (PASS) has asked the government to ban the cigarette advertisements on the PTV and in the print media, print warning against smoking on half of the cigarette packets and impose ban on the sale & purchase of cigarettes for the children below 18 years of age.

These demands were put forward by the office-bearers of the PASS, Dr Saeedul Majeed, advisor, Dr Sher Mohammad Khan, Dr Mukhtiar Zaman, Dr Akmal Naveed, and Dr Saifoora while addressing a press conference at the Peshawar Press

Campaigns were launched against the advertising of tobacco on the main roads. This was not easy, as two successive Presidents of Pakistan were chain smokers who smoked heavily while on television. Since health is a collective responsibility, schools, colleges and university students were also told about the harmful effects of tobacco use. Prayer leaders and Mullahs were asked to mention the deleterious effects of naswar, but they said its use was only forbidden in the mosques. People listen to religious leaders, but they have their own ways of giving sermons. For prevention of diseases, the examples of religious leaders and politicians are imperative.

CHAPTER TWENTY NINE

VISITS TO CHINA AND BURMA

☾⋆

To reiterate my earlier poing,it has been known for some hundreds of years that food pipe diseases are relatively common in the region of the world stretching from Caspian Sea to North China. Afghanistan and North West of Pakistan also comes in this belt of high prevalence of food pipe cancer - oesophageal cancer. Definite cause or causes are not known, but a lot of research, especially in China, is going on and hopefully one day the cause or causes will be found out and this serious malady can be prevented.

Treatment and giving solace to these very ill patients from Afghanistan and KP was a challenge for me, being head of the Institute, and for my colleagues, who were nurses, scientists and engineers. Instruments for examining the food pipe were procured which were also used by doctors, from other hospitals. An opportunity arose to visit China when a Chinese delegation visited Peshawar. They invited us to visit their country and see their health facilities, especially the facilities for treatment. I was very much looking forward to the visit, because during my childhood, I had heard about 'Da Cheen Khapere' - the fairies of China - meaning that the girls of China were very beautiful. I heard the people in the village hujra talk about the beauty of Chinese women and their soft, white, shining skin, but none of the villagers had seen a Chinese lady. Moreover in the village mosque, the prayer leader occasionally talked about the acquisition of knowledge in Islam and recited ha'dith: 'pursue the acquisition of knowledge, even if you have to go to China'.

In later life when I was a member of the selection board at Peshawar University, to lighten the tense and nervous atmosphere during the questions and answers in formal interviews, I asked the candidates who had done their medical or scientific qualifications in China whether they had brought 'Chinese fairies' with them, meaning whether they had married a Chinese girl or not. The invariable answer was that their Pukhtun parents had not given them permission to marry someone outside their circle.

The official formalities for the Chinese visit were not difficult, because China is one of the few countries where there is no excessive security or bureaucratic hurdles for visitors from Pakistan. I took a PIA flight, as those were the days when the PIA Airline had efficient management. The flight was over the snowcapped mountains of the Karakoram and Himalayan ranges. The captain pointed to the peaks of Rakapushi and K2 as we passed near these awe-inspiring mountains.

On arrival in Beijing, I was greeted by a courteous lady with a broad smile and whisked through the immigration counters, which were manned by women. To my surprise, for the first time I noticed that a green passport holder was not subjected to vigorous security checks.

I was escorted to a hotel in Beijing, overlooking the famous Tiananmen Square. The first night was quiet and I was left to rest and recover from jet lag. A meeting with one of the chairs of the Health Department was scheduled in the morning. The Chairperson happened to be a woman who had had her training in nursing partly in Cambridge, UK. The schedule of visits to hospitals was discussed and I was asked whether I wanted to visit special places. Besides healthcare facilities such as hospitals, I wanted to see the birthplace of Chairman Mao and the Great Wall of China.

At that first meeting I learned that anyone talented and with a good record can become a chairperson, as in the case of this woman, who belonged to the nursing profession, unlike in Pakistan, where kinship and patronage are considered. Society can only improve when merit becomes the criterion of selection and promotion. As I was writing this, I heard the news that a person by the name of Sajid Javed, of Pakistani origin, had become a Minister in the United Kingdom Cabinet. According to the BBC radio news, his father had one pound sterling in his pocket when he had landed in the UK in 1961. I had ten pounds sterling when I landed at Heathrow in the early sixties.

Visits to hospitals in China were rewarding. I found that usually a choice was given to the patient as to whether he wanted the traditional Chinese medicine or so-called 'modern medicine'. I was shown the 'brachytherapy' treatment for food pipe neoplastic diseases and the radiation treatment equipment, which was of German make. The National Institute of Health of the United States had collaborated in research regarding oesophageal cancer, which meant that cooperation between the capitalist system and the communist system is possible for the benefit of the common man. In our case in Pakistan, any cooperation with our eastern neighbour, India, has been discouraged and discarded, even if it is in the mutual interest of both countries.

On Friday I asked my escort to show me a mosque in Beijing and he was kind enough to agree, as Chinese people usually are. He took me to the mosque and waited outside. As I entered the place of ablution, a person put out his hand and asked for some money. This was the first time I had noticed someone begging. Whether Muslims had the habit of begging or whether poverty was still rampant in the general population, I could not discern, but I did know that the Government was trying to improve the standard of living of the people.

Before going to Beijing, I had met a PIA captain who had been my classmate in Lower Topa. He had come to Peshawar to seek help from bureaucracy and the Police Department, as he had been defrauded by the Pukhtun manager who was looking after his property in the Murree Hills. My schoolfriend volunteered to give me the names of his girlfriends in China, Malaysia and Singapore. He also mentioned that Chinese girls have two names, their real names and an English-sounding one. He also mentioned that a Pukhtun Air Force colleague had told him that an airline pilot should remember 'the three Fs', but he did not disclose what the 'Fs' were.

One always tries to visit the places where people have made history. I was no exception, and I wanted to see the birthplace of the person who had changed China from being a country known for its 'opium eaters' to an economic giant. My request was granted, and we set out for the birthplace of Chairman Mao Ze Dong. I was told of his interest in the mountains, where he got together with his comrades and discussed how to change the condition of the people, especially the peasants. The rest is history. Initially he had joined the nationalists, led by Chiang Kai-shek, against the Japanese. The Chinese, like Pukhtuns, are known to be individualistic, but they stick together whenever there is an external threat. Chairman Mao, along with his loyal friends, ultimately succeeded in the revolution, but at tremendous cost to Mao himself, as well as to other revolutionaries, although the benefits were much greater.

The visit to China was official, and was primarily meant for seeing their health facilities and specially how to learn from the Chinese and try to improve our health care system in the PAEC Medical Centres, but I was also interested in the history of the Chinese Nation.

On a subsequent official visit in the company of another colleague, I went to the south of China to see some hospitals where original research and treatment was conducted on a disease which was more common in that part. I had noticed that the Chinese were trying to find solutions to their problems in their own specific way rather than copying and adopting the solutions of other countries which might not be relevant.

I noticed that as we two foreigners were walking in the shopping area, the well-dressed sales girls came out of their shops and watch us. Was it because many foreigners would not visit the place at that time, or was it because we were two tall, well-built Pukhtuns, described by Olaf Caroe as the most handsome people? I also noticed that people would buy cooked rice and start eating with their chopsticks while walking in the bazaar. I had to be careful about my food, whether it was 'halal' or not. Religious people can be strict, moderate or liberal. I deliberately asked a liberal one who had some sense of humour what I should do if I was in the company of Chinese regarding halal food. He said 'everything becomes halal, if you say Bismillah'. I followed that rule, except with frogs' legs and pork. Pukhtuns usually quote a Persian proverb 'ala bala, ba gerdene Mullah'.

When delicious dishes of Chinese food are being served, it usually takes a long time to finish the dinner. I had to make excuses to my Chinese hosts for not eating the last dish, which was frogs' legs, and I had to say that I was allergic to frogs.

Tastes, likes and dislikes for food develop during childhood.

Our stay in the great city of Shanghai was enjoyable and rewarding. On the medical side the city had a centre for liver transplantation. Viral infections of the liver are relatively common in developing countries because of the lack of preventive measures. While I was walking through the well-paved streets of Shanghai, a boy came near me and started saying, 'girl, girl'. I did not know what he meant, but my companion from Waziristan, who after retirement grew a long beard and became very religious in later life, helped me by saying that the person meant that he could supply a prostitute. I asked for a price and he said 'hundred dollars', presumably thinking I was an American. Another person also overheard us speaking in Pushto and introduced himself as a trader from Nangarhar Jalal Abad. Entrepreneurship is built into the Pukhtun Ahmadzai tribe and I remember they used to bring gur - brown sugar - from down country to Swat on their camels. It was a very pleasant sight during my childhood watching graceful animals.

Aggressiveness and militancy is also built into other Pukhtun tribes, and this has been exploited by both external and internal vested interests and religious bigots. Leadership is important and in China, trade, commerce, industrialization, economic development and good neighbourly relations have always been encouraged. One wishes that the so-called leaders and rulers of Pakistan had done the same for the benefit of the common man and peace.

Not long thereafter I was sponsored for another official trip, this time by the International Atomic Energy Agency (IAEA) is a United Nations organization which is the watchdog for the nuclear users of the world. It has done much for the peaceful uses of atomic energy in medicine, agriculture and industry. The Pakistan Atomic Energy Commission (PAEC) is one of the competent organizations and headed by some fine people since its inception, has played its part in the higher managerial set up in Vienna, the headquarters of IAEA. Dr Aslam, who was seconded to the IAEA from the PAEC, was visiting Islamabad and I met him in the office of Dr Ashfaq, who was heading the PAEC. Dr Ashfaq mentioned to Dr Aslam that I would be able to help any developing country in upgrading their nuclear medicine facilities. Within a few weeks I received instructions for a visit to Burma (Myanmar) along with one scientist. I recommended Dr Iftikhar Ahmad, a physicist trained in the UK. IA has already been mentioned before because when he wanted to leave for Malaysia, and I had persuaded him to stay. He was happily married to a nice lady, a local Pukhtun girl (Iftikhar being from Punjab). They have three intelligent children who later in life began successful careers.

On reaching Colombo (Yangon), we were met by an official of the Foreign Ministry, and our entry to the country was easily facilitated. I noticed a lot of uniformed people in the airport, as Burma was governed by the Military. After spending the night in a small but comfortable hotel we went to the Nuclear Medicine Department, where we were introduced to the staff, who all spoke fluent English and were very courteous.

During my short stay in Myanmar, I noticed that there were usually girls working in the shops, restaurants and hospitals, unlike in NWFP (KP). Children were looked after very well. They were kept clean and dressed in clean multicoloured clothes, and some white local powder was put on their cheeks.

I asked one of the technicians to show me the house of Aung San Suu Kyi, who had become famous because of her struggle for democracy for her people. He took me to the house, but it was heavily guarded and visitors were not allowed. Ultimately the woman succeeded in her genuine struggle for her people. Most people in Myanmar are Buddhists, but there are also

Muslims and occasionally ethnic tensions crop up. The world famous Pagoda was inspiring, and its cupola, which is made of solid gold, is the hallmark of the city of Yangon. I knew that the last Mughal Emperor, Bahadar Shah Zafar, was buried in Yangon, and went to see his grave, which was well preserved. A Muslim in a green turban was sitting beside the grave reciting the holy Quran. On his grave was written:

Kitna ha badnaseeb Zafar qabar k lay
Do guz zameen bhi na meli kohy yar may

This means 'how unfortunate is Bahadar Shah Zafar that he could not get two yards into his beloved country for burial'.

Bahadar Shah Zafar was the last Muslim king who lost his kingdom to the British, partly because of the decadence of the Mughal kings, who instead of looking after their people indulged in all sorts of luxuries, and partly due to the expansionist role of the British, who ultimately succeeded in establishing the empire on which 'the sun never set'.

The Burmese were hospitable people, and one day we were introduced to a person in the hospital by a technician. We went to his house, where we were introduced to a middle-aged lady, and there were some pretty young girls. After taking some tea we thanked him and left the place. Later we learned that the place was a prostitution den. Both of us were naive when it came to sexual relations or acts. Iftikhar Ahmad was brought up in a strictly religious Punjabi family, whose parents had to leave everything and travel to Lahore during the partition of India through no fault of their own and then be called by all sorts of derogatory names in their newly-created country of Pakistan. The so called 'Muhajirs' had gone through many sacrifices: leaving their properties, illness and death, living without shelter or food. I was also brought up in a strict Pukhtun society where one was not supposed to talk to girls or look at someone else's spouse. So the shyness in both of us (Punjabi and Pukhtun) continued to adulthood and beyond. I also found Iftikhar Ahmad a thorough gentleman.

Our short official educational visit, thanks to the IAEA and the PAEC, was coming to an end and I was told to see the Health Minister. He was in Army uniform and his assistant, in civilian dress, was taking notes. I did most of the talking and mentioned to him that there was a need to upgrade the facilities in terms of equipment. The staff (medical, scientific and technical) needed to be educated and trained. I mentioned that I would ask the PAEC and especially Dr Abdullah Sadiq, the Rector of the Pakistan Institute of Applied Science (PIAS), if medical doctors from Burma could come and be trained in the PIAS. I also mentioned that some of the staff were not happy and wanted to leave because of their working conditions. Was it the right thing to say to a military person? I did not get a chance for further visits, but the Health Minister was a nice person who regularly sent me New Year good wishes cards. Or perhaps this was just expected politeness?

Before leaving Myanmar, I went to see the World War II Cemetery where lay many people who had died in that war, including people from the Indian sub-continent serving in the British Forces. The late world-famous malariologist MK Afridi was also serving in the British Army and he was mentioned in dispatches. Pukhtuns are good when serving away from their places of birth.

While walking in the cemetery, I was looking for Muslim and Pukhtun names on the graves. A person whom I had not noticed came to me and said in broken Urdu 'Are you Pakistani?' I said 'yes'. He said 'You look Angraiz' (English). I said spontaneously 'Dil, dil Pakistan' and then changed to Pushto. He was from the Khattak tribe and had two wives, one a Burmese and another in his hometown in KP. I also exchanged with him the proverbs about Khattaks and the love of music and dancing among the Khattak tribe.

When we were leaving, the staff gave us a farewell party and some came to the airport. The courtesy, hospitality, generosity and the love of the Myanmar people for their children will always be fondly remembered.

CHAPTER THIRTY

THE EXODUS FROM AFGHANISTAN

☾⋆

Afghanistan is interesting country. From Khyber to Herat, the people are generous, hospitable and hard-working. I say this because I used to travel by road from Peshawar to Herat every year and then onwards to Iran to see my in-laws. I always looked forward to the long journey by road. During those long journeys I had not faced any difficulty with the general public, with the officials of the country or the service providers in the hotels or restaurants. Was I lucky or were the people 'good'? Moreover, during my childhood, people in the hujra often talk about the amirs of Afghanistan, especially Amir Amanullah Khan. The tribe of Yusufzai, led by Malik Ahmad Khan, had also migrated from Afghanistan. However the country of Afghanistan has been subjected to manmade disasters, mainly through external forces and international vested interests, resulting in instability, infighting and misery for the people.

The rulers or amirs have either been West-leaning or Russian-leaning. Troubles have always been brewing, but these reached a peak when there were assassinations and a medically-qualified but Russian-trained doctor took over and Russian forces were invited in. It was the Cold War days, and the West, especially the USA, could not be expected to remain a silent spectator. General Zia was ruling Pakistan at the time. His religiosity was proverbial and at times he was labelled by his opponents as fanatic and bigoted. The West, especially the USA, found a pliable and religious military man ruling a country neighbouring the easily-penetrated thousand-mile border with Afghanistan. The West also knew from their experience in the fifties in Indonesia that only religion can defeat the power of Russia. The Russian presence and the effective propaganda against them caused a mass exodus of people to the neighbouring countries.

I used to ask the Afghans why they had left their country. Some of them told me that the Russians were going to get hold of all the young married girls and take them to Russia. The old people were also going to be taken to Moscow, killed and rendered into soap in Russian factories. Propaganda is known to play havoc. No wonder Hitler had a special minister for it.

Since the language, the dress, the religion and the way of life of Afghans were the same as the local population, they were not resented by Pukhtuns on the whole, but problems did occur occasionally. They were called 'Muhajirs'. Whenever a patient from Afghanistan was admitted to the hospital, I tried to make sure they received the same facilities as the local population without discrimination, as enunciated by the code of medical ethics to be followed by the medical and nursing professions. But negligence did occur in dealing with the so called 'Muhajir' patients, in spite of religion, culture and government advice to deal with them humanely. To be fair to the government of the day, headed by Zia-Ul-Haq and his team, they made sure that the Afghan refugees were dealt with in a proper manner at every level. The heads of the Afghan Refugees Commissionerate were handpicked in terms of managerial skills and religiosity. There was no dearth of money and support from Western countries, for political and humanitarian reasons. Ordinary people in Europe, the USA and Canada usually support humanitarian work because parents and teachers encourage children to take part in it.

Mr Abdullah was the Head of the Afghan Commissionerate, and he had a good reputation. His daughter Khudija happened to be a classmate and friend of my daughter Mah Muneer. Rustam Shah Momand became Commissioner later on and his colleagues were Ziarat Khan (ZK), a Yusufzai Pukhtun from the Swabi area, and Zaib Ullah Khan (ZUK) from Aloch Puran, Swat at the time, but later the area became Shangla, rightly or wrongly depending how you look at the division of people. I knew Ziarat Khan, a fine bureaucrat with managerial skills and other good Pukhtun characteristics. His daughter was also a classmate and friend of my daughter. Contacts, kinship and patronage work well if you want to get work done in Pakistan. For some unknown reason I had not acquired this habit, which at times resulted in personal difficulties, but life has been kind, by and large.

For the wider interests of the IRNUM Hospital I asked ZK whether they could help, as we were regularly treating Afghan refugees. He said he would try. He cleared the bureaucratic hurdles and the 'red tapism' because the Chief, Rustam Shah Momand, and ZK were both 'Mr. Clean'. Twenty million rupees were sanctioned, which was a large amount at the time. Some people suggested that I should put it in my account as it would bring a lot of interest, but I did not do so; I am not sure whether this was because I was scared of being caught or for some other reason. My previous boss in the IRNUM hospital used to call me *darpok* - a person who would not be corrupted for money. The Finance Member at the Pakistan Atomic Energy commission would later say that I had made them millionaires. The money was used for building a four-storey block for patients.

The influx of people from Afghanistan was never ending. People of all denominations and strata had come, from fine carpenters to highly-educated men like Sardar Roshan, Karzai and others. I was building a house at that time and the fine woodwork in it was done by Tajik Afghans. 'Mashooq', meaning lover, was the name of the fine woodwork craftsmen. There were complaints of overcrowding in Peshawar, but there were no bomb blasts, suicide attacks or target killings in Peshawar or any other part of the then NWFP, now KP. All the 'activities' were going on west of the Durand line.

My sources of information about the ongoing battles in Afghanistan were my patients and their relatives. It was no secret that people were trained in the borderlands and the interior of Pakistan to fight in Afghanistan. The then rulers of Pakistan were religiously and mentally averse to the rulers of Afghanistan at the time, and moreover they had all the backing of the West in terms of funding and political support. Internally the Army was behind them. So all sorts of organizations cropped up with religious names. The Middle Eastern countries were their strongest supporters. Once I asked the relatives of a patient who was introduced to me as commander of group of Mujahidin about their tactics of going inside Afghanistan and then fighting. He told me that sometimes they come so close to each other at night that they start abusing each other. I was curious what sort of abuses they hurl at each other: 'Da Rusiano, Kafirano bacho' - sons of infidel Russians. They would shout back 'da dalkhuro aw American anobacho' - sons of lentil eaters and Americans.

Later on when a documentary was being made about Osama bin Laden I found that he had lived opposite my house and medical clinic. Ahmad Shah Masood (ASM), known as 'the Lion of Punjsher', also used to visit the house. After the assassination of ASM, I said to my patients from Punjsher (five lions) that now they should call their area 'Char Sheri' (four lions), because one lion was no longer in this world.

I was too busy with my hospital work, education of the children and my private medical practice in Peshawar and Swat to be interested in making friendships and enquiring about my neighbours from other countries, though the Pukhtun culture and the religion of Islam teach one to support and help neighbours. Leaving one's abode or country unwillingly because of turmoil and going to another country must be awful, especially for children and women, but Afghans have suffered a lot because of external vested interests.

Chapter Thirty One

MY FIRST, BUT NOT MY LAST, VISIT TO THE USA

☪

As mentioned earlier, I had studied in a school that was run on the pattern of British public schools. Pakistan had earned a lot of foreign exchange during the Korean War because the jute of the then East Pakistan (Bengal) was in great demand for use in jute bags. Money was rightly spent on education by the then rulers of Pakistan. Most of the school teachers were British and they knew their jobs, not only teaching but inculcating discipline and good behaviour in students. Extracurricular activities were emphasized, and we were also taught table manners in the dining room. I always wanted to go to Britain and perhaps meet my teachers, and I succeeded in meeting some of them. Teachers are role models, and good teachers are always remembered by their students. So when I entered medical college, most of the teachers had their qualifications from the UK. Therefore, the first thing I wished to do was to try and go to the UK for postgraduate qualifications, but we also used to talk of trying to go to the USA, as some senior qualified students had gone there and they sent letters praising the healthcare system with its structured training, unlike the British at the time, as well as high salaries and beautiful nurses. While working in the UK I wanted to go to the USA, but did not succeed. On returning to my home country in the seventies, opportunity came: thanks to the well-run Pakistan Atomic Energy Commission, which had close relations with the International Atomic Energy Agency, I was offered a scholarship for training in nuclear medicine. A Pukhtun, by and large, is always hospitable and generous, but in return he expects hospitality and generosity from others.

I had two contacts in the USA. A younger brother of my school friend, Dr Roidad, was working in a hospital in Coney Island, New York. The name 'Coney' generated laughter as in Pushto 'Coney' means gay. Charles Lindholm was the other person with whom I had an exchange of correspondence in the sixties when he had reached Swat during the Vietnam War days, and ultimately came to our village because of his friendship with my stepbrother Zaman Khan. In the seventies I was host to him in Peshawar, when he had come with his wife Cherry and daughter Michelle to do research in Swat. As I mentioned earlier, CL later became an Anthropologist who wrote many books and papers, including *Generosity and Jealousy*, which was based on his residence in a Pukhtun village in a remote area of scenic Swat Valley. From a Pukhtun point of view he had not forgotten his 'Pukhto' of hospitality. If one looks at the positive aspects of Americans and Pukhtuns, then there are a lot of commonalities among them such as love of freedom, generosity, and love of religion. Whether Pukhtun values of revenge and vengeance are good or bad qualities depends on how you look at them. In my opinion, the sky will be the limit for peace, progress and prosperity all over the world if you combine the good qualities of Pukhtuns and Americans.

To give an example of how Americans and Pukhtuns can cooperate, below I reproduce interview I did with Charles Lindholm, which was published in the International Sunday edition of the English language newspaper *Jang* on October 26 of 2003.

In this interview, SM is Sher Muhammad Khan, while CL is Charles Lindholm.

SM: You have written extensively on the Middle East, Afghanistan and Pakistan, especially on the people of NWFP. Wrongly or rightly, this area has been in the news for a long time. What do you think the present and future generations of Afghanistan and Pakistan can learn from recent events in Afghanistan?

CL: I suppose you are asking here about the rise of the Taliban and Osama bin Laden. I think their success shows that desperate and hopeless people are likely to take refuge in radical social movements, which offer them at least a dream of peace and spiritual renewal. Years of war and rivalry had left the Afghan people without any faith in their traditional leaders. They were ready to try something new, and the Taliban and Osama filled the gap. The lesson is that fanaticism grows primarily where chaos reigns and where people have no sense of a viable future.

SM: Coming to the present, what can the government and the international community do to help Afghanistan and Pakistan on the road to peace, progress, and prosperity?

CL: Unhappily, there are great obstacles in the way of progress in the region, including endemic poverty, lack of opportunity and the forces of oppressive tradition, as well as continued class, religious and ethnic conflicts. However, there are also reasons for hope. The people of Pakistan and Afghanistan have a strong sense of themselves and their own value. They are famously self-reliant, creative, and entrepreneurial. The international community and national government ought to try to provide the space for people to realize their potentials. It is impossible for Pakistan and Afghanistan to immediately become modern, centralized states with rational bureaucracies and efficient Western-style institutions, but it is possible for them (with the help of outside aid) to provide roads, schools, and hospitals. It is also possible to provide a relatively safe environment. If some degree of security and a minimum possibility for a better life exists, I have every faith that the local people of Afghanistan and Pakistan will themselves work to transform their lives in pursuit of the peace, progress, and prosperity that they so deeply desire and deserve.

SM: In what way can jihad be used against illiteracy, poverty and ignorance and not against people of other religions, other countries and sects?

CL: Islam is indeed a religion in which the standard greeting is 'peace be upon you'. However, it is also a religion with a great history of expansion and warfare. This does not make it any different from other religions in the world, which also have mixed histories of peace and war. The real question is: what does the present time demand? To my mind, we are living in an era where the whole world is highly interdependent. In the present circumstances, violence is more destructive than in the past. Therefore, the notion of jihad as self-discipline and as a struggle against the fundamental sources of inequity is better suited to the modern condition. Such a concept of jihad has the potential to transform a world that is in danger of losing its bearings.

SM: Relations between Afghanistan and Pakistan are under strain these days. What can these countries do to be good neighbours and work for development rather than wasting time and energy on non-productive activities?

CL: Afghanistan and Pakistan have much in common. Not only do they share a border, a religion, a language and a past, they also have similar problems of development and security. Realization of shared interests offers the potential for alliance, which would be of advantage to both. Unfortunately, both Afghanistan and Pakistan have not had the degree of national coherence and unity that Western states have enjoyed. This has led each state to fear disintegration and attack and to consequently have a suspicious attitude toward the other. This destructive attitude can only be broken if far-sighted politicians on both sides realize that this antagonism is not a consequence of intrinsic divergence of interests, but is instead a product of entirely separate issues.

SM: In what way can one give appropriate education so that the citizens are not only useful to their own communities but also think of themselves as part of the 'global village'?

CL: A modern education needs to stress the capacity for individual initiative and creative thought, not rote learning. When a student gives the right answer only due to memorization, without understanding the reasoning at work, then schooling is producing robots. This is too often the case in Pakistan, where training for tradition and obedience often takes precedence in the classroom, producing a style of learning that is no longer functional in today's world. What is important instead is learning about the history, culture and beliefs of other peoples. This sort of knowledge gives the student a sense that the world is various and fascinating, breaks down prejudices, and, most important, can imbue a feeling of shared humanity with others who seem, at first, to be very different from oneself. Pakistan is no longer an isolated state. Its citizens travel and work everywhere in the world; in fact, without remittances from migrants, it would have trouble surviving. Given this, it is especially necessary for Pakistani schools to stress an internationally oriented curriculum that can prepare its young people for lives in a global community.

SM: Some young individuals in certain seminaries are recruited into extremist groups in Pakistan. Do you think economic development and raising the standard of living will minimize these tendencies?

CL: Evidence from all over the world indicates that economic development and a better standard of living, as well as a sense that life is meaningful and that there is hope for the future, is the best defense against extremism. Pakistan is no exception.

SM: We sometimes blindly follow the US, instead of adopting its good habits and avoiding its bad ones. In what way can we in the developing world (especially Pakistan and Afghanistan) avoid the so-called bad things of the West?

CL: Temptation to indulge in the 'bad things' (meaning, I suppose, sexual promiscuity, drug use, and so on) is usually increased by repression. But knowledge about immorality does not mean that one forgets about one's own standards. It only tests one's faith. Americans and people in the developing world all must face the same problem of acting morally in a world where the temptation to do wrong exists. The real difference is that young people in the developing world imagine that Americans are far more decadent than is the case. These young people are both repelled and attracted by a world they do not know, but that is presented to them in exaggerated form by the media. Again, this is a mistake that can be alleviated with education and experience.

SM: Islam and Muslims are not well thought of in the US. Is it because of ignorance or because of the tragic events of the recent past? What should Muslims individually as well as collectively do to reverse this?

CL: There is a history of mistrust and fear of Islam in the West. This is largely due to the fact that the Islamic world has long been the major rival of the West for temporal and spiritual authority. Of course, the terrorist attacks and continued violence in the Middle East only add to American fears and prejudice. To offset this, Muslims need to forcefully repudiate terrorism wherever it occurs. Muslims ought also to stress the democratic and egalitarian nature of their religion, and the high degree of personal responsibility that it demands. These aspects of Islam are aspects that Americans like to think are characteristic of themselves, and demonstrate that Muslims and Americans, although they may disagree, are actually very much alike in their fundamental attitudes toward life. It is also worth remembering that freedom of religion is a deep part of American culture, and that Americans will respect Islam as long as they do not feel threatened by Muslim militants.

SM: But then the Muslim world does not think well of the US either. In what ways can the US reverse this trend?

CL: A major help in improving relations between the US and the Muslim world would be a more realistic and even-handed policy in Israel. While the Israeli-Palestinian problem is a knotty one, there needs to be public recognition from America that Palestinians have suffered unjustly, and deserve some form of reparation. A successful democratization of Afghanistan and Iraq would also go a long way toward alleviating Muslim fears. The US must accept the fact that these nations must pursue their own pathways. American willingness to permit a degree of independence and political dissent would show that America does not desire to dominate, but rather wishes to foster democratic participation. At the moment, this seems rather unlikely given the agenda of the Bush administration, but

Muslims and Americans have been good friends in the past, and can be good friends again. They have a great deal in common, both in terms of interests and in terms of fundamental beliefs.

SM: In your opinion, what is the contribution of Muslim society to the human race in terms of science, architecture, and other human development?

CL: This is too vast a question for me to begin to answer. Any consideration of science and philosophy must give credit to Muslim thinkers, who accomplished so many great advances. Nor can I imagine the world without the brilliant mosques and palaces of Muslim dynasties. The music and art of the Muslim world is recognised everywhere. And, even for non-Muslims, the crowning triumph is the message of the Prophet himself, which has inspired so many people with its call for justice and equity. The world would be a much poorer place indeed without Islam.

Dr Roidad belonged to the Sahibzada family, which was respected in Swat as whenever the Pukhtun tribes Mamatkhel and Painda Khel used to leave their villages because of fighting, they left their womenfolk, along with their other precious material, in Sahibzada's and Mian's custody because of trust. I remembered that as a child, Roidad was quiet and well-behaved. He turned out to be intelligent and topped his class in medicine. A well-behaved child usually turns out to be successful, provided he or she is properly guided, and he was helped by his elder brother, my schoolfriend. I also had a small role in his education as well as in his medical treatment when Sahibzada Roidad was studying in the famous Jehan Zeb College in Swat, which had some excellent teachers and produced some successful personalities who in later life, like SR, not only made a name for himself but helped his kith and kin in acquiring education.

Before going to the USA, I had to go to my village to see my parents, as it was a Pukhtun tradition to seek the blessing not only of your relartives but also the neighbours and even the mosque prayer leader. People in the village heard that I was going to Charles's country as Charles, Cherry and Michelle were fondly remembered by the people. One of my cousins asked if Charles could send him more of the'nusha tablets' which he had given him years ago, when he felt so good that it was like floating on air. Sattar Khan of the village mentioned how grateful he was to Charles, because he taught him how to collect data in a field study. He was also thankful to him for helping him to get a job in an international organization. Qavi Khan (popularly known as Bacha Lala) and my brother Shad Muhammad, remembered the discussions on tribal system and Pukhtunwali. Khaista Dada (handsome daddy) remembered Cherry's charm and pretty face. Zaman was wondering what Michelle would be doing. Syed Mama's daughter, one of the 'outgoing' and non-purdah observing girls in the village, mentioned how she used to throw pebbles from the roof of the house to attract the attention of the handsome Charles. When my mother, Khaista Bibi, said to give her love to 'my son Charlus', I told her I hoped she did not mean that I had to share my inheritance with him. Pukhtuns are very particular about the matter of shares in inherited property. Land disputes among cousins and brothers can even lead to fighting and killing.

My departure from the Old World to the New World was well planned. Pakistan Airlines, which had been one of the best in the world, had deteriorated for many reasons, so I took Emirit Airlines, which was convenient from Peshawar; moreover I was also interested in seeing Dubai, as many people from Swat had taken jobs in the Middle East instead of going to India, as before the partition of India these workers used to talk about the luxuries in Dubai. The journey to New York was long but comfortable, thanks to the modern aviation industry and its engineers, the efficient crew and the pretty air hostesses of

Emirit Airlines. On arrival in New York, immigration and other formalities were neither tedious nor strict, as in later years when I was subjected to 'secondary checks' because of my name 'Khan' and Swat, the place of my birth. The officials have to do their job, but like everyone else, a Pukhtun perhaps unduly expects that he or she should be treated kindly and courteously.

As I stepped out after collecting my luggage, I was very pleased to see Charles and Roidad. He said 'Pakhair Raghle' - welcome. He had not forgotten his Pushto, and he had a knack of pleasing newcomers and guests, as Americans usually have. There were bear hugs and after exchanges of greetings about parents, brothers, sisters and cousins, followed by your spouse if you are educated and have seen the outside world, but traditionally Pukhtuns do not ask about wives.

The first night was spent in Roidad's apartment in Coney Island, and the next day he took me to the Lindholms' in Manhattan. They lived on the fifth floor of a building on 14th Street. Some of the streets are very famous in New York, depending on what you are interested in; the arts, museums, food, sports, shopping, the fair sex and so on. New York caters for the tastes of all sorts of people, as I learned during my brief stay.

My host gave me their bedroom, which was the biggest in their apartment. In the window, I noticed a pot containing a familiar small plant which is found wild in the Swat valley. It was a 'pot' plant, presumably to make me feel at home and remind my hosts of their tough but interesting time in a Pukhtun village.

The next two days were spent in getting to know the city and showing me a glimpse of life in one of the great American cities, which in the past had given refuge to Europeans when they were either persecuted or wanted a better life. This hospitality and generosity, one of the positive Pukhtun traditions, is being continued in the great city and great country of the USA for the people of Asia, Africa and other parts of the world, but at times it is abused, to devastating effect unfortunately.

The Lindholms showed me the precise details of how I should get to Staten Island Hospital, where I was to get training, or better still education in the peaceful uses of atomic energy. New York is of course also known for the 'Manhattan Project', concerning the not-so-peaceful uses of atomic energy.

As I was walking down the street with Cherry and Charles to the place where I would catch the boat for Staten Island, I was also carrying my briefcase. I heard the sound of running, and my briefcase was snatched from my hand. I saw Charles smiling ahead in the street with my briefcase. He wanted to show me that I had to be careful in a big city like New York, where all sorts of people live. I had been warned about 'mugging' and guns, but I had not come across these during my brief stay.

On one occasion I came across a phenomenon of a different kind; I was travelling by subway during the rush hour and was standing behind a black lady. As the train stopped, my body accidently touched the back of the lady, who was well built; she turned around with a bottle in her hand and started swearing. I could only understand a four-letter word and the phrase 'you whitey' as she was shouting incoherently. As I stepped out of the train, she threw the bottle at me, and it hit a pillar and broke into pieces. I realized the tensions between black and white communities. I had read and heard about these, but this was a first-hand experience. I also knew about Cassius Clay, or Mohammad Ali, the great boxer, Malcolm X, and of course about the historic speech of Dr King, 'we shall overcome'. People at that time could not imagine that one day America, a free democratic society, would have a black president.

After a few days with the Lindholms I was found a place in another apartment, as the owner had gone on holiday. Cherry put all the essential food, such as milk, eggs, butter and bread, in the fridge, not knowing that I was a spoiled Pukhtun khan who did not know even to fry an egg.

One day as I was entering the main gate to the multi-storey apartment, a blonde lady was coming down the stairs with her dog. On seeing me entering the apartment, she rushed back upstairs, probably thinking I was an intruder.

After spending a few days in the basement I moved, or rather I was moved to another place. The Lindholms arranged my stay without my having to pay rent. I did not know that Americans were so good. The new place was a house on 22nd Street which had been converted from a warehouse by a college professor who was now on holiday in the south of France with his family. Well-to-do westerners often have two houses, a summer house and a winter house, depending on where they live. Well-to-do Pukhtuns usually spend most of their time earning money and building property, without taking time off for holidays or sightseeing. The property is then left to their progeny, who may waste the hard-earned money of their parents (usually the father). One of my cousins was left a landed property that he sold bit by bit and spent the money on 'dancing girls'. Someone commented that he was not doing any work and asked what he was going to do when the property was finished. He showed him his pistol and said he would kill himself - which he did.

In the Professor's house, I met a nice gentleman by the name of Nathaniel Wander who was studying anthropology. We were sharing the house, as it consisted of a central hall, with a nicely polished wooden floor surrounded by living rooms. Nathanial told me that the Professor's wife was fond of giving parties and the hall had been specially made for her. A husband acceding to the wishes of a wife was strange for a Pukhtun's ears: the wife's place is in the secluded house, which is primarily meant for protection. However, sometimes the wife makes sure her presence is felt, as was in the case of my mother, who would not let my father get near his first wife. But in Islam, all the wives have to be treated equally.

I was taking an interest in what Mr. Wander was studying. 1 looked at his book and on the first two pages were portraits of people. I saw a portrait of a Pukhtun with a beard and headgear. I got more interested in the book and started to read it when he was not using it. He was kind and presented the book to me, writing on it, 'The world's first 'Anthropologist Medicalist'. I did not know that medical anthropology was a specialty until I met a tourist couple from America in the south of France. They said their son was teaching medical anthropology in Stanford University and he had written about cancer survivorship. So anthropologists are people of many talents, as the Iranians say.

Nathaniel would sometimes accompany me outside and show me the various places, but he would also advise me not to go out alone at night. He wanted to write a book, but the last I heard of him he was chasing and writing about birds (the feathered ones) in a place in Central America where a delicious dish of rodents is cooked. He had built a house for himself in a tree.

The Department of Nuclear Medicine where I was supposed to get training in advances in the field was part of the Radiology Department, headed by a Chinese-American radiologist. He was a nice person, as most Chinese are. I was interested in learning the techniques used in the investigations of heart disease, and he handed me to a pretty woman who taught me all the techniques.

The Chief of Radiology acceded to my other requests: one was to visit the world-famous Johns Hopkins Institute in Baltimore, and another was to attend a medical conference in Detroit, Michigan. A doctor who had settled in Baltimore facilitated my one-week stay and showed me around the port, mentioning that we Pushtuns also jump ship here to find new lives in the land of opportunity, America. He himself belonged to a famous tribe of Pushtuns, the Khattaks. In Johns Hopkins I spent a week in Henry Wagner's department, where world class research was going on in medicine.

The conference in Detroit was well organized in terms of the facilities for the audience, the speakers and the workshops. I took a taxi to go to a hotel in Dearborn. The taxi driver asked me where I was from and I said Afghanistan. Those were the days when there were Russian forces in Afghanistan and in America people had sympathies for Afghans. The driver said that if I wanted political asylum he would help me. In the hotel where I was staying I noticed familiar names of the staff working there. I learned later on that Henry Ford had recruited Palestinians in his automobile factories.

Before coming to the USA, I had collected the telephone numbers of friends and friends of friends. One was Dr Jan, who was settled in Michigan and living with his third or fourth wife. It was nice of him to come such a long way and take me to his house for dinner. I was surprised that his American wife did not greet me nor join us for dinner in the house, and there was a reason for it: she had been given the impression that her husband's Pukhtun friends had spoiled him by introducing him to girls.

Dr Jan took me to a Pukhtun restaurant in Detroit by the name of Sheikh. It belonged to Hassan Khan, who had come to the USA before the Second World War. Hassan Khan was from Garhi Kapoora Mardan. Dr Jan was free with the elderly gentleman, who was using pure Pushto words, and said that Hassan had wives in every big city in the USA. He had started from California and had now reached Detroit. He asked him about his son, who was admitted to hospital as an emergency because he took many sleeping tablets to try to kill himself. I asked the reason and Dr Jan said that his son was stupid, because the girlfriend did not want to marry him and he wanted to commit suicide. Jan continued that there are so many pretty girls around that he should find another girlfriend. In Pukhtun society, when love goes wrong, the male resorts to kidnapping or honour killing, but Hassan Khan's son could not do it. The last time I saw Dr Jan, he was in the cardiac unit in Peshawar following a heart attack. His devoted American wife came from the USA and took him there, but he could not survive and the property he left caused disputes regarding inheritance.

There is an end to everything, whether one likes it or not. My six-week stay in the great city of New York was coming to an end and I asked Cherry what sort of gift I should take for Shahnaz. In my previous visit to Sri Lanka and Burma, I had bought her sapphire and rubies, as I had enough money saved at that time. Cherry said, 'ladies like jewellery and precious stones.' She meant diamonds, but it had to wait for some other time, because I had spent all my allowances.

Physically, mentally, socially and even spiritually, my stay in New York was enjoyable and rewarding: I had generous hosts, the people I met were friendly and I learned the latest advances in nuclear medicine, which I did incorporate in my arsenal of weapons for dealing with diseases when I came back to Peshawar.

I felt heartfelt gratitude towards excellent organizations like the Pakistan Atomic Energy Organization, and to the American people who hosted me and met me socially. I could not prevent tears, but I did manage to avoid crying loudly as I said goodbye to Charles and Cherry. Pukhtuns can be sentimental and emotional at times, as in any other culture.

This was my first visit to the United States of America, but not the last. As they say, 'first impression is last impression'. On subsequent visits, my impression vacillated, because of the attitude of the border security people. The USA is a global power and anyone who has tasted power, individually or collectively, wants to keep it, perhaps at any cost. In my case, I was working in atomic energy at the time when there was talk of Pakistan smuggling materials for destructive uses of it, so my luggage was thoroughly checked. Then came the global terrorist activity and as I was from the Pukhtun belt and my name was Khan I had to be questioned twice, which was annoying, and sometimes I had to retaliate verbally because of my Pukhtun ego, but for some reason I did not have any harsh treatment and at times they were very polite; whether it was better training or better people in the Department I could not decipher. An interesting film from Bollywood has been made called 'My name is Khan, I am not a terrorist'. Shah Rukh Khan, from a Pukhtun family but settled in Mumbai, played the leading role excellently.

CHAPTER THIRTY TWO

INTERESTING TIMES

The foundation stone of our hospital was laid by Zulfiqar Ali Bhutto in the early seventies when he was Prime Minister. He had a soft spot for smaller provinces and was a charismatic but controversial leader. When he visited NWFP and delivered his fiery speeches, people, especially the Swatis and Hashtnagar people, rallied to him because he mentioned 'roti, kapra, makan' - bread, clothing and shelter. He tried but did not succeed, partly because of his own intolerance of people who did not subscribe to his ideas and the lack of humility in his character. The then Secretary of State of the USA praised him in his writing. According to some world leaders, especially those from Turkey, China and Iran, he did not deserve to be executed as some countries volunteered to give him asylum. A Pukhtun judge Safdar Shah resigned and did not want to be party to the concocted judgment.

In those days I sometimes saw the Registrar of the Supreme Court in Islamabad, who had showed me boxes full of intelligence documents and said that the regime of the day was bent on hanging Bhutto. The written confidential remarks by the High Commissioner of the UK in his dispatches released recently are interesting to read. During the Russian debacle in Afghanistan, our hospital had to cope with patients from Afghanistan who were suffering from serious diseases. Oesophageal cancer is common among them because of lifestyle, and moreover women with breast cancer only came in the last stages, because of ignorance, lack of resources and poverty. A medical doctor cannot and should not refuse a patient, and we made sure that the Afghan 'refugees' were given free treatment. Afghan patients were not only good patients but better workers, skilled in woodwork or construction work. They were very fond of General Zia and would display his picture in their shops. Pukhtuns cannot easily forget goodwill shown to them. General Zia did everything for the Mujahideen and Afghan refugees because of his religiosity or bigotry and for short-term advantage with foreign military aid. He could not or did not realize that his unilateral policies would have long-term devastating effects on the proud, freedom and religion-loving but poverty-stricken Tajiks, Pukhtuns, Uzbeks and Turkoman who have suffered greatly for years and are still suffering at the time of writing. They have been caught in the 'power game', and there is no end to it as yet.

These were interesting times in the sense that besides my professional medical work, I learned about the various 'hizbs' - groups - and their leaders. Some of them were living lives of luxury and would at times try to convince me themselves or their contacts to give them certificates that treatment was not available in the hospital and they were recommended to go to the USA and Europe. It was difficult to see people leaving their countries and houses and start living miserable lives of no fault of theirs. The word 'muhajir' was preferred by the Afghans because in Islam one is supposed to help them, but I joked with them that they had come to their own country and Peshawar was their winter capital, the Afghan kingdom extended to beyond Islamabad at one time and the Durand line was demarcated forcibly.

A book by Professor Toynbee, the Nobel Laureate, 'Between Oxus and Jumna', mentions how Durand, accompanied by some Khan Bahadars (KB), went to Kabul and forced Amir Abdur Rahman, the then King of Afghanistan, to put his thumbprint on the document of demarcation of the Durand line for ninety-nine years. Nawaz Sharif was the Prime Minister of Pakistan who intervened and talked to the leaders of the groups and some arrangements for forming the government were made, but as usual there was a lot of cruelty. Dr Najibullah Ahmadzai, the head of the Russian-backed government, was murdered and his body hung up in a public square. Other atrocities were also committed. Afghanistan is not the only country where there has been great cruelty of man to man. Examples include the French Revolution, the Nazis in Germany, the Russian Revolution, the division of the Subcontinent of India, the Chinese Revolution and the Japanese atrocities during World War II. The leaders of the West, China and Japan have set up systems of government where stability has occurred and the unstable countries have to learn from the past mistakes of other countries.

Talib is an Arab/Pushto word meaning a person who has studied in a religious seminary. I had known the word from childhood, as young talibs lived in the mosques and food were given in turn by us and the extended family when we were living in a large mudhouse. Taliban is the plural of talib.

Mujahidin rule in Afghanistan had to come to an end for many reasons, internal as well as external. They were not trained in governing people, and moreover the law and order situation was bad. They were not playing their cards very well vis-à-vis the USA and Pakistan. It was said that General Babar, a Pukhtun and a military man who was Home Minister, facilitated the coming of the Taliban through the well-trained military intelligence services known as ISI. The whole phenomenon started in Kandahar, a historical city where most of the population are of Pukhtun stock. Kandahar or Qandhar comes from 'qand', a Persian word meaning sweet and 'har' necklace, and it is said that the pretty damsels wore necklaces of sweet-smelling flowers. Mullah Omar, who had a religious education in Karachi, was made the Amir - head. His health minister was Mullah Abbas, who came to our hospital for medical advice. MA was a quiet, well-mannered person. As Taliban were in favour of strict purdah, I tried to indirectly impress on him the education of girls and positive role of women in the society. When Mullah Abbas came for a third follow up medical visit, I asked Lady Doctor Safoora and some nurses to come to the medical clinic. I introduced the ladies to him and mentioned to him how useful they were in the hospital set-up. There was no comment from his side - he just raised his head to look at the pretty girls.

A friend, Nang Yusufzai, told me that the Taliban phenomenon started one day in Kandahar when an elderly, bearded and turbaned man, accompanied by his burqa-clad women, came into the street and started shouting, 'Is this what you call Islam? Is this why we have lost our kith and kin because you said that Islam was in danger and you would eradicate injustices and cruelty in society?' People gathered around him, including Mullah Omar. People asked the man what had happened. He said, 'my young son has been taken forcibly by the Mujahid and is being used for sodomy. Is this the *ghairat* [honour] of Pushtuns?' At this, the women in their burqas began wailing and the old man threw his turban on the ground in disgust. When Pukhtuns are convinced of wrongdoings, especially when 'honour' is involved, they will get together to avenge them.

Since Kabul had no good facilities worth mentioning like our hospital, I wrote a request on their behalf to the International Atomic Energy Agency for the establishment of a cancer centre in Kabul, but Munir Ahmad was an intelligent man and said the IAEA would not agree. A 'Roving Ambassador' had also come in connection with the medical treatment of his father and wanted to know whether the Military Hospital in Rawalpindi could help as they had close and cordial relations with military personnel. A medical person has the privilege to know many people in the course of his or her work, but he or she has to concentrate on amelioration of the disease rather than becoming or acting like a mullah, priest, rabbi or politician. The people of Afghanistan, especially the Pukhtuns, liked the Taliban because there was anarchy during the Mujahidin time. Taliban had introduced Shariah (Islamic law) and criminal activities had reduced all over Afghanistan, especially in the Pukhtun-dominated areas. Pushtunwali was also followed whenever there was a question of honour involved. During their time some foreigners were imprisoned as they were thought to be spies, and there was one lady among them. Their treatment in the jail was so good that the lady was impressed and was said to have converted to Islam. But the Taliban did have their bad points in running the government. One was the extreme rigidity in their interpretation of Sharia law, especially the treatment of women and another was Pushtunwali, especially giving sanctuary to foreigners such as Osama bin Laden without asking whether they had committed a crime or not.

During Musharaf's time in Pakistan the Home Minister was Moin Haider, my schoolfriend in Lower Topa in the fifties. He was a fine man who was friendly to Musharaf and had joined his cabinet, but he did not agree with him on certain policies, although he had to obey orders. He was told to go and persuade Mullah Omar to hand over Osama bin Laden. Musharaf had been told by President Bush 'either you are with us or against us'. Moin Haider took Maulana Shamizai, from Swat, who settled in Karachi and was a teacher of Mullah Omar, I had been told. They asked Mullah Omar, but he did not agree because of his Pukhtunwali: a Pukhtun will not only give sanctuary to a person if it is sought but will protect him at any cost.

There is a story about the visit of Moin Haider, who had a great sense of humour, that he had also invited Kate Winslet, the pretty actress who was the heroine in the film 'Titanic', to help persuade Mullah Omar to give up OSB, but Mullah Omar still did not agree. MH's Pushtun friends told him that had he offered Leonardo di Caprio, the young hero of the Titanic film, in exchange for OBL, Mullah Omar would have not refused. I was told the story but could not corroborate it myself.

. The era of the Taliban had to end for many reasons, and it came to an end after 9/11, facilitated by the same countries who had encouraged the Taliban to fight against the Mujahidin. Straightforwardness was the hallmark of the Taliban and not diplomacy. The word 'Taliban' has found a permanent place in the dictionary, although as I mentioned it originally simply meant 'seeker of knowledge' and was not applied to all sorts of militants and insurgents.

The scenic Swat Valley has been through both manmade and natural disasters. Much has been written about manmade disasters lately, and people of all strata have witnessed the atrocities and suffered from them. As I mentioned earlier, my own house was raided by scores of young bearded so-called Taliban men at night. Household goods, including mattresses and crockery, were taken after they had blindfolded and tied the hands of the three people who were looking after the house, a part of which was used as a medical clinic. I was not living in the house at the time.

After a few days a person rang me; he sounded young on the phone and asked if I could recognize him. I had to say that I could not see his face on my phone. He said he was a commander with the Taliban and had studied in my school in the village. He returned all the stuff taken from the house except the mattresses, as those were very useful in the mountains for sleeping.

Since in the West and some countries in the East, the scholars are usually asked to look into problems and suggest solutions, I asked Professor Charles Lindholm if he could throw some light on the phenomena of 'Talibanisation' and the questions and answers were published in the International Sunday Edition of *Jang* on December 23, 2007. They are reproduced here.

The questions were sent by email and the answers are as follows, without any addition or omission. Again SMK is Sher Mohammad Khan and CL is Charles Lindholm.

SMK: Why have you have kept your academic interest in Swat? Is this because of your attachment to the place or because of a desire to find out the root causes of the problems, especially the militancy facing the region?

CL: From my point of view, Swat illustrates many of the difficulties that inevitably occur during the transformation of a traditional society, as old orders break down and new ones are not yet found. Because I know it best, I always refer to it when making larger comparative arguments about the Middle East or elsewhere. At the same time, if my thoughts can be of any help in minimizing suffering, I am very pleased to offer them. Whether they will be listened to is another matter.

SMK: In your academic work you have not mentioned anything about how to change the behaviour of the people for the better. Is that not the job of a social anthropologist?

CL: My first job is to attempt to record and analyze what actually occurs, trying to understand and clarify the reasons for action. Only with correct knowledge can adequate solutions be found. However, I cannot provide answers. I can only provide information and hope that it will help and not cause further oppression. That is the dilemma of my field. We never know how, or by whom, our investigations will be used.

SMK: Pukhtuns in general and Swat Pukhtuns in particular tend to gather around a religious person when they want to resist outside influences. Such men are often outsiders who do not belong to any well-known tribe. Examples include Sandakai Baba, Saidu Baba, his grandson Miangul Abdul Wadud and in 1994, Maulvi Sufi Mohammad, father-in-law of the present Maulvi Fazlullah of Swat. Can you throw some light on this?

CL: The Pukhtun - and Middle Eastern tribal people in general - are governed by strong loyalties to their own kin group (khel). It is very difficult for them to form long-lasting alliances with other related but opposing groups, and even more difficult for them to submit to a leader from another kin group. The basic axiom is that 'no one has the right to tell me what to do - except my own father'. However, religious figures from outside the kin group network do not partake of this rivalry. Furthermore, their claim to authority comes not from ancestry, but from their supposed closeness to God. As a result, they can overcome local kin loyalties and gather people around them, at least momentarily. This is most likely to occur when people are threatened and are looking for some way to unite without losing honour and autonomy. In general, loyalty to these leaders diminishes or vanishes once the threat is past or when the leaders seek to impose their own ideology on the tribal people.

SMK: Do you think the present phenomenon in Swat is of local origin, or is it fuelled by real or perceived threats to religion by the events in the rest of Pakistan, Afghanistan and the rest of the world?

CL: Taking the 'view from afar', it seems that both must be true. As the local authority of traditional landlords in Swat and elsewhere on the frontier has eroded, the authority of self-appointed mullahs and other religious teachers has expanded to fill the gap. These figures gain power by excoriating the corruption of the state. This strategy is very old - dating back to the earliest days of Islam - but has been fuelled and further inflamed by American incursions into Iraq and Afghanistan and the never-ending conflict in Israel. Because of these confrontations, ordinary complaints about injustice and poverty can easily be magnified and become identified with a moral jihad, which then tends to spiral into absolutism and violence.

SMK: A lot has been written and heard about Al-Qaeda. Hardly a day passes without Al-Qaeda being blamed for sponsoring outrages. Is this a ploy to draw attention away from injustices in the wider world?

CL: Certainly Al-Qaeda serves a valuable purpose as the new 'evil empire' par excellence, against whom a perpetual 'war on terror' can be waged. Such an elusive enemy serves to unite Americans who otherwise would have little interest in fighting battles so far from their own homeland. At the same time, Al-Qaeda has its own absolutist agenda of destruction, in which only those who are willing to adhere to a narrow and self-generated interpretation of Islam are judged Muslims - the rest are apostates who can legitimately be killed. This is a threat not only to the West, but to the whole Islamic world.

SMK: Is it fair to ask you what Al-Qaeda is?

CL: Anthropologists would call it a millennial movement. Its ambition is to bring the end of time and the advent of the Promised Land through the destruction of all opponents. Although the AQ is modern in its organization, in its absolutism and willingness to cast aside all worldly order it closely resembles the kharijites of early Islam, who saw themselves as 'the people of heaven' battling against 'the people of hell,' and who were willing to kill anyone who defied them. Another analogy from Islamic history is the Qaramati, whose blend of zealotry and communalism almost overthrew the Abbasid dynasty before they eventually collapsed. Like Al-Qaeda, these groups proclaimed the evil of the status quo and spread via diffuse secret networks. Like Al-Qaeda, they thrived on disorder and the corruption of the state. And like Al-Qaeda they were wholly unable to organize any viable alternative to the world they opposed so vehemently, and imploded due to their intransigence and profound disconnection from reality.

SMK: Historically in the West there have been movements such as the IRA in the UK, Afro-American Movements in the USA, ETA in Spain etc. What are the differences between those movements and Al-Qaeda?

CL: The movements you mention are primarily seeking justice and recognition for minorities within state systems. Al-Qaeda is not interested in such goals. Its aim is the total overthrow of the existing order. As such, it resembles transformational movements such as the Nazis or other charismatic cults much more than it resembles the IRA.

SMK: Coming back to Swat, your region of interest and the present uprising which the outsiders call 'Taliban', the local people call them 'Tor Patki' (Black Turbaned) and they call themselves 'Shari'ati' - Seekers of Shari'a (religious law). Some people are of the opinion that they are infiltrated by government agencies and the elite who want to perpetuate their hold by creating crisis after crisis. They also give the example of the 'dirty tricks' of the intelligence agencies, nationally as well as internationally. What is your opinion generally and specifically in the case of Swat?

CL: From this distance, I am not able to say how much the Black Turbans have been infiltrated by external agencies. Probably it is true that many different interests are seeking to further their own agendas by manipulating this movement. However, it is also true that it is notoriously difficult to control movements such as this one, which have popular support and express deep grievances. It is worth remembering that the German elite were sure they could control Hitler when they asked him to take over as Chancellor. In other words, it is not difficult to start a fire when the tinder is dry. It is very hard, however, to put it out once it begins to burn.

SMK: My personal view, for what it is worth, is that the majority of people in Swat are economically poor, they are unemployed, and getting justice is neither easy nor available. There is no good governance. These are the major reasons for the present uprising. What is your opinion on this?

CL: I agree. In general, religious fervor offers an apparent solution when all other options have failed.

SMK: Let me give you, if I may, an example. When the late Zulfikar Bhutto raised his slogan 'Roti, Kapra aur Makan' (bread, clothes and shelter), the people of Swat rallied behind him. When in 1994 Maulvi Fazlullah said that nobody would be poor and there would be no injustice, the people of Swat rallied behind him. Why don't the governments concentrate on the alleviation of poverty and ignorance, and sustainable development, rather than quick fixes?

CL: Your examples are good, but in fact none of these promises were realized. Politicians with a weak mandate in an unstable state are unable to pursue long-term goals because of the fragility of their base. Paradoxically, this means that to gain momentary advantage, politicians continually promise far more than can be delivered, and the disappointment that results further undermines the legitimacy of the political process. The answer is a more stable state featuring a secure legal system, a capable civil service and an independent judiciary. People need to believe they can rely on the infrastructure to continue and to pursue pragmatic goals, regardless of who holds the political reins.

SMK: As you know, the borderlands of Pakistan and Afghanistan are important sites historically, archeologically and culturally. They also feature some of the most beautiful scenery in the world. Yet it is also an area of high tension and has 'fault lines' that are natural as well as man-made. What do you think should be done nationally and internationally, specially by the USA, to help the people in the short term, medium term and long term?

CL: To accomplish anything, stability has to be achieved. This is a long-term project dependent upon larger developments in Pakistan and the region. In the short term, the government needs to reach a modus vivendi (way of living) with the less extreme elements in Swat and the frontier. The implementation of religious law in a version that is approved by mainstream clerics does not seem too far-fetched to me, and would give the government some legitimacy. The problem is whether religious law should then take precedence over custom (rewaj) or the law of the state. This can be decided by referendum. In the mid-range, regular referenda on matters of law and governance should be held, as well as local elections. At the same time pragmatic educational opportunities must be offered to offset or at least augment the narrow religious schooling presently provided by madrassas. And, of course, there should be efforts to provide opportunities for local people to earn a decent living. To this end, the wholesale destruction of forests must be stopped, a tourist industry developed (with the approval and participation of local communities), and the local agricultural infrastructure supported. It is, of course, very easy to make recommendations, very difficult to implement them. But it is important and encouraging to remember that the 'human capital' of the frontier, while presently ill-educated and backward, also has great stamina and discipline, as well as a strong desire for self-betterment. These capacities make them good workers and quick learners, willing to change if the changes make sense for them. The USA should do everything it can, financially and also by providing expert knowledge, to help further this important project. Peace on the frontier would go a long way toward assuring peace in the whole region.

SMK: Islam teaches peace and humanitarian values, and yet those who commit acts such as suicide bombings have a feeling of being morally right. In this day and age of science and technology and thinkers, cannot this trend be reversed at regional, national and international level?

CL: Recourse to terror is a desperate measure, arising from the depths of despair. It is compelling only among those who feel the world is so corrupt that it must be destroyed. The solution is not material wealth (the Arab adherents to Al-Qaeda are mostly middle class) but a sense of participation in the larger society. Social movements - even the Black Turbans - are efforts to take action in the world and to render it just and meaningful. If these activists can be brought into dialogue with the state, and if they can achieve at least some of their reforms, they then will feel a renewed sense of hope. Of course, some extremists will be satisfied with nothing less than carnage, but the vast majority can and will compromise if they discover that the world as it exists is not wholly indifferent to their suffering.

SMK: Pakistan has been an ally of the USA for many years and now it is an ally in the 'War on Terror.' Do you think the present-day animosity towards the USA is because of American government policies? How can these policies be changed to win the support of the people in Pakistan?

CL: The US government has long been unwilling to support a real democracy in Pakistan for fear that elections might bring elements hostile to its interests into power. This is a mistaken short-term policy that only serves to alienate the masses, who realize that their own government is not representing their interests. America should have more confidence in the processes of democracy that it says it supports. The US also must work harder to show an even-handed attitude in the Israeli-Palestinian conflict and throughout the Middle East. And, of course, the US intervention in Iraq has been a disaster. I hope that the election of a new President and the reversal of the harsh and clumsy policies of the Bush administration will offer new hope for achieving a better image of the United States in Pakistan and throughout the Muslim world.

SMK: Pakistan is passing through a dangerous phase. In what way do you think it can be helped or can help itself so that democratic government is ushered in, militancy is controlled and prevented and sustainable progress and prosperity attained?

CL: Pakistan is a weak state with serious internal subdivisions based on language, culture and ethnicity. The reliance on military power and the degree of corruption in the political arena bear witness to that weakness. For the state to survive, it should extend greater autonomy to its provinces, reach a permanent peace agreement with India, shore up its legal infrastructure and focus on providing services to its people. But above all, a culture of participation needs to be nurtured. This can be accomplished by encouraging volunteer organizations, of whatever form, which can negotiate with the state for their own special interests. Through this process, people begin to feel they belong to something larger than themselves, and to develop a sense of trust in the public arena that is necessary for any state to thrive.

Chapter Thirty Three

FINAL THOUGHTS

☪

Such voluntary organizations favoring local participation were once widespread in Pakistan. For example, in our village there were many hujras, the places where men came to sit in charpais, chat and discuss any decisions to be made. The younger unmarried boys slept there at night. These hujras were also used for guests and others who wanted to stay overnight. They were communal places of entertainment where musical instruments were played. The popular instruments were sitars and rababs - stringed instruments. In the hujera, the younger ones learned to respect their elders, help those who were in need and also learned to make decisions on a collective basis. However, as the population increased, people started building their own small places next to their homes, which were called *baitaks*. Our hujra, which was built in a common property of the village probably in the early 1920s, had beautiful woodwork on cedar wood brought from Kalam Kohistan. The khan chieftain who was the eldest and most experienced person in the family played the role of a leader and arbitrator of disputes. In our case, when the elders passed away, the younger ones were now too busy in their own separate careers, resulting in the so called 'headless' extended family. The result was that the common hujra was divided and converted into separate houses. The socialization of the young into the collective no longer took place.

I started a separate hujra of my own next to my newly-built house, which had reasonable amenities, unlike the previous hujras, which did not have toilet facilities and the people passed urine in a corner of the courtyard squatting on a raised platform, making sure their clothes were not soiled. As the hujra was not much used, in 1997 I converted it to a school for underprivileged children. I tried to make sure that children were taught in their mother tongue. Religious studies were also taught, but character building and humanitarian values were emphasized. Guests from other regions of the country and from abroad were invited so that the teachers and children had exposure to the idea of global citizenship. During the manmade disasters in Swat, more than 200 schools were either burnt or bombed, but this Shin Bagh school was not touched. Why the school was spared I could not decipher.

In Europe and North America, most people look forward to retirement, but in Pakistan people always try to extend the retirement age, and I was no exception. One avenue for continuing meaningful work is business, but I had no had no experience, as my primary profession was medicine. The meaning of 'business' is given in one dictionary as 'the principal activity in your life that you do to earn money'. I heard 'Tijarat' - trade - in sermons in mosques, when it was described as 'kare swab'. So I was drawn to attempt to start a chicken business (poultry farming) by my neighbour Ghulam Nabi Khan (GNK) who was from an illustrious family of Yusufzai of Mardan. His grandfather was 'Khan Bahadar' in British time and had accompanied Durand to see Amir Abdur Rahman in Kabul. He had also been given a revolver engraved in gold when a member of the British Royal Family visited Delhi. GNK had no experience, but his elder brother Ghulam Muhammad Khan (GMK) was successful in setting up a ghee oil factory and other businesses. GMK was an intelligent person who also took part in politics. A Pukhtun always tries to be like his close relations, even if he or she is not talented in the same field. Jealousy even of close relatives also plays a part. GNK was not as talented as his brother, but he persuaded me to join him in business. Preliminary work such as inspection of the poultry farms and the advice of a veterinary surgeon who was an expert in diseases of chickens was also sought. It was interesting to find out about all aspects of poultry farming and to know about successful men like Abbasi, a politician who made his mark not only in the poultry business but in politics, becoming a government minister and later on Governor of the Province.

We started the poultry farm in hired premises, and a manager was appointed; there were also some female workers. It was run for a few months and for a while our fridges at home were full of chickens, but losses occurred and we could not continue. The reasons were inexperience, lack of supervision and corruption among the managerial staff. As they say 'it is not your business', and chicken farming was clearly not my business.

There is a Pushto proverb, 'Pa mogi sarae yawa pera ghurzegi' - one falls only once on a pig. In other words one does not repeat a mistake, but greed is part and parcel of human nature. I was lured into another business with a twenty per cent share in a venture started by GNK and his brother Ghulam Rasool Khan (GSK), who had no children but was intelligent and very easy to deal with. Money was borrowed from the bank through my nephew Adalat Khan, who had connections. I had to pledge my shares and defence saving certificates, and ultimately lost them to the banks because the factory could not be started on time to pay the loan. I used to hear, and still hear, that billions of rupees are 'written off' to rich and powerful people. I thought the well-placed family of my partners would use their patronage links and kinship ties to come to the rescue, but this did not occur. In the end a nephew of GNK sold the factory to a Pakistani Canadian who made millions out of the deal but has yet to pay a portion of my share money.

Farooq Khan, a schoolfriend whose profession is in finance, rightly told me that one can never go wrong if one invests in property, gold and raw gemstones. Since that time I have invested whatever I have brought from the UK after working there for ten years, and whatever I could save from private medical practice, in agricultural land in Swat and residential plots. The price of land generally, and particularly in Swat, has gone up, and land which I had bought for twenty rupees a square foot was sold recently for 350 rupees a square foot to a person working in the Middle East. The advice of Virgin Conglomerate for young entrepreneurs is well worth reading and digesting.

So I decided to stay in medicine. I tried to advance through approaching my immediate boss, Dr Samar Mubarakmand, a well-known Oxford University-educated scientist, who at a later stage in the Pakistan Atomic Energy Commission (PAEC) was given the task of missile production. He also had a major role in making the nuclear bomb. He recommended the extension of my services in the PAEC, but the conditions were not in my favour.

General Qidwai was the main person looking after PAEC affairs. I had met him at one of the conferences arranged by Dr Abdullah Sadiq in PIEAS, but did not know that he was a powerful man and was close to General Musharaf, who was ruling the country at the time. Living in Pakistan, one has to know the mighty and powerful army personnel, and I knew a fine and very influential person, General Moin Haider, who happened to be my schoolfriend, but I did not feel like asking him to 'put in a word' for me because of my Pukhtun ego. One can call it a false ego, but still it exists. Moreover there were factors working against me; a doctor relative of an Army General was interested in a directorship at the Faisal Abad Medical Centre and the sitting Director, a Pukhtun, had to be shifted to Peshawar in my place to make room for him.

Dr. Sher M. Khan – a brief sketch by
Lt Gen Moin Uddin Haider

I saw Sher Khan for the first time at Pakistan Air Force Public School, Lower Topa Murree Hills in March 1954. He was one year senior to me and joined the school in 1953. Our fellow boarders hailed from all parts of Pakistan, including East Pakistan. Since Sher Khan was from Swat, he was addressed by us as Sher Khan Sawati. Our ages were between 12-13 years. I remember him as a kind, helpful and well-disciplined senior.

On leaving the school in 1956-57, we lost contact as Sher Khan belonged to another house in the school. We re-established contact after many years. He had become a doctor and I was a major in the Pakistan Army. Our school had been closed down by Air Headquarters in 1968. We then founded the Lower Topian Old Boys Association in early 70s in the Provincial Capital Cities and met regularly. We put together a telephone and address directory and re-established our lost contacts. We learnt that Dr. Sher Khan had married a British lady and was practising in the UK. Later, he returned to Pakistan and became in charge of nuclear medicine facilities at Peshawar.

Our school was revived in 1998 after a gap of 30 years and we had our Alma Mater available to us for reunion every year, and developed closer contacts with each other. On retirement, Dr. Khan was appointed as Head of Red Crescent in KPK Province. I made it a point to see him every time I visited Peshawar, and we always had a meal together.

I am happy to see him engaged in positive social and professional work. He is working in a hospital at Peshawar. I was impressed by his social and philanthropic work in his native place in Swat. His wife assists him in running the school and a dispensary for the poor people of the area.

It is always a great pleasure to meet Dr. Sher Khan as he has a very loveable personality, soft and pleasing manners. He is very sincere, balanced in his thoughts and views and likes to remain in touch with his schoolmates and maintain friendships formed over 60 years ago.

I am very proud of his association with me and thankful to him for sending me delicious peaches and apples from his fruit farms in Swat every year, no matter where I am posted as a General, Governor or Federal Minister of Interior. There was a disruption in the supply of fresh fruit as Swat was taken over by the militants and terrorists for several years. But due to a very bold and effective military operation the authority of the Government is fully restored in Swat and the area has returned to normality. I hope Dr. Khan can now resume his yearly gift of excellent quality fresh fruits. I assure him, this is the best way of cementing a long-standing friendship of 61 years.

I pray for good health and prosperity to the family.

Lt Gen Moin Uddin Haider
Ex-Governor Sindh and Ex-Federal Minister of Interior

As I have already said, in the West people make preparations for their retirements in terms of the place where they would spend the rest of their lives, medical insurance and pension. My previous boss in England told me that he was looking forward to retirement on a beautiful island off the coast of Spain. He lived with his younger friend in Menorca, which was at one time under Muslim rule. In my case, I was not prepared for retirement and had not made any formal preparations. In the West the retirement age is sixty-five years, while in Pakistan it is sixty. There is a Pushto saying: 'che da shpato shi na da weshto shi' - when someone gets to sixty years old he needs to be shot, meaning that he is no longer of any use. This might have been true a long time ago, but is no longer true, thanks to medical and scientific advancements. For example, Alzheimer's disease (brain degenerative disease of old age) can be kept at bay with mental as well as physical exercise

When one is watching a live show sitting in a big decorated hall, whether it is a cinema or another building, a curtain is opened and one sees scenes depicting struggles, rivalries, jealousies, generosities, political intrigues and so one. Then the curtain is closed. The audience judges whether it was an entertaining show, and some would also ask whether they had learned something from it or may give advice or educate younger people about the good episodes or otherwise in the play. Then there are committees who decide whether the film or the show deserves a prize or award or is a flop. The main characters are also judged.

In my case, looking back, I was born and bred in a small Pukhtun village, getting the 'right education' and then making use of it in the 'right way' for the benefit of myself and other people, however little this was worth. Charles Lindholm once remarked to me that 'you are lucky to be what you are in this society'. However, if a Pukhtun is oriented in the right direction by a quality education, the inculcation of humanitarian qualities, has acquired broad thinking as a citizen of the 'global village' and makes use of his 'Pukhtunwali' in a positive sense, then the sky is the limit, as they say. There are national as well as international examples, as in other nationalities. However at the time of writing, Pukhtuns are subjected to all sorts of negative external as well as internal forces, which make their advancement more difficult, but not impossible.

Retirement is not the end of the world, as they say; retirement, physically, mentally, socially and spiritually, can be the end, but once again, thanks to medical and scientific advances, the average useful age is increasing. Once again the 'curtain' has been opened thanks to some good friends (it is very useful as well as pleasurable to have sincere friends), and the opportunity has come for me to do humanitarian work supporting clinics and schools in my home village. About these opportunities, I shall say, as a Swati always says when he is confronted with the future, 'Ka khair ye' - if all is well - or better still, INSHALLAH.